Eighth International Joint Conference on Natural Language Processing (IJCNLP 2017)

Shared Tasks

Taipei, Taiwan
1 December 2017

ISBN: 978-1-5108-5295-2

IJCNLP 2017

The Eighth International Joint Conference on Natural Language Processing

Proceedings of the IJCNLP 2017, Shared Tasks

November 27 – December 1, 2017
Taipei, Taiwan

Introduction

The 8th International Joint Conference on Natural Language Processing (IJCNLP 2017) took place in Taipei, Taiwan from November 27 to December 1, 2017. It was organized by the National Taiwan Normal University and by the Association for Computational Linguistics and Chinese Language Processing (ACLCLP), and it was hosted by the Asian Federation of Natural Language Processing (AFNLP).

For a first time in the history of IJCNLP, the conference featured shared tasks. We received a total of ten task proposals, and after a rigurous review, we accepted the following five of them:

- **Task 1: Chinese Grammatical Error Diagnosis.** Participants were asked to build systems to automatically detect the errors in Chinese sentences made by Chinese-as-Second-Language learners, i.e., redundant word, missing word, word selection and word ordering. (*Organized by: Gaoqi Rao, Baolin Zhang, and Endong Xun*)

- **Task 2: Dimensional Sentiment Analysis for Chinese Phrases.** Given a word or a phrase, participants were asked to generate a real-valued score between 1 and 9, indicating the degree of valence, from most negative to most positive, and for the degree of arousal, from most calm to most excited. (*Organized by Liang-Chih Yu, Lung-Hao Lee, Jin Wang, and Kam-Fai Wong*)

- **Task 3: Review Opinion Diversification.** Participants were asked to build systems to rank product reviews based on a summary of opinions in two domains: books and electronics. (*Organized by Anil Kumar Singh, Julian McAuley, Avijit Thawani, Mayank Panchal, Anubhav Gupta, and Rajesh Kumar Mundotiya*)

- **Task 4: Customer Feedback Analysis.** Participants were asked to train classifiers for the detection of meaning in customer feedback in English, French, Spanish, and Japanese: comment, request, bug, complaint, meaningless, and undetermined. (*Organized by Chao-Hong Liu, Yasufumi Moriya, Alberto Poncelas, and Declan Groves*)

- **Task 5: Multi-choice Question Answering in Examinations.** Participants were asked to build systems to choose the correct option for a multi-choice question: for English and Chinese. (*Organized by Jun Zhao, Kang Liu, Shizhu He, Zhuoyu Wei, and Shangmin Guo*)

A total of 40 teams participated in the five tasks (and many more registered to participate, but ended up not submitting systems), submitting hundreds of runs for the different tasks and their subtasks: 5 for task 1, 13 for task 2, 3 for task 3, 12 for task 4, and 7 for task 5. Moreover, most of the participating teams contributed a system description paper: 3 for task 1, 10 for task 2, 3 for task 3, 9 for task 4, and 6 for task 5. Finally, the organizers of each task prepared a task description paper. All these appear in the present proceedings.

We thank the shared task participants, as well as the task organizers, for all their great work. We further take the opportunity to thank the program committee and all reviewers for their thorough reviews.

The IJCNLP'2017 Shared Task Co-Chairs:

Chao-Hong Liu, ADAPT Centre, Dublin City University, Ireland
Preslav Nakov, Qatar Computing Research Institute, HBKU, Qatar
Nianwen Xue, Brandeis University, USA

Organizing Committee

Shared Task Workshop Co-Chairs

Chao-Hong Liu, ADAPT Centre, Dublin City University
Preslav Nakov, Qatar Computing Research Institute, HBKU
Nianwen Xue, Brandeis University

Task 1: Chinese Grammatical Error Diagnosis (CGED) Organizers

Gaoqi Rao, Beijing Language and Culture University
Baolin Zhang, Beijing Language and Culture University
Endong Xun, Beijing Language and Culture University

Task 2: Dimensional Sentiment Analysis for Chinese Phrases (DSAP) Organizers

Liang-Chih Yu, Yuan Ze University
Lung-Hao Lee, National Taiwan Normal University
Jin Wang, Yunnan University
Kam-Fai Wong, The Chinese University of Hong Kong

Task 3: Review Opinion Diversification Organizers

Anil Kumar Singh, Indian Institute of Technology (BHU) Varanasi
Julian McAuley, University of California, San Diego
Avijit Thawani, Indian Institute of Technology (BHU) Varanasi
Mayank Panchal, Indian Institute of Technology (BHU) Varanasi
Anubhav Gupta, Indian Institute of Technology (BHU) Varanasi
Rajesh Kumar Mundotiya, Indian Institute of Technology (BHU)

Task 4: Customer Feedback Analysis Organizers

Chao-Hong Liu, ADAPT Centre, Dublin City University
Yasufumi Moriya, ADAPT Centre, Dublin City University
Alberto Poncelas, ADAPT Centre, Dublin City University
Declan Groves, Microsoft Dublin

Task 5: Multi-choice Question Answering in Examinations Organizers

Jun Zhao, Institute of Automation, Chinese Academy of Sciences
Kang Liu, Institute of Automation, Chinese Academy of Sciences
Shizhu He, Institute of Automation, Chinese Academy of Sciences
Zhuoyu Wei, Institute of Automation, Chinese Academy of Sciences
Shangmin Guo, Institute of Automation, Chinese Academy of Sciences

Program Committee

Reviewers

Alberto Poncelas, ADAPT Centre, Dublin City University
Anil Kumar Singh, Indian Institute of Technology (BHU) Varanasi
Anubhav Gupta, Indian Institute of Technology (BHU) Varanasi
Avijit Thawani, Indian Institute of Technology (BHU) Varanasi
Baolin Zhang, Beijing Language and Culture University
Chao-Hong Liu, ADAPT Centre, Dublin City University
Endong Xun, Beijing Language and Culture University
Gaoqi Rao, Beijing Language and Culture University
Haithem Afli, ADAPT Centre, Dublin City University
Jin Wang, Yunnan University
Julian McAuley, University of California, San Diego
Jun Zhao, Institute of Automation, Chinese Academy of Sciences
Kam-Fai Wong, The Chinese University of Hong Kong
Kang Liu, Institute of Automation, Chinese Academy of Sciences
Liang-Chih Yu, Yuan Ze University
Lung-Hao Lee, National Taiwan Normal University
Mayank Panchal, Indian Institute of Technology (BHU) Varanasi
Monalisa Dey, Jadavpur University
Nianwen Xue, Brandeis University
Preslav Nakov, Qatar Computing Research Institute, HBKU
Pruthwik Mishra, International Institute of Information Technology, Hyderabad
Rajesh Kumar Mundotiya, Indian Institute of Technology (BHU) Varanasi
Shangmin Guo, Institute of Automation, Chinese Academy of Sciences
Shih-Hung Wu, Chaoyang University of Technology
Yasufumi Moriya, ADAPT Centre, Dublin City University

Invited Talk

Public Health Surveillance Using Twitter: The Case for Biosurveillance and Pharmacovigilance

Antonio Jimeno Yepes

IBM Research, Australia

Abstract

Public health surveillance using clinical data is challenging due to issues related to accessing health care data in a homogeneous way and in real-time, which is further affected by privacy concerns. Yet, it is still relevant to access this data in real-time to model potential disease outbreaks and to detect post-marketing adverse events of drugs. Social networks such as Twitter provide a large quantity of information that can be relevant as an alternative to clinical data. We have researched the usage of Twitter in several tasks related to public health surveillance. In this talk, I will present the work that we have done in IBM Research Australia using Twitter in public health related problems and the challenges that we have faced using Twitter. Specifically, I will show results related to the prediction of the prevalence of flu in the USA and related to the identification of post-marketing adverse events of drugs.

Biography

Dr Antonio Jimeno Yepes is a senior researcher in text analytics in the Biomedical Data Science team at IBM Research Australia. Before joining IBM, he worked as software engineer at CERN from 2000 to 2006, then as software engineer at the European Bioinformatics Institute (EBI) from 2006 to 2010, as a post-doctoral researcher at the USA National Library of Medicine (NIH/NLM) from 2010 to 2012, as a researcher at National ICT Australia from 2012 to 2014 and as researcher at the CIS department at the University of Melbourne in 2014. He obtained his Masters degree in Computer Science in 2001, a master in Intelligent systems in 2008 and his PhD degree related to biomedical natural languages and ontologies in 2009 from University Jaume I.

Table of Contents

Shared Tasks Program

Friday, December 1, 2017, Room 503

08:00–09:00 *Registration*

09:10–09:30 *Opening Remarks*

09:30–10:30 *Keynote Talk by Antonio Jimeno Yepes on "Public Health Surveillance Using Twitter: the Case for Biosurveillance and Pharmacovigilance"*

10:30–11:00 *Coffee Break*

Session 1: Shared Tasks Overview

11:00–11:20 *IJCNLP-2017 Task 1: Chinese Grammatical Error Diagnosis*
Gaoqi RAO, Baolin Zhang, Endong XUN and Lung-Hao Lee

11:20–11:40 *IJCNLP-2017 Task 2: Dimensional Sentiment Analysis for Chinese Phrases*
Liang-Chih Yu, Lung-Hao Lee, Jin Wang and Kam-Fai Wong

11:40–12:00 *IJCNLP-2017 Task 3: Review Opinion Diversification (RevOpiD-2017)*
Anil Kumar Singh, Avijit Thawani, Mayank Panchal, Anubhav Gupta and Julian McAuley

12:00–12:20 *IJCNLP-2017 Task 4: Customer Feedback Analysis*
Chao-Hong Liu, Yasufumi Moriya, Alberto Poncelas and Declan Groves

12:20–12:40 *IJCNLP-2017 Task 5: Multi-choice Question Answering in Examinations*
Shangmin Guo, Kang Liu, Shizhu He, Cao Liu, Jun Zhao and Zhuoyu Wei

12:40–13:20 *Lunch*

Friday, December 1, 2017, Room 503 (continued)

Session 2: IJCNLP-2017 Shared Tasks Oral Session

13:20–13:40   *Alibaba at IJCNLP-2017 Task 1: Embedding Grammatical Features into LSTMs for Chinese Grammatical Error Diagnosis Task*
Yi yang, Pengjun Xie, Jun tao, Guangwei xu, Linlin li and Si luo

13:40–14:00   *THU_NGN at IJCNLP-2017 Task 2: Dimensional Sentiment Analysis for Chinese Phrases with Deep LSTM*
Chuhan Wu, Fangzhao Wu, Yongfeng Huang, Sixing Wu and Zhigang Yuan

14:00–14:20   *IIIT-H at IJCNLP-2017 Task 3: A Bidirectional-LSTM Approach for Review Opinion Diversification*
Pruthwik Mishra, Prathyusha Danda, Silpa Kanneganti and Soujanya Lanka

14:20–14:40   *Bingo at IJCNLP-2017 Task 4: Augmenting Data using Machine Translation for Cross-linguistic Customer Feedback Classification*
Heba Elfardy, Manisha Srivastava, Wei Xiao, Jared Kramer and Tarun Agarwal

14:40–15:00   *ADAPT Centre Cone Team at IJCNLP-2017 Task 5: A Similarity-Based Logistic Regression Approach to Multi-choice Question Answering in an Examinations Shared Task*
Daria Dzendzik, Alberto Poncelas, Carl Vogel and Qun Liu

15:00–15:30   ***Coffee Break***

15:30–16:50   ***Session 3: IJCNLP-2017 Shared Tasks Poster Session***

    YNU-HPCC at IJCNLP-2017 Task 1: Chinese Grammatical Error Diagnosis Using a Bi-directional LSTM-CRF Model
Quanlei Liao, Jin Wang, Jinnan Yang and Xuejie Zhang

    CVTE at IJCNLP-2017 Task 1: Character Checking System for Chinese Grammatical Error Diagnosis Task
Xian Li, Peng Wang, Suixue Wang, Guanyu Jiang and Tianyuan You

    LDCCNLP at IJCNLP-2017 Task 2: Dimensional Sentiment Analysis for Chinese Phrases Using Machine Learning
Peng Zhong and Jingbin Wang

    CKIP at IJCNLP-2017 Task 2: Neural Valence-Arousal Prediction for Phrases
Peng-Hsuan Li, Wei-Yun Ma and Hsin-Yang Wang

16:50–17:00   *Closing Session*

IJCNLP-2017 Task 1: Chinese Grammatical Error Diagnosis

Gaoqi Rao[1], Baolin Zhang[2], Endong Xun[3]
{[1]Center for Studies of Chinese as a Second Language, [2]Faculty of Language Sciences,
[3]College of Information Science} Beijing Language and Culture University
raogaoqi-fj@163.com, zhangbl@blcu.edu.cn, edxun@126.com

Abstract

This paper presents the IJCNLP 2017 shared task for Chinese grammatical error diagnosis (CGED) which seeks to identify grammatical error types and their range of occurrence within sentences written by learners of Chinese as foreign language. We describe the task definition, data preparation, performance metrics, and evaluation results. Of the 13 teams registered for this shared task, 5 teams developed the system and submitted a total of 13 runs. We expected this evaluation campaign could lead to the development of more advanced NLP techniques for educational applications, especially for Chinese error detection. All data sets with gold standards and scoring scripts are made publicly available to researchers.

1 Introduction

Recently, automated grammar checking for learners of English as a foreign language has attracted more attention. For example, Helping Our Own (HOO) is a series of shared tasks in correcting textual errors (Dale and Kilgarriff, 2011; Dale et al., 2012). The shared tasks at CoNLL 2013 and CoNLL 2014 focused on grammatical error correction, increasing the visibility of educational application research in the NLP community (Ng et al., 2013; 2014).

Many of these learning technologies focus on learners of English as a Foreign Language (EFL), while relatively few grammar checking applications have been developed to support Chinese as a Foreign Language(CFL) learners.

Those applications which do exist rely on a range of techniques, such as statistical learning (Chang et al, 2012; Wu et al, 2010; Yu and Chen, 2012), rule-based analysis (Lee et al., 2013) and hybrid methods (Lee et al., 2014). In response to the limited availability of CFL learner data for machine learning and linguistic analysis, the ICCE-2014 workshop on Natural Language Processing Techniques for Educational Applications (NLP-TEA) organized a shared task on diagnosing grammatical errors for CFL (Yu et al., 2014). A second version of this shared task in NLP-TEA was collocated with the ACL-IJCNLP-2015 (Lee et al., 2015) and COLING-2016 (Lee et al., 2016). In conjunction with the IJCNLP 2017, the shared task for Chinese grammatical error diagnosis is organized again. The main purpose of these shared tasks is to provide a common setting so that researchers who approach the tasks using different linguistic factors and computational techniques can compare their results. Such technical evaluations allow researchers to exchange their experiences to advance the field and eventually develop optimal solutions to this shared task.

The rest of this paper is organized as follows. Section 2 describes the task in detail. Section 3 introduces the constructed datasets. Section 4 proposes evaluation metrics. Section 5 reports the results of the participants' approaches. Conclusions are finally drawn in Section 6.

2 Task Description

The goal of this shared task is to develop NLP techniques to automatically diagnose grammatical errors in Chinese sentences written by CFL learners. Such errors are defined as redundant words (denoted as a capital "R"), missing words ("M"), word selection errors ("S"), and word

Proceedings of the 8th International Joint Conference on Natural Language Processing, Shared Tasks, pages 1–8,
Taipei, Taiwan, November 27 – December 1, 2017. ©2017 AFNLP

ordering errors ("W"). The input sentence may contain one or more such errors. The developed system should indicate which error types are embedded in the given unit (containing 1 to 5 sentences) and the position at which they occur. Each input unit is given a unique number "sid". If the inputs contain no grammatical errors, the system should return: "sid, correct". If an input unit contains the grammatical errors, the output format should include four items "sid, start_off, end_off, error_type", where start_off and end_off respectively denote the positions of starting and ending character at which the grammatical error occurs, and error_type should be one of the defined errors: "R", "M", "S", and "W". Each character or punctuation mark occupies 1 space for counting positions. Example sentences and corresponding notes are shown as Table 1 shows. This year, we only have one track of HSK.

<table>
<tr><td colspan="1" align="center">HSK (Simplified Chinese)</td></tr>
<tr><td>

Example 1
Input: (sid=00038800481) 我根本不能<u>了解这</u>妇女辞职回家的现象。在这个时代，为什么放弃自己的工作，就回家当家庭主妇？
Output: 00038800481, 6, 7, S
      00038800481, 8, 8, R
(Notes: "了解"should be "理解". In addition, "这" is a redundant word.)

Example 2
Input: (sid=00038800464)我真不明白。她们可能是追求一些前代的浪漫。
Output: 00038800464, correct

Example 3
Input: (sid=00038801261)人战胜了饥饿，才努力为了下一代<u>作</u>更好的、更健康的东西。
Output: 00038801261, 9, 9, M
      00038801261, 16, 16, S
(Notes: "能" is missing. The word "作"should be "做". The correct sentence is "才<u>能</u>努力为了下一代<u>做</u>更好的")

Example 4
Input: (sid=00038801320)饥饿的问题也是应该解决的。世界上每天<u>由于饥饿很多人</u>死亡。
Output: 00038801320, 19, 25, W
(Notes: "由于饥饿很多人" should be "很多人由于饥饿")

</td></tr>
</table>

Table 1: Example sentences and corresponding notes.

3 Datasets

The learner corpora used in our shared task were taken from the writing section of the Hanyu Shuiping Kaoshi(HSK, Test of Chinese Level)(Cui et al, 2011; Zhang et al, 2013).

Native Chinese speakers were trained to manually annotate grammatical errors and provide corrections corresponding to each error. The data were then split into two mutually exclusive sets as follows.

(1) Training Set: All units in this set were used to train the grammatical error diagnostic systems. Each unit contains 1 to 5 sentences with annotated grammatical errors and their corresponding corrections. All units are represented in SGML format, as shown in Table 2. We provide 10,449 training units with a total of 26,448 grammatical errors, categorized as redundant (5,852 instances), missing (7,010), word selection (11,591) and word ordering (1,995).

In addition to the data sets provided, participating research teams were allowed to use other public data for system development and implementation. Use of other data should be specified in the final system report.

```
<DOC>
<TEXT id="200307109523200140_2_2x3">
因为养农作物时不用农药的话，生产率较低。那肯定价格要上升，那有钱的人想吃
多少，就吃多少。左边的文中已提出了世界上的有几亿人因缺少粮食而挨饿。
</TEXT>
<CORRECTION>
因为种植农作物时不用农药的话，生产率较低。那价格肯定要上升，那有钱的人想
吃多少，就吃多少。左边的文中已提出了世界上有几亿人因缺少粮食而挨饿。
</CORRECTION>
<ERROR start_off="3" end_off="3" type="S"></ERROR>
<ERROR start_off="22" end_off="25" type="W"></ERROR>
<ERROR start_off="57" end_off="57" type="R"></ERROR>
</DOC>

<DOC>
<TEXT id="200210543634250003_2_1x3">
对于"安乐死"的看法，向来都是一个极具争议性的题目，因为毕竟每个人对于死亡
的观念都不一样，怎样的情况下去判断，也自然产生出很多主观和客观的理论。每
个人都有着生存的权利，也代表着每个人都能去决定如何结束自己的生命的权利。
在我的个人观点中，如果一个长期受着病魔折磨的人，会是十分痛苦的事，不仅是
病人本身，以致病者的家人和朋友，都是一件难受的事。
</TEXT>
<CORRECTION>
对于"安乐死"的看法，向来都是一个极具争议性的题目，因为毕竟每个人对于死亡
的观念都不一样，无论在怎样的情况下去判断，都自然产生出很多主观和客观的理
论。每个人都有着生存的权利，也代表着每个人都能去决定如何结束自己的生命。
在我的个人观点中，如果一个长期受着病魔折磨的人活着，会是十分痛苦的事，不
仅是病人本身，对于病者的家人和朋友，都是一件难受的事。
</CORRECTION>
<ERROR start_off="46" end_off="46" type="M"></ERROR>
<ERROR start_off="56" end_off="56" type="S"></ERROR>
<ERROR start_off="106" end_off="108" type="R"></ERROR>
<ERROR start_off="133" end_off="133" type="M"></ERROR>
<ERROR start_off="151" end_off="152" type="S"></ERROR>
</DOC>
```

Table 2: A training sentence denoted in SGML format.

(2) Test Set: This set consists of testing sentences used for evaluating system performance. Table 3 shows statistics for the testing set for this year. About half of these sentences are correct and do not contain grammatical errors, while the other half include at least one error. The distributions of error types (shown in Table 4) are similar with that of the training set. The proportion of the correct sentences is sampled from data of the online Dynamic Corpus of HSK[1].

#Units	#Correct	#Erroneous
3,154 (100%)	1,173 (48.38%)	1,628 (51.62%)

Table 3: The statistics of correct sentences in testing set.

Error Type	
#R	1,062 (21.78%)
#M	1,274 (26.13%)
#S	2,155 (44.20%)
#W	385

---

[1] http://202.112.195.192:8060/hsk/login.asp

	(7.90%)
#Error	4,876 (100%)

Table 4: The distributions of error types in testing set.

4 Performance Metrics

Table 5 shows the confusion matrix used for evaluating system performance. In this matrix, TP (True Positive) is the number of sentences with grammatical errors are correctly identified by the developed system; FP (False Positive) is the number of sentences in which non-existent grammatical errors are identified as errors; TN (True Negative) is the number of sentences without grammatical errors that are correctly identified as such; FN (False Negative) is the number of sentences with grammatical errors which the system incorrectly identifies as being correct.

The criteria for judging correctness are determined at three levels as follows.

(1) Detection-level: Binary classification of a given sentence, that is, correct or incorrect, should be completely identical with the gold standard. All error types will be regarded as incorrect.

(2) Identification-level: This level could be considered as a multi-class categorization problem. All error types should be clearly identified. A correct case should be completely identical with the gold standard of the given error type.

(3) Position-level: In addition to identifying the error types, this level also judges the occurrence range of the grammatical error. That is to say, the system results should be perfectly identical with the quadruples of the gold standard.

The following metrics are measured at all levels with the help of the confusion matrix.
- False Positive Rate = FP / (FP+TN)
- Accuracy = (TP+TN) / (TP+FP+TN+FN)
- Precision = TP / (TP+FP)
- Recall = TP / (TP+FN)
- F1 = 2*Precision*Recall / (Precision + Recall)

Confusion Matrix		System Results	
		Positive (Erroneous)	Negative(Correct)
Gold Standard	Positive	TP (True Positive)	FN (False Negative)
	Negative	FP (False Positive)	TN (True Negative)

Table 5: Confusion matrix for evaluation.

For example, for 4 testing inputs with gold standards shown as "00038800481, 6, 7, S", "00038800481, 8, 8, R", "00038800464, correct", "00038801261, 9, 9, M", "00038801261, 16, 16, S" and "00038801320, 19, 25, W", the system may output the result as "00038800481, 2, 3, S", "00038800481, 4, 5, S", "00038800481, 8, 8, R", "00038800464, correct", "00038801261, 9, 9, M", "00038801261, 16, 19, S" and "00038801320, 19, 25, M". The scoring script will yield the following performance.
- False Positive Rate (FPR) = 0 (=0/1)
- Detection-level
  - Accuracy = 1 (=4/4)
  - Precision = 1 (=3/3)
  - Recall = 1 (=3/3)
  - F1 = 1 (=(2*1*1)/(1+1))
- Identification-level
  - Accuracy = 0.8333 (=5/6)
  - Precision = 0.8 (=4/5)
  - Recall = 0.8 (=4/5)
  - F1 = 0.8 (=(2*0.8*0.8)/(0.8+08))
- Position-level
  - Accuracy = 0.4286 (=3/7)
  - Precision = 0.3333 (=2/6)
  - Recall = 0.4 (=2/5)
  - F1 = 0.3636 (=(2*0.3333*0.4)/(0.3333+0.4))

5 Evaluation Results

Table 6 summarizes the submission statistics for the 13 participating teams including 10 from universities and research institutes in China (NTOUA, BLCU, SKY, PkU-Cherry, BNU_ICIP, CCNUNLP, CVTER, TONGTONG, AL_I_NLP), 1 from the U.S. (Harvard University) and 1 private firm (Lingosail Inc.). In the official testing phase, each participating team was allowed to submit at most three runs. Of the

13 registered teams, 5 teams submitted their testing results, for a total of 13 runs.

Participant (Ordered by abbreviations of names)	#Runs
ALI_NLP	3
BLCU	0
BNU_ICIP	3
CCNUNLP	0
Cherry	0
CVTER	2
Harvard University	0
NTOUA	2
PkU	0
SKY	0
TONGTONG	0
YNU-HPCC	3
Lingosail	0

Table 6: Submission statistics for all participants.

Table 7 shows the testing results of CGED2017. The BNU team achieved the lowest false positive rate (denoted as "FPR") of 0.098. Detection-level evaluations are designed to detect whether a sentence contains grammatical errors or not. A neutral baseline can be easily achieved by always reporting all testing sentences as correct without errors. According to the test data distribution, the baseline system can achieve an accuracy of 0.5162. However, not all systems performed above the baseline. The system result submitted by ALI_NLP achieved the best detection accuracy of 0.6465. We use the F1 score to reflect the tradeoffs between precision and recall. The ALI_NLP provided the best error detection results, providing a high F1 score of 0.8284. For identification-level evaluations, the systems need to identify the error types in a given sentences. The system developed by YNU-HPCC provided the highest F1 score of 0.7829 for grammatical error identification. For position-level evaluations, ALI_NLP achieved the best F1 score of 0.2693. Perfectly identifying the error types and their corresponding positions is difficult in part because no word delimiters exist among Chinese words in the given sentences.

NTOUA, CVTE and ALI_NLP submit reports on their develop systems. Though neural networks achieved good performances in various NLP tasks, traditional pipe-lines were still widely implemented in the CGED task. LSTM+CRF has been a standard implementation. Unlike CGED2016, though CRF model in pipe-line were only equipped with simple designed feature templates.

In summary, none of the submitted systems provided superior performance using different metrics, indicating the difficulty of developing systems for effective grammatical error diagnosis, especially in CFL contexts. From organizers' perspectives, a good system should have a high F1 score and a low false positive rate. Overall, ALI_NLP, YNU-HPCC and CVTE achieved relatively better performances.

TEAM	RUNs	False Positive Rate	Accuracy	Precision	Recall	F1	Accuracy	Precision	Recall	F1	Accuracy	Precision	Recall	F1
				Detection Level				Identification Level				Position Level		
YNU-HPCC	run3	0.6104 (716/1173)	0.5311	0.6298	0.6148	0.6222	0.3979	0.4086	0.3298	0.365	0.1702	0.0981	0.0698	0.0816
	run2	0.7383 (866/1173)	0.5891	0.6417	0.7829	0.7053	0.3879	0.3825	0.4575	0.4167	0.1426	0.1056	0.1191	0.112
	run1	0.6513 (764/1173)	0.5796	0.65	0.7163	0.6816	0.4218	0.4219	0.4217	0.4218	0.1778	0.1262	0.1191	0.1225
NTOUA	run2	1 (1173/1173)	0.6281	0.6281	1	0.7716	0.3889	0.3889	0.506	0.4398	0.018	0.018	0.082	0.0295
	run1	1 (1173/1173)	0.6281	0.6281	1	0.7716	0.3211	0.3211	0.6099	0.4207	0.0212	0.0212	0.0958	0.0348
CVTE	run2	0.3154 (370/1173)	0.539	0.708	0.4528	0.5523	0.4711	0.5391	0.2057	0.2978	0.2602	0.1093	0.0465	0.0653
	run1	0.1441 (169/1173)	0.4756	0.7459	0.2504	0.3749	0.4461	0.606	0.1214	0.2023	0.3314	0.118	0.0204	0.0348
BNU	run3	0.1893 (222/1173)	0.5181	0.7547	0.3448	0.4733	0.4696	0.5707	0.1786	0.2721	0.3798	0.2968	0.0715	0.1152
	run2	0.1355 (159/1173)	0.4794	0.758	0.2514	0.3776	0.4412	0.5527	0.131	0.2118	0.3735	0.2818	0.0515	0.0871
	run1	0.098 (115/1173)	0.4721	0.7894	0.2176	0.3411	0.4337	0.5474	0.106	0.1776	0.3775	0.2773	0.0418	0.0727
AL_I_N LP	run3	0.3052 (358/1173)	0.6173	0.7597	0.5714	0.6523	0.5513	0.6007	0.3756	0.4622	0.4121	0.3663	0.213	0.2693
	run2	0.6607 (775/1173)	0.6465	0.6792	0.8284	0.7464	0.4654	0.453	0.6006	0.5164	0.2264	0.1949	0.2941	0.2344
	run1	0.6172 (724/1173)	0.6439	0.686	0.7986	0.738	0.488	0.4791	0.5657	0.5188	0.2547	0.2169	0.2752	0.2426

Table 7: Testing results of CGED2017.

6 Conclusions

This study describes the NLP-TEA 2016 shared task for Chinese grammatical error diagnosis, including task design, data preparation, performance metrics, and evaluation results. Regardless of actual performance, all submissions contribute to the common effort to develop Chinese grammatical error diagnosis system, and the individual reports in the proceedings provide useful insights into computer-assisted language learning for CFL learners.

We hope the data sets collected and annotated for this shared task can facilitate and expedite future development in this research area. Therefore, all data sets with gold standards and scoring scripts are publicly available online at http://www.cged.science.

Acknowledgments

We thank all the participants for taking part in our shared task. We would like to thank Kuei-Ching Lee for implementing the evaluation program and the usage feedbacks from Bo Zheng (in proceeding of NLPTEA2016). Gong Qi, Tang Peilan, Luo Ping and Chang Jie contributed in the proofreading of data.
This study was supported by the projects from P.R.C: High-Tech Center of Language Resource(KYD17004), BLCU Innovation Platform(17PT05), Institute Project of BLCU(16YBB16) Social Science Funding China (11BYY054, 12&ZD173, 16AYY007), Social Science Funding Beijing (15WYA017), National Language Committee Project (YB125-42, ZDI135-3), MOE Project of Key Research Institutes in Univ(16JJD740004).

References

Ru-Yng Chang, Chung-Hsien Wu, and Philips Kokoh Prasetyo. 2012. Error diagnosis of Chinese sentences usign inductive learning algorithm and decomposition-based testing mechanism. ACM Transactions on Asian Language Information Processing, 11(1), article 3.

Xiliang Cui, Bao-lin Zhang. 2011. The Principles for Building the " International Corpus of Learner Chinese". Applied Linguistics, 2011(2), pages 100-108.

Robert Dale and Adam Kilgarriff. 2011. Helping our own: The HOO 2011 pilot shared task. In Proceedings of the 13th European Workshop on Natural Language Generation(ENLG'11), pages 1-8, Nancy, France.

Reobert Dale, Ilya Anisimoff, and George Narroway. 2012. HOO 2012: A report on the preposiiton and determiner error correction shared task. In Proceedings of the 7th Workshop on the Innovative Use of NLP for Building Educational Applications(BEA ' 12), pages 54-62, Montreal, Canada.

Hwee Tou Ng, Siew Mei Wu, Ted Briscoe, Christian Hadiwinoto, Raymond Hendy Susanto, and Christopher Bryant. 2014. The CoNLL-2014 shared task on grammatical error correction. In Proceedings of the 18th Conference on Computational Natural Language Learning (CoNLL'14): Shared Task, pages 1-12, Baltimore, Maryland, USA.

Hwee Tou Ng, Siew Mei Wu, Yuanbin Wu, Christian Hadiwinoto, and Joel Tetreault. 2013. The CoNLL-2013 shared task on grammatical error correction. In Proceedings of the 17th Conference on Computational Natural Language Learning(CoNLL ' 13): Shared Task, pages 1-14, Sofia, Bulgaria.

Lung-Hao Lee, Li-Ping Chang, and Yuen-Hsien Tseng. 2016. Developing learner corpus annotation for Chinese grammatical errors. In Proceedings of the 20th International Conference on Asian Language Processing (IALP'16), Tainan, Taiwan.

Lung-Hao Lee, Li-Ping Chang, Kuei-Ching Lee, Yuen-Hsien Tseng, and Hsin-Hsi Chen. 2013. Linguistic rules based Chinese error detection for second language learning. In Proceedings of the 21st International Conference on Computers in Education(ICCE'13), pages 27-29, Denpasar Bali, Indonesia.

Lung-Hao Lee, Liang-Chih Yu, and Li-Ping Chang. 2015. Overview of the NLP-TEA 2015 shared task for Chinese grammatical error diagnosis. In Proceedings of the 2nd Workshop on Natural Language Processing Techniques for Educational Applications (NLP-TEA ' 15), pages 1-6, Beijing, China.

Lung-Hao Lee, Liang-Chih Yu, Kuei-Ching Lee, Yuen-Hsien Tseng, Li-Ping Chang, and Hsin-Hsi Chen. 2014. A sentence judgment system for grammatical error detection. In Proceedings of the

25th International Conference on Computational Linguistics (COLING ' 14): Demos, pages 67-70, Dublin, Ireland.

Lung-Hao Lee, Rao Gaoqi, Liang-Chih Yu, Xun, Eendong, Zhang Baolin, and Chang Li-Ping. 2016. Overview of the NLP-TEA 2016 Shared Task for Chinese Grammatical Error Diagnosis. The Workshop on Natural Language Processing Techniques for Educational Applications (NLP-TEA' 16), pages 1-6, Osaka, Japan.

Chung-Hsien Wu, Chao-Hong Liu, Matthew Harris, and Liang-Chih Yu. 2010. Sentence correction incorporating relative position and parse template language models. IEEE Transactions on Audio, Speech, and Language Processing, 18(6), pages 1170-1181.

Chi-Hsin Yu and Hsin-Hsi Chen. 2012. Detecting word ordering errors in Chinese sentences for learning Chinese as a foreign language. In Proceedings of the 24th International Conference on Computational Linguistics (COLING'12), pages 3003-3017, Bombay, India.

Liang-Chih Yu, Lung-Hao Lee, and Li-Ping Chang. 2014. Overview of grammatical error diagnosis for learning Chinese as foreign language. In Proceedings of the 1stWorkshop on Natural Language Processing Techniques for Educational Applications (NLP-TEA ' 14), pages 42-47, Nara, Japan.

Bao-lin Zhang, Xiliang Cui. 2013. Design Concepts of " the Construction and Research of the Inter-language Corpus of Chinese from Global Learners". Language Teaching and Linguistic Study, 2013(5), pages 27-34.

IJCNLP-2017 Task 2: Dimensional Sentiment Analysis for Chinese Phrases

Liang-Chih Yu[1,2], Lung-Hao Lee[3], Jin Wang[4], Kam-Fai Wong[5]
[1]Department of Information Management, Yuan Ze University, Taiwan
[2]Innovative Center for Big Data and Digital Convergence, Yuan Ze University, Taiwan
[3]Graduate Institute of Library and Information Studies, National Taiwan Normal University
[4]School of Information Science and Engineering, Yunnan University, Yunnan, China
[5]The Chinese University of Hong Kong, Hong Kong, China
Contact: lcyu@saturn.yzu.edu.tw, lhlee@ntnu.edu.tw,
wangjin@ynu.edu.cn, kfwong@se.cuhk.edu.hk

Abstract

This paper presents the IJCNLP 2017 shared task on Dimensional Sentiment Analysis for Chinese Phrases (DSAP) which seeks to identify a real-value sentiment score of Chinese single words and multi-word phrases in the both valence and arousal dimensions. Valence represents the degree of pleasant and unpleasant (or positive and negative) feelings, and arousal represents the degree of excitement and calm. Of the 19 teams registered for this shared task for two-dimensional sentiment analysis, 13 submitted results. We expected that this evaluation campaign could produce more advanced dimensional sentiment analysis techniques, especially for Chinese affective computing. All data sets with gold standards and scoring script are made publicly available to researchers.

1 Introduction

Sentiment analysis has emerged as a leading technique to automatically identify affective information within texts. In sentiment analysis, affective states are generally represented using either categorical or dimensional approaches (Calvo and Kim, 2013). The categorical approach represents affective states as several discrete classes (e.g., positive, negative, neutral), while the dimensional approach represents affective states as continuous numerical values on multiple dimensions, such as valence-arousal (VA) space (Russell, 1980), as shown in Fig. 1. The valence represents the degree of pleasant and unpleasant (or positive and negative) feelings, and the arousal represents the degree of excitement and calm. Based on this two-dimensional representation, any affective state can be represented as a point in the VA coordinate plane by determining the degrees of valence and arousal of given words (Wei et al., 2011; Malandrakis et al., 2011; Wang et al., 2016a) or texts (Kim et al., 2010; Paltoglou et al, 2013; Wang et al., 2016b). Dimensional sentiment analysis has emerged as a compelling topic for research with applications including antisocial behavior detection (Munezero et al., 2011), mood analysis (De Choudhury et al., 2012) and product review ranking (Ren and Nickerson, 2014)

The IJCNLP 2017 features a shared task for dimensional sentiment analysis for Chinese words, providing an evaluation platform for the development and implementation of advanced techniques for affective computing. Sentiment lexicons with valence-arousal ratings are useful resources for the development of dimensional sentiment applications. Due to the limited availability of such VA lexicons, especially for Chinese, the objective of the task is to automatically acquire the valence-arousal ratings of Chinese affective words and phrases.

The rest of this paper is organized as follows. Section II describes the task in detail. Section III introduces the constructed datasets. Section IV proposes evaluation metrics. Section V reports the results of the participants' approaches. Conclusions are finally drawn in Section VI.

9

Proceedings of the 8th International Joint Conference on Natural Language Processing, Shared Tasks, pages 9–16,
Taipei, Taiwan, November 27 – December 1, 2017. ©2017 AFNLP

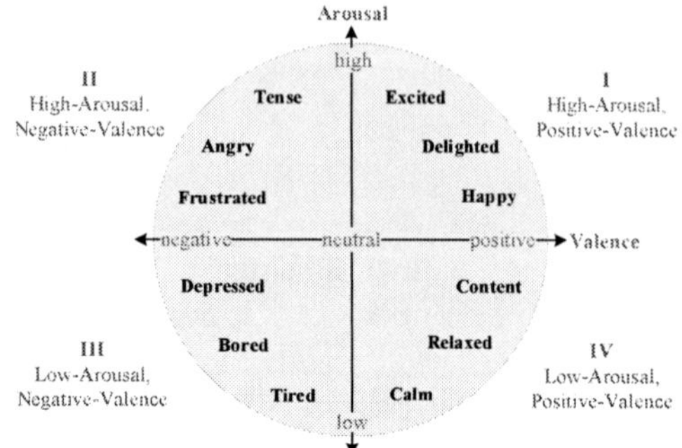

Figure 1: Two-dimensional valence-arousal space.

2   Task Description

This task seeks to evaluate the capability of systems for predicting dimensional sentiments of Chinese words and phrases. For a given word or phrase, participants were asked to provide a real-valued score from 1 to 9 for both the valence and arousal dimensions, respectively indicating the degree from most negative to most positive for valence, and from most calm to most excited for arousal. The input format is "term_id, term", and the output format is "term_id, valence_rating, arousal_rating". Below are the input/output formats of the example words "好" (good), "非常好" (very good), "满意" (satisfy) and "不满意" (not satisfy).

Example 1:
 Input: 1, 好
 Output: 1, 6.8, 5.2
Example 2:
 Input: 2, 非常好
 Output: 2, 8.500, 6.625
Example 3:
 Input: 3, 满意
 Output: 3, 7.2, 5.6
Example 4:
 Input: 4, 不满意
 Output: 4, 2.813, 5.688

3   Datasets

Training set: For single words, the training set was taken from the Chinese Valence-Arousal Words (CVAW)[1] (Yu et al., 2016a) version two, which contains 2,802 affective words annotated

---

[1] http://nlp.innobic.yzu.edu.tw/resources/cvaw.html

with valence-arousal ratings. For multi-word phrases, we first selected a set of modifiers such as negators (e.g., *not*), degree adverbs (e.g., *very*) and modals (e.g., *would*). These modifiers were combined with the affective words in CVAW to form multi-word phrases. The frequency of each phrase was then retrieved from a large web-based corpus. Only phrases with a frequency greater than or equal to 3 were retained as candidates. To avoid several modifiers dominating the whole dataset, each modifier (or modifier combination) can have at most 50 phrases. In addition, the phrases were selected to maximize the balance between positive and negative words. Finally, a total of 3,000 phrases were collected by excluding unusual and semantically incomplete candidate phrases, of which 2,250 phrases were randomly selected as the training set according to the proportions of each modifier (or modifier combination) in the original set, and the remaining 750 phrases were used as the test set.

Test set: For single words, we selected 750 words that were not included in the CVAW 2.0 from NTUSD (Ku and Chen, 2007) using the same method presented in our previous task on Dimensional Sentiment Analysis for Chinese Words (Yu et al, 2016b).

Each single word in both training and test sets was annotated with valence-arousal ratings by five annotators and the average ratings were taken as ground truth. Each multi-word phrase was rated by at least 10 different annotators. Once the rating process was finished, a corpus clean up procedure was performed to remove outlier ratings that did not fall within the mean plus/minus 1.5 standard deviations. They were then excluded from the calculation of the average ratings for each phrase.

The policy of this shared task was implemented as is an open test. That is, in addition to the above official datasets, participating teams were allowed to use other publicly available data for system development, but such sources should be specified in the final technical report.

4   Evaluation Metrics

Prediction performance is evaluated by examining the difference between machine-predicted ratings and human-annotated ratings, in which valence and arousal are treated independently. The evaluation metrics include Mean Absolute Error (MAE)

Team	Affiliation	#Run
AL_I_NLP	Alibaba	2
CASIA	Institute of Automation, Chinese Academy of Sciences	1
CIAL	Academia Sinica & Taipei Medical University	2
CKIP	Institute of Information Science, Academia Sinica	2
DeepCybErNet	Amrita University, India	0
Dlg	IIT Hyderabad	0
DCU	ADAPT Centre, Dublin City University, Ireland	0
G-719	Yunnan University	0
LDCCNLP	Fuzhou University	2
Mainiway AI	Shanghai Mainiway Corp.	2
NCTU-NTUT	National Chiao Tung University & National Taipei University of Technology	2
NCYU	National Chiayi University	2
NLPSA	Institute of Information Science, Academia Sinica	2
NTOU	National Taiwan Ocean University	2
SAM	Soochow University	1
THU_NGN	Department of Electronic Engineering, Tsinghua University	2
TeeMo	Southeast University	0
UIUC	University of Illinois at Urbana Champaign	0
XMUT	Xiamen University of Technology	1

Table 1: Submission statistics for all participating teams.

and Pearson Correction Coefficient (PCC), as shown in the following equations.

- **Mean absolute error (MAE)**

$$MAE = \frac{1}{n}\sum_{i=1}^{n} | A_i - P_i | \qquad (1)$$

- **Pearson correlation coefficient (PCC)**

$$PCC = \frac{1}{n-1}\sum_{i=1}^{n}(\frac{A_i - \overline{A}}{\sigma_A})(\frac{P_i - \overline{P}}{\sigma_P}) \qquad (2)$$

where A_i is the actual value, P_i is the predicted value, n is the number of test samples, $\overline{A}$ and $\overline{P}$ respectively denote the arithmetic mean of A and P, and σ is the standard deviation. The MAE measures the error rate and the PCC measures the linear correlation between the actual values and the predicted values. A lower MAE and a higher PCC indicate more accurate prediction performance.

5 Evaluation Results

5.1 Participants

Table 1 summarizes the submission statistics for 19 participating teams including 7 from universities and research institutes in China (CASIA, G-719, LDCCNLP, SAM, THU_NGN, TeeMo and XMUT), 6 from Taiwan (CIAL, CKIP, NCTU-NTUT, NCYU, NLPSA and NTOU), 2 private films (AL_I_NLP and Mainiway AI), 2 teams from India (DeepCybErNet and Dlg), one from Europe (DCU) and one team from USA (UIUC). Thirteen of the 19 registered teams submitted their testing results. In the testing phase, each team was allowed to submit at most two runs. Three teams submitted only one run, while the other 10 teams submitted two runs for a total of 23 runs.

Word-Level	Valence MAE	Valence PCC	Arousal MAE	Arousal PCC
Baseline	0.984	0.643	1.031	0.456
AL_I_NLP-Run1	0.547	0.891	**0.853**	0.667
AL_I_NLP-Run2	0.545	0.892	0.857	0.678
CASIA-Run1	0.725	0.803	1.069	0.428
CIAL-Run1	0.644	0.853	1.039	0.423
CIAL-Run2	0.644	0.85	1.036	0.426
CKIP-Run1	0.602	0.858	0.949	0.576
CKIP-Run2	0.665	0.855	1.133	0.569
LDCCNLP-Run1	0.811	0.769	0.996	0.479
LDCCNLP-Run2	1.219	0.521	1.235	0.346
MainiwayAI-Run1	0.715	0.796	1.032	0.509
MainiwayAI-Run2	0.706	0.800	0.985	0.552
NCTU-NTUT-Run1	0.632	0.846	0.952	0.543
NCTU-NTUT-Run2	0.639	0.842	0.94	0.566
NCYU-Run1	0.922	0.645	1.155	0.428
NCYU-Run2	1.235	0.663	1.177	0.402
NLPSA-Run1	1.108	0.561	1.207	0.351
NLPSA-Run2	1.000	0.604	1.207	0.351
NTOU-Run1	0.913	0.700	1.133	0.163
NTOU-Run2	1.061	0.544	1.114	0.35
SAM-Run1	1.098	0.639	1.027	0.378
THU_NGN-Run1	0.610	0.857	0.940	0.623
THU_NGN-Run2	**0.509**	**0.908**	0.864	**0.686**
XMUT-Run1	0.946	0.701	1.036	0.451

Table 2: Comparative results of valence-arousal prediction for single words.

5.2 Baseline

We implemented a baseline by training a linear regression model using word vectors as the only features. For single words, the regression was implemented by directly training word vectors to determine VA scores.

Given a word w_i, the baseline regression model is defined as

$$Val_{w_i} = W_w^{val} \cdot vec(w_i) + b_w^{val}$$
$$Aro_{w_i} = W_w^{aro} \cdot vec(w_i) + b_w^{aro} \quad (3)$$

where Val_{wi} and Aro_{wi} respectively denote the valence and arousal ratings of w_i. W and b respectively denote the weights and bias. For phrases, we first calculate the mean vector of the constituent words in the phrase, considering each modifier word can also obtain its word vector. Give a phrase p_j, its representation can be obtained by,

$$vec(p_j) = mean[vec(w_1), vec(w_2),..., vec(w_n)] \quad (4)$$

where $w_i \in p_j$ is the word in phrase p_j. The regression was then trained using $vec(p_j)$ as a feature, defined as

$$Val_{p_j} = W_p^{val} \cdot vec(p_i) + b_p^{val}$$
$$Aro_{p_j} = W_p^{aro} \cdot vec(p_i) + b_p^{aro} \quad (5)$$

Phrase-Level	Valence MAE	Valence PCC	Arousal MAE	Arousal PCC
Baseline	1.051	0.610	0.607	0.730
AL_I_NLP-Run1	0.531	0.900	0.465	0.855
AL_I_NLP-Run2	0.526	0.901	0.465	0.854
CASIA-Run1	1.008	0.598	0.816	0.683
CIAL-Run1	0.723	0.835	0.914	0.756
CIAL-Run2	1.152	0.647	1.596	0.286
CKIP-Run1	0.492	0.921	**0.382**	0.908
CKIP-Run2	0.444	0.935	0.395	0.904
LDCCNLP-Run1	0.822	0.762	0.489	0.828
LDCCNLP-Run2	0.916	0.632	0.605	0.742
MainiwayAI-Run1	0.612	0.861	0.554	0.793
MainiwayAI-Run2	0.577	0.874	0.524	0.813
NCTU-NTUT-Run1	0.454	0.928	0.488	0.847
NCTU-NTUT-Run2	0.453	0.931	0.517	0.832
NCYU-Run1	1.035	0.725	0.735	0.670
NCYU-Run2	1.175	0.670	0.801	0.666
NLPSA-Run1	0.709	0.818	0.632	0.732
NLPSA-Run2	0.689	0.829	0.633	0.727
NTOU-Run1	0.472	0.910	0.420	0.882
NTOU-Run2	0.453	0.929	0.441	0.870
SAM-Run1	0.960	0.669	0.722	0.704
THU_NGN-Run1	0.349	0.960	0.389	0.909
THU_NGN-Run2	**0.345**	**0.961**	0.385	**0.911**
XMUT-Run1	1.723	0.064	1.163	0.084

Table 3: Comparative results of valence-arousal prediction for multi-word phrases.

The word vectors were trained on the Chinese Wiki Corpus [2] using the CBOW model of word2vec [3] (Mikolov et al., 2013a; 2013b) (dimensionality=300 and window size=5).

5.3 Results

Tables 2 shows the results of valence-arousal prediction for single words. The three best performing systems are summarized as follows.

- Valence MAE: THU_NGN, AL_I_NLP and CKIP.
- Valence PCC: THU_NGN, AL_I_NLP and CKIP.

- Arousal MAE: AL_I_NLP, THU_NGN and NCTU-NTUT.
- Arousal PCC: THU_NGN, AL_I_NLP and CKIP.

Tables 3 shows the results of valence-arousal prediction for multi-word phrases. The three best performing systems are summarized as follows.

- Valence MAE: THU_NGN, CKIP and NCTU-NTUT.
- Valence PCC: THU_NGN, CKIP and NCTU-NTUT.
- Arousal MAE: CKIP, THU_NGN and NTOU.
- Arousal PCC: THU_NGN, CKIP and NTOU.

[2] https://dumps.wikimedia.org/
[3] http://code.google.com/p/word2vec/

All-Level	V-MAE	V-MAE Rank	V- PCC	V- PCC Rank	A-MAE	A-MAE Rank	A-PCC	A-PCC Rank	Mean Rank
THU_NGN-Run2	0.427	1	0.9345	1	0.6245	1	0.7985	1	1
THU_NGN-Run1	0.4795	2	0.9085	2	0.6645	4	0.766	3	2.75
AL_I_NLP-Run2	0.5355	3	0.8965	3	0.661	3	0.766	2	2.75
AL_I_NLP-Run1	0.539	4	0.8955	4	0.659	2	0.761	4	3.5
CKIP-Run1	0.547	7	0.8895	6	0.6655	5	0.742	5	5.75
NCTU-NTUT-Run1	0.543	5	0.887	7	0.72	6	0.695	8	6.5
NCTU-NTUT-Run2	0.546	6	0.8865	8	0.7285	7	0.699	7	7
CKIP-Run2	0.5545	8	0.895	5	0.764	10	0.7365	6	7.25
MainiwayAI-Run2	0.6415	9	0.837	10	0.7545	9	0.6825	9	9.25
MainiwayAI-Run1	0.6635	10	0.8285	11	0.793	13	0.651	11	11.25
LDCCNLP-Run1	0.8165	14	0.7655	13	0.7425	8	0.6535	10	11.25
NTOU-Run2	0.757	13	0.7365	15	0.7775	12	0.61	12	13
CIAL-Run1	0.6835	11	0.844	9	0.9765	21	0.5895	14	13.75
NTOU-Run1	0.6925	12	0.805	12	0.7765	11	0.5225	22	14.25
CASIA-Run1	0.8665	16	0.7005	17	0.9425	19	0.5555	15	16.75
NLPSA-Run2	0.8445	15	0.7165	16	0.92	17	0.539	20	17
Baseline	1.0175	20	0.6265	22	0.819	14	0.593	13	17.25
NLPSA-Run1	0.9085	18	0.6895	18	0.9195	16	0.5415	18	17.5
NCYU-Run1	0.9785	19	0.685	19	0.945	20	0.549	16	18.5
SAM-Run1	1.029	21	0.654	21	0.8745	15	0.541	19	19
CIAL-Run2	0.898	17	0.7485	14	1.316	24	0.356	23	19.5
LDCCNLP-Run2	1.0675	22	0.5765	23	0.92	18	0.544	17	20
NCYU-Run2	1.205	23	0.6665	20	0.989	22	0.534	21	21.5
XMUT-Run1	1.3345	24	0.3825	24	1.0995	23	0.2675	24	23.75

Table 4: Comparative results of valence-arousal prediction for both words and phrases.

Table 4 shows the overall results for both single words and multi-word phrases. We rank the MAE and PCC independently and calculate the mean rank (average of MAE rank and PCC rank) for ordering system performance. The three best performing systems are THU_NGN, AL_I_NLP and CKIP.

Table 5 summarizes the approaches for each participating system. CASIA, SAM and XMUT did not submit reports on their developed methods. Nearly all teams used word embeddings. The most commonly used word embeddings were word2vec (Mikolov et al., 2013a; 2013b) and GloVe (Pennington et al., 2014). Others included FastText [4] (Bojanowski et al., 2017), character-enhanced word embedding (Chen et al., 2015) and Cw2vec (Cao et al., 2017). For machine learning algorithms, six teams used deep neural networks such as feed-forward neural network (CKIP), boosted neural network (BNN) (AL_I_NLP), convolutional neural network (CNN) (NLPSA), long short-term memory (LSTM) (NCTU-NTUT and THU_NGN) and ensembles (Mainiway AI and THU_NGN). Three teams used regression-based methods such as support vector regression (CIAL, CKIP, LDCCNLP) and linear regression (CIAL). Other methods included a lexicon-based

---

[4] https://github.com/facebookresearch/fastText

Team	Approach		Word/ Character Embedding
	Word-Level	**Phrase-level**	
AL_I_NLP	Boosted neural networks		Word2Vec GloVe Character-enhanced Cw2vec
CIAL	Valence 1.WVA+CVA 2.kNN Arousal 1.Linear regression 2.SVR	ADV Weight List	Word2vec
CKIP	1.E-HowNet-based predictor 2.Word embedding with kNN	1.SVR-RBF 2.Feed-forward neural networks	GloVe
LDCCNLP	SVR		GloVe
Mainiway AI	Ensembles of deep neural networks		FastText (character-level)
NCTU-NTUT	Variable length/Bi-directional LSTM		Word2vec (order-aware) Phrase2vec
NCYU	Vector-based method	sentiment phrase-like unit	—
NLPSA	CNN (integration of words and images)		GloVe
NTOU	Co-occurrence, sentiment scores	Word, sentiment scores Random forest	—
THU_NGN	Densely connected deep LSTM with model ensemble		Word2vec

Table 5: Summary of approaches used by the participating systems.

E-HowNet (Huang et al., 2008) predictor (CKIP) and heuristic-based ADV Weight List (CIAL).

6   Conclusions

This study describes an overview of the IJCNLP 2017 shared task on dimensional sentiment analysis for Chinese phrases, including task design, data preparation, performance metrics, and evaluation results. Regardless of actual performance, all submissions contribute to the common effort to develop dimensional approaches for affective computing, and the individual report in the proceedings provide useful insights into Chinese sentiment analysis.

We hope the data sets collected and annotated for this shared task can facilitate and expedite future development in this research area. Therefore, all data sets with gold standard and scoring script are publicly available[5].

Acknowledgments

This work was supported by the Ministry of Science and Technology, Taiwan, ROC, under Grant No. MOST 105-2221-E-155-059-MY2 and MOST 105-2218-E-006-028, and the National Natural Science Foundation of China (NSFC) under Grant No.61702443 and-No.61762091.

References

Piotr Bojanowski, Edouard Grave, Armand Joulin, and Tomas Mikolov. 2017. Enriching word vectors with subword information. *Transactions of the Association for Computational Linguistics* 5:135–146.

---

[5] http://nlp.innobic.yzu.edu.tw/tasks/dsa_p/

Rafael A. Calvo and Sunghwan Mac Kim. 2013. Emotions in text: dimensional and categorical models. *Computational Intelligence*, 29(3):527-543.

Shaosheng Cao, Wei Lu, Jun Zhou, and Xiaolong Li. 2017. Investigating chinese word embeddings based on stroke information.

Xinxiong Chen, Lei Xu, Zhiyuan Liu, Maosong Sun, and Huan-Bo Luan. 2015. Joint learning of character- and word embeddings. In *Proc. of the 25th International Joint Conference on Artificial Intelligence (IJCAI-15)*, pages 1236–1242.

Munmun De Choudhury, Scott Counts, and Michael Gamon. 2012. Not all moods are created equal! Exploring human emotional states in social media. In *Proc. of the 6th International AAAI Conference on Weblogs and Social Media (ICWSM-12)*, pages 66-73.

Shu-Ling Huang, Yueh-Yin Shih, and Keh-Jiann Chen. 2008. Knowledge representation for comparative constructions in extended-HowNet. *Language and Linguistics*, 9(2):395-413, 2008.

Sunghwan Mac Kim, Alessandro Valitutti, and Rafael A. Calvo. 2010. Evaluation of unsupervised emotion models to textual affect recognition. In *Proc. of the NAACL HLT 2010 Workshop on Computational Approaches to Analysis and Generation of Emotion in Text*, pages 62-70.

Lun-Wei Ku and Hsin-Hsi Chen. 2007. Mining Opinions from the Web: Beyond Relevance Retrieval. Journal of American Society for Information Science and Technology, *Special Issue on Mining Web Resources for Enhancing Information Retrieval*, 58(12):1838-1850.

Nikos Malandrakis, Alexandros Potamianos, Elias Iosif, and Shrikanth Narayanan, 2011. Kernel models for affective lexicon creation. In *Proc. of INTERSPEECH-11*, pages 2977-2980.

Tomas Mikolov, Kai Chen, Greg Corrado, and Jeffrey Dean. 2013a. Distributed representations of words and phrases and their compositionality. In *Proceedings of the Annual Conference on Advances in Neural Information Processing Systems (NIPS-13)*, pages 1-9.

Tomas Mikolov, Greg Corrado, Kai Chen, and Jeffrey Dean. 2013b. Efficient estimation of word representations in vector space. In *Proceedings of the International Conference on Learning Representations (ICLR-2013)*, pages 1-12.

Myriam Munezero, Tuomo Kakkonen, and Calkin S. Montero. 2011. Towards automatic detection of antisocial behavior from texts. In *Proc. of the Workshop on Sentiment Analysis where AI meets Psychology (SAAIP) at IJCNLP-11*, pages 20-27.

Georgios Paltoglou, Mathias Theunis, Arvid Kappas, and Mike Thelwall. 2013. Predicting emotional responses to long informal text. *IEEE Trans. Affective Computing*, 4(1):106-115.

Jeffrey Pennington, Richard Socher, and Christopher D. Manning. 2014. GloVe: Global vectors for word representation. In *Proceedings of the Conference on Empirical Methods in Natural Language Processing (EMNLP-14)*, pages 1532-1543.

Jie Ren and Jeffrey V. Nickerson. 2014. Online review systems: How emotional language drives sales. In *Proc. of the 20th Americas Conference on Information Systems (AMCIS-14)*.

James A. Russell. 1980. A circumplex model of affect. *Journal of Personality and Social Psychology*, 39(6):1161.

Wen-Li Wei, Chung-Hsien Wu, and Jen-Chun Lin. 2011. A regression approach to affective rating of Chinese words from ANEW. In *Proc. of the 4th International Conference on Affective Computing and Intelligent Interaction (ACII-11)*, pages 121-131.

Liang-Chih Yu, Lung-Hao Lee, Shuai Hao, Jin Wang, Yunchao He, Jun Hu, K. Robert Lai, and Xuejie Zhang. 2016a. Building Chinese affective resources in valence-arousal dimensions. In *Proc. of NAACL/HLT-16*, pages 540-545.

Liang-Chih Yu, Lung-Hao Lee and Kam-Fai Wong. 2016b. Overview of the IALP 2016 shared task on dimensional sentiment analysis for Chinese words, in *Proc. of the 20th International Conference on Asian Language Processing (IALP-16)*, pages 156-160.

Jin Wang, Liang-Chih Yu, K. Robert Lai and Xuejie Zhang. 2016a. Community-based weighted graph model for valence-arousal prediction of affective words, *IEEE/ACM Trans. Audio, Speech and Language Processing*, 24(11):1957-1968.

Jin Wang, Liang-Chih Yu, K. Robert Lai, and Xuejie Zhang. 2016b. Dimensional sentiment analysis using a regional CNN-LSTM model. In *Proc. of the 54th Annual Meeting of the Association for Computational Linguistics (ACL-16)*, pages 225-230.

IJCNLP-2017 Task 3: Review Opinion Diversification (RevOpiD-2017)

Anil Kumar Singh, Avijit Thawani
Mayank Panchal, Anubhav Gupta
IIT (BHU), Varanasi, India

Julian McAuley
University of California, San Diego

Abstract

Unlike Entity Disambiguation in web search results, Opinion Disambiguation is a relatively unexplored topic. RevOpiD shared task at IJCNLP-2107 aimed to attract attention towards this research problem. In this paper, we summarize the first run of this task and introduce a new dataset that we have annotated for the purpose of evaluating Opinion Mining, Summarization and Disambiguation methods.

1 Introduction

In the famous Asch Conformity experiment, individuals were first shown a line segment on a card. Next, they were shown another card with 3 line segments (with a significant difference in length) and were asked to decide which of the 3 matched the length of the previously shown line. The same task was then to be performed in the presence of a group of 8 people (where the remaining 7 were confederates/actors, all of whom were instructed beforehand to give the wrong answer). The error rate soared from a bare 1 percent in the case the subject was alone, to 36.8 percent when the people around expressed the wrong perception (Asch and Guetzkow, 1951). This goes to show how heavily can others' opinions influence our own. With the ever growing influence of sources of opinion today, the need to regulate them is also at an all time high. Documents in the form of social media posts, web blogs, biased or fake news articles, tweets and product reviews can be listed as the primary sources of opinionated information one encounters on a daily basis. Vidulich et. al (Vidulich and Kaiman, 1961) also reported similar results in experiments with the sources of conformity. They found that dogmatists are influenced by the status of the source of information.

The domains of Search Result Ranking and Document Summarization then possess a great potential (and bear a great responsibility) in influencing popular opinion about a target entity. For example, if on searching for 'iPhone reviews', we see results (ranked by, say, PageRank) that coincidentally happen to be against the product, then one might form a perception of the general opinion around the world regarding the smartphone. This perception may or may not be in line with the original composition of the opinion worldwide. What, then, should be the basis of document ranking in Information Retrieval methods?

To delve deeper into addressing this problem, we chose to limit ourselves to a single type of documents: Product Reviews. The reason behind this choice is manifold: Product Reviews are concise, targeted, opinionated (though sometimes descriptive and sometimes objective), diverse (in terms of the category of product), readily available as datasets, and easily comprehended (which makes annotating such data relatively easier). Besides, finding a diverse subset of product review documents (in terms of opinions) provides a good application, which might be of commercial interest to e-commerce websites.

For a product with several reviews, it can get cumbersome for a user to browse through them all. According to an internet source, 90 percent of consumers form an opinion by reading at most 10 reviews, while 68 percent form their opinion after reading just 1-6 reviews.[1] It leads to a natural curiosity into the manner in which reviews are ordered. Order by date (most recent reviews first), order by upvotes (reviews voted 'helpful' the most are ranked first), group by words (show only those reviews which contain specific words, eg. 'battery'), group by stance (segregate reviews

---

[1] https://www.brightlocal.com/learn/local-consumer-review-survey/

Proceedings of the 8th International Joint Conference on Natural Language Processing, Shared Tasks, pages 17–25,
Taipei, Taiwan, November 27 – December 1, 2017. ©2017 AFNLP

into positive and negative), group by stars (filter reviews which gave a certain number of stars to the product) are some of the techniques used in sorting and ranking of online customer reviews.

However, only the last two of these take into account the difference of opinions in reviews. And not even these take into account the overall opinion about the product. What we propose is a ranked list that aims to represent a gist of opinions of the whole set of reviews (for any given product). To this end, we will present a novel dataset that can be used as a benchmark for evaluating such a ranked list in Section 3. We will also summarize the details of RevOpiD 2017, the first run of Review Opinion Diversification shared task in Section 4.

2 Related Work

Many researchers have undertaken the study of opinion diversity, but most exhibit limited scope owing to the absence of a standard dataset among the community. The Blog Track Opinion Finding Task (TREC 6-8) has a favourable corpus, and was initially meant to judge systems on their Re-ranking approach on web search results, based on opinion diversity.

The Aspect Based Sentiment Analysis task at SemEval 2014-2016 (Pontiki et al., 2014) was an initiative towards the objective evaluation of sentiment expressed in product reviews. In a wide enough corpora of 39 datasets, ranging across 7 domains and 8 languages, the task was to identify target entity and pick the attribute commented upon (from a list of attributes already provided to annotators).

Our aim differs slightly in that we reward systems which ultimately produce an opinion diversified (and representative) ranking of a subset of the review corpora. The motivation for this statement bases itself on two targeted benefits:

1. Due to absence of an inventory of aspects or opinions for the participants to 'identify', the systems must mine new 'aspects' that vary enormously for different products. Thus, vague aspects in the form of topics modelled will be rewarded equivalently to another approach that, say, manages to match exact lexicons to the subtopics retrieved.

2. We avoid evaluating the opinions on the opinions mined since the number of opinions expressed is a subjective choice made by annotators in the labelling process. For instance, if one annotator suggests having 'affordable' and 'worth the money' as two different opinions whereas a system assumes both to express the same opinion, it may still perform well on diversifying the ranked list. Hence our evaluation on the final ranked list prevents systems from over-fitting on the opinions mined.

Despite the limitations in previous opinion mining evaluations, a recurring and fundamental feature in most of these methodologies is the identification of nuggets (in summarization jargon) or subtopics (in indexing terminology) or attributes (in product reviews); and their subsequent application in having a fine-grained view at the relevance contained in a document. In our pursuit of a tested and suitable data collection, we observed the small-scale attempts at similar data annotation (Marcheggiani et al., 2014) (Täckström and McDonald, 2011) (a few tens of reviews at most, for evaluation of their own opinion mining and discourse analysis systems respectively). The most well known among these is the 'Mining and Summarizing Customer Reviews' paper by Bing et. al. (Hu and Liu, 2004). The experimentation in this publication is based on a compilation of the first 100 reviews of 5 products from Amazon.com and cnet.com. Initially, there were 9 and then 3 more products were added in subsequent years (Ding et al., 2008) (Liu et al., 2015). These reviews were sentence-wise annotated with the following:

1. feature on which opinion is expressed, if any

2. orientation of opinion (+ or -)

3. opinion strength (on a scale of 1 to 3)

An example of annotation by the human taggers (the authors of the paper themselves) for a Digital Camera is: "affordability[+3]while , there are flaws with the machine , the xtra gets five stars because of its affordability ."

3 Dataset

The dataset labelled by Bing et. al. is created through a fairly suitable and scalable annotation procedure, despite the inherent flaws associated with subjectivity of human annotation. A

Sterling Silver Cubic Zirconia Eternity Ring		
Product Reviews		**Rating**
1. Alex Date : 24/07/2016		
This ring is pretty, it can go good with another ring. It narrow and the stone size is small by it self. It would be a good thumb ring. Again nice ring that does not have alot of bling.		3.0/5.0
2. Bran Date : 20/07/2016		
The ring was a gift and my daughter loved it!!! It is very sparkly and fit just right! I would highly recommend this product.		4.0/5.0
3. Chau Date : 14/07/2016		
This ring is amazing for the price. It doesn't turn my finger white, and the sizing is great. It's just a little bling that isn't too flashy. I wear it as a thumb ring. I think it's really pretty, and very sparkly.		3.0/5.0
4. Dany Date : 29/06/2016		
This sterling ring is not too wide, it has a nice touch with the CZ all the way around, making it easier to wear for my wife, because she doesn't worry about it spinning and cutting into the fingers to the side. The CZ stones are recessed a bit making it pretty smooth.		1.0/5.0

Table 1: A Sample Ranking of Product Reviews

few drawbacks are yet to be addressed before we present our Opinion Labelling procedure:

1. Bing et. al. aimed to mine features and opinions from review texts, and hence it is justifiable to practice sentence-wise labelling. On the other hand, for evaluation of opinion diversity in reviews (or any document), labelling of each statement is less of a benefit and very time consuming.

2. The referred dataset contained 96 unique features for a total of 95 reviews (product: Digital Camera 2). Such an exhaustive labelling is again detrimental to the annotation efforts, and is of limited benefits. A reasoning behind this can be observed from the way commercial websites continue to sort their reviews. TripAdvisor, for instance, uses a common set of just 6 attributes: 'Location', 'Service'...

Note that identification of opinions on a per-product basis is a key point of the procedure described in this paper.

3.1 Labelling Procedure

Having established our primary objectives behind the need for a opinion-labelled dataset, we now propose our opinion labelling procedure. Labelling process can be broken down into 2 steps. Note that this procedure is to be iterated for each product individually.

1. Make an opinion list, i.e., a set of popular opinions recurrently occurring in the reviews.

2. Make an opinion matrix. The opinion-document matrix (or simply the opinion matrix) is a tabular output of the labelling process, with each row corresponding to a review and each column corresponding to an opinion from the opinion list of the product.

Due to the space constraints, we avoid full textual description and complete specification of guidelines for the dataset. We proceed to show a sample Opinion List (Table 2) and a sample Opinion-Document matrix (Table 3).

3.2 Proportion

Our opinion annotated dataset is derived from a subset of Amazon SNAP online reviews dataset (McAuley and Leskovec, 2013). The original SNAP dataset contains more than 34 million reviews spanning over 2 million products. 85 products were chosen from among these, spanning 12 categories, and were labelled with opinions. The number of reviews per product is shown in Table 4 and the number of opinions taken (as considered by annotators) for each product are shown in Table 5. The products in both these tables have been grouped by their category. Eg. Office category has 6 products which are included in our dataset.

Opinion List
Realistic look
Good deal
Thumb ring replacement
Preference of sizes
Good for gifts
Matches with jewelry collection
Dainty and sparkly ring
Comfortable fit
Quality product
Long lasting and durable
Great substitute for wedding ring
Cleans easy
Not upto the pic
Looks expensive
Stones are small
'Made in China' on the interior looks bad
Stones fallen out
Not much sparkly

Table 2: Opinion List for "Sterling Silver Cubic Zirconia Eternity Ring"

Opinion Matrix					
	Realistic Look	Good deal	Many sizes	Good for gifts	Sparkly ring
Review1	X	X			X
Review2		X			
Review3			X	X	
Review4	X				X
Review5	X	X	X		
Review6	X			X	
Review7				X	X
Review8	X		X		
Review9					X
Review10		X	X	X	
Overall	5	4	5	4	4

Table 3: Opinion Matrix for "Sterling Silver Cubic Zirconia Eternity Ring"

3.3 Inter Annotator Confidence

Our proposed evaluation framework relies heavily on the labelling procedure described above, which in turn has the major factor of human subjectivity. What one annotator deems as an opinion (as expressed in a certain number of reviews for a product) might not seem significant enough for another annotator. Thus inter annotator agreement studies are crucial for judging our dataset's reliability. We conducted an experiment asking 5 of our annotators to annotate a single product's review files (only the first 25 reviews). Since opinion lists are not marked 0s or 1s but contain natural language (opinions in the form of text), it is difficult to measure their agreement objectively. Instead, we checked the inter-annotator confidence on whether specific opinions occur in a given review or not. For every pair of annotators A and B, whose inter annotator agreement is to be calculated, we manually select certain opinions from O1 (opinion list of A) which have more or less equivalent opinions in O2 (opinion list of B). Let this set be called O3. Thereafter, presence or absence of opinion o_i in a review r_i in opinion matrix M1 (matrix of A) is compared with that in M2 (matrix of B).

Cohen's Kappa inter-rater agreement (Fleiss and Cohen, 1973) for different pairs of annotators is summarized in Table 6. For example annotators A1 and A2 show a Cohen's Kappa coefficient of 0.77 for the commonly occurring opinion "Realistic look". Some blank cells exist (for example, in A1-A3 and A2-A3 under 'Moderate') since not all opinions occur in the opinion lists of all annotators.

4   RevOpiD-2017

RevOpiD-2017 is a part of the 8th International Joint Conference on Natural Language Processing (November 27 to December 1, 2017) at Taipei, Taiwan. The shared task consists of three independent subtasks. Participating systems are required to produce a top-k summarized ranking of reviews (one ranked list for each product for a given subtask) from amongst the given set of reviews. The redundancy of opinions expressed in the review corpus must be minimised, along with maximisation of a certain property. This property can be one of the following (one property corresponds to one subtask):

1. usefulness rating of the review (Subtask A)

2. representativeness of the overall corpus of reviews (Subtask B)

3. exhaustiveness of opinions expressed (Subtask C)

Some Definitions:

1. Review: Review text and any other relevant metadata as may be considered necessary to be used by the participating system, from the given data.

Reviews per Product									
Baby	133	113	111	103	132	124	100	107	125	111
Automotive	149	147	150	110	123	103	101	105	150
Health	112	114	104	101	127	120	103	126	107
Grocery	114	118	147	117	122	115	100	146
PetSupplies	105	132	100	128	120	146	105
Beauty	137	143	123	137	109	102	102
PatioLawn	143	115	109	104	105	119	150
Office	135	124	131	119	101	131
ToolsHome	123	99	146	138	135	131
DigitalMusic	130	129	102	125	142	102
VideoGames	117	108	108	101	116
ToysGames	114	126	138	149	111

Table 4: Reviews per Product

Opinions per Product									
Baby	19	27	23	27	17	12	20	20	16	23
Automotive	22	23	23	14	23	13	17	18	23
Health	22	26	23	20	22	39	11	21	18
Grocery	21	26	14	21	27	11	17	22
PetSupplies	17	27	12	16	22	15	21
Beauty	22	26	13	16	23	18	20
PatioLawn	22	26	17	30	13	19	26
Office	19	27	18	15	11	18
ToolsHome	21	18	25	15	29	21
DigitalMusic	25	31	18	22	15	18
VideoGames	20	24	11	27	28
ToysGames	19	24	32	14	16

Table 5: Opinions per Product

2. Corpus: All the reviews for a given product.

3. Feature: A ratable aspect of the product.

4. Opinion: An ordered pair of an aspect and sentiment (for that aspect) in any review.

For the purpose of RevOpiD 2017, our derived dataset was split into three parts:

1. Training Data: was the same as the SNAP dataset, except it being a subset of the latter. Statistics of the training data has been shown in Table 7.

2. Development Data: contained annotated opinion matrices along with the text review files for 30 products. These matrices were used by an evaluation script to measure the performance of participating systems in Subtasks B and C (for representativeness and exhuastiveness).

3. Test Data: The test data contained the review text files alone (also devoid of usefulness scores) of 50 products. The opinion matrices were withheld by us to evaluate final scores based on this test data.

4.1 Task Description

4.1.1 Subtask A (Usefulness Ranking)

Usefulness rating is a user-collected field in the provided training dataset. Given a corpus of reviews for a particular product, the goal is to rank the top-k of them, according to predicted usefulness rating, while simultaneously penalizing redundancy among the ranked list of reviews. An essential subsection of this task obviously includes predicting the usefulness rating for a particular review.

Kappa Inter Rater Agreement (on opinion matrix) scores for 3 of our annotators			
	A1-A2	A2-A3	A3-A1
Looks Real	0.77	0.77	0.61
Perfect Fit	0.43	0.38	0.29
Moderate	1.0		
Pretty	0.30		
Light Weight	1.0		
Good Deal			0.34
Different from Image	0.64		
Looks Cheap	0.0		
Affordable		0.66	
Alternate to wedding ring		0.78	
Not bright			1.0
No Maintenance		-0.05	
Looks Expensive	1.0	1.0	1.0
Alternate to thumb ring			0.62
Good Gift			1.0
Matches with Jwellery			0.64
Cleans Easy			0.0
Overall	0.59	0.59	0.61

Table 6: Inter Rater Agreement (on opinion matrix) Kappa scores for 3 of our annotators. Product category: Automotive. Number of reviews: 25

Data Statistics			
	Products	Reviews	Avg Reviews per Products
Automotive	569	172106	302
Baby	1000	352231	352
Beauty	1000	316536	316
Digital music	468	145075	309
Grocery	800	293629	367
Health	1000	357669	357
Office	1000	327556	327
Patio lawn	859	263489	306
Pet supplies	1000	398658	398
Tools home	1000	320162	320
Toys games	1000	314634	314
Video games	1000	358235	358

Table 7: Data Statistics

4.1.2 Subtask B (Representativeness Ranking)

Given a corpus of reviews for a particular product, the goal is to rank the top-k of them, so as to maximize representativeness of the ranked list. The ranking should summarize the perspectives expressed in the reviews given as input, incorporating a trade-off between diversity and novelty.

An ideal representation would be one that covers the popular perspectives expressed in the corpus, in proportion to their expression in the corpus (for that product), e.g. if 90 reviews claim that the iPhone cost is low, and 10 reviews claim that it is high, the former perspective should have 90 percent visibility in the final ranking and the latter should have 10 percent (or may even be ignored owing to low popularity) in the final ranking. The ranking should be such that for every i in $1 <= i <= k$, the top i reviews best represent the overall set of reviews for the product. That is, the #1 review should be the best single review to represent the overall opinion in the corpus; The combination of #1 and #2 reviews should be the best pair of reviews to represent the corpus, and so on.

4.1.3 Subtask C (Exhaustive Coverage Ranking)

Given a corpus of reviews for a particular product, the goal is to rank the top-k of them, so as to include the majority of popular perspectives in the corpus regarding the product, while simultaneously penalizing redundancy among the ranked list of reviews. This is similar to Subtask B, except that:

In Subtask B, the final ranking is judged on the basis of how well the ranked list represents the most popular opinions in the review corpus, in proportion. In Subtask C, the final ranking is judged on the basis of the exhaustive coverage of the opinions in the final ranking. That means, most of the significant (not necessarily all very popular) perspectives should be covered regardless of their proportions of popularity in the review corpus, e.g. if 90 reviews claim that the iPhone cost is low, and 10 reviews claim that it is high, both perspectives should be more or less equally reflected in the final ranked list.

4.2 Evaluation

This being the first run of RevOpiD, we experimented with several measures of evaluation (Singh et al.) and 8 of them were shortlisted to study their variations with the system submissions:

1. mth (More than half's): The fraction of reviews included (in submitted ranked list) with more than half votes in favour. In other words, if upvotes on a review be counted as the number of users who found it helpful, and downvotes be counted as the number of users who didn't find it helpful; then the mth count will be incremented by one if upvotes > downvotes.

2. Cosine similarity: Cosine similarity between Overall Vector and Opinion Vector

3. Discounted Cosine similarity: Cosine similarity between Overall Vector and Discounted Opinion Vector

4. Cumulative Proportionality: Based on Saint Lague method, used in Electoral seat alloca-

tion. (Dang and Croft, 2012). A ranking S is said to be proportional to the corpus D, or a proportional representation of D, with respect to opinions/aspects T, if and only if the number of documents in S that is relevant to each of the aspects $t_i \in T$ is proportional to its overall popularity $p_i \in D$.

5. α-DCG: A measure that rewards novel information (to be covered incrementally in each review) (Clarke et al., 2008).

6. Weighted Relevance: Discounted Cumulative Gain with the relevance of a review given by sum of weights of the opinions covered in the review (weight of an opinion = Number of reviews in which it appears in the whole opinion matrix / corpus size).

7. UnWeighted Relevance: A discounted sum of number of opinions present in the ranked list.

8. Recall: The fraction of opinions/columns covered by the ranking. An opinion is said to be covered if atleast a single 1 appears in that column in the ranked list submission.

4.3 Systems

There were 3 participating systems at RevOpiD-2017, namely JUNLP, CYUT and FAAD. Also included in our analysis is the official baseline (Subtasks B and C) [2]. The last row shows the scores obtained for a random submission script averaged over 5 runs.

While CYUT and FAAD have attempted Subtask A alone, JUNLP has submitted runs for each of Subtasks A, B and C.

1. JUNLP (Dey et al.): Instead of posing this as a regression problem, they have modeled it as a classification task where the aim is to identify whether a review is useful or not. They've employed a bi-directional LSTM to represent each review which is used with a softmax layer to predict the usefulness score. First they choose the review with highest usefulness score, then they find its cosine similarity score with rest of the reviews. This is done in order to ensure diversity in the selection of top-k reviews.

---

[2] https://github.com/shreyansh26/RevOpiD/tree/master

<table>
<tr><td colspan="9" align="center">RevOpiD final scores</td></tr>
<tr><td></td><td>mth</td><td>cos_d</td><td>cos</td><td>cpr</td><td>a-dcg</td><td>wt</td><td>unwt</td><td>recall</td></tr>
<tr><td>CYUT 1</td><td>0.71</td><td>0.83</td><td>0.84</td><td>0.7</td><td>4.28</td><td>504.18</td><td>14.31</td><td>0.71</td></tr>
<tr><td>CYUT 2</td><td>0.84</td><td>0.87</td><td>0.88</td><td>0.7</td><td>5.22</td><td>575.58</td><td>17.67</td><td>0.83</td></tr>
<tr><td>FAAD 1</td><td>0.78</td><td>0.86</td><td>0.87</td><td>0.49</td><td>4.27</td><td>494.03</td><td>14.04</td><td>0.76</td></tr>
<tr><td>FAAD 2</td><td>0.78</td><td>0.85</td><td>0.86</td><td>0.52</td><td>4.34</td><td>495.35</td><td>14.34</td><td>0.75</td></tr>
<tr><td>FAAD 3</td><td>0.78</td><td>0.84</td><td>0.85</td><td>0.51</td><td>4.11</td><td>486.51</td><td>13.35</td><td>0.72</td></tr>
<tr><td>JUNLP A</td><td>0.8</td><td>0.83</td><td>0.85</td><td>0.46</td><td>4.05</td><td>475.54</td><td>13.12</td><td>0.74</td></tr>
<tr><td>JUNLP B</td><td>0.7</td><td>0.86</td><td>0.87</td><td>0.71</td><td>4.98</td><td>556.94</td><td>16.9</td><td>0.81</td></tr>
<tr><td>JUNLP C</td><td>0.53</td><td>0.8</td><td>0.81</td><td>0.3</td><td>3.58</td><td>390.44</td><td>10.94</td><td>0.67</td></tr>
<tr><td>Baseline 0</td><td>0.64</td><td>0.84</td><td>0.84</td><td>0.74</td><td>4.53</td><td>533.41</td><td>15.33</td><td>0.73</td></tr>
<tr><td>Baseline 1</td><td>0.64</td><td>0.87</td><td>0.87</td><td>0.56</td><td>4.61</td><td>564.02</td><td>15.81</td><td>0.76</td></tr>
<tr><td>Baseline 2</td><td>0.65</td><td>0.86</td><td>0.86</td><td>0.54</td><td>4.6</td><td>566.68</td><td>15.85</td><td>0.75</td></tr>
<tr><td>Baseline 3</td><td>0.63</td><td>0.86</td><td>0.87</td><td>0.56</td><td>4.6</td><td>572.27</td><td>15.97</td><td>0.75</td></tr>
<tr><td>Expected</td><td>0.61</td><td>0.79</td><td>0.81</td><td>0.11</td><td>3.4</td><td>393.07</td><td>10.45</td><td>0.64</td></tr>
</table>

Table 8: System and Baseline Scores

2. CYUT (Wu et al.): This team (with prior work in helpfulness rating prediction of Chinese online reviews) implemented two models using linear regression with two different loss functions: least squares (CYUT 1) and cross entropy (CYUT 2).

3. FAAD (Mishra et al.): Two supervised classifiers (Naıve Bayes and Logistic Regression) are fitted on top of several extracted features such as the number of nouns, number of verbs, and the number of sentiment words etc. from the provided development and training datasets. Three runs (FAAD 1,2,3) vary only in the weightage given to the two classifiers.

4. Baseline: A feature based opinion extraction based on the work of Bing et al. This task is done in three steps:

(i) Identify the features of the product that customers have expressed opinions on (called opinion features) and rank the features according to their frequencies that they appear in the reviews.

(ii) For each feature, identify how many customer reviews have positive, negative or neutral opinions. The specific reviews that express these opinions are attached to the feature.

(iii) Generate an opinion matrix based on these predicted occurrences of opinions and greedily select the best representative and exhaustive rankings.

4.4 Results

The results of RevOpiD-2017 have been summarized in Table 8 for the chosen metrics already described above.

Based on the system performances, the feature selection mechanism in CYUT's submission using Cross Entropy loss function proves the leader in Subtask A. JUNLP's submission (representative ranking) outperforms others marginally in Subtask B and Subtask C. Not a lot of improvement is reported over the baseline, therefore there exists a lot of scope for improvement in Subtasks B and C.

Acknowledgments

This project was assisted upon by several enthusiastic students as well as lab annotators: Shreyansh Singh (for developing the baseline), Shashwat Trivedi, Shivam Arora, Avijeet Diwaker, Divyanshu Gupta, Avi Chawla, Ayush Sharma, Tara Hemaliya, Vandana Singh, Neelam and Rajesh Kumar Mundotiya.

References

Solomon E Asch and H Guetzkow. 1951. Effects of group pressure upon the modification and distortion of judgments. *Groups, leadership, and men*, pages 222–236.

Charles LA Clarke, Maheedhar Kolla, Gordon V Cormack, Olga Vechtomova, Azin Ashkan, Stefan Büttcher, and Ian MacKinnon. 2008. Novelty and diversity in information retrieval evaluation. In *Proceedings of the 31st annual international ACM SIGIR conference on Research and development in information retrieval*, pages 659–666. ACM.

Van Dang and W Bruce Croft. 2012. Diversity by proportionality: an election-based approach to search result diversification. In *Proceedings of the 35th international ACM SIGIR conference on Research and development in information retrieval*, pages 65–74. ACM.

Monalisa Dey, Anupam Mondal, and Dipankar Das. Junlp: Ijcnlp-2017 revopid- a rank prediction model for review opinion diversification. In *Proceedings of the IJCNLP-2017 Shared Tasks*.

Xiaowen Ding, Bing Liu, and Philip S Yu. 2008. A holistic lexicon-based approach to opinion mining. In *Proceedings of the 2008 international conference on web search and data mining*, pages 231–240. ACM.

Joseph L Fleiss and Jacob Cohen. 1973. The equivalence of weighted kappa and the intraclass correlation coefficient as measures of reliability. *Educational and psychological measurement*, 33(3):613–619.

Minqing Hu and Bing Liu. 2004. Mining and summarizing customer reviews. In *Proceedings of the tenth ACM SIGKDD international conference on Knowledge discovery and data mining*, pages 168–177. ACM.

Qian Liu, Zhiqiang Gao, Bing Liu, and Yuanlin Zhang. 2015. Automated rule selection for aspect extraction in opinion mining. In *Proceeding of the IJCAI*, pages 1291–1297.

Diego Marcheggiani, Oscar Täckström, Andrea Esuli, and Fabrizio Sebastiani. 2014. Hierarchical multi-label conditional random fields for aspect-oriented opinion mining. In *Proceeding of the European Conference on Information Retrieval*, pages 273–285. Springer.

Julian McAuley and Jure Leskovec. 2013. Hidden factors and hidden topics: understanding rating dimensions with review text. In *Proceedings of the 7th ACM conference on Recommender systems*, pages 165–172. ACM.

Pruthwik Mishra, Prathyusha Danda, Silpa Kanneganti, and Soujanya Lanka. Ijcnlp-2017 revopid shared task: A bidirectional-lstm approach for review opinion diversification. In *Proceedings of the IJCNLP-2017 Shared Tasks*.

Maria Pontiki, Dimitris Galanis, John Pavlopoulos, Harris Papageorgiou, Ion Androutsopoulos, and Suresh Manandhar. 2014. Semeval-2014 task 4: Aspect based sentiment analysis. *Proceedings of SemEval*, pages 27–35.

Anil Kumar Singh, Avijit Thawani, Anubhav Gupta, and Rajesh Kumar Mundotiya. Evaluating opinion summarization in ranking. In *Proceeding of the 13th Asia Information Retrieval Societies Conference (AIRS 2017)*.

Oscar Täckström and Ryan McDonald. 2011. Discovering fine-grained sentiment with latent variable structured prediction models. In *Proceeding of the European Conference on Information Retrieval*, pages 368–374. Springer.

Robert N Vidulich and Ivan P Kaiman. 1961. The effects of information source status and dogmatism upon conformity behavior. *The Journal of Abnormal and Social Psychology*, 63(3):639.

Shih-Hung Wu, Su-Yu Chang, and Liang-Pu Chen. System report of cyut team at revopid-2017 shared task in ijcnlp-2017. In *Proceedings of the IJCNLP-2017 Shared Tasks*.

IJCNLP-2017 Task 4: Customer Feedback Analysis

Chao-Hong Liu, Yasufumi Moriya, Alberto Poncelas

ADAPT Centre, Ireland
Dublin City University

{chaohong.liu, yasufumi.moriya,
alberto.poncelas}@adaptcentre.ie

Declan Groves

Microsoft Ireland
Leopardstown, Dublin 18

degroves
@microsoft.com

Abstract

This document introduces the IJCNLP 2017 Shared Task on Customer Feedback Analysis. In this shared task we have prepared corpora of customer feedback in four languages, i.e. English, French, Spanish and Japanese. They were annotated in a common meanings categorization, which was improved from an ADAPT-Microsoft pivot study on customer feedback. Twenty teams participated in the shared task and twelve of them have submitted prediction results. The results show that performance of prediction meanings of customer feedback is reasonable well in four languages. Nine system description papers are archived in the shared tasks proceeding.

1 Introduction

In this paper we introduce the results of IJCNLP 2017 Shared Task on Customer Feedback Analysis. The shared task is a follow-up of an ADAPT-Microsoft joint pilot study on multilingual customer feedback analysis. We have improved the categorization and the classes (tags) used in the corpora are the five-class "comment", "request", "bug", "complaint", "meaningless", and the "undetermined" tag. By undetermined we mean that the feedback could be annotated as one of the five classes but due to lack of contexts it was annotated as undetermined. Table 1 shows the numbers of customer feedback sentences curated in the corpora and how many they are grouped into training, development and test sets. We also provided unannotated customer feedback sentences in the corpora. Table 2 shows the statistics of each class in the meaning categorization in the training set. Noted we cannot find "meaningless" feedback

sentence in Japanese corpus. On the contrary, there is no "undetermined" feedback sentence in Spanish corpus. These might reflect some linguistic and/or cultural differences in the curated customer feedback corpora. Abbreviations EN, ES, FR and JP are used interchangeably with English, Spanish, French and Japanese where applicable.

Lang.	Train.	Dev.	Test	Unanno.
English	3,065	500	500	12,838
French	1,950	400	400	5,092
Spanish	1,631	301	299	6,035
Japanese	1,526	250	300	4,873
TOTAL	8,172	1,451	1,499	28,838

Table 1: Statistics of the curated Customer Feedback Analysis Corpora for the shared task.

	EN	FR	ES	JP
Comment	276	259	224	142
Request	21	6	12	22
Bug	21	13	5	18
Complaint	148	112	39	73
Meaningless	48	36	1	0
Undetermined	3	1	0	9

Table 2: Numbers of customer feedback tags that were annotated in the training set.

The purpose of the shared task is to try to answer the question that if we need to 1) train native systems for different languages (using the same meanings categorization of customer feedback), or it is good enough to 2) use Machine Translation (MT) to translate customer feedback in other languages into English and use English based systems to do the detection of meanings of customer feedback. If the answer is 1, we will have to prepare corpora for different languages using the same categorization. If the answer is 2, then it would be more reasonable to put more efforts to

Proceedings of the 8th International Joint Conference on Natural Language Processing, Shared Tasks, pages 26–33,
Taipei, Taiwan, November 27 – December 1, 2017. ©2017 AFNLP

enhance the performance of English based systems and try to further improve the quality of MT results.

There are several categorizations that could be used for customer feedback analysis. First, different kinds of sentiment categorizations that were used in sentiment analysis in Microsoft Office and many other institutions (Salameh et al., 2015) Customer feedback analysis is now an industry in its own right (Freshdesk, 2016; Burns, 2016). One commonly used categorization is the Excellent-Good-Average-Fair-Poor and its various kinds of variants (Yin et al., 2016; Survey-Monkey, 2016). (Freshdesk, 2016) and (Keatext, 2016) used a combined categorization of Positive-Neutral-Negative-Answered-Unanswered. (Sift, 2016) has the Refund-Complaint-Pricing-Tech Support-Store Locator-Feedback-Warranty Info categorization in seven classes. We can also have observed that there are many other categorizations that are not publicly available (Equiniti, 2016; UscResponse, 2016; Inmoment, 2016).

In this shared task, we followed (Liu et al., 2017)'s five-class customer feedback meanings categorization which is generalized from English, Spanish and Japanese customer feedback, add an "undetermined" class and prepared the corpora in four languages (English, French, Spanish and Japanese). The resulting categorization is as follows.

1. Comment
2. Request
3. Bug
4. Complaint
5. Meaningless
6. Undetermined

2 Measures

In this shared task, we concluded the results in four different measures. The details of the results can be download from the shared task website.

- Exact-match Accuracy: Feedback is considered correct only when "all its oracle tags" are predicted correctly.
- Partial-match Accuracy: Feedback is considered correct if 'any' of its oracle tags is predicted.
- Micro-Average of Precision, Recall and F1
- Macro-Average of Precision, Recall and F1: As the number of instances of each tag varies a lot this measure might not be suitable for comparisons in the shared task.

In this paper we show mainly the results of 1) Exact-match Accuracy and 2) Micro-Average of Precision, Recall and F1, which are more suitable measures in our consideration.

3 Baseline and Submitted Systems

A baseline system was implemented using similarity based method. It uses trigrams to calculate the similarity of an input sentence and all the annotated customer feedback sentences in the corpora and uses the annotation of the one (in the annotated training corpora) with highest similarity score as the input sentence's predicted annotation. The baseline system is referred to as "Baseline-Similarity" in this paper.

In this shared task, an initial team name was given to each team in the release of results. For example, TA was used to designate Team A. In the report of these results, i.e. this paper, a team name is revealed only when consent from its corresponding team is granted.

The mapping of each team name and its corresponding system description paper is shown as follows. Please refer to each paper for details of the system/method they used for the problem of customer feedback analysis

- ADAPT: (Lohar et al., 2017)
- Bingo: (Elfardy et al., 2017)
- IIIT-H: (Danda et al., 2017)
- OhioState: (Dhyani, 2017)
- Plank: (Plank, 2017)
- SentiNLP: (Lin et al., 2017)
- YNU-HPCC: (Wang et al., 2017)

4 Results in Exact-Match Accuracy

Tables 3-6 shows the results of each team-method in exact-match accuracy in English, Spanish, French and Japanese, respectively. The details of each method implemented by each team are described in their associated system description papers. The method denoted as "entrans" is the one that used machine translated sentences to do the prediction of meanings of customer feedback. For example, in the "Plank-entrans" system in Table 4, the sentences in Spanish test set are machine translated from Spanish to English using Google Translate, and then use Plank's English based system to predict their tags.

It is observed that for exact-accuracy, the best performers of submitted systems can achieve 71.00%, 88.63%, 73.75% and 75.00% in English, Spanish, French and Japanese, respectively. First, we can observe that the task seems to be easier in

Spanish which is the same phenomenon reported in (Liu et al., 2017). Second, performances in English, French and Japanese are also good and around the same level. Third, using machine translation the systems can achieve comparable results for Spanish and French, which are only 4 and 2 points behind native systems, respectively. For Japanese there is about 12 points behind the best native system.

English	Exact-Accuracy
YNU-HPCC-glove	**71.00%**
YNU-HPCC-EmbedConcatNoWeight	71.00%
SentiNLP-bilstmcnn	70.80%
SentiNLP-bilstm	70.40%
SentiNLP-bicnn	70.20%
IITP-CNN	70.00%
SentiNLP-cnnlstm	69.00%
Plank-monolingual	68.80%
Plank-multilingual	68.60%
YNU-HPCC-EmbedConcatWeight	68.60%
SentiNLP-cnn	68.20%
TJ-single-cnn	67.40%
IIIT-H-SVM	65.60%
TJ-ensemble-sentiment	65.40%
ADAPT-Run3	65.40%
IIIT-H-biLSTM	65.20%
TJ-ensemble-2	65.20%
YNU-HPCC-hotelWeight	65.00%
TJ-ensemble-epoch5	64.60%
TJ-ensemble-7	64.60%
TJ-ensemble-1	64.60%
TJ-ensemble-epoch10	64.40%
TJ-ensemble-5	64.20%
YNU-HPCC-hotel	64.00%
YNU-HPCC-gloveWeight	64.00%
TJ-ensemble-epoch5n10	64.00%
ADAPT-Run2	64.00%
TJ-ensemble-8	63.80%
TJ-ensemble-6	63.80%
TJ-ensemble-3	63.80%
TJ-ensemble-4	63.60%
OhioState-FastText	63.40%
ADAPT-Run1	63.40%
YNU-HPCC-SVM	63.00%
OhioState-biLSTM3	62.80%
YNU-HPCC-bayes	62.60%
TJ-single-cbow	62.00%

	Exact-Accuracy
OhioState-biLSTM2	61.60%
IITP-RNN	61.40%
YNU-HPCC-hotelNoATT	61.20%
OhioState-biLSTM1	61.20%
Bingo-logistic-reg	55.80%
Bingo-lstm	54.40%
OhioState-CNN	54.20%
TD-M1	52.20%
TF-nn	51.20%
Baseline-Similarity	**48.80%**
Bingo-rf	47.40%
TF-ss-svm	41.00%
TF-ss-lr	41.00%
TF-ss-nb	40.40%
TF-ss	40.40%
TB-en-run2	38.80%
TB-en-run1	37.40%
TB-en-run3	37.00%

Table 3: Resulting scores of each team-method in exact-match accuracy in English.

Spanish	Exact-Accuracy
Plank-multilingual	**88.63%**
Plank-monolingual	88.29%
IIIT-H-biLSTM	86.29%
IITP-RNN	85.62%
OhioState-biLSTM2	85.28%
Plank-entrans	84.62%
IITP-CNN	84.62%
IIIT-H-SVM	84.62%
ADAPT-Run1	83.61%
OhioState-FastText	82.94%
IITP-CNN-entrans	82.61%
OhioState-biLSTM1	82.61%
IITP-RNN-entrans	81.94%
ADAPT-Run2	81.61%
OhioState-CNN	81.27%
OhioState-biLSTM3	79.93%
Baseline-Similarity	**77.26%**
TF-ss-lr-entrans	76.25%
Bingo-rf	75.92%
Bingo-logistic-reg	72.91%
Bingo-lstm	71.57%
TF-ss	62.21%
TF-cnn-entrans	60.54%
TF-nn	59.53%
TF-ss-svm	57.19%
TF-ss-nb	57.19%

TF-ss-lr	57.19%

Table 4: Resulting scores of each team-method in exact-match accuracy in Spanish.

French	Exact-Accuracy
Plank-monolingual	**73.75%**
IITP-CNN-entrans	71.75%
Plank-multilingual	71.50%
OhioState-biLSTM1	70.00%
IIIT-H-SVM	69.75%
ADAPT-Run1	69.50%
IITP-CNN	69.00%
OhioState-biLSTM2	68.50%
Plank-entrans	68.25%
IITP-RNN-entrans	68.25%
IITP-RNN	68.25%
OhioState-FastText	68.00%
TB-fr-run1	66.75%
ADAPT-Run2	66.75%
IIIT-H-biLSTM	65.25%
OhioState-biLSTM3	65.00%
OhioState-CNN	65.00%
TB-fr-run4	63.50%
TB-fr-run3	62.25%
Bingo-lstm	61.25%
TB-fr-run2	60.50%
Bingo-logistic-reg	59.00%
Baseline-Similarity	**54.75%**
Bingo-rf	48.75%
TF-ss-nb	48.25%
TF-ss-lr	48.25%
TF-nn2	47.75%
TF-nn	47.25%
TF-ss	44.50%
TF-nn3	39.00%

Table 5: Resulting scores of each team-method in exact-match accuracy in French.

Japanese	Exact-Accuracy
Plank-multilingual	**75.00%**
Plank-monolingual	73.33%
ADAPT-Run1	67.67%
Plank-entrans	63.67%
IITP-CNN-entrans	63.00%
Bingo-logistic-reg	60.67%
IITP-RNN-entrans	58.67%
ADAPT-Run2	57.67%
Baseline-Similarity	**56.67%**
IIIT-H-biLSTM	56.67%
OhioState-CNN	56.67%
IIIT-H-SVM	56.33%
OhioState-biLSTM1	56.33%
OhioState-biLSTM2	56.33%
IITP-RNN	56.00%
OhioState-biLSTM3	56.00%
OhioState-FastText	56.00%
TF-nn	55.67%
TF-ss-svm	55.00%
TF-ss-nb	55.00%
TF-ss	55.00%
IITP-CNN	54.00%
TF-cnn-entrans	53.33%
TF-ss-lr-entrans	53.00%
Bingo-lstm	53.00%
Bingo-rf	45.00%
TF-ss-lr	28.67%

Table 6: Resulting scores of each team-method in exact-match accuracy in Japanese.

5 Results in Micro-Average Precision, Recall and F1 measures

Likewise, Tables 7-10 show the results of each team-method in micro-average precision, recall and F1 measures in English, Spanish, French and Japanese, respectively.

For micro-average F1, the best systems achieved 75.57%, 88.63%, 76.59% and 77.05% in English, Spanish, French and Japanese, respectively. The results in Spanish exhibit the same phenomenon as in exact-match accuracy results and in (Liu et al., 2017). The performances in English, French and Japanese are also good and around the same level. Using machine translation, the systems can also achieve comparable results in this measure for Spanish and French, which are 4 and 2 points behind native systems, respectively. There is 11 points behind in Japanese in this regard.

English	A.P	A.R	A.F1
SentiNLP-bilstmcnn	**74.86%**	**76.30%**	**75.57%**
SentiNLP-bicnn	73.83%	76.11%	74.95%
SentiNLP-bilstm	73.77%	75.34%	74.55%
SentiNLP-cnn	72.12%	74.76%	73.42%

	A.P	A.R	A.F1
SentiNLP-cnnlstm	73.04%	73.60%	73.32%
YNU-HPCC-EmbedConcat-NoWeight	74.60%	71.87%	73.21%
YNU-HPCC-glove	74.40%	71.68%	73.01%
IITP-CNN	73.80%	71.10%	72.42%
Plank-mono-lingual	72.40%	69.75%	71.05%
Plank-multi-lingual	72.20%	69.56%	70.85%
TJ-single-cnn	70.85%	70.71%	70.78%
YNU-HPCC-EmbedConcat-Weight	72.00%	69.36%	70.66%
TJ-ensemble-2	69.10%	69.36%	69.23%
TJ-ensemble-senti-ment	68.22%	67.82%	68.02%
TJ-ensemble-epoch10	68.02%	68.02%	68.02%
TJ-ensemble-8	67.82%	68.21%	68.01%
TJ-ensemble-epoch5n10	66.73%	69.17%	67.93%
ADAPT-Run3	69.20%	66.67%	67.91%
IIIT-H-biLSTM	67.82%	67.82%	67.82%
TJ-ensemble-epoch5	67.62%	68.02%	67.82%
IIIT-H-SVM	69.22%	66.28%	67.72%
YNU-HPCC-hotel-Weight	68.60%	66.09%	67.32%
TJ-ensemble-1	67.77%	66.86%	67.31%
TJ-ensemble-4	67.18%	67.44%	67.31%
TJ-ensemble-6	66.92%	67.44%	67.18%
TJ-ensemble-7	67.18%	67.05%	67.12%
TJ-ensemble-3	66.79%	67.44%	67.11%
TJ-ensemble-5	66.99%	66.47%	66.73%
YNU-HPCC-hotel	67.60%	65.13%	66.34%
YNU-HPCC-gloveWeight	67.40%	64.93%	66.14%
ADAPT-Run2	67.40%	64.93%	66.14%
ADAPT-Run1	66.87%	64.55%	65.69%
YNU-HPCC-SVM	66.60%	64.16%	65.36%
OhioState-FastText	66.60%	64.16%	65.36%
OhioState-biLSTM3	66.20%	63.78%	64.97%
YNU-HPCC-bayes	66.00%	63.58%	64.77%
TJ-single-cbow	65.11%	64.35%	64.73%
Bingo-rf	54.35%	79.38%	64.53%
OhioState-biLSTM2	65.20%	62.81%	63.98%
OhioState-biLSTM1	65.00%	62.62%	63.79%
IITP-RNN	64.60%	62.24%	63.40%
YNU-HPCC-hotelNoATT	63.40%	61.08%	62.22%
Bingo-lo-gistic-reg	60.47%	63.97%	62.17%
TD-M1	55.78%	68.79%	61.60%
Bingo-lstm	56.97%	65.32%	60.86%
OhioState-CNN	57.20%	55.11%	56.13%
Baseline-Similarity	**53.73%**	**54.14%**	**53.93%**
TF-nn	54.40%	52.41%	53.39%
TB-en-run1	42.70%	44.51%	43.58%
TF-ss-svm	44.20%	42.58%	43.38%
TF-ss-lr	44.20%	42.58%	43.38%
TF-ss-nb	43.60%	42.00%	42.79%
TF-ss	43.60%	42.00%	42.79%
TB-en-run2	42.77%	42.77%	42.77%
TB-en-run3	41.32%	42.20%	41.75%

Table 7: Resulting scores of each team-method in micro-average precision (A.P), recall (A.R) and F1 (A.F1) measures in English.

Spanish	A.P	A.R	A.F1
Plank-mul-tilingual	**88.63%**	**88.63%**	**88.63%**
Plank-mono-lingual	88.29%	88.29%	88.29%

	A.P	A.R	A.F1
IIIT-H-biLSTM	86.29%	86.29%	86.29%
IITP-RNN	85.62%	85.62%	85.62%
OhioState-biLSTM2	85.28%	85.28%	85.28%
Plank-en-trans	84.62%	84.62%	84.62%
IITP-CNN	84.62%	84.62%	84.62%
IIIT-H-SVM	84.62%	84.62%	84.62%
ADAPT-Run1	83.61%	83.61%	83.61%
OhioState-FastText	82.94%	82.94%	82.94%
IITP-CNN-entrans	82.61%	82.61%	82.61%
OhioState-biLSTM1	82.61%	82.61%	82.61%
IITP-RNN-entrans	81.94%	81.94%	81.94%
ADAPT-Run2	81.61%	81.61%	81.61%
OhioState-CNN	81.27%	81.27%	81.27%
Bingo-logistic-reg	82.29%	79.26%	80.75%
OhioState-biLSTM3	79.93%	79.93%	79.93%
Bingo-lstm	71.35%	86.62%	78.25%
Bingo-rf	75.00%	81.27%	78.01%
Baseline-Similarity	**77.26%**	**77.26%**	**77.26%**
TF-ss-lr-en-trans	76.25%	76.25%	76.25%
TF-ss	62.21%	62.21%	62.21%
TF-cnn-en-trans	60.54%	60.54%	60.54%
TF-nn	59.53%	59.53%	59.53%
TF-ss-svm	57.19%	57.19%	57.19%
TF-ss-nb	57.19%	57.19%	57.19%
TF-ss-lr	57.19%	57.19%	57.19%

Table 8: Resulting scores of each team-method in micro-average precision (A.P), recall (A.R) and F1 (A.F1) measures in Spanish.

French	A.P	A.R	A.F1
Plank-monolingual	**78.50%**	**74.76%**	**76.59%**
IITP-CNN-entrans	76.50%	72.86%	74.63%
Plank-multilingual	76.25%	72.62%	74.39%
OhioState-biLSTM1	75.00%	71.43%	73.17%

French	A.P	A.R	A.F1
ADAPT-Run1	74.50%	70.95%	72.68%
IIIT-H-SVM	74.68%	70.24%	72.39%
IITP-CNN	73.50%	70.00%	71.71%
OhioState-biLSTM2	73.50%	70.00%	71.71%
Plank-en-trans	73.00%	69.52%	71.22%
IITP-RNN	72.75%	69.29%	70.98%
IITP-RNN-entrans	72.25%	68.81%	70.49%
OhioState-FastText	72.25%	68.81%	70.49%
TB-fr-run1	70.94%	69.76%	70.35%
Bingo-lstm	62.04%	79.76%	69.79%
ADAPT-Run2	71.00%	67.62%	69.27%
IIIT-H-biLSTM	72.63%	65.71%	69.00%
TB-fr-run4	68.10%	68.10%	68.10%
OhioState-CNN	69.50%	66.19%	67.80%
OhioState-biLSTM3	69.25%	65.95%	67.56%
Bingo-rf	58.03%	80.00%	67.27%
TB-fr-run3	66.75%	65.95%	66.35%
Bingo-logistic-reg	64.84%	67.62%	66.20%
TB-fr-run2	65.02%	62.86%	63.92%
Baseline-Similarity	**60.05%**	**60.48%**	**60.26%**
TF-nn3	56.48%	53.80%	55.11%
TF-ss-nb	52.25%	49.76%	50.98%
TF-ss-lr	52.25%	49.76%	50.98%
TF-nn2	51.75%	49.29%	50.49%
TF-nn	51.50%	49.05%	50.24%
TF-ss	48.75%	46.43%	47.56%

Table 9: Resulting scores of each team-method in micro-average precision (A.P), recall (A.R) and F1 (A.F1) measures in French.

Japanese	A.P	A.R	A.F1
Plank-multilingual	**79.12%**	**75.08%**	**77.05%**
Plank-monolingual	77.70%	73.48%	75.53%
ADAPT-Run1	71.67%	68.69%	70.15%
IITP-CNN-entrans	70.21%	63.26%	66.55%
Bingo-rf	56.36%	79.23%	65.87%

	67.46%	63.58%	65.46%
Plank-en-trans	67.46%	63.58%	65.46%
Bingo-lo-gistic-reg	63.86%	65.50%	64.67%
Bingo-lstm	58.38%	71.25%	64.17%
IITP-RNN-entrans	65.60%	59.11%	62.18%
ADAPT-Run2	62.24%	58.47%	60.30%
Baseline-Similarity	**59.24%**	**59.42%**	**59.33%**
OhioState-CNN	58.00%	55.59%	56.77%
IIIT-H-biLSTM	57.33%	54.95%	56.12%
IIIT-H-SVM	57.33%	54.95%	56.12%
OhioState-biLSTM1	57.00%	54.63%	55.79%
OhioState-biLSTM2	57.00%	54.63%	55.79%
IITP-RNN	56.67%	54.31%	55.46%
OhioState-biLSTM3	56.67%	54.31%	55.46%
OhioState-FastText	56.67%	54.31%	55.46%
TF-nn	56.33%	53.99%	55.14%
TF-ss-svm	55.67%	53.35%	54.49%
TF-ss-nb	55.67%	53.35%	54.49%
TF-ss	55.67%	53.35%	54.49%
IITP-CNN	55.00%	52.72%	53.83%
TF-cnn-en-trans	54.67%	52.40%	53.51%
TF-ss-lr-en-trans	53.67%	51.44%	52.53%
TF-ss-lr	32.67%	31.31%	31.97%

Table 10: Resulting scores of each team-method in micro-average precision (A.P), recall (A.R) and F1 (A.F1) measures in Japanese.

6 Conclusions

In this shared task, we address the problem if we should 1) train native systems for different languages, or 2) use MT to translate customer feedback into English and use English based systems to predict meanings of customer feedback. By using the same categorization, we concluded that using native systems, the performances in the four languages are all good. For Spanish and French, using MT can achieve comparable results as using native systems. Therefore, we would suggest improving English based systems and probably preparing the corpora in finer categorizations that would help us understand customer feedbacks.

However, for Japanese or other languages where MT still does not produce high quality translations, preparing native corpora and building native systems are still highly recommended.

Acknowledgements

This research is supported by the ADAPT Centre for Digital Content Technology, funded under the Science Foundation Ireland (SFI) Research Centres Programme (Grant 13/RC/2106). We are grateful to ADAPT colleagues Anna Kostekidou, Julie Connelly, Clare Conran, among others, for their support to the project. We would like to thank Ms Sara Garvey and Ms Rachel Costello of Trinity College Dublin who prepared the English and French parts of corpora and helped improve the categorization. They also built an initial system using a nascent version of the corpora to help understand the performance that might be in both English and French. Special thanks to Dr Barbara Plank and Ms Shuying Lin for spotting the bug in the calculation of exact-match accuracy. Barbara also provided helpful comments on the use of these measures, among others, which are much appreciated. We are also grateful to Dr Heba Elfardy and her team from Amazon who identified several issues of the corpora and helped improve the corpora for the shared task. Finally, all participants are much appreciated to take part of this shared task and together help us better understand the task questions.

References

Barbara Plank. All-In-1 at IJCNLP-2017 Task 4: Short Text Classification with One Model for All Languages. In *the Proceedings of IJCNLP, Shared Tasks,* pp. 143–148, 2017. AFNLP.

Bentley, Michael and Batra, Soumya. Giving Voice to Office Customers: Best Practices in How Office Handles Verbatim Text Feedback. In *IEEE International Conference on Big Data.* pp. 3826–3832, 2016.

Burns, Michelle. (2016, February). Kampyle Introduces the NebulaCX Experience Optimizer. Retrieved from http://www.kampyle.com/kampyle-introduces-the-nebulacx-experience-optimizer/

Chao-Hong Liu, Declan Groves, Akira Hayakawa, Alberto Poncelas and Qun Liu. Understanding Meanings in Multilingual Customer Feedback. In *the Proceedings of First Workshop on Social Media and User Generated Content Machine Translation (Social MT 2017),* Prague, Czech Republic.

Dushyanta Dhyani. OhioState at IJCNLP-2017 Task 4: Exploring Neural Architectures for Multilingual

Customer Feedback Analysis. In *the Proceedings of IJCNLP, Shared Tasks*, pp. 170–173, 2017. AFNLP.

Equiniti. (2017, April). Complaints Management. Retrieved from https://www.equiniticharter.com/services/complaints-management/#.WOH5X2_yt0w

Freshdesk Inc. (2017, February). Creating and sending the Satisfaction Survey. Retrieved from https://support.freshdesk.com/support/solutions/articles/37886-creating-and-sending-the-satisfaction-survey

Heba Elfardy, Manisha Srivastava, Wei Xiao, Jared Kramer and Tarun Agarwal. Bingo at IJCNLP-2017 Task 4: Augmenting Data using Machine Translation for Cross-linguistic Customer Feedback Classification. In *the Proceedings of IJCNLP, Shared Tasks*, pp. 59–66, 2017. AFNLP.

Inmoment. (2017, April). Software to Improve and Optimize the Customer Experience. Retrieved from http://www.inmoment.com/products/

Keatext Inc. (2016, September). Text Analytics Made Easy. Retrieved from http://www.keatext.ai/

Nan Wang, Jin Wang and Xuejie Zhang. YNU-HPCC at IJCNLP-2017 Task 4: Attention-based Bi-directional GRU Model for Customer Feedback Analysis Task of English. In *the Proceedings of IJCNLP, Shared Tasks*, pp. 174–179, 2017. AFNLP.

Pintu Lohar, Koel Dutta Chowdhury, Haithem Afli, Mohammed Hasanuzzaman and Andy Way. ADAPT at IJCNLP-2017 Task 4: A Multinomial Naive Bayes Classification Approach for Customer Feedback Analysis task. In *the Proceedings of IJCNLP, Shared Tasks*, pp. 161–169, 2017. AFNLP.

Potharaju, Rahul, Navendu Jain and Cristina Nita-Rotaru. Juggling the Jigsaw: Towards Automated Problem Inference from Network Trouble Tickets. In *10th USENIX Symposium on Network Systems Design and Implementation (NSDI 13)*. pp. 127–141, 2013.

Prathyusha Danda, Pruthwik Mishra, Silpa Kanneganti and Soujanya Lanka. IIIT-H at IJCNLP-2017 Task 4: Customer Feedback Analysis using Machine Learning and Neural Network Approaches. In *the Proceedings of IJCNLP, Shared Tasks*, pp. 155–160, 2017. AFNLP.

Salameh, Mohammad, Saif M Mohammad, and Svetlana Kiritchenko. Sentiment after translation: A case-study on Arabic social media posts. In *Proceedings of the 2015 Annual Conference of the North American Chapter of the ACL*, pp. 767–777, 2015.

Shuying Lin, Huosheng Xie, Liang-Chih Yu and K. Robert Lai. SentiNLP at IJCNLP-2017 Task 4: Customer Feedback Analysis Using a Bi-LSTM-CNN Model. In *the Proceedings of IJCNLP, Shared Tasks*, pp. 149–154, 2017. AFNLP.

SurveyMonkey Inc. (2017, April). Customer Service and Satisfaction Survey. Retrieved from https://www.surveymonkey.com/r/BHM_Survey

UseResponse. (2017, April). Customer Service & Customer Support are best when automated. Retrieved from https://www.useresponse.com/

Yin, Dawei, Yuening Hu, Jiliang Tang, Tim Daly, Mianwei Zhou, Hua Ouyang, Jianhui Chen, Changsung Kang, Hongbo Deng, Chikashi Nobata, Jean-Mark Langlois, and Yi Chang. Ranking relevance in yahoo search. In *Proceedings of the 22nd ACM SIGKDD International Conference on Knowledge Discovery and Data Mining*. pp. 323–332, 2016. ACM.

IJCNLP-2017 Task 5: Multi-choice Question Answering in Examinations

Shangmin Guo[†], Kang Liu[†‡], Shizhu He[†], Zhuoyu Wei[†], Cao Liu[†‡] and Jun Zhao[†‡]
[†] National Laboratory of Pattern Recognition, Institute of Automation,
Chinese Academy of Sciences, Beijing, 100190, China
[‡] University of Chinese Academy of Sciences, Beijing, 100049, China

Abstract

The IJCNLP-2017 Multi-choice Question Answering(MCQA) task aims at exploring the performance of current Question Answering(QA) techniques via the real-world complex questions collected from Chinese Senior High School Entrance Examination papers and CK12 website[1]. The questions are all 4-way multi-choice questions writing in Chinese and English respectively that cover a wide range of subjects, e.g. Biology, History, Life Science and etc. And, all questions are restrained within the elementary and middle school level. During the whole procedure of this task, 7 teams submitted 323 runs in total. This paper describes the collected data, the format and size of these questions, formal run statistics and results, overview and performance statistics of different methods.

1 Introduction

One critical but challenging problem in natural language understanding (NLU) is to develop a question answering(QA) system which could consistently understand and correctly answer general questions about the world. "Multi-choice Question Answering in Exams"(MCQA) is a typical question answering task that aims to test how accurately the participant QA systems could answer the questions in exams. All questions in this competition come from real examinations. We collected multiple choice questions from several curriculums, such as Biology, History, Life-Science, with a restrain that all questions are limited in the elementary and middle school level. For every question, four answer candidates are provided,

---

[1]http://www.ck12.org/browse/

> Peach trees have sweet-smelling blossoms and produce rich fruit. What is the main purpose of the flowers of a peach tree? (Answer is A.)
>
> (A) to attract bees for pollination.
> (B) to create flower arrangements.
> (C) to protect the tree from disease.
> (D) to feed migratory birds.

Figure 1: An example question from English Subset.

where each of them may be a word, a value, a phrase or even a sentence. The participant QA systems are required to select the best one from these four candidates. Fig 1 is an example. To answer these questions, participants could utilize any public toolkits and any resources on the Web, but manually annotation is not permitted.

As for the knowledge resources, we encourage participants to utilize any resource on Internet, including softwares, toolboxes, and all kinds of corpora. Meanwhile, we also provide a dump of Wikipedia[2] and a collection of related Baidu Baike Corpus[3] under a specific license. These corpora and released questions are all provided in the XML format, which will be explained in section 2.2.

Main characteristics of our task are as follow:

- All the questions are from real word examinations.

- Most of questions require considerable inference ability.

- Some questions require a deep understanding of context.

- Questions from different categories have different characteristics, which makes it harder

---

[2]https://www.wikipedia.org/
[3]https://baike.baidu.com/

Proceedings of the 8th International Joint Conference on Natural Language Processing, Shared Tasks, pages 34–40,
Taipei, Taiwan, November 27 – December 1, 2017. ©2017 AFNLP

for a model to have a good performance on all kinds of questions.

- It concentrates only on the textual content, as questions with figures and tables are all filtered out.

2 Task and Data Description

All questions in MCQA consist of 2 parts, a question and 4 answer candidates, without any figure or table. The participant systems are required to select the only right one from all candidates.

2.1 Languages and Subjects

In order to explore the influence of diversity of questions, we collect questions from seven subjects in two languages, including an English subset and a Chinese subset. The subjects of English subset contain biology, chemistry, physics, earth science and life science. And the subjects of Chinese subset only contain biology and history. The total number of questions is 14,447.

2.2 Format

All questions in our dataset are consisted by the following 7 parts:

1. ID, i.e. the identical number of a specific question;

2. Question, i.e. the question to be answered;

3. Option A, i.e. the content of first answer candidate;

4. Option B, i.e. the content of second answer candidate;

5. Option C, i.e. the content of third answer candidate;

6. Option D, i.e. the content of fourth answer candidate;

7. Correct Answer No., i.e. the number of the correct candidate(0, 1, 2 and 3, which corresponds to four options respectively).

Take a question in Figure 1 for example. Roles of every part are as follow:

1. ID: wb415;

2. Question: "Peach trees have sweet-smelling blossoms and produce rich fruit. What is the main purpose of the flowers of a peach tree?";

3. Option A: "to attract bees for pollination.";

4. Option B: "to create flower arrangements.";

5. Option C: "to protect the tree from disease.";

6. Option D: "to feed migratory birds.";

7. Correct Answer No.: 0.

It needs to be specified that we exclude the Correct Answer No. in the validation and test set.

2.3 Data Size

The dataset totally contains 14,447 multiple choice questions. In detail, English subset contains 5,367 questions and Chinese subset contains 9,080 questions. We randomly split the dataset into Train, Validation and Test sets. And more detail statistics is showed in Table 1.

	Train	Valid	Test	Total
English Subset				
Biology	281	70	210	561
Chemistry	775	193	581	1549
Physics	299	74	224	597
Earth Science	830	207	622	1659
Life Science	501	125	375	1001
English Total	2686	669	2012	5367
Chinese Subset				
Biology	2266	566	1699	4531
History	2275	568	1706	4549
Chinese Total	4541	1134	3405	9080
Complete Dataset				
Total	7227	1803	5417	14447

Table 1: The statistics of dataset.

2.4 English Subset

We collected all the downloadable quiz from CK12 and only reserved 5367 4-way multi-choice questions with their tags which are also the basis of classifying the questions. For every subject, we randomly separate questions into 3 parts, train set, valid set and test set with 50%, 12.5% and 37.5% questions respectively.

2.5 Chinese Subset

As questions in Senior High School Entrance Examination(SHSEE) differs among different cities, we collected questions in SHSEE from as many cities as we can. After filtering out the questions containing more information than textual content, the answers of left questions were labeled by human. Finally, we got 4,531 questions in Biology and 4,549 questions in History. For every subject, we randomly separate questions into 3 parts, train

English Subset					
Biology	Chemistry	Physics	Earth Science	Life Science	All English
30%	21.24%	25.68%	31.88%	40%	29.45%
Chinese Subset					
Biology		History		All Chinese	
34.81%		54.42%		44.63%	
All Datasets					
39%					

Table 2: The detail performance of the baseline method.

set, valid set and test set with same ratio stated above.

2.6 Evaluation

This challenge employs the accuracy of a method on answering questions in test set as the metric, the accuracy is calculated as follow.

$$Accuracy = \frac{n_{correct}}{N_{total}} \times 100\%$$

where $n_{correct}$ is the number of correctly answered questions and N_{total} is the total number of all questions.

To automatically evaluate the performance of QA systems, we built a web-site for participants to submit solutions for valid and test data set and get accuracy immediately on the page.

2.7 Baseline

We employ a simple retrieval based method as a baseline, and it is implemented based on Lucene[4] which is an open-source information retrieval software library. We employ the method to build reverse-index on the whole Wikipedia dump[5] for English questions and on the Baidu Baike corpus[6] for Chinese questions.

This method scores pairs of the question and each of its option, the detail steps are shown as follows.

- concatenate a question with an option as the query;

- use Lucene to search relevant documents with the query;

- score relevant documents by the similarity between the query q and the document d, noted as $Sim(q, d)$;

- choose at most three highest scores to calculate the score of the pair of the question and the option as

$$score(q, a) = \frac{1}{n} \sum_{1}^{n} Sim(q, d)$$

where $n \leqslant 3$ and $if\, n = 0, score(q, a) = 0$;

All questions and options are preprocessed by Stanford CoreNLP[7]. The detail result of the baseline on the validation set is shown in Table 2.

3 Participation

7 teams as shown in Table 3 were participated in the end.

Team Name	Affliation
YNU-HPCC	Yunnan University
CASIA-NLP	Institute of Automation, Chinese Academy of Sciences
Cone	Dublin City University
G623	Yunnan University
JU_NITM	Jadavpur University
TALN	Universit de Nantes
QA_challenge	Free

Table 3: Active Participating Teams (as of Aug. 31, 2017)

The details of participation of different language subsets are listed in the following Table 4.

4 Submission

In order to avoid the situation that participants submit different permutation of answers to sniff the correct answer labels, we limited the times that a team can submit their solutions. Before the release of test set, a team can submit no more than 5 solutions for valid set in 24 hours. After the release of test set, a team can submit as many as 30 solutions

---

[4]http://lucene.apache.org/
[5]https://dumps.wikimedia.org/
[6]http://www.nlpr.ia.ac.cn/cip/ijcnlp/baidubaike_corpus.html
[7]https://stanfordnlp.github.io/CoreNLP/

Team Name	Language
YNU-HPCC	Both
CASIA-NLP	Chinese
Cone	English
G623	English
JU_NITM	English
TALN	English
QA_challenge	English

Table 4: Language Selection of Teams (as of Aug. 31, 2017)

for valid set per 24 hours, but no more than 5 solutions for test set in 24 hours. Finally, we got 323 runs in total, in which there are 219 runs for valid set and 104 runs for test set.

5 Results

In our evaluation system, only the best performance of participants were reserved. The detail results of every subset is listed in the following subsections.

5.1 All Questions

There is only one team, "YNU-HPCC", that took the challenge of both English subset and Chinese subset. And, the performance of their system is listed in Table 5.

5.2 English Subset

Totally, there are 5 teams that only took the challenge of English subset and details of their performance are listed in the Table 6.

5.3 Chinese Subset

There are 1 team that only took the challenge of Chinese subset and their performance is listed in the Table 7.

6 Overview of Participant Systems

6.1 YNU-HPCC, An Attetion-based LSTM

YNU-HPCC (Yuan et al., 2017) proposed an attention-based LSTM(AT-LSTM) model for MCQA. According to them, this model can easily capture long contextual information with the help of an attention mechanism. As illustrated in Figure 2, LSTM layer takes the vector representions of question and answers as input and then calculates out the hidden vectors which are the input of attention layer to calculate the weight vector α and weighted hidden representation r.

Finally, an softmax layer takes r as input to select the right answer.

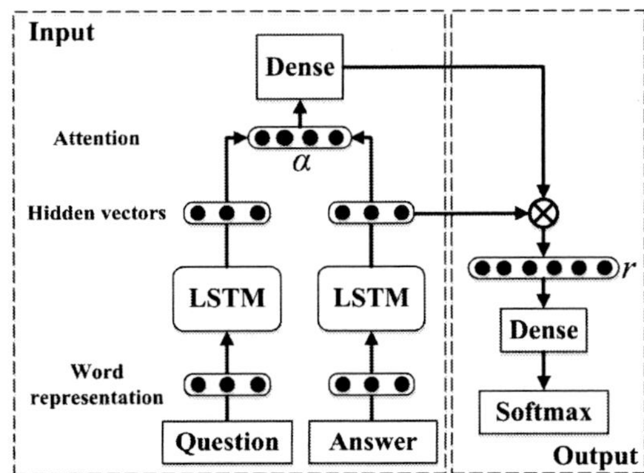

Figure 2: Architecture of AT-LSTM proposed by team YNU-HPCC(Yuan et al., 2017).

6.2 CASIA-NLP, Internet Resources and Localization Method

Based on the phenomenon that many web pages containing answers of the questions in MCQA, CASIA-NLP (Li and Kong, 2017) crawled on Internet and analyzed the content in these pages. When analyzing these pages, they use a localization method to locate the positions of sentences that have same meaning of questions in MCQA by merging a score given by edit distance that evaluates the structural similarity and a cosine score given by a CNN network that evaluates the semantic similarity. Finally, the system can analyze answers to find out the right one. The overview of the system is illustrated in Figure 3 and the CNN network they used is demonstrated in Figure 4.

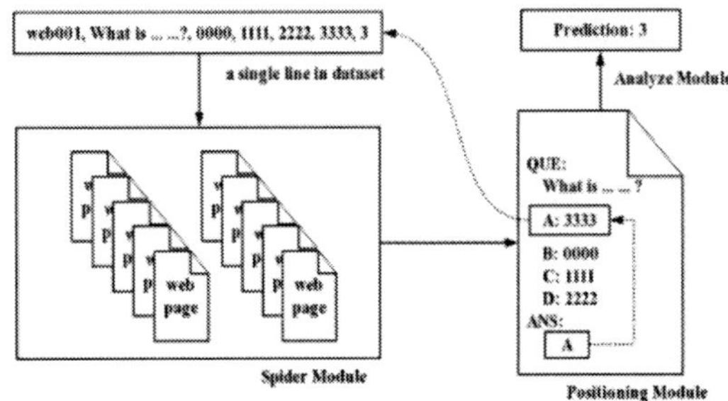

Figure 3: Overview of CAISA-NLP's system (Li and Kong, 2017). Communication between modules is indicated by arrows.

Valid Set			Test Set		
English	Chinese	All	English	Chinese	All
34.5%	46.5%	42.1%	35.5%	46.5%	42.3%

Table 5: Performance of YNU-HPCC (as of Aug. 31, 2017)

Team Name	Valid Set	Test Set
Cone	48.7%	45.6%
G623	42.8%	42.2%
JU_NITM	40.7%	40.6%
TALN	34.7%	30.3%
QA_challenge	21.5%	N/A

Table 6: Performance on English Subset (as of Aug. 31, 2017)

Team Name	Valid Set	Test Set
CASIA-NLP	60.1%	58.1%

Table 7: Performance on English Subset (as of Aug. 31, 2017)

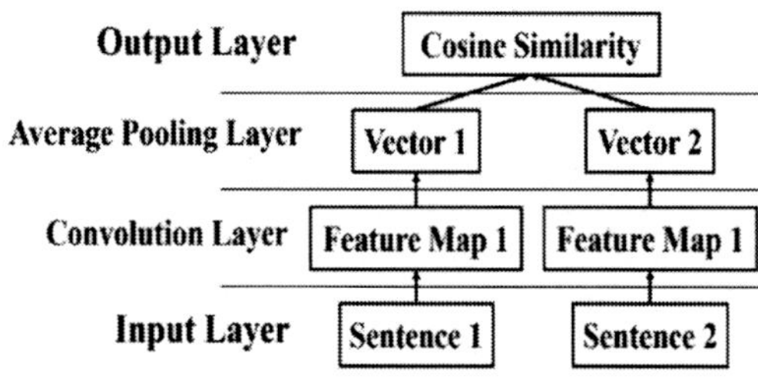

Figure 4: Convolutional architecture used in CASIA-NLP's system (Li and Kong, 2017).

6.3 Cone, Wikipedia and Logistic Regression

The system of Cone (Dzendzik et al., 2017), a team from ADAPT Centre, based on a logistic regression over the string similarities between question, answer, and additional text. Their model is constructed as a four-step pipeline as follow.

1. Preprocessing cleaning of the input data;

2. Data selection relative sentences are extracted from Wikipedia based on key words from question;

3. Feature Vector Concatenation for every question, a feature vector is built as a concatenation of similarities between the answer candidates and sentences obtained in the previous step;

4. Logistic Regression a logistic regression over the feature vector.

The features they employed includes term frequencyinverse document frequency (Tf-IDf) metric, character n-grams (with n ranging from 1 to 4), bag of words,and windows slide (a ratio between answer and substrings of extracted data). While their model is trained in two ways, combining training over all domains and separate model training from each domain, the later one got the best performance.

6.4 G623, A CNN-LSTM Model with Attention Mechanism

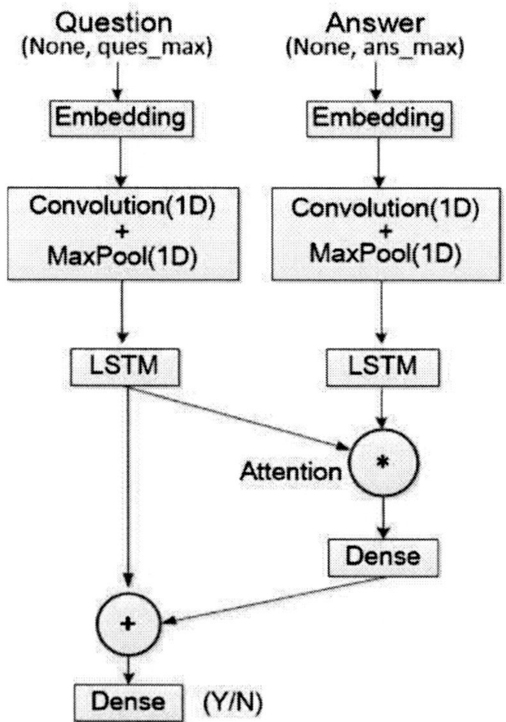

Figure 5: Architecture of the model proposed by G623(Min et al., 2017).

The system of G623 (Min et al., 2017) combined CNN with LSTM network and took into account the attention mechanism. Fistly , question and answer pairs are fed into a CNN network and produce joint representations of these pairs which are then fed into a LSTM network. The two separate vector representations of question and answer are then calculated to generate the weight vector by dot multiplication. Finally, a softmax layer is applied to classify the join representations with the help of attention weight. The diagram of their system is illustrated in Figure 5.

6.5 JU_NITM, Complex Decision Tree

To handle the questions in MCQA, JU_NITM (Sarkar et al., 2017) built a complex decision tree classifier using word embedding features to predict the right answer. The overview of the whole system is demonstrated in Figure 6. In distributed semantic similarity module, they trained a word embedding dictionary containing 3 million words in 300-dimensional space on GoogleNews. Then, a complex decision tree is used to select the right answer in step2, classification.

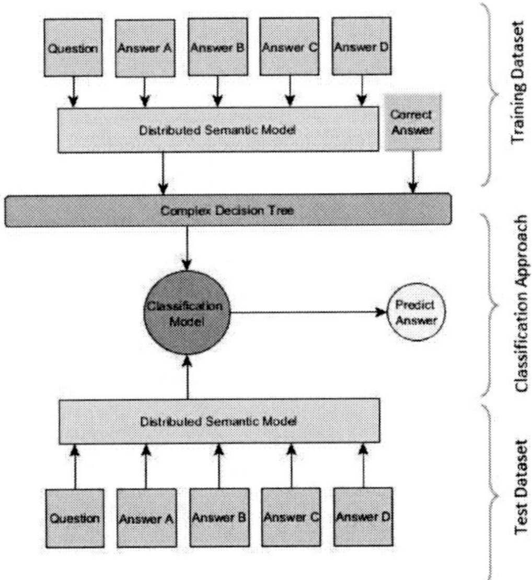

Figure 6: System Framework proposed by JU_NITM(Sarkar et al., 2017).

6.6 TALN, MappSent

Mappsent is proposed in a previous work of TALN, (Hazem et al., 2017). To adapt to the characteristics of MCQA, they retrofitted MappSent model in two different ways(Hazem, 2017). The first approach illustrated in Figure 7 is to follow the same procedure as the question-to-question similarity task, i.e. using anatated pairs of questions and their corresponding answers to build the mapping matrix. The second approach illustrated in Figure 8 tends to keep the strong hypothesis of sentence pairs similarity. They built two mapping matrices, one that represent similar question pairs and ther other one to represent similar answers pairs. For a give test question, the system can extracted the most similar quesiont in the training data and select the candidate with highest similarity score as correct answer.

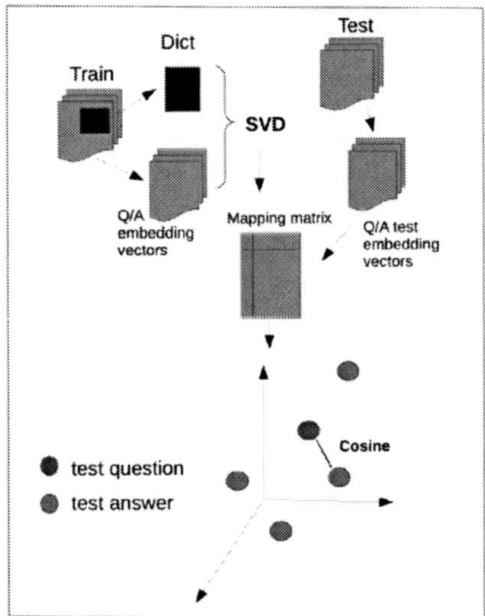

Figure 7: Fist adaptation of MappSent(Hazem, 2017).

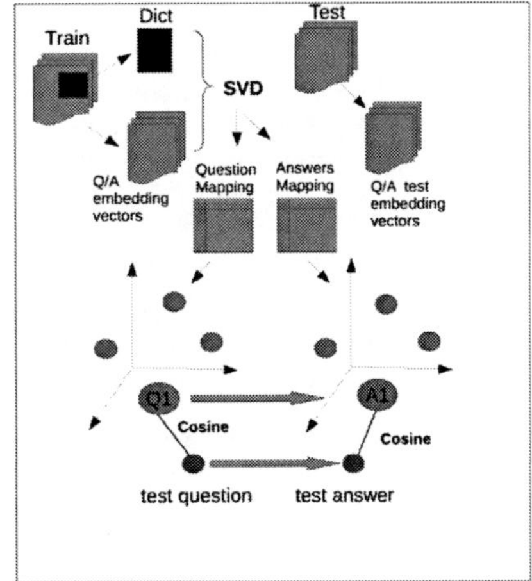

Figure 8: Second adaptation of MappSent(Hazem, 2017).

7   Conclusions

We described the overview of the Multi-choice Question Answering task. The goal is exploring the performance of current Question Answering(QA) techniques via the real-world complex questions collected from Chinese Senior High School Entrance Examination(SHSEE) papers and CK12 website. We collected 14,447 questions covering 2 language in 7 different subjects. 7 teams submitted 323 runs in total. We describe the collected data, the format and size of these questions, formal run statistics and results, overview and performance statistics of different methods in this paper.

Acknowledgments

Our thanks to participants. This task organization was supported by the Natural Science Foundation of China (No.61533018) and the National Basic Research Program of China (No. 2014CB340503). And this research work was also supported by Google through focused research awards program.

References

Daria Dzendzik, Alberto Poncelas, Carl Vogel, and Qun Liu. 2017. A similarity-based logistic regression approach to multi-choice question answering in an examinations shared task. In *IJCNLP-2017, Shared Task 5*.

Amir Hazem. 2017. A textual similarity approach applied to multi-choice question answering in examinations shared task. In *IJCNLP-2017, Shared Task 5*.

Amir Hazem, Basma el amel Boussaha, and Niclas Hernandez. 2017. Mappsent: a textual mapping ap-proach for question-toquestion similarity. In *Proceedings of the International Conference Recent Advances in Natural Language Processing RANLP 2017*.

Changliang Li and Cunliang Kong. 2017. Answer localization for multi-choice question answering in exams. In *IJCNLP-2017, Shared Task 5*.

Wang Min, Qingxun Liu, Peng Ding, Yongbin Li, and Xiaobing Zhou. 2017. A cnn-lstm model with attention for multi-choice question answering in examinations. In *IJCNLP-2017, Shared Task 5*.

Sandip Sarkar, Dipankar Das, and Partha Pakray. 2017. Ju nitm: A classification approach for answer selection in multi-choice question answering system. In *IJCNLP-2017, Shared Task 5*.

Hang Yuan, You Zhang, Jin Wang, and Xuejie Zhang. 2017. Using an attention-based lstm for multi-choice question answering in exams. In *IJCNLP-2017, Shared Task 5*.

Alibaba at IJCNLP-2017 Task 1: Embedding Grammatical Features into LSTMs for Chinese Grammatical Error Diagnosis Task

Yi Yang and **Pengjun Xie** and **Jun Tao** and **Guangwei Xu** and **Linlin Li** and **Si Luo**
{zongchen.yy, Jun.Tao, linyan.lll, luo.si}@alibaba-inc.com
chengchen.xpj, kunka.xgw@taobao.com@taobao.com

Abstract

This paper introduces Alibaba NLP team system on IJCNLP 2017 shared task No. 1 Chinese Grammatical Error Diagnosis (CGED). The task is to diagnose four types of grammatical errors which are redundant words (R), missing words (M), bad word selection (S) and disordered words (W). We treat the task as a sequence tagging problem and design some handcraft features to solve it. Our system is mainly based on the LSTM-CRF model and 3 ensemble strategies are applied to improve the performance. At the identification level and the position level our system gets the highest F1 scores. At the position level, which is the most difficult level, we perform best on all metrics.

1 Introduction

Chinese is one of the old and versatile languages in the world. In its long use of history, it has accumulated a lot of difference from other languages. For example, compared to English, Chinese has neither singular/plural change, nor the tense changes of the verb. It has more flexible expression but loose structural grammar, uses more short sentences but less clauses. It also has more repetitions, while English omits a lot. e.g. "Ambition is the mother of destruction as well as of evil. 野心不仅是罪恶的根源，同时也是毁灭的根源。" In English, "the mother of" evil is completely omitted. But in Chinese, it need be expressed clearly in the sentence. All these differences bring a lot of trouble to new learners. With the surging of Chinese Foreign Language(CFL)

Learners, an automatic Chinese Grammatical Error Diagnosis will be very helpful. English Grammar Check has been studied for many years, with a lot of progress being made, while Chinese Grammar Check, Error Detection and Correction study is much less until very recently. Though the two languages have a lot of difference between them, they also share similarities, such as the fixed collocation of words. Experience can be obtained from the English NLP study. The CGED Task gives Chinese NLP researchers an opportunity to build and develop the Chinese Grammatical Error Diagnosis System, compare their results and exchange their learning methods.

This paper is organized as follows: Section 2 describes the Shared Task. Section 3 introduces some related work both in English and in Chinese. Section 4 describes our methodology, including feature generation, model architecture and ensemble. Section 5 shows the data analysis and final result on the evaluation data set. Section 6 concludes the paper and shows future work.

2 Chinese Grammatical Error Diagnosis

The NLPTea CGED has been held since 2014. It provides several sets of training data written by Chinese Foreign Language(CFL) leaner. In these training data sets, 4 kinds of error have been labeled: R(redundant word error), S(word selection error), M(missing word error) and W(word ordering error). With a test data set provided, an automatic Chinese Grammatical Error Diagnosis System need to be developed to detect: (1) If the sentence is correct or not; (2) What kind of errors the sentence contains; (3) the exact error position. One thing need additional attention is that each sentence may contain more than one error. Some

Proceedings of the 8th International Joint Conference on Natural Language Processing, Shared Tasks, pages 41–46,
Taipei, Taiwan, November 27 – December 1, 2017. ©2017 AFNLP

Table 1: Typical Error Examples.

Error Type	Original Sentence	Correct Sentence
M(missing word)	我河边散步的时候。	我在河边散步的时候。
R(redundant word)	流行歌曲告诉我们现在的我们的心理状态。	流行歌曲告诉我们现在的心理状态。
S(word selection)	还有其他的人也受被害。	还有其他的人也受伤害。
W(word order)	听多流行歌就会对唱那首歌的歌手痴迷。	多听流行歌就会对唱那首歌的歌手痴迷。

typical examples are shown in table 1:

All these metrics are measured in the test results: False Positive Rate, Accuracy, Precision, Recall and F1.

3 Related Works

Grammatical Error Detection and Correction in CoNLL2013 and CoNLL2014 shared Task attracts a lot of English NLP researchers and different approaches were adopted by the participants, e.g. hand-crafted rules, statistical model, translation model and language model(Ng et al., 2014). The study on collocation also shows great improvement in Grammatical Error Detection(Chen et al., 2016; Ferraro et al., 2014). The long short term memory (LSTM) has proved its efficiency in NLP general sequence related modeling(Hochreiter and Schmidhuber, 1997) and Grammatical Error Diagnosis(Zheng et al., 2016). Chinese Grammatical Error Detection research is much less compared with English, and lack of large publicly published data also hinders its study. In 2012, a CRF based Classifier is proposed to detect the word ordering error(Yu and Chen, 2012). In 2014, Cheng etc propose a rule based Diagnosis System(Chang et al., 2014). NLPTea 2014/2015/2016 CGED shared task also provides the Chinese NLP researchers a chance to publish their progress on this topic(Yu et al., 2014; Lee et al., 2015, 2016). HIT propose a CRF+BiLSTM model based on character embedding on bigram embedding(Zheng et al., 2016). CYUT propose a CRF based model on collocation, Part-Of-Speech (POS) linguistic features(Ferraro et al., 2014).

4 Methodology

4.1 Model Description

Same with the method of most teams in 2016, we treat the CGED problem as a sequence tagging problem. Specifically, given a sentence x, we generate a corresponding label sequence y using the BIO encoding (Kim et al., 2004). The HIT

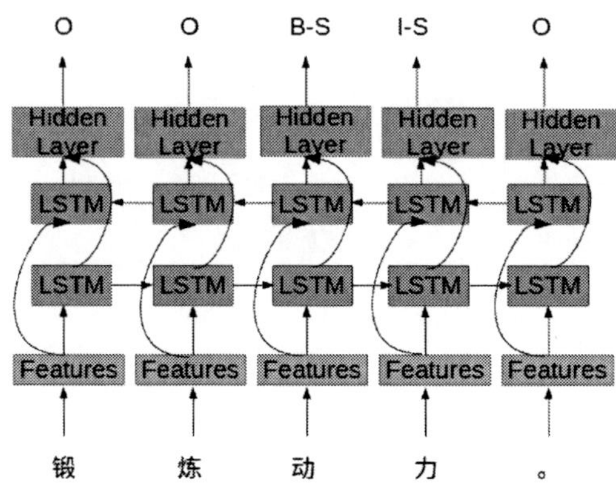

Figure 1: The LSTM-CRF model we applied. Note that we use bi-directional LSTM as the basic neural unit.

team (Zheng et al., 2016) had used traditional CRF model and LSTM-based models to solve the sequence tagging problem. However, it's straightforward to combine the two models, that results to a relatively new model named LSTM-CRF (Huang et al., 2015). With the help of the CRF, the LSTM-CRF model can predict the tagging sequence better. For instance, the LSTM-CRF model can avoid predicting the 'I-X' error compared with single LSTM model. Same with the HIT team, we use the bidirectional LSTM unit as the RNN unit to model the input sequence. The model architecture is illustrated in figure 1. As you can see from the figure, the features are not specific in the architecture, we will explain them in the next section.

4.2 Feature Engineering

Since the lack of training data, the task heavily depends on the prior knowledge, such as POS feature, provided by external data or domain expert. In another word, the feature engineering is very important in this task. We designed several features. Figure 2 illustrates the features we used. Next we will introduce each feature one by one.

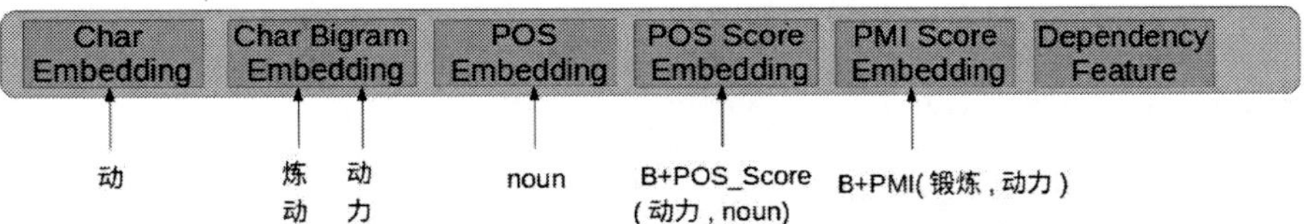

Figure 2: The features we used in this task. Use the feature at "动" in "锻炼动力 。" as an example.

- Char: We solved the sequence tagging problem at the character level, it's straightforward to use the char embedding as an input feature. We randomly initialized the char embedding.

- Char Bigram: Bigram is an informative and discriminating feature in this task because it makes the model easily to learn the degree of collocation between neighbor chars. We obtained the bigram embeddings the same way as the HIT team.

- POS: Part-of-speech-tagging (POST) of words containing verb, adverb, adjective, noun. character's POS tag is decided by its word POS tag, B-pos indicating the beginning character's POS tag while I-pos indicating the middle and end characters'.

- POS Score: By analyzing the training data, we found that the POS tag of lots of error words are not the tag the word showing most of times. For example, the POS tag for the word "损伤" in the sentence "抽烟明显损伤身体健康" is VV, which is not its usual tag. This is a S error and the word should be changed to "损害". We used the discrete probability of the word's tag as a feature. The probabilities are calculated by the Gigawords dataset (Graff and Chen, 2005). Note that we also attached position indicators to this feature in the same way as the POS feature.

- Adjacent Word Collocation: In the training data, we found that wrong collocation happens between the neighbor words. Based on this observation, we calculated a pointwise mutual information (PMI) (Church and Hanks, 1990) score using the Gigawords dataset for each adjacent words pair. The formula for calculating the PMI score is:

$$PMI(w1, w2) = log(\frac{p(w1, w2)}{p(w1) * p(w2)}) \quad (1)$$

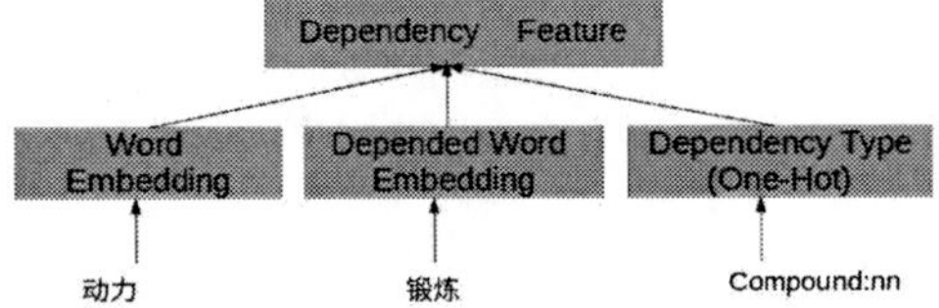

Figure 3: The dependency feature sub-network.

For example, the score of the words pair <"锻炼", "动力"> in the sentence "天天锻炼动力 。" is very low, while the score of < "锻炼", "能力"> is much higher. Similarly, the score of <"一部", "电影"> is much higher than <"一台", "电影">. We embedded the discrete PMI score into a low dimension vector as one of input features for our LSTM-CRF model. Since we solved the task at the character level, we also added the position indicators to the discrete PMI score.

- Dependent Word Collocation: The adjacent word PMI score represents the collocation between adjacent words. However the collocation relationship is not limited to the adjacent words. For example, the word "一个" in sentence "他刚刚出版了一个新的小说." is used to modify the word "小说". By using dependency parser, we can get the dependent word for each word. At each position, we model the collocation relationship feature through a sub-network. The input of the sub-network is a concatenation of the word's embedding, the dependent word's embedding and the dependent type. Figure 3 illustrates the sub-network.

4.3 Model Ensemble

Because of random initialization, random dropout (Srivastava et al., 2014) and random training order, the model result may be different at the end of each training. After the experiments, we found that each model gave very different predicted result even they share the same set of pre-trained parameters. According to this situation, we designed 3 different ensemble methods to improve the result.

The first ensemble method was just simple merging all results. We found that the precision of a single model was much higher than the recall. It's straightforward to merge different model results to increase the recall. After applying the merging-all strategy, the recall was increased as expected, but the precision decreased greatly. So we designed a second ensemble method to balance the precision and the recall. We used the score generated by the LSTM-CRF to rank the errors generated by each model. We deleted the final ranking 20% errors for each single model and then merged the rest results. The second ensemble method can increase the precision to some extent, but it is hard to exceed the single model. In order to increase the precision further, the third ensemble method we applied was voting. Voting is really a powerful method in this task because it can greatly increase the precision while keep the recall same as long as the model quantity is big enough.

In all of our experiments, we used 4 different groups of parameters and trained 2 models for each parameter groups, so totally we used 8 models. Surprisingly, we found that the 3 different ensemble methods achieved the best F1-score respectively in the detection level, identification level and position level.

5 Experiments

5.1 Data Split and Experiment Settings

We collected data sets of year 2015, 2016, and 2017, of which 20% data of year 2017 are used for validation and the rest for training. In our experiments, we found that adding the correct sentence could improve the result, so all correct sentence were added into the training set.

We pretrained bigram-char embeddings and word embeddings using the Gigawords dateset and fixed them when training models. For other parameters, we randomly initialized them.

The performance metrics were calculated at three levels, detection-level, identification-level and position-level. For each level, false positive rate, accuracy, precision, recall and F1-score were included.

5.2 Experiment Results

5.2.1 Results on Validation Dataset

We used the validation dataset to select the best hyper-parameters for single LSTM-CRF model. Among the parameters, we chose 4 groups of parameters and trained 2 models for each parameters group to ensemble. There exists a certain degree of difference among the 4 groups, while the model performance is also good for each single parameters group. Table 2 shows the result. As we can see, the ensemble method 1 (simple merging all) has the highest recall at all 3 levels as intended. It gets the best F1-score at detection level at the same time. The ensemble method 2 (merging after removing low-score errors) has relatively good performance at all 3 levels, especially gets the highest F1-score at detection level. The ensemble method 3 (voting) gets the best precision at all 3 levels. It gets the best F1-score at position level. As intended, we can figure out that the precision is increasing from ensemble method 1 to method 3, and the recall is decreasing. Furthermore, all 3 ensemble methods are very effective compared with single model and achieve great improvement on F1-score at all 3 levels.

5.2.2 Results on Evaluation Dataset

When testing on the final evaluation dataset, we merged our training dataset and validation dataset, and retrained our models. Table 3 shows the results of our 3 submissions, each submission corresponds to an ensemble method.

Our system achieves the best F1 scores at identification level and position level, and achieve the best recall rates in all 3 levels. At detection level, if not taking all sentences to be error into consideration, our F1 score is also the highest. At the position level, our system perform best on all the metrics. It is a little pity that the best F1-score we have gotten at position level is just 0.2693. To some extent, it is because that the problem is very hard and the training data is not enough. However, we are optimistic about the solving the CGED problem completely.

6 Conclusion and Future Work

This article describes our system approach in IJC-NLP TASK1, CGED. We combined some hand-craft features, like the POS, dependency features and PMI Score, etc, and trained LSTM-CRF models based on these features. Later, we designed

Table 2: Results on Validation Dataset. Single Model refers to the LSTM-CRF model. Ensemble Method 1 refers to merging results of 8 models. Ensemble Method 2 refers to merging results after removing the 20% low-score errors. Ensemble Method 3 refers to voting. We keep errors occurred at least 2 times among 8 results when voting.

Method	Detection Level			Identification Level			Position Level		
	Precision	Recall	F1	Precision	Recall	F1	Precision	Recall	F1
Single Model	0.66	0.46	0.54	0.52	0.26	0.36	0.31	0.13	0.19
Ensemble Method 1	0.55	**0.84**	**0.6745**	0.25	**0.62**	0.36	0.15	**0.29**	0.202
Ensemble Method 2	0.56	0.81	0.66	0.39	0.58	**0.47**	0.17	0.27	0.21
Ensemble Method 3	**0.67**	0.56	0.61	**0.54**	0.36	0.43	**0.30**	0.20	**0.24**

Table 3: Results on Evaluation Dataset

Method	Detection Level			Identification Level			Position Level		
	Precision	Recall	F1	Precision	Recall	F1	Precision	Recall	F1
Ensemble Method 1	0.6792	**00.8284**	**0.7464**	0.453	**0.6006**	0.5164	0.1949	**0.2941**	0.2344
Ensemble Method 2	0.686	0.7986	0.738	0.4791	0.5657	**0.5188**	0.2169	0.2752	0.2426
Ensemble Method 3	**0.7597**	0.5714	0.6523	**0.6007**	0.3756	0.4622	**0.3663**	0.213	**0.2693**

different ensemble strategies for the 3 levels. The results show that our strategies are valid. At the identification level and the position level we get the highest F1 scores. At detection level, without taking all sentences to be error into consideration, our F1 score is also the highest. At the position level, which is the most difficult level, our accuracy, precision, recall, and F1 score are the highest.

In the future, with more training data, we hope not only to identify the error, but also directly correct the error based on models like seq2seq (Sutskever et al., 2014). Chinese Grammatic Error Correction will be more helpful for the non-native language learners to learn Chinese. Currently, We used many handcraft features in this task. In the future, we will design a more automatic neural architecture to get an end-to-end grammatical error recognition system by combining the pre-trained language model and other related multi-task models, which will help the recognition and correction of grammatical errors.

7 References

References

Tao Hsing Chang, Yao Ting Sung, Jia Fei Hong, and Jen I Chang. 2014. Knged: A tool for grammatical error diagnosis of chinese sentences. In *22nd International Conference on Computers in Education, ICCE 2014*. Asia-Pacific Society for Computers in Education.

Po-Lin Chen, Shih-Hung Wu, Liang-Pu Chen, and Ping-Che Yang. 2016. Improving the selection error recognition in a chinese grammar error detection system. In *Information Reuse and Integration (IRI), 2016 IEEE 17th International Conference on*, pages 525–530. IEEE.

Kenneth Ward Church and Patrick Hanks. 1990. Word association norms, mutual information, and lexicography. *Computational linguistics*, 16(1):22–29.

Gabriela Ferraro, Rogelio Nazar, Margarita Alonso Ramos, and Leo Wanner. 2014. Towards advanced collocation error correction in spanish learner corpora. *Language resources and evaluation*, 48(1):45–64.

David Graff and Ke Chen. 2005. Chinese gigaword. *LDC Catalog No.: LDC2003T09, ISBN*, 1:58563–58230.

Sepp Hochreiter and Jürgen Schmidhuber. 1997. Long short-term memory. *Neural computation*, 9(8):1735–1780.

Zhiheng Huang, Wei Xu, and Kai Yu. 2015. Bidirectional lstm-crf models for sequence tagging. *arXiv preprint arXiv:1508.01991*.

Jin-Dong Kim, Tomoko Ohta, Yoshimasa Tsuruoka, Yuka Tateisi, and Nigel Collier. 2004. Introduction to the bio-entity recognition task at jnlpba. In *Proceedings of the international joint workshop on natural language processing in biomedicine and its applications*, pages 70–75. Association for Computational Linguistics.

Lung-Hao Lee, RAO Gaoqi, Liang-Chih Yu, XUN Endong, Baolin Zhang, and Li-Ping Chang. 2016. Overview of nlp-tea 2016 shared task for chinese grammatical error diagnosis. In *Proceedings of the 3rd Workshop on Natural Language Processing Techniques for Educational Applications (NLPTEA2016)*, pages 40–48.

Lung Hao Lee, Liang Chih Yu, and Li Ping Chang. 2015. Overview of the nlp-tea 2015 shared task for chinese grammatical error diagnosis. In *Overview of the NLP-TEA 2015 Shared Task for Chinese Grammatical Error Diagnosis*.

HT Ng, SM Wu, and Y Wu. Ch. hadiwinoto, and j. tetreault. 2013. the conll-2013 shared task on grammatical error correction. *Proceedings of CoNLL: Shared Task*.

Hwee Tou Ng, Siew Mei Wu, Ted Briscoe, Christian Hadiwinoto, Raymond Hendy Susanto, and Christopher Bryant. 2014. The conll-2014 shared task on grammatical error correction. In *CoNLL Shared Task*, pages 1–14.

Nitish Srivastava, Geoffrey E Hinton, Alex Krizhevsky, Ilya Sutskever, and Ruslan Salakhutdinov. 2014. Dropout: a simple way to prevent neural networks from overfitting. *Journal of machine learning research*, 15(1):1929–1958.

Ilya Sutskever, Oriol Vinyals, and Quoc V Le. 2014. Sequence to sequence learning with neural networks. In *Advances in neural information processing systems*, pages 3104–3112.

Chi-Hsin Yu and Hsin-Hsi Chen. 2012. Detecting word ordering errors in chinese sentences for learning chinese as a foreign language. In *COLING*, pages 3003–3018.

Liang-Chih Yu, Lung-Hao Lee, and Li-Ping Chang. 2014. Overview of grammatical error diagnosis for learning chinese as a foreign language. In *Proceedings of the 1st Workshop on Natural Language Processing Techniques for Educational Applications*, pages 42–47.

Bo Zheng, Wanxiang Che, Jiang Guo, and Ting Liu. 2016. Chinese grammatical error diagnosis with long short-term memory networks. *NLPTEA 2016*, page 49.

THU_NGN at IJCNLP-2017 Task 2: Dimensional Sentiment Analysis for Chinese Phrases with Deep LSTM

Chuhan Wu[1], **Fangzhao Wu**[2], **Yongfeng Huang**[1], **Sixing Wu**[1] and **Zhigang Yuan**[1]

[1]Tsinghua National Laboratory for Information Science and Technology,
Department of Electronic Engineering, Tsinghua University, Beijing 100084, China
{wuch15,wu-sx15,yuanzg14}@mails.tsinghua.edu.cn, yfhuang@mail.tsinghua.edu.cn
[2]Microsoft Research Asia, wufangzhao@gmail.com

Abstract

Predicting valence-arousal ratings for words and phrases is very useful for constructing affective resources for dimensional sentiment analysis. Since the existing valence-arousal resources of Chinese are mainly in word-level and there is a lack of phrase-level ones, the Dimensional Sentiment Analysis for Chinese Phrases (DSAP) task aims to predict the valence-arousal ratings for Chinese affective words and phrases automatically. In this task, we propose an approach using a densely connected LSTM network and word features to identify dimensional sentiment on valence and arousal for words and phrases jointly. We use word embedding as major feature and choose part of speech (POS) and word clusters as additional features to train the dense LSTM network. The evaluation results of our submissions (1st and 2nd in average performance) validate the effectiveness of our system to predict valence and arousal dimensions for Chinese words and phrases.

1 Introduction

Sentiment analysis is an important task in opinion mining for both academic and business use. Traditional sentiment analysis approaches mainly intend to identify the positive or negative sentiment polarities of text. This field has been widely researched and has many effective approaches based on rules or statistical methods. However, analyzing only the polarities of sentiments is rough and can't differ sentiment distinctions in fine-grained. In order to go further in fine-grained sentiment analysis, some approaches were proposed to address this problem in more categories or in real-value, such as dimensional sentiment analysis. Evaluating sentiment in valence-arousal (VA) space was first proposed by Ressel (1980). As shown in Figure 1, the valence dimension represents the degree of positive or negative sentiment, while the arousal dimension indicates the intensity of sentiment. Based on this two-dimensional representation, any affective state can be represented as a point in the VA coordinate plane by determining the degrees of valence and arousal of given words (Wei et al., 2011; Malandrakis et al., 2011; Yu et al., 2015; Wang et al., 2016) or texts(Kim et al., 2010; Paltoglou et al., 2013).

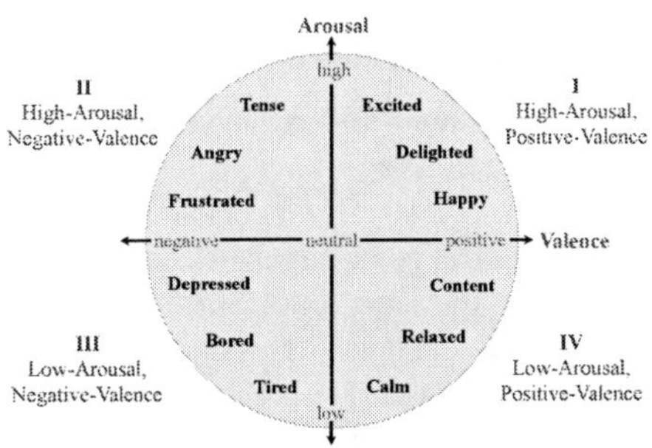

Figure 1: Two-dimensional valence-arousal space.

External VA resources like lexicons are necessary to VA sentiment evaluation. However, there is a lack of these resources especially for Chinese, and it's usually difficult to construct them manually. Thus in order to get large scale lexicons in a reasonable cost, the objective of the shared task DSAP is to automatically acquire the valence-arousal ratings of Chinese affective words and phrases. Some typical approaches to word-level VA rating task are based on statistical observations like linear regression (Wei et al., 2011) and kernel function (Malandrakis et al., 2011). However, these methods deeply rely on the affective lex-

Proceedings of the 8th International Joint Conference on Natural Language Processing, Shared Tasks, pages 47–52,
Taipei, Taiwan, November 27 – December 1, 2017. ©2017 AFNLP

icons and may ignore some high level sentimen-t features. After an effective word representation proposed by Mikolov et al. (2013), some meth-ods based on word embedding were introduced to this task such as weighted graph (Yu et al., 2015; Wang et al., 2016). And in recent years, NN-based methods (Chou et al., 2016; Du and Zhang, 2016) were employed for this task and show better per-formance.

However, deep learning methods haven't been applied to such word-level and phrase-level task yet. Motivated by the successful applications of deep learning such as DenseNet proposed by Huang et al. (2016), we propose a densely con-nected deep LSTM network to predict VA ratings for words and phrases jointly. We segment al-l words and phrases and pad them to the same length for joint training. In network training, we use word embedding as the representation of word and add POS embedding and word clusters as ad-ditional features. The evaluation results of our sys-tem (1st and 2nd of two runs) in this task show the effectiveness of our method.

2 Densely Connected LSTM with Word Features

2.1 Network Architecture

Due to the feature self-extraction ability of deep network, features in different level can be learned by different layers. If we concatenate these fea-tures, layers can learn linguistic features of differ-ent levels at the same time. Since the input is se-quential data, the layers of network can be imple-mented with LSTM. The architecture of our dense LSTM network is shown in Figure 2. Output from every top LSTM layer will be concatenated togeth-er as the input for bottom layers. Thus for a N-layer dense LSTM, there will be $\frac{N(N-1)}{2}$ connec-tions.

The input of our network is word embedding concatenated with additional features. The details of features will presents in the following subsec-tions. In this dense network, we pad all N LSTM layers to the same length L. We mark the output hidden state of i-th LSTM layer as h_i. Thus, the fitting function of h_i can be represented as follows:

$$h_i = \mathcal{F}_i(h_1; h_2; ...; h_{(i-1)}) \tag{1}$$

where $\mathcal{F}_i$ denotes the fitting function of i-th LSTM layer. Finally, a linear decoder is used to dense the output from the bottom LSTM layer into VA ratings. So the final output y is:

$$y = W \cdot h_{NL} + b \tag{2}$$

Where h_{NL} denotes the last hidden state of the N-th layer. From Eq. 1 we can see that each layer can learn all levels of features from previous layers at the same time. Thus it may be easier for the net-work to learn a better representation by combining low-level semantic and high-level sentiment infor-mation.

2.2 Word Features

In our method, word embedding is the major fea-ture for network's training, while POS embedding and the one-hot representation of word cluster are chosen as additional linguistic features. We con-catenate these features of each word to feed the network. These features are described as follows.

2.2.1 Word Embedding

In our model, we embed each word into a v_1-dim vector. The word embedding model is trained on a mixed corpus including SogouCA News dump[1] and wiki dump[2]. Since the linguistic features for out-vocabulary word are missing, and the miss segments can also cause similar problem. So we use 500 collected sentences from the Internet to fix this problem in run2 submission. The embed-ding we use is Google Embedding (Mikolov et al., 2013) proposed by Mikolov et al. We use the open source word2vec tool[3] to train word embedding and get word clusters.

2.2.2 POS Embedding

We get the POS tags of words and phrases after parsing. Since the POS tags of words also car-ry rich linguistic information, we embed POS tags into a v_2-dim vector when training on the dataset instead of using one-hot representation.

2.2.3 Word Cluster

After getting the embedding of words, we cluster all words in the dictionary into k classes by K-means method. The selection of k is based on the 10-fold cross validation results in our experiment. The class of a word will be one-hot encoded and then merged directly with other features.

---

[1] https://www.sogou.com/labs/resource/ca.php
[2] http://download.wikipedia.com/zhwiki/latest/zhwiki-latest-pages-articles.xml.bz2
[3] https://code.google.com/archive/p/word2vec/

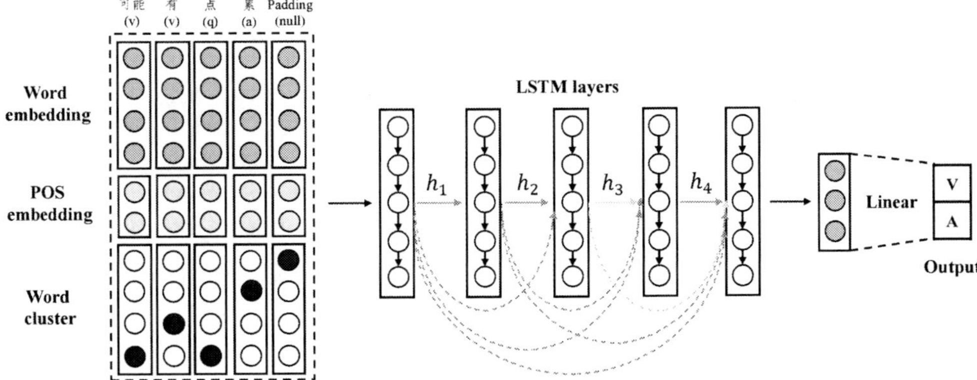

Figure 2: Dense LSTM network architecture. This figure shows a 5 layers dense LSTM as an example. The dashed lines represent the highway connection of different layers.

3 Experiment

3.1 Experiment Settings

3.1.1 Dataset and Metrics

In this task we use the dataset provided by the organizer which contains 2,802 words and 2,250 phrases for training, 750 words and 750 phrases for test. This dataset is based on the Chinese valence-arousal words (CVAW) dataset with 1,654 words and its later extensions. The annotations of valence and arousal are real-value from 1 to 9.

Prediction performance is evaluated by examining the difference between machine-predicted ratings and human annotated ratings. The evaluation metrics include Mean Absolute Error (MAE) and Pearson Correlation Coefficient (PCC), as shown in the following equations.

- Mean absolute error(MAE)

$$MAE = \frac{1}{n} \sum_{i=1}^{n} |A_i - P_i|$$

- Pearson correlation coefficient(PCC)

$$PCC = \frac{1}{n-1} \sum_{i=1}^{n} (\frac{A_i - \bar{A}}{\sigma_A})(\frac{P_i - \bar{P}}{\sigma_P})$$

where A_i is the actual value, P_i is the predicted value, n is the number of test samples, $\bar{A}$ and $\bar{P}$ respectively denote the arithmetic mean of A and P, and σ is the standard deviation.

3.1.2 Preprocessing

Since we don't have enough corpus of traditional Chinese, we first translate the data into simplified Chinese. We use the ANSJ tool[4] to segment all words and phrases, because some words can also be splited into smaller subwords. Finally we pad all of them to the length of 5 for network training.

3.1.3 Network Training

In our experiment, the word embedding dimension v_1 is set to 300 and the POS embedding dimension v_2 is set to 50. The hidden states of every LSTM layer are 100-dim. The word cluster classes k is set to 250 for word-level prediction and 350 for phrase-level prediction. The objective function in our experiment is MAE and we use RMSProp optimizer to train the network. In order to prevent overfitting, we apply dropout after embedding and all LSTM layers. And specially in our run2 submission, we use a randomly selected dropout rate in every model, and the training samples are randomly selected from the whole training set. In order to suppress data noise and the randomicity introduced by dropout, we train our model for 100 times and ensemble all the model outputs by mean as the final predictions.

3.2 Performance Evaluation

The evaluation results of our system are shown in Table 1. Our approach shows effectiveness in both word and phrase level and significantly outperforms these baselines. Besides, in the averaging performance, we reach 0.427 and 0.6245 of

---

[4]https://github.com/NLPchina/ansj_seg.git

MAE, 0.9345 and 0.7985 of PCC in the valence and arousal dimension respectively. And especially in phrase-level, our approach reach very low MAE (0.345 and 0.385) and very high PCC (0.961 and 0.911). We can see that our approach works better in phrase-level, which may indicate that our recurrent-NN based method makes better use of sequential information. And the word-level results in run1 are much lower than our cross validation results. It may due to the out-dictionary words or network overfitting. To solve these problems in run2, we use our collected sentences from the Internet to re-train the embedding, and ensemble models that trained by randomly selected data and dropout rate to reduce the risk of overfitting. The final evaluation results show the significant improvement made by these processes.

Model	Valence		Arousal	
	MAE	PCC	MAE	PCC
Word				
Baseline	0.984	0.643	1.031	0.456
MLP	0.728	0.802	0.955	0.577
CNN	0.765	0.772	0.992	0.537
LSTM	0.707	0.804	1.055	0.588
Our Run1	0.610	0.857	0.940	0.623
Our Run2	**0.509**	**0.908**	**0.864**	**0.686**
Phrase				
Baseline	1.051	0.610	0.607	0.730
MLP	0.831	0.763	0.449	0.872
CNN	0.512	0.911	0.471	0.861
LSTM	0.429	0.939	0.450	0.869
Our Run1	0.349	0.960	0.389	0.909
Our Run2	**0.345**	**0.961**	**0.385**	**0.911**

Table 1: Evaluation results of our two submissions and some baselines for comparison.

3.3 Influence of Network Depth

We compare the validation MAE performance of network with different depth, as shown in Figure 3. Note that we don't use word cluster here. When $N = 1$ this network is equal to a single LSTM layer, and when $N = 2$ it's equal to a 2-layer deep LSTM. From two figures, we can see that the dense LSTM network has better performance than a single LSTM or a standard deep LSTM, and a 5-layer dense LSTM network is the most suitable for this task. This result indicates that our dense LSTM network can learn a better representation of sentiment by combining different levels of features.

Model	Valence		Arousal	
	MAE	PCC	MAE	PCC
Word				
+POS	**0.516**	**0.898**	**0.719**	**0.748**
w/o POS	0.540	0.874	0.732	0.721
Phrase				
+POS	**0.335**	**0.968**	**0.387**	**0.918**
w/o POS	0.364	0.960	0.402	0.911

Table 2: Performance with POS embedding or not.

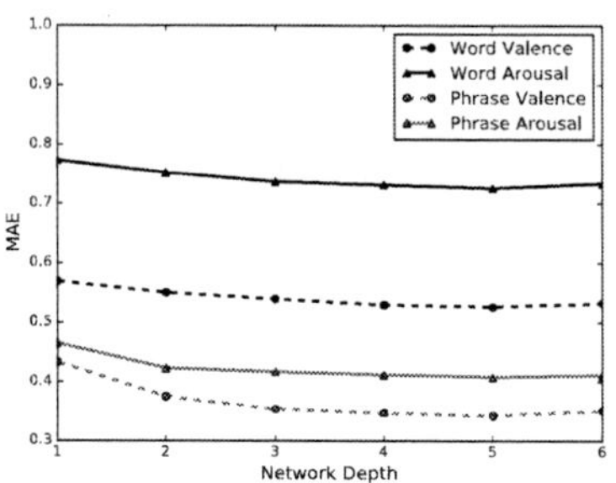

Figure 3: Validation MAE with different network depth.

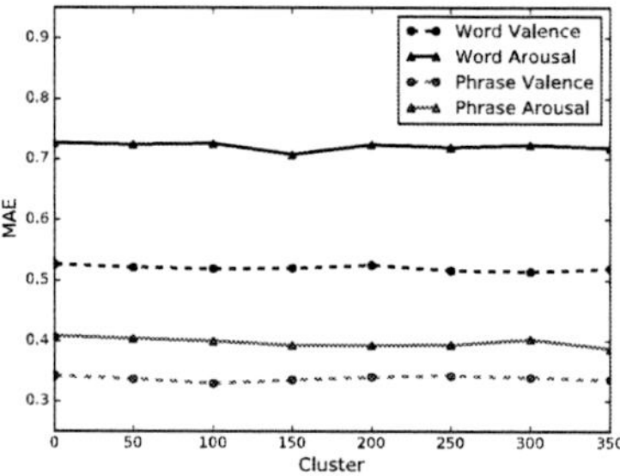

Figure 4: Validation MAE with cluster size k.

3.4 Influence of Word Features

3.4.1 POS embedding

We compare the validation performance of network with POS embedding and without. From Table 2, We can see that the significant improvement made by POS feature. This result indicates that POS tags of words contain very useful linguistic information and can improve the performance of deep model in DSA task.

3.4.2 Word cluster

We choose the cluster size k according to the validation performance and we use the network settings in run1. See Figure 4. The validation MAE results show that word cluster can improve the performance of network. We found the cluster size $k = 250$ is slightly better for word-level prediction while $k = 350$ is slightly better for phrase-level prediction.

3.5 Model Ensemble

We ensemble the output predictions of models trained by different hyper-parameters and training data. The results is shown in Table 3. We can see that the model ensembling can improve the performance very siginicicantly. This may because the ensembled model have a better generalization ablility and is more stable with the data noise.

Model	Valence		Arousal	
	MAE	PCC	MAE	PCC
Word				
+ensemble	**0.469**	**0.927**	**0.688**	**0.767**
w/o ensemble	0.516	0.898	0.719	0.748
Phrase				
+ensemble	**0.286**	**0.975**	**0.348**	**0.930**
w/o ensemble	0.335	0.968	0.387	0.918

Table 3: The influence of model ensembling.

4 Conclusion

In this paper, we introduce a novel approach using a densely connected LSTM network with word features to DSAP shared task for Chinese words and phrases. We combine deep network and word features including POS and word cluster to address this task. In addition, we also use a random model ensemble strategy to improve the performance of our approach. The evaluation results (1st and 2nd averaging performance in two runs) show the effectiveness of our approach.

Acknowledgments

This research is supported by the Key Program of National Natural Science Foundation of China under Grant No. U1405254 and U1536201.

References

Stefano Baccianella, Andrea Esuli, and Fabrizio Sebastiani. 2010. Sentiwordnet 3.0: An enhanced lexical resource for sentiment analysis and opinion mining. In *LREC*, volume 10, pages 2200–2204.

Margaret M Bradley and Peter J Lang. 1999. Affective norms for english words (anew): Instruction manual and affective ratings. Technical report, Technical report C-1, the center for research in psychophysiology, University of Florida.

Wei-Chieh Chou, Chin-Kui Lin, Yih-Ru Wang, and Yuan-Fu Liao. 2016. Evaluation of weighted graph and neural network models on predicting the valence-arousal ratings of chinese words. In *Asian Language Processing (IALP), 2016 International Conference on*, pages 168–171. IEEE.

Junyoung Chung, Caglar Gulcehre, KyungHyun Cho, and Yoshua Bengio. 2014. Empirical evaluation of gated recurrent neural networks on sequence modeling. *arXiv preprint arXiv:1412.3555*.

Steven Du and Xi Zhang. 2016. Aicyber's system for ialp 2016 shared task: Character-enhanced word vectors and boosted neural networks. In *Asian Language Processing (IALP), 2016 International Conference on*, pages 161–163. IEEE.

Andrea Esuli and Fabrizio Sebastiani. 2006. Sentiwordnet: A publicly available lexical resource tor opinion mining. In *In Proceedings of the 5th Conference on Language Resources and Evaluation (LREC06*, pages 417–422.

Gao Huang, Zhuang Liu, Kilian Q Weinberger, and Laurens van der Maaten. 2016. Densely connected convolutional networks. *arXiv preprint arXiv:1608.06993*.

Sunghwan Mac Kim, Alessandro Valitutti, and Rafael A Calvo. 2010. Evaluation of unsupervised emotion models to textual affect recognition. In *Proceedings of the NAACL HLT 2010 Workshop on Computational Approaches to Analysis and Generation of Emotion in Text*, pages 62–70. Association for Computational Linguistics.

Baoli Li. 2016. Learning dimensional sentiment of traditional chinese words with word embedding and support vector regression. In *Asian Language Processing (IALP), 2016 International Conference on*, pages 324–327. IEEE.

Nikos Malandrakis, Alexandros Potamianos, Elias Iosif, and Shrikanth Narayanan. 2011. Kernel models for affective lexicon creation. In *Twelfth Annual Conference of the International Speech Communication Association*.

Tomas Mikolov, Kai Chen, Greg Corrado, and Jeffrey Dean. 2013. Efficient estimation of word representations in vector space. *arXiv preprint arXiv:1301.3781*.

Georgios Paltoglou, Mathias Theunis, Arvid Kappas, and Mike Thelwall. 2013. Predicting emotional responses to long informal text. *IEEE transactions on affective computing*, 4(1):106–115.

JA Ressel. 1980. A circumplex model of affect. *J. Personality and Social Psychology*, 39:1161–78.

Jin Wang, Liang-Chih Yu, K Robert Lai, and Xuejie Zhang. 2016. Community-based weighted graph model for valence-arousal prediction of affective words. *IEEE/ACM Transactions on Audio, Speech, and Language Processing*, 24(11):1957–1968.

Wen-Li Wei, Chung-Hsien Wu, and Jen-Chun Lin. 2011. A regression approach to affective rating of chinese words from anew. *Affective Computing and Intelligent Interaction*, pages 121–131.

Liang-Chih Yu, Lung-Hao Lee, Shuai Hao, Jin Wang, Yunchao He, Jun Hu, K Robert Lai, and Xue-jie Zhang. 2016. Building chinese affective resources in valence-arousal dimensions. In *HLT-NAACL*, pages 540–545.

Liang-Chih Yu, Jin Wang, K Robert Lai, and Xue-jie Zhang. 2015. Predicting valence-arousal ratings of words using a weighted graph method. In *ACL (2)*, pages 788–793.

IIIT-H at IJCNLP-2017 Task 3: A Bidirectional-LSTM Approach for Review Opinion Diversification

Pruthwik Mishra[1]
IIIT-Hyderabad
Hyderabad, India
500032

Prathyusha Danda[1]
IIIT-Hyderabad
Hyderabad, India
500032

Silpa Kanneganti[2]
i.am+ LLC.
Bangalore, India
560071

Soujanya Lanka[3]
i.am+ LLC.
37 Mapex building
Singapore - 577177

Abstract

The Review Opinion Diversification (Revopid-2017) shared task (Singh et al., 2017b) focuses on selecting top-k reviews from a set of reviews for a particular product based on a specific criteria. In this paper, we describe our approaches and results for modeling the ranking of reviews based on their usefulness score, this being the first of the three subtasks under this shared task. Instead of posing this as a regression problem, we modeled this as a classification task where we want to identify whether a review is useful or not. We employed a bi-directional LSTM to represent each review and is used with a softmax layer to predict the usefulness score. We chose the review with highest usefulness score, then find its cosine similarity score with rest of the reviews. This is done in order to ensure diversity in the selection of top-k reviews. On the top-5 list prediction, we finished 3rd while in top-10 list one, we are placed 2nd in the shared task. We have discussed the model and the results in detail in the paper.

1 Introduction

With the increase in usage of e-commerce websites like Amazon, the views of the consumers on products that they purchase, have become both massive and vital to the on-line purchasing community. The facility to express one's views on a purchased product, helps the community members gain perspective on the features as well as quality of the product. This helps them in their decision making of buying the product. Hence, product reviews have tremendous effect on the sales of a product. Due to all these factors, it is very important for the sellers to know which reviews are immediately visible to the buyers. A review should not be given importance just based on its recency. For someone, it might not be very informative compared to not so recent or old reviews. It is vital that the top k reviews that are displayed to the customer are as descriptive as possible.

In view of the above, the IJCNLP shared task: Review Opinion Diversification focuses on ranking the product reviews based on certain criteria. The criteria is unique for each of the three subtasks under this shared task. Ranking must be done based on usefulness score in the case of Subtask A, where as in Subtask B, the goal is to rank the top-k, so as to maximize representativeness of the ranked list. In both Subtask A and B there should also be less redundancy among the top ranked reviews. The goal of Subtask C is to get the top-k reviews which will cover majority of the popular perspectives that are in the data. Similar to Subtask A and B, Subtask C should also have less redundancy among the ranked reviews. In this paper we have aimed for the Subtask A- Usefulness Ranking. Usefulness score of a review is the ratio of number of people who have found the review useful to the total number of people who have assessed the review as useful or not.

We built a model for the Usefulness Ranking subtask using neural networks. We have posed the ranking task as a regression problem in the early stage and then used cosine similarity to achieve the goal. We used bi-directional Long Short-Term Memory units (bi-LSTM) to get a representation of the reviews. Using these vector representations we obtained the top-k most useful, less redundant reviews for each product.

The paper is organized as per the following - section 2 explains the related work and details about the corpus. Different approaches employed are explained in the subsequent sections. Results

Proceedings of the 8th International Joint Conference on Natural Language Processing, Shared Tasks, pages 53–58,
Taipei, Taiwan, November 27 – December 1, 2017. ©2017 AFNLP

and Error Analysis constitute sections 5 and 6 respectively. The evaluation metrics are detailed in section 7. We conclude our paper with the Conclusion & Future Work section.

2   Related Work

(Zhou and Xu) dealt with classification of Amazon Fine Food reviews, based on usefulness score of the review. The classification of a review is binary, it will be classified as either useful or not useful. In their training data they have tagged a review as useful if it has been voted by at least on user as well as more than 50% percent of the users find it helpful. They have employed both feed-forward neural networks (Bishop, 2006) and LSTMs (Hochreiter and Schmidhuber, 1997) for classifying the products. In feed-forward neural networks, they used GloVe (Pennington et al., 2014) as embedding for word vectors and in LSTM model, self-trained word vectors were used to represent the reviews. The best feed-forward model had F1 score of 0.78 where as the LSTM model had 0.86.

In (Hu et al., 2017) a multi-text summarization technique is proposed. The idea is to identify the top-k most informative sentences to use them to summarize the reviews. The training data used are hotel reviews obtained from online sites like TripAdvisor. The novelty of the approach is to consider critical factors like author reliability, review time, review usefulness along with conflicting opinions. Their research method starts by collecting hotel reviews and then proceeds to review preprocessing. Next, sentence importance and sentence similarity are calculated by taking author credibility and usefulness scores into consideration. The last task is the selection of the top-k sentences, which involves grouping the sentences into k clusters, which is done by using k-medoids (Ester et al., 1996) algorithm. Human evaluation was done and the results showed that the proposed approach provided more comprehensive hotel information.

3   Corpus Details

The corpus provided for the task was extracted and annotated from Amazon SNAP Review Dataset[1] (McAuley and Leskovec, 2013). Examples of some reviews in the training data are given below-

---

[1]https://snap.stanford.edu/data/web-Amazon.html

- 'reviewerID': 'A30O9Z1A927GZK', 'asin': 'B00004TFT1', 'helpful': [0, 0], 'reviewText': 'Good price. Nice to have one charging when the other one is being used. They were more expensive in the stores, if you can find it.', 'overall': 5.0, 'summary': 'Power wheels 12 volt battery', 'unixReviewTime': 1405209600, 'reviewTime': '07 13, 2014'

  - 'reviewerID' gives the ID of the reviewer
  - 'asin' is ID of the product reviewed
  - 'name' field gives the name of the reviewer
  - 'helpful' is the usefulness rating of the review which is a list of two numbers 1st being the number of people who found the product helpful and 2nd denotes the total number of people who accessed the review
  - 'reviewText' is the text of the review
  - 'overall' is the overall rating of the product
  - 'summary' is summary of the review
  - 'unixReviewTime' is the time of the review
  - 'reviewTime' is time of the review (raw)

- 'reviewerID': 'A1D9U33OHQTO18', 'asin': 'B00000016W', 'reviewerName': 'Julie L. Friedman', 'helpful': [0, 6], 'reviewText': 'This album is the Beach Boys at their best. The genius of Brian Wilson, the beautiful voice of Carl Wilson, Denis Wilson on the Drums, Al Jardine with rhythm guitar and Mike Love with the Lyrics. A true classic. By Gregg L. Friedman MD, Psychiatrist, Hallandale Beach, FL', 'overall': 5.0, 'summary': 'Gregg L. Friedman MD, Psychiatrist, Hallandale Beach, FL', 'unixReviewTime': 1343865600, 'reviewTime': '08 2, 2012' This review got a usefulness score of 0 because 6 persons who accessed the review did not find the review useful.

The training corpus details are shown in table 3

- Product_Type → Type of the product

- MaxLen → Maximum Length of a review

Product_Type	MaxLen	Non-Useful	Total Reviews	Total Products
Automotive	2974	112035	172016	569
Beauty	4399	185061	316536	1000
Toys Games	5853	217766	314634	1000
Grocery	5532	183146	293629	800
Video Games	7785	169455	358235	1000
Baby Products	5217	236950	352231	1000
Office	5043	195627	327556	1000
Patio Lawn	3963	152329	263489	859
Health	5566	200859	357669	1000
Tools Home	5939	205331	320162	1000
Digital Music	6397	56502	145075	468
Pet Supplies	5263	271616	398658	1000

Table 1: Training Corpus Details

- Non-Useful $\rightarrow$ the total number of reviews with a usefulness score $= [0, 0]$

- Total Reviews $\rightarrow$ total number of reviews of a product-type

- Total Products $\rightarrow$ Total number of products under a product-type

We did not include the Non-useful reviews defined above in training our network.

4 Approach

The main task here is to predict the usefulness of a review. The usefulness score describes the fraction of people who found the review useful. e.g. if 5 users have seen a review and 3 of them have found it useful, then the usefulness score $= 3/5 = 0.6$. The usefulness score is a continuous value.

We implemented a bi-directional LSTM (bi-LSTM) (Graves and Schmidhuber, 2005) for this task. The architecture and model details are explained in the following sections.

4.1 Architecture

Each review is modeled as a sequence of Glove vectors (Pennington et al., 2014). Bi-LSTMs present better semantic representations for a sequence where future and past information are encoded. Figure 4.1 shows the architecture of the bi-LSTM. We used glove embeddings trained on amazon reviews data for each word.

4.2 Model

We implemented a bi-LSTM using keras deep learning library (Chollet et al., 2015). We label any review as useful if its usefulness score is

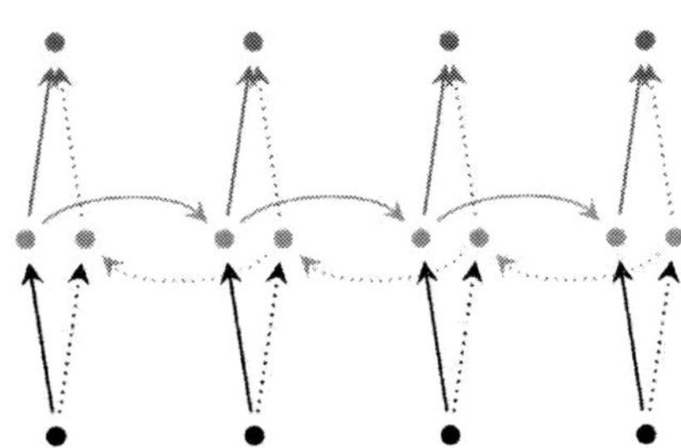

Figure 1: Bidirectional-LSTM [2]

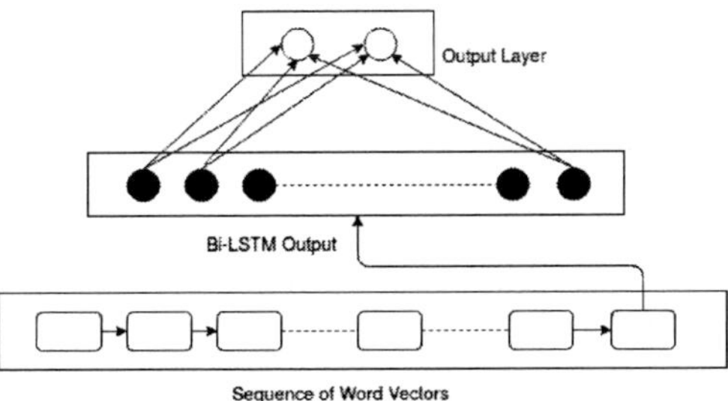

Figure 2: System Architecture

greater than 0.5, non-useful otherwise. The loss function used is binary cross entropy which is the most common loss function for binary classification tasks. Each glove vector is of 300 dimensions. The maximum sequence length is found from the the training set. The output layer uses softmax (Bishop, 2006) activation function. The dropout (Srivastava et al., 2014) rate in the network is 20% or 0.2. Adam (Kingma and Ba, 2014) optimizer was used to model the network.

---

[1] http://www.wildml.com/2015/09/recurrent-neural-networks-tutorial-part-1-introduction-to-rnns/

System	mth	cos_d	cos	cpr	a-dcg	wt	unwt	recall
S1-Top-5	0.71	0.81	0.82	0.63	6.77	670.16	21.27	0.70
S2-Top-5	0.69	0.81	0.83	**0.73**	**6.88**	**681.75**	**21.54**	**0.73**
S3-Top-5	**0.79**	**0.82**	**0.84**	**0.74**	6.65	678.66	21.16	0.68
S1-Top-10	0.80	**0.89**	**0.91**	0.73	8.25	1768.09	54.77	**0.88**
S2-Top-10	0.77	0.88	0.90	**0.78**	**8.28**	1759.26	**55.14**	**0.88**
S3-Top-10	**0.84**	0.88	0.89	0.77	8.24	**1772.34**	54.99	0.86

Table 2: Results on Development Data

4.3 Scoring Measures

The main task here is to pick top-k reviews maximizing the usefulness score and minimizing the overall redundancy among the selected reviews. So we used 3 different weighting schemes where the hyper-parameters are tuned using Grid-Search technique. We used a linear interpolated weights for the overall usefulness estimate.

4.3.1 Basic Scoring Measure

In this scoring scheme, we sorted the reviews of any product based on it predicted usefulness score. The proposed model assigned a classification probability to any incoming review based on its usefulness. The probability score of deciding whether a review is useful or not is directly proportional to the usefulness of the review. The assignment of higher usefulness score to a review with high classification probability of being useful seemed a fair assumption. We chose top-N useful reviews (N=20 for this experiment). We pick the bi-LSTM representation of the review which has the maximum score. Then the cosine similarity between each of the rest of the vectors of reviews with the most useful review was evaluated. We picked the k-reviews which had least cosine similarity with the highest one. This ensured diversity as well as usefulness in the selected reviews. The cosine similarity between two sequences with Bag-Of-Words (BOW) representation many times fails to capture the semantic similarity between them. So the bidirectional-LSTM representation of a sequence which captures long range dependencies in the both the directions proved to be a better alternative.

4.3.2 Weighted Scoring Measure

To have a better weighted score with usefulness and diversity, we used two scoring measures which are explained below.

$$u_i = \alpha * p_i - \beta * cosim(v_{max}, v_i) \quad (1)$$

- $u_i \rightarrow$ usefulness score of the ith review

- $p_i \rightarrow$ predicted usefulness score of the ith review
- $cosim(a, b) \rightarrow$ Cosine-Similarity between vectors a and b, $v_{max} \rightarrow$ bi-LSTM output vector of the review with maximum usefulness score
- $v_i \rightarrow$ bi-LSTM output vector of ith review
- $\alpha, \beta \rightarrow$ tunable hyper-parameters

$$u_i = \alpha * (p_i) - \beta * (cosim(v_{max}, v_i) - 1.0) \quad (2)$$

The variables in equation 2 are the same as those defined in equation 1. We introduced an additional discounting factor while considering the cosine similarity between the vectors. The best values of the hyper-parameters were empirically found at $\alpha = 0.8$ and $\beta = 0.2$ through grid search cross-validation. Equation 2 refers to the relative difference between the cosine similarity between the most useful reviews and i^{th} review and the maximum possible cosine similarity score i.e. 1.0. The cosine similarity has nothing to do with the cosine similarity between overall vector representation of the review and opinion vector according to opinion matrix terminology defined by the evaluation system provided by the organizers.

5 Results

The results on the test and development data is tabulated in Table 2.

The systems described in tables 2 and 3 are defined as per the following.

- S1 $\rightarrow$ Predictions using basic scoring measure
- S2 $\rightarrow$ Predictions using scoring scheme defined in equation 1
- S3 $\rightarrow$ Predictions using scoring scheme defined in equation 2
- Top-5 $\rightarrow$ List of Top 5 predictions
- Top-10 $\rightarrow$ List of Top 10 predictions

We observed that the weighted scoring measures have a positive impact on most of the metrics used

System	mth	cos_d	cos	cpr	a-dcg	wt	unwt	recall
S1-Top-5	0.78	**0.86**	**0.87**	0.49	4.27	494.03	14.04	**0.76**
S2-Top-5	0.78	0.85	0.86	**0.52**	**4.34**	**495.35**	**14.34**	0.75
S3-Top-5	0.78	0.84	0.85	0.51	4.11	486.51	13.35	0.72
S1-Top-10	0.81	**0.92**	0.93	0.61	5.18	**1325.2**	37.54	0.89
S2-Top-10	**0.84**	0.91	0.92	**0.65**	**5.2**	1318.8	**37.8**	0.9
S3-Top-10	0.83	**0.92**	**0.94**	**0.65**	5.16	1317.5	36.8	**0.92**

Table 3: Results on Test Data

for evaluation. The evaluation of the mentioned metrics are done against an opinion matrix for each product. This opinion matrix has been created by evaluators. The evaluation code was provided by the shared task organizers.

6 Error Analysis

There are some reviews where the 'reviewText' field is blank. The input sequence in this case were a series of zero vectors. The usefulness score for these reviews were wrongly predicted. There were cases where the system incorrectly assigned highest probability score to non-useful review.

- 'reviewerID': 'A3S3HYY3BDTYA7', 'asin': 'B00003XAKR', 'reviewerName': 'Shellzbell', 'helpful': [0, 0], 'reviewText': 'Love this thing.. what a bed saver... I was finishing potty training my 2 year old and bed time was my biggest concern. But with this I do not have to worry about the foam mattress I have on my daughters bed. It is easy to wash and put back on the bed.. love this thing.', 'overall': 5.0, 'summary': 'What a find', 'unixReviewTime': 1365292800, 'reviewTime': '04 7, 2013'.

- This review is given highest usefulness during the prediction. Then an incorrect list of reviews were returned which was not be representative of any product.

The usefulness score for a review is very subjective. e.g if 6 out of 7 people have found a review useful, then the usefulness score $= 6/7 = 0.86$. If 1 out of 1 person found one review helpful, it is assigned higher score $1/1 = 1.0$ compared to the previous review. So the usefulness score should not be concerned only with the usefulness score, but it should also take into account the total number of people who access a review.

7 Evaluation

The organizers provided an evaluation system (Singh et al., 2017a) for evaluating the performance of the submitted systems [3]. There were different evaluation metrics for different subtasks. Those evaluation metrics are briefly described here

- SubTaskA
  - mth (More Than Half's) - The fraction of reviews where more than half of the reviewers voted in favour of them.

- SubTaskB
  - Cosine Similarity - The cosine similarity between the overall vector and the opinion vector. The opinion vectors were designed by human evaluators. This vectors are different from the vector representation used after training our bi-LSTM network
  - Discounted Cosine Similarity - The cosine similarity between the overall vector and the discounted opinion vector.
  - Cumulative Proportionality - This metric is based on Saint Lague method and widely used in Electoral Seat Allocation (Dang and Croft, 2012)
  - Alpha-DCG - This measures the diversity and novelty in ranking (Clarke et al., 2008)
  - Weighted Relevance - This is a discounted cumulative gain where the relevance of a review is evaluated by summing the weights of the opinions expressed in the review

- SubTaskC
  - Unweighted Relevance - This metric captures a discounted sum of number of opinion covered in a ranked reviews list
  - Recall - This is a measure of how many opinions are actually covered out of all possible opinions in the ranking

---

[3] https://sites.google.com/itbhu.ac.in/revopid-2017/evaluation

8 Conclusion & Future Work

In this paper, we showed that bi-directional LSTMs perform decently for a task of ranking the top-k reviews based on their usefulness score. This showed that a sequence of word vectors presented a good alternative for training systems without any hand-crafted features.

We can remove the blank reviews and train our system for further analysis. We intend to use character embedding along with the word embeddings to get better representation of a sequence, in this case a review. This will also help in getting a better representation for out-of-vocabulary(OOV) words. We can also include some linguistic regularization (Qian et al., 2016) while learning the bi-LSTM to take advantage of intensifiers, negative words, positive words, sentiment words and other cue words.

Acknowledgements

We thank Vandan Mujadia and Pranav Dhakras for their valuable inputs and feedback for us on the paper.

References

Christopher M Bishop. 2006. *Pattern recognition and machine learning.* springer.

François Chollet et al. 2015. Keras. `https://github.com/fchollet/keras`.

Charles LA Clarke, Maheedhar Kolla, Gordon V Cormack, Olga Vechtomova, Azin Ashkan, Stefan Büttcher, and Ian MacKinnon. 2008. Novelty and diversity in information retrieval evaluation. In *Proceedings of the 31st annual international ACM SIGIR conference on Research and development in information retrieval*, pages 659–666. ACM.

Van Dang and W Bruce Croft. 2012. Diversity by proportionality: an election-based approach to search result diversification. In *Proceedings of the 35th international ACM SIGIR conference on Research and development in information retrieval*, pages 65–74. ACM.

Martin Ester, Hans-Peter Kriegel, Jörg Sander, Xiaowei Xu, et al. 1996. A density-based algorithm for discovering clusters in large spatial databases with noise. In *Kdd*, volume 96, pages 226–231.

Alex Graves and Jürgen Schmidhuber. 2005. Framewise phoneme classification with bidirectional lstm and other neural network architectures. *Neural Networks*, 18(5):602–610.

Sepp Hochreiter and Jürgen Schmidhuber. 1997. Long short-term memory. *Neural computation*, 9(8):1735–1780.

Ya-Han Hu, Yen-Liang Chen, and Hui-Ling Chou. 2017. Opinion mining from online hotel reviews–a text summarization approach. *Information Processing & Management*, 53(2):436–449.

Diederik Kingma and Jimmy Ba. 2014. Adam a method for stochastic optimization. *arXiv preprint arXiv:1412.6980*.

Julian McAuley and Jure Leskovec. 2013. Hidden factors and hidden topics: understanding rating dimensions with review text. In *Proceedings of the 7th ACM conference on Recommender systems*, pages 165–172. ACM.

Jeffrey Pennington, Richard Socher, and Christopher Manning. 2014. Glove: Global vectors for word representation. In *Proceedings of the 2014 conference on empirical methods in natural language processing (EMNLP)*, pages 1532–1543.

Qiao Qian, Minlie Huang, and Xiaoyan Zhu. 2016. Linguistically regularized lstms for sentiment classification. *arXiv preprint arXiv:1611.03949*.

Anil Kumar Singh, Avijit Thawani, Anubhav Gupta, and Rajesh Kumar Mundotiya. 2017a. Evaluating Opinion Summarization in Ranking. In *Proceeding of the 13th Asia Information Retrieval Societies Conference (AIRS 2017)*, Jeju island, Korea.

Anil Kumar Singh, Avijit Thawani, Mayank Panchal, Anubhav Gupta, and Julian McAuley. 2017b. Overview of the IJCNLP-2017 Shared Task on Review Opinion Diversification (RevOpiD-2017). In *Proceedings of the IJCNLP-2017 Shared Tasks*, Taipei, Taiwan. AFNLP.

Nitish Srivastava, Geoffrey E Hinton, Alex Krizhevsky, Ilya Sutskever, and Ruslan Salakhutdinov. 2014. Dropout: a simple way to prevent neural networks from overfitting. *Journal of machine learning research*, 15(1):1929–1958.

Zhenxiang Zhou and Lan Xu. Amazon food review classification using deep learning and recommender system.

Bingo at IJCNLP-2017 Task 4: Augmenting Data using Machine Translation for Cross-linguistic Customer Feedback Classification

Heba Elfardy, Manisha Srivastava, Wei Xiao, Jared Kramer, Tarun Agarwal
`{helfardy,mansri,weixiaow,jaredkra,tagar}@amazon.com`
Amazon
Seattle, WA, USA

Abstract

The ability to automatically and accurately process customer feedback is a necessity in the private sector. Unfortunately, customer feedback can be one of the most difficult types of data to work with due to the sheer volume and variety of services, products, languages, and cultures that comprise the customer experience. In order to address this issue, our team built a suite of classifiers trained on a four-language, multi-label corpus released as part of the shared task on "Customer Feedback Analysis" at IJCNLP 2017. In addition to standard text preprocessing, we translated each dataset into each other language to increase the size of the training datasets. Additionally, we also used word embeddings in our feature engineering step. Ultimately, we trained classifiers using Logistic Regression, Random Forest, and Long Short-Term Memory (LSTM) Recurrent Neural Networks. Overall, we achieved a Macro-Average $F_{\beta=1}$ score between 48.7% and 56.0% for the four languages and ranked 3/12 for English, 3/7 for Spanish, 1/8 for French, and 2/7 for Japanese.

1 Introduction

Customer feedback constitutes the primary back-channel for improving most business offerings. Due to the sheer volume that is typical for customer feedback, there is a strong industry need for systems that can automatically classify this data. Unfortunately, this classification task is not straightforward; every product has a unique customer experience and every company has particular goals when extracting constructive information from feedback. These targets vary across not only products and services, but across the languages and cultures of their customers as well. To complicate the matter further, the private nature of businesses in need of this classification–as well as businesses offering this classification as a service–has resulted in a lack of any agreed-upon classification standards.

To address this gap, IJCNLP 2017 hosted a shared task and released a corpus of multi-lingual, multi-label customer feedback. This data is organized according to a five-plus-one label schema consisting of the following labels: "bug", "comment", "complaint", "meaningless", "request" or "undetermined" across four languages; English (en), Spanish (es), French (fr) and Japanese (jp). As part of this shared task, our team has trained a suite of classifiers over this corpus and here reports the performance of our system. In the remainder of this paper, we will first describe related work in Section 2 before briefly describing the dataset in Section 3. In Section 4, we describe our classification approach, including the translation of the data, our approach to feature engineering, and the learning methods used to train our classifiers, before offering results and discussion in Section 5.

2 Related Work

While text classification is a well-established field, its application on customer feedback is somewhat less mature. One area that has received a fair amount of attention is the task of sentiment classification of customer feedback (Gupta et al., 2010; Gamon, 2004; Kiritchenko et al., 2014). However, sentiment classification enjoys the use of established labeling schemas, typically two, three, or five-way labeling to indicate the presence

Proceedings of the 8th International Joint Conference on Natural Language Processing, Shared Tasks, pages 59–66,
Taipei, Taiwan, November 27 – December 1, 2017. ©2017 AFNLP

	lang	bug	comment	complaint	meaningless	request	undeter.	# Posts	Avg Post Len.
	train	73	1,624	877	283	97	20	2,851	13.1
en	dev	19	410	219	71	25	5	714	13.3
	test	10	285	145	62	13	4	500	13.0
	train	15	997	460	8	64	0	1,544	11.1
es	dev	4	250	115	2	17	0	388	11.3
	test	2	229	53	1	14	0	299	11.5
	train	48	1,192	512	171	36	8	1,877	10.0
fr	dev	13	300	129	43	8	3	473	10.3
	test	8	255	104	40	11	2	400	12.1
	train	85	775	484	0	94	43	1,419	13.3
jp	dev	22	193	120	0	25	11	357	12.7
	test	14	170	94	0	26	9	300	12.6

Table 1: Number of posts per class and average post length in the training (folds 1-4), development (fold 5) and held-out test sets of the dataset

or intensity of positivity, negativity, or neutrality of customer text (Balahur et al., 2014).

More recently, several customer feedback labeling schemas have been published, including Bentley and Batra (2016) who make the distinction between Customer Service data and Customer Feedback such as product reviews and in-app comments. The authors classify text according to product-specific labels defined by domain experts. Potharaju et al. (2013) built a system to identify three distinct labels in network trouble tickets including problem symptoms, troubleshooting activities and resolution actions. Arora et al. (2009) classify product reviews as qualified claims or bald claims depending on how quantifiable a customer claim is. Other labeling schema do of course exist, though they are kept private as part of private products that help users analyze and synthesize customer complaints and comments.

3 Data

In an effort to close the gap in a unified labeling schema for customer feedback, this shared task on Customer Feedback Analysis aims to organize customer feedback according to a more universally applicable label set. This label set includes: "bug", "comment", "complaint", "meaningless", "request" or "undetermined". This label set is multi-label where each customer utterance can belong to one or more of these classes. For example, "*We didn't eat there again and thankful it was only 1 night.*" is both a "comment" and a "complaint" while "*Transactions made on weekend are updated on Tuesday Please improve.*" is a "request" and a "complaint". The corpus that was created for this shared task consists of data for four languages: English (en), Spanish (es), French (fr), and Japanese (jp).

For each language, we first combine the training and development sets together. We then perform stratified sampling based on the label to split the combined dataset into five folds. Each fold contains roughly 20% of the utterances and all folds have similar label distribution. We then pick one fold as a development set and use all the other four folds for training. Table 1 shows the complete statistics of the dataset. For all languages, the utterances are quite short–~10 to 13 words–which makes the task more challenging. Another challenge is the skewed distribution of the class labels: some labels are much more common than others, with "comment" and "complaint" being the most common classes and only a few utterances per language–if any–belonging to the "meaningless" and "undetermined" classes. Indeed, the "undetermined" label does not exist in the Spanish data and the "meaningless" class is not found in the Japanese data. The shared task systems' performance were evaluated according to Accuracy, Micro and Macro-Average $F_{\beta=1}$ score. In this paper, we do not report on the accuracy because the dataset is highly unbalanced and $F_{\beta=1}$ score is thus a better indicator of

Language	Without Translations	With Translations	Percentage Increase
en	3,565	9,623	170%
es	1,932	9,623	390%
fr	2,350	9,623	309%
jp	1,776	9,623	442%

Table 2: Number of utterances in the training data before and after including the translations from all other three languages

performance. For the development set, we tune our systems using the unweighted average $F_{\beta=1}$ score of all six class labels. However, on the test set we also report Micro and Macro averages.

4 Approach

We train classifiers using three different learning methods: Random Forest, Logistic Regression, and Long Short-Term Memory Recurrent Neural Network (LSTM). In this section, we describe our data preprocessing (including machine translation of the sub-corpora), our use of word embedddings, and each of the learning methods used to train our classifiers.

4.1 Preprocessing

We tokenize and stem the English and Spanish data using Stanford Core NLP toolkit (Manning et al., 2014) . For French, we use an in-house tool for both tokenization and stemming while for Japanese, we use MeCab (Kudo, 2005) to tokenize the data.

4.2 Translation

We translate the data in each language pairwise to the other three languages to increase the size of the training data. Our assumption here was that the increased amount of data would more than make up for the introduction of noise that comes from using machine translation. We use the Neural Machine Translation (NMT) model in Google Cloud Translation API [1] to perform the translations.

Table 2 shows the number of labeled sentences that were provided in each language, and the number of labeled sentences after translation.

[1] https://cloud.google.com/translate/docs

4.3 Word Embeddings

Word-embeddings convert the high-dimensional n-grams space to a low-dimensional continuous vector space by calculating the distributional similarity of words. Accordingly, words that tend to occur in similar contexts will be close to each other in the resulting vector space. Word-embeddings have been shown to help with a variety of NLP tasks (Socher et al., 2011; Turian et al., 2010; Collobert et al., 2011; Baroni et al., 2014). For each language, we use Facebook's FastText embeddings (Bojanowski et al., 2016) that were trained on that language's Wikipedia articles to generate a vector of 300 dimensions for each word in a given tokenized utterance. As opposed to Word2Vec (Mikolov et al., 2013) which assigns a vector to each word, FastText represents each word as a bag of character n-grams and maps each character n-gram to a vector. Accordingly, it is able to model the morphology of words.

4.4 Learning Methods

We train classifiers using three learning methods: Random Forest, Logistic Regression, and LSTM. In this section, we provide a brief overview of each learning method.

4.4.1 Random Forest

Random Forest (Breiman, 2001) is an ensemble learning method. It averages over a large collection of de-correlated decision trees. Thus, it can model interaction effects among features while avoiding over-fitting the data. Random forests build decision trees on bootstrapped samples. In each split of the tree, the Random Forest randomly selects a proportion of predictors as the candidates. This approach makes the decision trees generated by Random Forest de-correlated. When averaging over these de-correlated trees, we get a stable predictor with low variance. Compared with boosting, Random Forest is easier to train and tune

(Friedman et al., 2001).

4.4.2 Logistic Regression

For our Logistic Regression classifier we use the implementation included in the Scikit-Learn toolkit (Pedregosa et al., 2011) [2]. Logistic Regression is a regression model for classification problems where a logistic function is used to model the probabilities of all possible class labels of a data instance. We use L2 regularization and set the inverse of regularization strength (C) to 100.

4.4.3 LSTM

We also experiment with an LSTM classifier. A sentence is a sequence of words, and LSTM is a now common approach for sequence classification. It encodes an entire sentence into a feature vector which is used to classify the sentence instead of using bigrams/trigrams occurring in the sentence. LSTMs use the embeddings of the words, hence encode the semantic similarity between words that occur in similar contexts. Using embeddings also helps in reducing the sparsity problem that we encounter with bigrams/trigrams models.

For this classifier, we map each input sentence to a sequence of maximum length 30, and pad the sequence with zeros if the length is less than 30. We initialize the embedding using the pre-trained embeddings presented earlier in Section 4.3. Our final LSTM architecture has 80 nodes–except for French, where each LSTM has 100 nodes–and 0.1 dropout on both the input and hidden layer weights. Using the same hyper parameters for the French model resulted in a poor performance, so the number of nodes in the LSTM was increased to 100. The last layer is a fully-connected layer with six output nodes corresponding to the six output classes. We used RMSProp optimizer to train the model. For prediction, we create a one-hot-encoding for the output labels. For each multi-label utterance, we create two samples, one for each label. We use a sigmoid function at the final layer instead of softmax, in order to be able to threshold each output node individually to decide whether the input sentence belongs to that class or not.

---

²`http://scikit-learn.org/`
`stable/modules/linear_model.html#`
`logistic-regression`

class	en	es	fr	jp
bug	31.2	14.3	31.9	56.0
comment	77.8	87.6	81.7	76.9
complaint	62.4	72.3	62.3	60.7
meaningless	36.5	4.5	45.5	0.0
request	20.2	33.9	22.4	38.4
undetermined	2.6	0.0	0.0	20.9
Avg	38.5	35.4	40.6	42.2

Table 3: Development Set Performance of Random Forest measured in $F_{\beta=1}$ score

class	en	es	fr	jp
bug	31.2	40.0	21.1	45.0
comment	79.7	88.6	81.8	81.4
complaint	60.4	61.4	58.2	57.7
meaningless	41.9	0.0	37.3	0.0
request	30.3	53.3	32.0	50.9
undetermined	0.0	0.0	0.0	20.0
Avg	40.6	40.6	38.4	42.5
Micro Avg	64.5	78.0	67.2	65.9
Macro Avg	42.5	50.0	39.7	52.3

Table 4: Held-Out Test Set Performance of Random Forest measured in $F_{\beta=1}$ score

Since the labels' distribution in the training data is skewed, we weight the classes inversely by the number of utterances of the class in the training data. The weights assigned to the classes are as follows: "bug": 20.0, "complaint": 2.0, "comment": 1.0, "meaningless": 10.0, "request": 20.0, "undetermined": 50.0

We train a separate LSTM for each language. The vocabulary size for all four LSTMs is 7,000. All models are trained for 10 epochs with a learning rate of 0.001 and optimized using a categorical cross-entropy loss function.

5 Results & Discussion

For each classifier, we vary the experimental setups and feature sets.

	en	es	fr	jp
Ngram	37.5	34.8	33.8	**43.4**
Ngram-Stem	39.2	33.6	31.8	-
Ngram+Stem	36.2	36.6	36.0	-
EMB	32.0	29.1	36.3	30.5
Ngram+EMB	40.7	38.6	**39.2**	40.1
Ngram-Stem+EMB	40.2	**41.9**	34.3	-
Ngram+Stem+EMB	**41.6**	39.2	36.2	-

Table 5: Development Set Performance of different setups of Logistic Regression measured in $F_{\beta=1}$ score

	en	es	fr	jp
bug	40.0	22.3	21.1	57.9
comment	78.7	90.6	82.3	83.6
complaint	59.1	71.6	68.7	68.0
meaningless	38.5	16.7	43.8	0.0
request	33.3	50.0	15.4	41.9
undetermined	0.0	0.0	4.3	8.9
Avg	41.6	41.9	39.2	43.8

Table 6: Per-class Development Set Performance of Logistic Regression measured in $F_{\beta=1}$ score

	en	es	fr	jp
bug	55.6	57.1	46.2	62.1
comment	76.8	91.7	82.1	78.3
complaint	59.1	57.7	59.8	63.2
meaningless	32.6	0.0	32.8	0.0
request	50.0	35.3	23.5	46.2
undetermined	2.8	0.0	0.0	6.8
Avg	46.1	40.3	40.8	42.7
Micro Avg	62.1	80.8	32.6	64.7
Macro Avg	48.8	56.0	41.3	53.7

Table 7: Held-Out Test Set Performance of Logistic Regression measured in $F_{\beta=1}$ score

5.1 Random Forest

We use standard n-gram features (1 to 3) and pre-trained FastText word-embeddings to train a binary Random Forest classifier for each of the different classes. For word embeddings, we calculate the average of embeddings of all words in a given training/test instance and use the resulting scores as features. In this experiment, we do not augment each language's training data with the translations and only rely on each language's training data. Here we choose separate cutoff point for each class. The cutoff point for a class is defined in such a way that if the predicted probability is larger than the cutoff point, then the corresponding label is added to the prediction for the sentence. The cutoff point for a class is chosen by maximizing the average $F_{\beta=1}$ score of the corresponding class over the five pairs of training and development datasets. The performance of Random Forest on the development and test sets is given in Tables 3 and 4.

5.2 Logistic Regression

For this model, we experiment with the following feature sets for each language:

- N-grams: For this feature-set, we use the TFIDF score of n-grams (1 to 3) that appear in more than five training instances. For Japanese data, we use the MeCab-tokenized text while for the other three languages we use the white-space tokenzied text.

- Stemmed N-grams: In addition to tradional n-grams, we use the stemmed English, French and Spanish data to extract stemmed n-grams.

- Word Embeddings: Similar to the Random Forest experiment, we use the average of embeddings of all words in a given training/test instance as features in our classifier.

For all languages we combine the original data

for each language with the translations of the other three languages data into this language. As noted earlier, our assumption is that the increase in the size of each dataset would lead to improved performance despite the noisey nature of machine translation. This assumption was born out in that adding translated data resulted in 8.82% average $F_{\beta=1}$ improvement on the English development dataset.

Table 5 shows the average $F_{\beta=1}$ score for the different experimental setups. Table 6 shows the $F_{\beta=1}$ for each of the six classes for the best development setup for each language.

For English, Spanish and French, combining n-grams with word-embeddings yields best results. The only difference between each of the three languages is whether the best setup involves using basic n-grams, stemmed n-grams or both. For Japanese, adding word-embeddings degrades the performance. This could be due to a discrepancy in our tokenization scheme and the tokenization scheme used to train the embeddings' model. The best performance is achieved on "comment" class since it is the most dominant class in the training data and the worst performance is on "undetermined" class since the percentage of training instances that have that class is almost negligible.

Table 7 shows the results using the best development setup on the held-out test set. Similar to the development set, the performance of each class directly correlates with how well it is represented in the training data.

5.3 LSTM

For all languages and all classes a threshold of 0.7 is used. The threshold was chosen to maximize the average $F_{\beta=1}$ score on the development set. If the sigmoid value of the output node is more than the threshold, the corresponding output label is added to the input sentence. If none of the output nodes crosses the threshold, the input sentence is labeled as "comment" which is the majority class in all languages.

Table 8 shows the $F_{\beta=1}$ score of the model on the development set. The model performs significantly better on the Japanese data. Across all

	en	es	fr	jp
bug	38.8	30.7	36.3	58.8
comment	78.7	92.1	83.0	82.5
complaint	61.1	73.8	67.4	68.3
meaningless	44.2	5.8	41.2	0.0
request	36.3	41.1	14.2	43.3
undetermined	0.0	0.0	0.0	24.3
Avg	43.2	40.6	40.3	46.2

Table 8: Development Set performance of LSTM model measured in $F_{\beta=1}$ score

	en	es	fr	jp
bug	45.1	21.0	28.5	48.0
comment	78.7	92.6	67.2	80.0
complaint	45.0	66.0	84.8	60.4
meaningless	45.7	0.0	49.1	0.0
request	27.1	52.0	34.7	44.7
undetermined	0.0	0.0	6.8	20.0
Avg	40.3	38.6	45.2	42.1
Micro Avg	60.8	78.2	69.7	64.1
Macro Avg	45.1	52.0	48.7	53.8

Table 9: Test Set performance of LSTM model measured in $F_{\beta=1}$ score

languages, and similar to the previous two models, the model performs best on the most dominant classes—"complaint" and "comment". Also, the performance of the model on "meaningless" and "undetermined" classes is significantly worse because there is not enough training examples for the model to be able to distinguish these classes. Table 9 shows the performance of the model on the held-out test data. Similar to the development set, the model performs best on Japanese.

5.4 Ranking

The performance of our classifiers varied a fair amount with respect to the different metrics. The metrics used to evaluate the systems were announced after the submission of the systems hence the system was tuned using a different one; unweighted average $F_{\beta=1}$ score. Macro average $F_{\beta=1}$ score is the closest metric to the one we used for tuning hence we report our ranking using Macro average $F_{\beta=1}$ score. LSTM performed best on French and Japanese and ranked 1/8 and 2/7 on each of them while Logistic Regression performed best on English where it ranked 3/12 and Spanish ranking 3/7.

6   Conclusion

This shared task was created with the intent of establishing a labeling schema that is both widely applicable and publicly available. Ultimately, the performance of our classifiers varied a fair amount with respect to the different metrics. Overall, using Macro-Average $F_{\beta=1}$, we ranked 3/12, 3/7, 1/8 and 2/7 on English, Spanish, French and Japanese datasets respectively. The inclusion of word embeddings and machine translation offered the largest boosts to system performance. Future directions for work in this area could include expanding the amount of data, which in turn might improve the performance of deep learning methods. Included in this shared task was an unannotated dataset for each language. Though our team did not explore a semi-supervised approach, our experiments with translated data indicate this would be low-hanging fruit.

References

Shilpa Arora, Mahesh Joshi, and Carolyn P Rosé. 2009. Identifying types of claims in online customer reviews. In *Proceedings of the Annual Conference of the North American Chapter of the Association for Computational Linguistics*.

Alexandra Balahur, Rada Mihalcea, and Andrés Montoyo. 2014. Computational approaches to subjectivity and sentiment analysis: Present and envisaged methods and applications. *Computer Speech & Language*, 1(28):1–6.

Marco Baroni, Georgiana Dinu, and Germán Kruszewski. 2014. Don't count, predict! a systematic comparison of context-counting vs. context-predicting semantic vectors. In *Proceedings of the 52nd Annual Meeting of the Association for Computational Linguistics*.

Michael Bentley and Soumya Batra. 2016. Giving voice to office customers: Best practices in how office handles verbatim text feedback. In *2016 IEEE International Conference on Big Data*, pages 3826–3832. IEEE.

Piotr Bojanowski, Edouard Grave, Armand Joulin, and Tomas Mikolov. 2016. Enriching word vectors with subword information. *arXiv preprint arXiv:1607.04606*.

Leo Breiman. 2001. Random forests. *Machine Learning*, 45(1):5–32.

Ronan Collobert, Jason Weston, Léon Bottou, Michael Karlen, Koray Kavukcuoglu, and Pavel Kuksa. 2011. Natural language processing (almost) from scratch. *Journal of Machine Learning Research*, 12(Aug):2493–2537.

Jerome Friedman, Trevor Hastie, and Robert Tibshirani. 2001. *The Elements of Statistical Learning*, volume 1. Springer series in statistics New York.

Michael Gamon. 2004. Sentiment classification on customer feedback data: noisy data, large feature vectors, and the role of linguistic analysis. In *Proceedings of the 20th International Conference on Computational Linguistics*.

Narendra Gupta, Mazin Gilbert, and Giuseppe Di Fabbrizio. 2010. Emotion detection in email customer care. In *Proceedings of the NAACL HLT 2010 Workshop on Computational Approaches to Analysis and Generation of Emotion in Text*.

Svetlana Kiritchenko, Xiaodan Zhu, Colin Cherry, and Saif Mohammad. 2014. Nrc-canada-2014: Detecting aspects and sentiment in customer reviews. In *Proceedings of the 8th International Workshop on Semantic Evaluation (SemEval)*.

Taku Kudo. 2005. Mecab: Yet another part-of-speech and morphological analyzer.

Christopher D Manning, Mihai Surdeanu, John Bauer, Jenny Rose Finkel, Steven Bethard, and David McClosky. 2014. The stanford corenlp natural language processing toolkit. In *ACL (System Demonstrations)*.

Tomas Mikolov, Ilya Sutskever, Kai Chen, Greg S Corrado, and Jeff Dean. 2013. Distributed representations of words and phrases and their compositionality. In *Advances in neural information processing systems*.

Fabian Pedregosa, Gaël Varoquaux, Alexandre Gramfort, Vincent Michel, Bertrand Thirion, Olivier Grisel, Mathieu Blondel, Peter Prettenhofer, Ron Weiss, Vincent Dubourg, et al. 2011. Scikit-learn: Machine learning in python. *Journal of Machine Learning Research*, 12(Oct):2825–2830.

Rahul Potharaju, Navendu Jain, and Cristina Nita-Rotaru. 2013. Juggling the jigsaw: Towards automated problem inference from network trouble tickets. In *Proceedings of the 10th USENIX Symposium on Network Systems Design and Implementation (NSDI'13)*, pages 127–141.

Richard Socher, Jeffrey Pennington, Eric H Huang, Andrew Y Ng, and Christopher D Manning. 2011. Semi-supervised recursive autoencoders for predicting sentiment distributions. In *Proceedings of the 2011 Conference on Empirical Methods in Natural Language Processing*.

Joseph Turian, Lev Ratinov, and Yoshua Bengio. 2010. Word representations: A simple and general method for semi-supervised learning. In *Proceedings of the 48th Annual Meeting of the Association for Computational Linguistics*.

ADAPT Centre Cone Team at IJCNLP-2017 Task 5:
A Similarity-Based Logistic Regression Approach to Multi-choice Question Answering in an Examinations Shared Task

Daria Dzendzik
ADAPT Centre
School of Computing
Dublin City University
Dublin, Ireland
daria.dzendzik@adaptcentre.ie

Alberto Poncelas
ADAPT Centre
School of Computing
Dublin City University
Dublin, Ireland
alberto.poncelas@adaptcentre.ie

Carl Vogel
School of Computer Science and Statistics
Trinity College Dublin the University of Dublin
Dublin, Ireland
vogel@tcd.ie

Qun Liu
ADAPT Centre
School of Computing
Dublin City University
Dublin, Ireland
qun.liu@adaptcentre.ie

Abstract

We describe the work of a team from the ADAPT Centre in Ireland in addressing automatic answer selection for the Multi-choice Question Answering in Examinations shared task. The system is based on a logistic regression over the string similarities between question, answer, and additional text. We obtain the highest grade out of six systems: 48.7% accuracy on a validation set (vs. a baseline of 29.45%) and 45.6% on a test set.

1 Introduction

This paper describes the participation of the ADAPT Centre team in the Multi-choice Question Answering in Examinations Shared Task 2017.[1] This is a typical question answering task that aims to test how accurately the answers of the questions in exams could be selected. Any additional sources, such as knowledge base, textbooks or articles, can be used to exploit support information. The English subset contains 5,367 questions from five domains: Biology, Chemistry, Earth Science, Life Science and Physical Science. The questions come from real exams. Every question has four answer candidates which may be a word, a value, a phrase or a sentence. This challenge is an important step towards a rational, quantitative assessment of natural language understanding capabilities.

Our approach is to extract relevant information from Wikipedia[2] and to apply logistic regression over string similarities. We used an adaptation of methods developed for a comparable task in relation to question answering about films (Dzendzik et al., 2017). The features we employ are similarities of a term frequency–inverse document frequency ($\mathtt{TF\text{-}IDF}$) metric, character n-grams (with n ranging from 2 to 5), bag of words, and windows slide (a ratio between answer and substrings of extracted data) – the window slide ratio is described in further detail below (section 2.3). We train our model in two ways: combining training over all domains and separate model training for each domain. The second way yields a better result on the validation set: 48.7% of accuracy vs. 43.6%. Finally, we obtained 45.6% accuracy on the test set, and this is the best result for the English dataset of the six competing systems.

The paper is organized as follows: We detail our approach in Section 2. In Section 3, we describe experiments and results on the training, validation and test data. In Section 4, we compare our approach to previous research in answering examination questions. Finally, Section 5 contains conclusions and directions of future work.

2 Approach

We constructed our model as a four-step pipeline:

1. Preprocessing – cleaning of the input data.

2. Data selection – based on key words from the question we extract relative sentences from

---

[1]See http://www.nlpr.ia.ac.cn/cip/ijcnlp/Multi-choice_Question_Answering_in_Exams.html – October 2017.

[2]wikipedia.org– September 2017

Proceedings of the 8th International Joint Conference on Natural Language Processing, Shared Tasks, pages 67–72,
Taipei, Taiwan, November 27 – December 1, 2017. ©2017 AFNLP

Wikipedia.

3. Feature Vector Concatenation – for every question, a feature vector is built as a concatenation of vectors of similarities between the answer candidates and sentences obtained in the previous step.

4. Logistic Regression – a logistic regression over the feature vector.

Later in this section, we describe our approach to multi-choice question answering in detail.

2.1 Preprocessing

The first step is to clean the question and answers statements. Using regular expressions, the existing serial numbers and letters of the question and answer candidates are deleted. See the examples (1)-(3).

(1) *"3. What ..."* → *"What ... "*

(2) *"8) Who ..."* → *"Who ... "*

(3) *"a) Paper: Paper degrades ... "* → *"Paper: Paper degrades ..."*

2.2 Data Selection

A list of keywords are extracted from the question statement using Natural Language Toolkit (nltk)[3] implementation of the Rapid Automatic Keyword Extraction (RAKE) algorithm (Rose et al., 2010). These words are used to retrieve a list of sentences from an information source. For each question, we select the top-50 sentences as ranked by containing (unweighted) keywords related to the item

The information source used in this system is a set of sentences from articles of Wikipedia. Each sentence is stored as a document in an inverted index data structure using Lucene.[4]

2.3 Feature Vector Creation

The data is organized in triplets (q, a, S) where a is a candidate answer, q is the question that a belongs to, and S is the set of sentences retrieved from Wikipedia by querying the keywords of the question q.

Then, for every triplet a feature vector is created by concatenating different features. Each feature is a function of two arguments and encodes

---

[3]https://github.com/csurfer/rake-nltk – September 2017

[4]https://lucene.apache.org/core/ – September 2017

the similarity between two strings. The first argument is either the answer a or a concatenation of the question and the answer $q + a$ and the second argument is S. The value of every feature is between 0 and 1: the higher the value, the more similar the strings are.

The five similarities are based on the work of (Dzendzik et al., 2017), and are described below.

- **TF-IDF cosine similarity** - the cosine similarity between `TF-IDF` representations as defined in Equation (4).

$$cos\_tfidf(a, S) = \frac{w_a \cdot w_S}{|w_a||w_S|} \quad (4)$$

where w_a and w_S are `TF-IDF` vector representations of the answer (or question + answer) and the sentences correspondingly.

- **Bag of words ratio similarity** - a bag of words measure shows the ratio of sentences words which exist in the answer (or question + answer) as shown in Equation (5).

$$bow(a, S) = \frac{|W_a \cap W_S|}{|W_a|} \quad (5)$$

where W_a - bag of words from the answer (or the question + the answer) and W_S bag of words from sentences.

- **Window slide ratio similarity** - returns the highest ratio of sequence match between answer (or question + answer) and all sentences substrings. The window of the substrings has a size equal to a length of the answer. See the Equation (6).

$$wSlide(a, S) = max_i(\frac{2 * M_i}{T_i}) \quad (6)$$

where $T_i = |a| + |s_i|$ is the total number of character elements in both sequences: the answer a and s_i. s_i is i–substring of S, $\forall i s_i \in S, |s_i| = |a|$ and M_i is the number of matches between all substrings of a and s_i.

- **Character N-gram** - similar to `Window Slide` but on character level. The size of the window is limited by parameter n (We consider n = 2,3,4,5 characters). As a result, we get the ratio of n-grams overlap including white spaces in the answer (or the question + the answer) and the sentences.

- **Word2vec cosine similarity** The cosine distance similarity (as in Equation (7)) between skip-gram representations (Mikolov et al., 2013).

$$w2v\_cos(a, S) = \frac{v_a \cdot v_S}{|v_a||v_S|} \quad (7)$$

where v_a and v_S are $\texttt{Word2vec}$ representations of the answer (or the question + the answer) and the sentences correspondingly.

We use a pre-trained word2vec model based on small subset of Wikipedia (Tapaswi et al., 2016).

Using this metrics 17 different features are built:

1. $f_1 = w2v\_cos(q, S) + w2v\_cos(a, S)$
2. $f_2 = w2v\_cos(a, S)$
3. $f_3 = cos\_tfidf(a, S)$
4. $f_4 = bow\_overlap(a, S)$
5. $f_5 = windowSlide(a, S)$
6. $f_6 = charNgramm_2(a, S)$
7. $f_7 = charNgramm_3(a, S)$
8. $f_8 = charNgramm_4(a, S)$
9. $f_9 = charNgramm_5(a, S)$
10. $f_{10} = w2v\_cos(q + a, S)$
11. $f_{11} = cos\_tfidf(q + a, S)$
12. $f_{12} = bow\_overlap(q + a, S)$
13. $f_{13} = windowSlide(q + a, S)$
14. $f_{14} = charNgramm_2(q + a, S)$
15. $f_{15} = charNgramm_3(q + a, S)$
16. $f_{16} = charNgramm_4(q + a, S)$
17. $f_{17} = charNgramm_5(q + a, S)$

Here $q+a$ is the concatenation of q and a. Some questions from the dataset are presented as sentences with one or many gaps. If the question q includes gaps, instead of concatenating, the candidate answer a will be used to fill the gaps in the question. See the example (8).

(8) Question: *"_____ obtain energy by using the chemical energy stored in inorganic compounds"*

Answer candidates:

1. *Photoautotrophs*
2. *Chemoautotrophs*
3. *Heterotrophs*
4. *None of the above*

Concatenation strings:

1. *Photoautotrophs obtain energy by using the chemical energy stored in inorganic compounds*
2. *Chemoautotrophs obtain energy by using the chemical energy stored in inorganic compounds*
3. *Heterotrophs obtain energy by using the chemical energy stored in inorganic compounds*
4. *None of the above obtain energy by using the chemical energy stored in inorganic compounds*

For a question q the similarity features of its answer candidates a_1, a_2, a_3, a_4 are concatenated into one single vector as shown in Figure 1.

Following this method, for each question, there is one feature vector which contains information for all answer candidates inside.

2.4 Logistic Regression

The final step of our system is logistic regression over the vector. It returns the eventual answer. We use a scikit-learn[5] implementation with liblinear core and one-versus-rest schemes.

3 Experiments

In this section, we describe the data and results of our experiments.

3.1 Data

The dataset provides examination questions in two languages: English and Chinese. We focus our research on English subset of data which contains 5,367 questions from five domains: Biology, Chemistry, Earth Science, Life Science and Physical Science. Table 1 presents the division of the dataset into training, validation and test sets.

As mentioned before, we use Wikipedia dump as source of additional data.

---

[5]`http://scikit-learn.org/stable/`
`modules/generated/sklearn.linear_model.`
`LogisticRegression.html` – September 2017

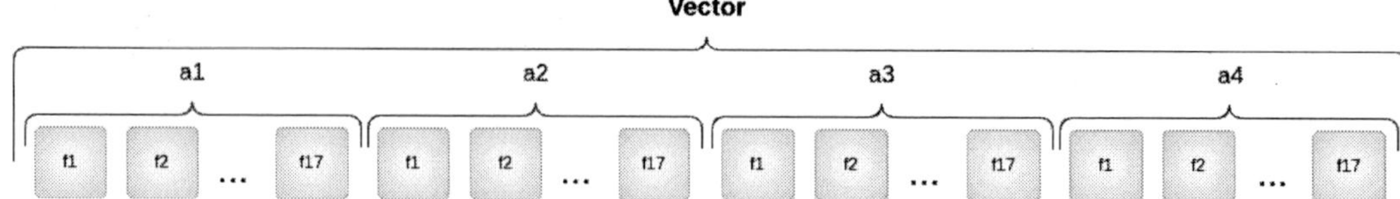

Figure 1: Feature vector concatenation.

Domain	Train	Val	Test	Total
Biology	281	70	210	561
Chemistry	775	193	581	1549
Physical	299	74	224	597
Earth Science	830	207	622	1659
Life Science	501	125	375	1001
Total	2686	669	2012	5367

Table 1: The number of questions for each domain and a division for training, validation and test sets.

3.2 Results

The systems built are the following:

- **Combined training:** Data from all domains is combined together to train one single model.

- **Domain training:** Use separate models trained in each domain. The parameters of the logistic regressions are the same for every domain.

The results obtained by these systems and the baseline[6] are presented in tables 2 and 3.

Using the Combined training approach we obtained 44.82% accuracy on the training data and 43.6% on the validation set (table 2 line 2). This result significantly outperforms the baseline (table 2 line 1). Using the Domain training approach we observe that the average score is better (51.71%) than Combined training. In addition, this approach enables evaluation of the method in each domain. The best performance is obtained in the Chemical subset – 69.55% accuracy. However, for Earth Science and for Life Science we obtained 41.08% and 42.91%, respectively. Unfortunately, we can obtain the results of separate domains only for the trainin set; we cannot compare it with the published baseline on the validation set. Finally, by concatenating the results from separate domains

---

[6]The baseline is provided by the shared task organizers–see footnote 1.

we obtain 48.7% accuracy on the validation set and 45.6% on the test set.

System	Train	Valid	Test
Baseline	–	29.45	–
Combined training	44.82	43.6	–
Domain training	**51.71**	**48.7**	**45.6**

Table 2: Results of all English subset of the baseline system on the validation set and our system for combined and domain training on the training, validation and test sets.

	Bio	Chem	Phys	Earth	Life
			Baseline		
Valid	30	21.24	25.68	31.88	40
			Domain training		
Train	49.47	69.55	51.84	41.08	42.91

Table 3: Results of the baseline system on the validation set and results of domain training on the train set for each domain.

4 Related Work

As mentioned before, this system is based on the work of (Dzendzik et al., 2017). The main difference is the data selection module: in the earlier work we select sentences from movie plot using similarities; here we extract relevant sentences from Wikipedia. Another difference is that we do not build semantic features in this shared task.

The core of our method is text similarity. We consider only five types of similarities. Gomaa and Fahmy (2013) consider more than 25 text similarity metrics in five categories: character-based similarity, term-based similarity, corpus-based similarity, knowledge-based similarity, and hybrid similarity measures. They also mention cosine similarity (for the mathematical function that determines the metric), Tf-IDf (which we deem to be a hybrid of term-based and corpus-based) and `N-grams` similarities (which may be character-based or term based), all of which we use, too.

There is interest in answering examination questions automatically. Wang et al. (2014) describe CMUs UIMA-based[7] modular automatic question answering system to automatically answer multiple-choice questions for the entrance exam in world history in English. The approach relies on two different test collection: the original test collection provided by NTCIR (NII Testbeds and Community for Information access Research)[8] organizers and the collection created by the authors.

Li et al. (2013) described the system that was used in the Entrance Exams task of Question Answering for Machine Reading Evaluation on Conference and Labs of the Evaluation Forum 2013 (QA4MRE CLEF) (Sutcliffe et al., 2013). It consists of three components, Character Resolver, Sentence Extractor and Recognizing Textual Entailment. In the system, the documents are processed by the Character Resolver in order to tag each story with a character as ID. The Sentence Extractor then extracts related sentences for each question and creates a Hypothesis (H) and Text (T). Finally it inputs this T/H pair into the Recognizing Textual Entailment system to select an answer.

5 Conclusions and Future Work

In this paper, we described the work of ADAPT Centre for the multi-choice question answering in examination shared task. In this work we have used a sentence retrieval approach with combination of logistic regression over string similarities. Our submission shows an improvement over the baseline system. According to the shared task leader board, six teams submitted their results for English subset. Our submission shows the best result on validation and test dataset and significantly outperform the baseline system.

At the same time, we believe that our system can be improved in the future: a) Using more in-domain data, for this system a set of Wikipedia articles has been used as the information source, the accuracy may be improved by using technical books or manuals; b) exploring different methods for selecting sentences from the information source (such as considering the keywords from the candidate answers); or c) Extracting a different set of keywords (for example, maximizing semantic distance among keywords selected).

Acknowledgments

This research is supported by the Science Foundation Ireland (Grant 12/CE/I2267) as part of ADAPT centre (www.adaptcentre.ie) at Dublin City University. The ADAPT Centre for Digital Content Technology is funded under the SFI Research Centres Programme (Grant 13/RC/2106) and is cofunded under the European Regional Development Fund.

References

Daria Dzendzik, Carl Vogel, and Qun Liu. 2017. Who framed roger rabbit? answering questions about movie plot. The Joint Video and Language Understanding Workshop: MovieQA and The Large Scale Movie Description Challenge (LSMDC), at ICCV 2017, 23th of October, Venice, Italy.

Wael H. Gomaa and Aly A. Fahmy. 2013. Article: A survey of text similarity approaches. *International Journal of Computer Applications*, 68(13):13–18. Full text available.

Xinjian Li, Ran Tian, Ngan L. T. Nguyen, Yusuke Miyao, and Akiko Aizawa. 2013. Question answering system for entrance exams in QA4MRE. In *Working Notes for CLEF 2013 Conference , Valencia, Spain, September 23-26, 2013*.

Tomas Mikolov, Kai Chen, Greg Corrado, and Jeffrey Dean. 2013. Efficient estimation of word representations in vector space. *CoRR*, abs/1301.3781.

Stuart Rose, Dave Engel, Nick Cramer, and Wendy Cowley. 2010. Automatic keyword extraction from individual documents.

Richard FE Sutcliffe, Anselmo Peñas, Eduard H Hovy, Pamela Forner, Álvaro Rodrigo, Corina Forascu, Yassine Benajiba, and Petya Osenova. 2013. Overview of qa4mre main task at clef 2013. In *CLEF (Working Notes)*.

Makarand Tapaswi, Yukun Zhu, Rainer Stiefelhagen, Antonio Torralba, Raquel Urtasun, and Sanja Fidler. 2016. Movieqa: Understanding stories in movies through question-answering. In *IEEE Conference on Computer Vision and Pattern Recognition (CVPR)*.

Di Wang, Leonid Boytsov, Jun Araki, Alkesh Patel, Jeff Gee, Zhengzhong Liu, Eric Nyberg, and Teruko Mitamura. 2014. CMU multiple-choice question answering system at NTCIR-11 qa-lab. In *Proceedings of the 11th NTCIR Conference on Evaluation*

---

[7]https://uima.apache.org/ – September 2017

[8]`http://research.nii.ac.jp/ntcir/ index-en.html` – September 2017

of Information Access Technologies, NTCIR-11, National Center of Sciences, Tokyo, Japan, December 9-12, 2014.

YNU-HPCC at IJCNLP-2017 Task 1: Chinese Grammatical Error Diagnosis Using a Bi-directional LSTM-CRF Model

Quanlei Liao, Jin Wang, Jinnan Yang and **Xuejie Zhang**
School of Information Science and Engineering
Yunnan University
Kunming, P.R. China
Contact:xjzhang@ynu.edu.cn

Abstract

Building a system to detect Chinese grammatical errors is a challenge for natural-language processing researchers. As Chinese learners are increasing, developing such a system can help them study Chinese more easily. This paper introduces a bi-directional long short-term memory (BiLSTM) - conditional random field (CRF) model to produce the sequences that indicate an error type for every position of a sentence, since we regard Chinese grammatical error diagnosis (CGED) as a sequence-labeling problem. Among the participants this year of CGED shard task, our model ranked third in the detection-level and identification-level results. In the position-level, our results ranked second among the participants.

1 Introduction

With China's rapid development, more and more foreign people have begun to learn Chinese. Writing is an important part of language learning, and grammar is the basis of writing. Traditional learning methods rely on artificial work to point out grammatical errors in an article. This requires more time and labor costs. Thus, it is quite practical to develop a system that can automatically correct the grammatical errors in an article. This is the aim of the CGED shared task.

In the shared task, Chinese-grammar errors are divided into four types: redundant words, word-selection errors, missing words, and incorrect word order (Lee et al., 2016). They are represented as uppercase letters "R", "S", "M", and "W", respectively. For each sentence, the task should first determine whether the sentence is correct. If the sentence is incorrect, it should indicate the specific error types and their locations.

In this paper, the CGED task is treated as a sequence labeling problem, which is a classic natural language processing problem. The traditional solutions are a series of statistical learning methods, including the hidden Markov model (HMM), the maximum-entropy Markov model (MEMM), and the conditional random field.

The HMM model makes two assumptions. First, that the current implicit state is only related to the last implied state; second, that the current output state is only related to the current implied state (Dugad and Desai, 1996). However, the reality is not so simple. A CRF uses the entire output sequence and two adjacent implicit states to find a conditional probability (Lafferty et al., 2001). It can fit more complex situations. Practice has proven that the CRF works better than other models.

Recently, artificial neural networks have been used to do natural language processing tasks. For the sequence labeling problem, because of its equal length output, a recurrent neural network (RNN) is an appropriate model. It is more capable of understanding the information context; however, this is not a good method for learning state transfer laws. To improve the problems of exploding and vanishing gradients, new RNN units, e.g., long short-term memory (LSTM) and gated recurrent units (GRUs) (Chung et al., 2014), have been proposed.

In this study, we propose a BiLSTM-CRF model. Our model combines statistical learning with neural networks. The BiLSTM is used to obtain information about long or short distances in two directions (Huang et al., 2015). It then feeds the information to the CRF. Thus, the CRF can better use conditional probabilities to fit the data without handmade features. The CRF and LSTM models

Proceedings of the 8th International Joint Conference on Natural Language Processing, Shared Tasks, pages 73–77,
Taipei, Taiwan, November 27 – December 1, 2017. ©2017 AFNLP

are also used as part of the experiment to compare the models' performance.

The rest of this paper is organized as follows. Section 2 describes our model in detail. Section 3 presents our experiment, including the data pre-processing and results. Conclusions are drawn in Section 4.

2 Proposed Model

The proposed model consists of three major parts: the word-embedding layer, the bi-directional LST-M layer, and the CRF layer. CRF is a traditional s-tatistical learning method for sequence labeling. It has two limits. First, it heavily depends on hand-crafted features. Second, it cannot capture long distance context information. The context infor-mation for a CGED task is very important. For example, here are two correct sentences.

- "只有努力，才能过的更好。" (Only you work hard, you can be better.)

- "只要努力，就能过的更好。" (As long as you work hard, you will be able to be better.)

It is impossible to determine whether the sentence, "才能过的更好。" is correct without the previous context information. On the other hand, handcraft-ed features greatly increase the workload. Thus, our model combines an RNN with a CRF to im-prove the above problems. To capture informa-tion from two directions (Ma and Hovy, 2016), we use a bi-directional RNN instead of a unidirection-al RNN. In addition, an LSTM cell is selected to avoid vanishing and exploding gradients (Sunder-meyer et al., 2012).

We trained four models for four error types be-cause there may be two or more errors in one posi-tion. Each model is given the original text index as input, its label sequence outputs 0 for correct and 1 for error.

The model includes three layers: a word-embedding layer to transfer the word index into word embedding, a BiLSTM layer to extract the information and features for each position, and a CRF layer to decode and produce labels. The three layers are introduced in the following sections.

2.1 Embedding Layer

A diagram of the embedding layer's structure is shown in Figure 1. It shows a pre-trained word-embedding lookup table. Every line of this table

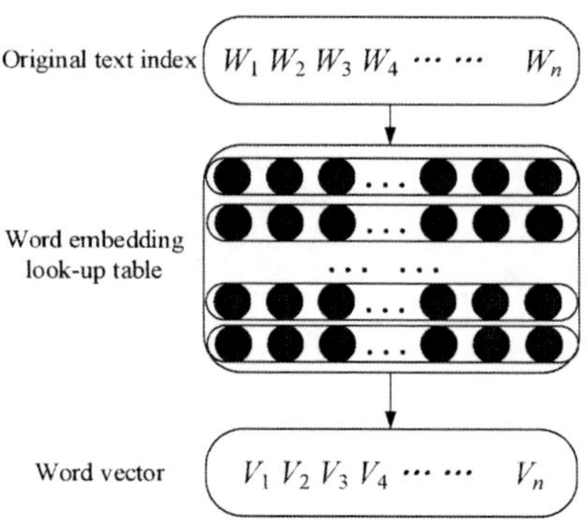

Figure 1: Embedding Layer

stands for one Chinese word. Therefore, the orig-inal text of the training data should be turned into a sequence of indexes for every word. This lay-er takes a sequence that contains the word indices, e.g., w_1, w_2,..., w_i,..., w_n where w_i, is an in-dex number indicating the position of the original word in the table. Then, the layer finds the word vector for every index and outputs them in a new sequence, e.g., v_1, v_2,..., v_i,..., v_n where v_i is a word vector.

If the dimensionality of the original text index is N and the dimensionality of the word vector is M, the dimensionality of the output sequence should be $M * N$.

2.2 Bi-directional LSTM Layer

An RNN can effectively extract features from the entire sentence because of its ability to capture context information. For the reasons mentioned above, a bi-directional LSTM network was cho-sen.

An LSTM is a special type of RNN unit that can learn long-term dependency information. It is designed to avoid the long-term dependence prob-lem. An LSTM can remove or increase the infor-mation to a cell state using a well-designed struc-ture called a "gate". The gate determines whether information should pass. The LSTM uses the following formulas (Hochreiter and Schmidhuber, 1997):

$$i_t = \sigma(W_{vi}v_t + W_{hi}h_{t-1} + b_i) \quad (1)$$

$$f_t = \sigma(W_{vf}v_t + W_{hf}h_{t-1} + b_f) \quad (2)$$

$$c_t = f_t c_{t-1} + i_t \tanh(W_{vc}v_t + W_{hc}h_{t-1} + b_c) \quad (3)$$

$$o_t = \sigma(W_{vo}v_t + W_{ho}h_{t-1} + b_o) \quad (4)$$

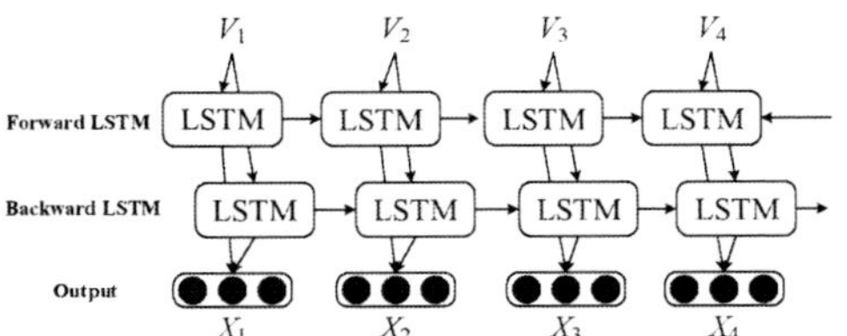

Figure 2: Bi-directional LSTM Layer

$$h_t = o_t \tanh(c_t) \qquad (5)$$

where v is the input vector from the embedding layer. σ is the sigmoid activation function. i is the input gate, f is the forget gate, and o is the output gate. Parameters $\{W_{vi}, W_{hi}, W_{vf}, W_{hf}, W_{vc}, W_{hc}, W_{vo}, W_{ho}, b_i, b_f, b_c, b_o\}$ are the weights and biases of an LSTM cell. c is the cell vector and h is the hidden cell. K represents the output dimensionality of the LSTM unit. N is the dimensionality of the word vector. The size of the last four bias vectors are K and the others are $N * K$. Figure 2 shows a bi-directional LSTM network. The embedding output is fed into two LSTM layers with forward and backward directions. Two outputs from two layers at one position are linked into a new vector as the layer's output.

The dimensionality of the input is $M * N$. M is the length of the original text. Each word vector of input is also called an RNN time step. For instance, v_1, v_2,..., v_i,..., v_n is input, each v_i is a time step. For each time step, v_i is fed into two LSTMs; the forward LSTM layer produces an output vector $o_{i-forward}$ with dimensionality K, and the backward LSTM layer produces $o_{i-backward}$. Therefore, the result of a time step is $x_i(o_{i-forward}, o_{i-backward})$ and the dimensionality is $2 * K$, which is the result of combining the two layers' output. Thus, the dimensionality of the final output is $M * (2 * K)$.

2.3 CRF Layer

Because of the importance of the relationships between neighboring tags in CGED, a CRF is selected to capture the relationship. The CRF is a type of undirected discriminative graph model. In general, a CRF is a Markov random field with an observation set. A general CRF is defined as a Markov random field with random variable Y under the condition of random variable X. Y constitutes a Markov random field represented by an undirected graph, as in the formula below (Sutton and Mccal-

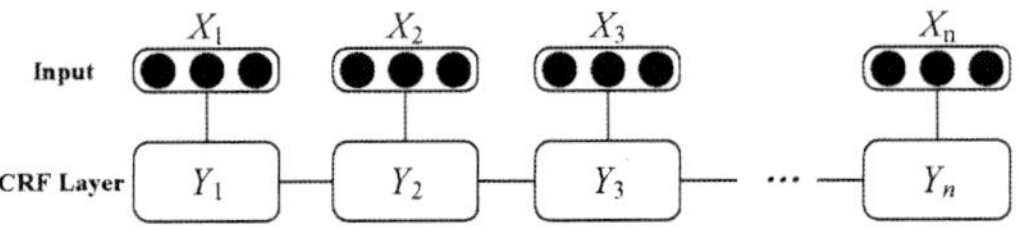

Figure 3: CRF Layer

lum, 2010):

$$P(Y_v|X, Y_w, w \neq v) = P(Y_v|X, Y_w, w \sim v) \quad (6)$$

where operator $\sim$ means that w and v have a public edge. X is the input variable or state sequence, and Y is the output variable or tag sequence. In our problem, we assume that X and Y have the same linear structure, as shown in Figure 3.

The conditional probability of random variable y with value x is given as follows:

$$P(y|x) = \frac{\prod\limits_{i=1}^{n} M_i(y_{i-1}, y_i, x)}{Z(x)} \qquad (7)$$

The denominator is a normalization item:

$$Z(x) = \sum_{y} \prod_{i=1}^{n} M_i(y_{i-1}, y_i, x) \qquad (8)$$

where $M_i(y', y'', x)$ is a potential function, x is the input vector produced by the BiLSTM layer and y is the labeling of the input sentence.

3 Experiment

This section describes the contents of the experiment, including the training data processing, choice of parameters, experimental results, etc.

3.1 Dataset

The word embedding was trained using the word2vec toolkit with the Chinese Wikipedia corpus. According to the experimental results, the word-embedding results from word2vec are better than GloVe (Yang et al., 2016). In addition to the CGED17 training data, the HSK (i.e., Chinese Proficiency Test) training data from CGED16 was used. The number of training sets is 20,048, with 10,447 from CGED17 and 9,601 from CGED16.

For the reasons mentioned above, four models for every error type were selected. Thus, we preprocessed training sets for four error type models. For each error type, the position's label is 0 if correct, or 1 if erroneous. The training-data text was transferred into the word-index sequence, according to the pre-trained word-embedding table.

Model	Acc	Pre	Rec	F1
CRF	0.1805	0.1136	0.1483	0.1287
LSTM	0.1696	0.1824	0.0816	0.1128
BiLSTM-CRF	0.3325	0.2769	0.3502	0.3093

Table 1: Comparative results of three models.

Parameter	Dataset	LSTM cell	Epoch
Run1	CGED16,17	120	22
Run2	CGED16,17	100	18
Run3	CGED16	100	18

Table 2: Parameter selection for BiLSTM-CRF models.

Results	Detection-Level			
	Acc	Pre	Rec	F1
Run1	0.5796	**0.65**	0.7163	0.6816
Run2	**0.5891**	0.6417	**0.7829**	**0.7053**
Run3	0.5311	0.6298	0.6148	0.6222

Table 3: Comparative results on detection-level.

3.2 Implementation Details

The experiment contains three models for comparison: CRF, LSTM, and BiLSTM-CRF. CRF represents the statistical learning method, which is the best simple statistical learning model in a variety of sequence labeling tasks. LSTM is a typical neural network model for sequence labeling. The above two models were used as the baseline for the experiment. The last model, proposed in this paper, combines both neural network and statistical learning models.

The CRF model was implemented using the CRF++ toolkit. CRF++ is an open-source, easy-to-use implementation of CRF, written in C++. The LSTM model and the BiLSTM-CRF model were implemented using the Keras framework with a Tensorflow backend. The CRF layer implementation in the BiLSTM-CRF model used Keras_contrib.

The training data for the three models comes from CGED16 or CGED17. Hence, the training data is regarded as a hyper-parameter. It will be CGED16 or CGED17 or a combination of both. In addition, there is a public hyper-parameter for the three models. The hyper-parameter for the CRF model is c, which controls the over-fitting of the training data. The hyper-parameters for LSTM and BiLSTM-CRF include the LSTM cell number and the training epoch.

Some empirical parameters are given as candidate values for the model. A grid search algorithm was used to find the best hyper-parameter combinations.

To evaluate the model's performance, we used four metrics such as accuracy (Acc), precision (Pre), recall (Rec) and F1-score (F1) for all three models on CGED16 HSK test data. Table 1 shows the best results for each model on position-level. The results show that the BiLSTM-CRF model has the best results in Table 1.

3.3 Experimental Results

Five teams submitted 13 results. We submitted three running results. The three results were produced by the three BiLSTM-CRF models that had the best three results on the CGED16 HSK test data. The three results have different hyper-parameters, as shown in Table 2.

The next three tables show the final test results for the three BiLSTM-CRF models. Table 3 shows the detection-level results. Table 4 shows the identification-level results. Table 5 shows the position-level results.

The false positive (FP) rates of the three results of BiLSTM-CRF models are 0.5796, 0.7383, and 0.614 shown in Table 6. The highest one is over 70%. This is because the model uses four sub-models to generate the sentence label. If only one model misjudges the label of one position, from 0 to 1, it will produce a false negative (FN) sample. Thus, the model produces a high false positive rate. In addition, the experimental results show that the recall of the first two results is better than the previous in the detection level. This model is more likely to produce positive examples.

4 Conclusion

Compared with most previous models (Lee et al., 2016), the F1-score of the position level greatly increased with the CGED16 HSK test data. It was observed that neural network and statistical-learning methods could be combined to obtain better results. Among the participants this year, our model ranked third in the detection-level and identification-level results. In the position-level,

Results	Identification-Level			
	Acc	Pre	Rec	F1
Run1	**0.4218**	**0.4219**	0.4217	**0.4218**
Run2	0.3819	0.3825	**0.4575**	0.4167
Run3	0.3979	0.4086	0.3298	0.365

Table 4: Comparative results on identification-level.

Results	Position-Level			
	Acc	**Pre**	**Rec**	**F1**
Run1	**0.1778**	**0.1262**	**0.1191**	**0.1225**
Run2	0.1426	0.1056	**0.1191**	0.112
Run3	0.1702	0.0981	0.0698	0.0816

Table 5: Comparative results on position-Level.

Result	False Positive Rate
Run1	0.5796
Run2	0.7383
Run3	0.614

Table 6: False positive rates of three results.

our results ranked second among the participants.

Our model is a combination of BiLSTM and CRF. It combines the extraction capabilities of the LSTM context information and the conditional probability of CRF's local features. More complex models contain more parameters that need to be trained. Thus, more training data can improve the model; too little training data may cause overfitting.

The shared task provided us with more in-depth understanding about CGED. Our next step is to obtain more training data to enhance the model.

Acknowledgments

This work was supported by the National Natural Science Foundation of China (NSFC) under Grant No.61702443 and No.61762091, and in part by Educational Commission of Yunnan Province of China under Grant No.2017ZZX030.The authors would like to thank the anonymous reviewers and the area chairs for their constructive comments.

References

Junyoung Chung, Caglar Gulcehre, KyungHyun Cho, and Yoshua Bengio. 2014. Empirical evaluation of gated recurrent neural networks on sequence modeling. In *arXiv preprint arXiv:1412.3555*.

Rakesh Dugad and U B Desai. 1996. A tutorial on hidden markov models. In *Proceedings of the IEEE*, pages 257–286.

Sepp Hochreiter and Jürgen Schmidhuber. 1997. Long short-term memory. *Neural Computation*, 9(8):1735–1780.

Zhiheng Huang, Wei Xu, and Kai Yu. 2015. Bidirectional lstm-crf models for sequence tagging. In *arXiv preprint arXiv:1508.01991*.

John Lafferty, Andrew Mccallum, and Fernando Pereira. 2001. Conditional random fields: Probabilistic models for segmenting and labeling sequence data. In *Proceedings of the International Conference on Machine Learning (ICML-01)*, pages 282–289.

Lung-Hao Lee, Liang-Chih Yu, and Li-Ping Chang. 2016. Overview of nlp-tea 2016 shared task for Chinese grammatical error diagnosis. In *Proceedings of the 3rd Workshop on Natural Language Processing Techniques for Educational Applications (NLP-TEA-16)*, pages 40–48.

Xuezhe Ma and Eduard Hovy. 2016. End-to-end sequence labeling via bi-directional lstm-cnns-crf. In *Proceedings of the 54th Annual Meeting of the Association for Computational Linguistics (ACL-16)*, pages 1064–1074.

Martin Sundermeyer, Ralf Schluter, and Hermann Ney. 2012. Lstm neural networks for language modeling. In *Proceedings of INTERSPEECH 2013*, pages 601–608.

Charles Sutton and Andrew Mccallum. 2010. *An Introduction to Conditional Random Fields*. Now Publishers Inc.

Jinnan Yang, Bo Peng, Jin Wang, Jixian Zhang, and Xuejie Zhang. 2016. Chinese grammatical error diagnosis using single word embedding. In *Proceedings of the 3rd Workshop on Natural Language Processing Techniques for Educational Applications (NLP-TEA-16)*, pages 155–161.

CVTE at IJCNLP-2017 Task 1: Character Checking System for Chinese Grammatical Error Diagnosis Task

Xian Li, Peng Wang, Suixue Wang, Guanyu Jiang, Tianyuan You
CVTE Central R&D Institute
lixian@cvte.com

Abstract

Grammatical error diagnosis is an important task in natural language processing. This paper introduces CVTE Character Checking System in the NLP-TEA-4 shared task for CGED 2017, we use Bi-LSTM to generate the probability of every character, then take two kinds of strategies to decide whether a character is correct or not. This system is probably more suitable to deal with the error type of bad word selection, which is one of four types of errors, and the rest are words redundancy, words missing and words disorder. Finally the second strategy achieves better F1 score than the first one at all of detection level, identification level, position level.

1 Introduction

Nowadays, Chinese language gains more popularity in the world, many foreigners begin to learn Chinese. Unlike English, Chinese has no verb tenses and pluralities, and a sentence can be expressed in many ways, a native Chinese speaker can handle well all of these different grammatical phenomena, but for the foreigners, these are difficult parts to learn the Chinese well. In the HSK (Hanyu Shuiping Kaoshi), which is an international standard test for Chinese language proficiency of non-native speakers, after analyzing a considerable number of examination papers, it shows that foreigners who study Chinese often make grammatical mistakes by having redundant words, missing words, bad word selection and disorder words due to their language false analogy, over-generalization, teaching methods, learning strategies and other reasons. For all grammatical errors, it is proposed that a task named CGED (Chinese Grammatical Error Diagnosis) as one of share task of NLPTEA in three consecutive years 2014-2016, CGED 2014 (Yu etal., 2014) defined four kinds of grammatical errors: words redundancy, words missing, bad word selection and words disorder. At most one error occurred in one sentence. The evaluation was based on error detection and error classification in sentence level. CGED 2015 (Lee et al., 2015) further required the positions of the errors. CGED 2016 tested on the ability to detect multiple errors in one sentence.

2 Task Definition

The shared task of CGED is defined as below: There are four types of grammatical errors in a sentence, which are redundancy (R), words missing (M), bad selection (S) and disorder (D). The systems participating this shared task should detect whether the sentence contains errors (Detection-level), find out which type the error belongs to (Identification-level), and where the errors are (Position-level).

Table1 and Table2 show two examples in test data:

	我$_1$真$_2$不$_3$明$_4$白$_5$。$_6$她$_7$们$_8$可$_9$能$_{10}$是$_{11}$追$_{12}$求$_{13}$一$_{14}$些$_{15}$前$_{16}$代$_{17}$的$_{18}$浪$_{19}$漫$_{20}$	
Correction	我$_1$真$_2$不$_3$明$_4$白$_5$。$_6$她$_7$们$_8$可$_9$能$_{10}$是$_{11}$追$_{12}$求$_{13}$一$_{14}$些$_{15}$前$_{16}$代$_{17}$的$_{18}$浪$_{19}$漫$_{20}$	
Detection-level	correct	
Identification-level	-	-
Position-level	-	-

Table 1: The sentence is correct.

Proceedings of the 8th International Joint Conference on Natural Language Processing, Shared Tasks, pages 78–83,
Taipei, Taiwan, November 27 – December 1, 2017. ©2017 AFNLP

	我$_1$根$_2$本$_3$不$_4$能$_5$了$_6$解$_7$这$_8$妇$_9$女$_{10}$辞$_{11}$职$_{12}$回$_{13}$家$_{14}$的$_{15}$现$_{16}$象$_{17}$	
Correction	我$_1$根$_2$本$_3$不$_4$能$_5$理$_6$解$_7$妇$_8$女$_9$辞$_{10}$职$_{11}$回$_{12}$家$_{13}$的$_{14}$现$_{15}$象$_{16}$	
Detection-level	-	
Identification-level	S	R
Position-level	6,7	8,8

Table 2: Two errors are found in the sentence above, one is bad word selection (S) error from position 6 to 7, the other one is redundant words (R) error at position 8.

3 The Unified Framework of CVTE Character Checking System

For this shared task, we propose a unified framework called CVTE Character Checking System in Figure 1, just as its name implies, the system can handle with Chinese character errors which are almost S errors in CGED-2017, hence our system mainly focuses on S errors for the moment.

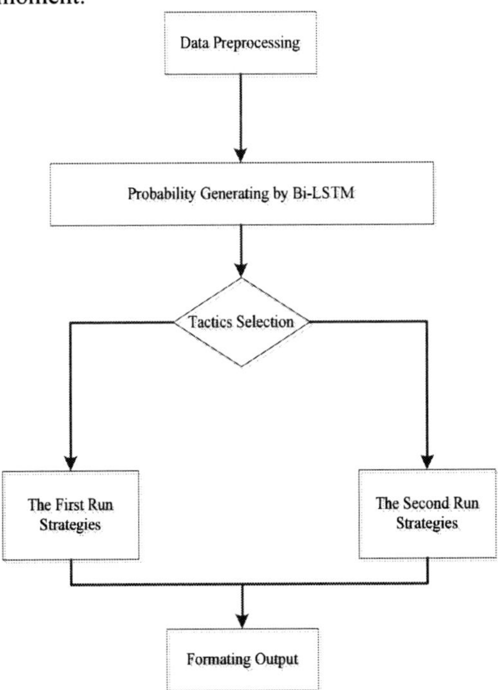

Figure 1: A unified framework of CVTE Character Checking System

Data preprocessing step is to split a sentence into sub-sentences by punctuation. Probability Generating by Bi-LSTM step generates the probability of each character of the input sub-sentence. In Tactics Selection step, the sole purpose is to choose which error deciding strategy we are going to use. The First Run Strategies and The Second Run Strategies are error deciding steps. Format output step is to format the output into CGED-2017 style.

3.1 Data preparation

Data provided by organizer is in the form of long sentences and contains some non-Chinese characters. In our system, only short sentences are supported, and they can't contain non-Chinese characters and punctuations. In order to meet the input requirement of our system, long sentences were splitted into some short sub-sentences by punctuation, and non-Chinese characters were removed determined by its unicode.

This task is an open test and some training data is provided, but considering that a larger training set can improve the performance of our framework, we crawl corpus in addition from composition website and novel website as our training data.

3.2 Probability Generating by Bi-LSTM Model

In order to achieve good performance of neural network language model (Bengio Y.,2003), we implement RNN neural network (Mikolov T.,2012) to train our language model. A Bi-LSTM multi-layer network is applied into the structure of training model, so that both previous and posterior sub-sentences could be taken into consideration.

In the Chinese information processing, the performance of word segmentation determines the upper bound of tasks. In addition, the number of words is much larger than the number of characters. Words based features will bring sparseness to the training data, and will also reduce the training speed of the neural network. In order to get rid of these problems, the Chinese characters are taken as the input of the neural network language model. $S = C_1C_2...C_n$ stands for the sentence to be detected, as shown in figure 1, and

C_i is a single Chinese character. After sentence S is put into the neural network, the probability of every character at its position will be exported, which we name "position probability distribution". The forward input sequence is $<s>C_1...C_{n-1}$, and the backward input sequence is $C_2...C_{n-1}</s>$, and the label sequence is $C_1C_2...C_n$. In all of forward and backward input sequences, $<s>$ and $</s>$ represent the start and the end of a sequence respectively. Taking the probability distribution of position of C_2 as an example, Bi-LSTM utilizes the context information of both $<s>C_1$ and $C_3...</s>$.

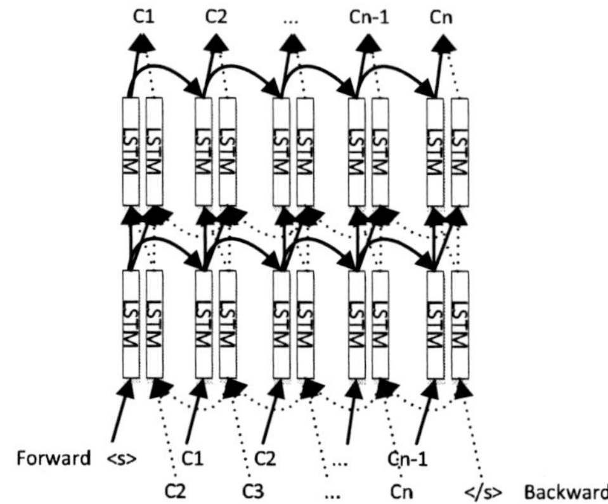

Figure 2: The Bi-LSTM language model based on characters

3.3 Error Detection Strategies

Based on the neural network language model mentioned in the previous section, we propose two Strategies for the final detection of the error position.

3.3.1 The First Run Strategy

After a sequence is input, we can get the position probability distribution and the probability of each character. The main process of this strategy has two parts. Firstly, whether a character is correct may be judged directly by the character probability. Secondly, if it is hard to make such a decision, generating the scores of all candidate sentences which are built by replacing certain characters with confusion characters which own the top 3 probability values in confusion set, and choosing the one with top score in candidate sentences and original sentence. Confusion characters share the same Pinyin with each other. The score of a sentence is computed by multiplying every character probability which is the output of Bi-LSTM model in the sentence. The same position where the character is different between top score sentence and original sentence is the error position the system finds out. The details are shown as pseudo code in Table 3.

3.3.2 The Second Run Strategy

We also put forward another strategy which can improve the recall rate. The specific process is shown in the pseudo code of Table 4 and Table 5.

The pseudo code of the first strategy
1: FOR each character C_i^{origin} with probability P_i^{origin} in sentence S_{origin}:
IF $P_i^{origin} \geq 0.1$ THEN:
C_i^{origin} correct and continue
IF $0.001 \leq P_i^{origin} < 0.1$ THEN:
Get the maximum probability value Q_{C_i} of character in confusion set F_{C_i}
IF $P_i^{origin} == Q_{C_i}$ THEN:
C_i^{origin} correct and continue
Select the characters $T_1^{C_i^{origin}}$, $T_2^{C_i^{origin}}$, $T_3^{C_i^{origin}}$ with top 3 probability values in F_{C_i}
3: Generate the candidate sentences by replace C_i^{origin} with $T_1^{C_i^{origin}}$, $T_2^{C_i^{origin}}$, $T_3^{C_i^{origin}}$ in S_{origin}
4: Input these candidate sentences $S_{T_j^{C_i^{origin}}}$ back into model，and get $Score_{T_j^{C_i^{origin}}}$,
where $Score_{T_j^{C_i^{origin}}} = \sum_1^N \log P_k^{T_j^{C_i^{origin}}}$
5: FOR position i in S_{origin}:
IF $Score_{C_i^{origin}} > Score_{T_j^{C_i^{origin}}}$ THEN:

C_i correct
IF $Score_{C_i^{origin}} <= Score_{T_j^{C_i^{origin}}}$ THEN:
C_i error

Table 3: The pseudo code of the firs strategy

Rule_Top_3
FOR position i, Bi-LSTM output set of softmax probabilities is D_i, p_1, p_2, p_3 are top three probabilities in D_i THEN:

$$sum\_top\_3 = p_1 + p_2 + p_3$$

IF $sum\_top\_3 \geq 0.99$ THEN:

$N_1 = 10$ and $M_1 = 30$

select top N_2 characters that make the sum of probabilities is greater than 0.998

select top M_2 characters that make the sum of probabilities is just greater than 0.97

IF $sum\_top\_3 < 0.99$ AND $sum\_top\_3 \geq 0.95$ THEN:

$N_1 = 20$ and $M_1 = 40$

select top N_2 characters that make the sum of probabilities is greater than 0.995

select top M_2 characters that make the sum of probabilities is greater than 0.965

IF $sum\_top\_3 < 0.95$ AND $sum\_top\_3 \geq 0.65$ THEN:

$N_1 = 30$ and $M_1 = 70$

select top N_2 characters that make the sum of probabilities is greater than 0.992

select top M_2 characters that make the sum of probabilities is greater than 0.96

IF $sum\_top\_3 < 0.65$ THEN:

$N_1 = 50$ and $M_1 = 100$

select top N_2 characters that make the sum of probabilities is greater than 0.99

select top M_2 characters that make the sum of probabilities is greater than 0.95

$N = min\ (N_1, N_2)$

$M = min\ (M_1, M_2)$

The N number of characters make up set one U_1

The M number of characters make up set two U_2

Table 4: The pseudo code of Rule_Top_3

The process of strategy two
1: FOR each character C_i^{origin} with probability P_i^{origin} in sentence S_{origin}:

IF $P_i^{origin} \geq 0.1$ THEN:

C_i^{origin} correct and continue

IF $P_i^{origin} \leq 0.0001$ THEN:

C_i^{origin} error and continue

Select two sets based on Rule_Top_3 shown in Table 4

IF C_i^{origin} in U_1 THEN:

C_i^{origin} correct and continue

IF C_i^{origin} not in U_2 THEN:

C_i^{origin} error and continue

2: Generate the candidate sentences $S_{T_j^{C_i^{origin}}}$ by replace C_i^{origin} with all character T_j in confusion set F_{C_i}

3: Input these candidate sentences $S_{T_j^{C_i^{origin}}}$ back into model，and get $Score_{T_j^{C_i^{origin}}}$，

$$\text{where } Score_{T_j^{C_i^{origin}}} = \sum_1^N \log P_k^{T_j^{C_i^{origin}}}$$

$$\text{IF } Score_{C_i^{origin}} \text{ is in top 20 percent of set } \left(Score_{C_i^{origin}}, Score_{T_j^{C_i^{origin}}} \right) \text{ THEN:}$$

$$C_i^{origin} \text{ correct and continue}$$

$$\text{ELSE:}$$

$$C_i^{origin} \text{ error and continue}$$

Table 5: The pseudo code of the second strategy

4 Experiments

In the formal run of CGED2017 shared task, there are 5 participants in HSK, 13 runs in total. Two runs (CVTE-Run1, Run2) of HSK were submitted to CGED 2017 shared task for official evaluation. The submission of Run1 is generated by The First Run Strategies system and the Run2 is generated by The Second Run Strategies system. Table 6 shows the false positive rate, our system has relatively low false positive rate comparing with other participants.

Table 7, Table 8, and Table 9 show the formal run result of our system in Detection level, Identification level and Position level, respectively. Our system mainly focuses on the Detection level, as for this task, Run2 plays better than Run1, and it has relatively better performance on Accuracy, Precision and F1-score indicators. As for Identification level task, Run1 achieves the highest precision rate comparing with other teams, but the recall rate of our system is fare.

Submission	False Positive Rate
CVTE-Run1	0.1441 (169/1173)
CVTE-Run2	0.3154 (370/1173)

Table 6: False Positive Rate

Submission	Acc	Pre	Rec	F1
CVTE-Run1	0.475	0.745	0.250	0.374
CVTE-Run2	0.539	0.708	0.452	0.552

Table 7: Detection Level

Submission	Acc	Pre	Rec	F1
CVTE-Run1	0.446	**0.606**	0.121	0.202
CVTE-Run2	0.471	0.539	0.205	0.297

Table 8: Identification Level

Submission	Acc	Pre	Rec	F1
CVTE-Run1	0.331	0.118	0.020	0.034
CVTE-Run2	0.260	0.109	0.046	0.065

Table 9: Position Level

5 Conclusion

This paper proposes a unified framework called CVTE Character Checking System which only aims to handle with bad word selection error. Bi-LSTM and two kinds of strategies are applied into our system. However, the other types of errors such as words redundancy, words missing, and words disorder are not considered in the system, which may not give fine results. Chinese character error and Chinese grammatical error are different levels of error in a sentence, so the solutions are quite different.

In future studies, works on both Chinese character check and Chinese grammatical error diagnosis could be done to improve our system, which include: (1) Taking the word level Bi-LSTM model for Chinese character check. (2) Containing a sequence to sequence model for Chinese grammatical error diagnosis. (3) Implementing an online toolkit and service for Chinese character check and Chinese grammatical error diagnosis as a stimulator for this empirical research topic.

Acknowledgments

This research was funded by the Guangzhou Huangpu Postdoctoral Science Foundation.

References

Liang-Chih Yu, Lung-Hao Lee, and Li-Ping Chang (2014). Overview of Grammatical Error Diagnosis for Learning Chinese as a Foreign Language. *Proceedings of the 1st Workshop on Natural Language Processing Techniques for Educational Applications (NLPTEA'14), Nara, Japan, 30 November, 2014, pp. 42-47.*

Lung-Hao Lee, Liang-Chih Yu, and Li-Ping Chang. 2015. Overview of the NLP-TEA 2015 shared task for Chinese grammatical error diagnosis. *In Proceedings of the 2nd*

Workshop on Natural Language Processing Techniques for Educational Applications (NLP-TEA'15), pages 1-6, Beijing, China.

Bengio Y, Ducharme R, Vincent P, et al. A neural probabilistic language model[J]. *Journal of machine learning research*, 2003, 3(Feb): 1137-1155.

Mikolov T. Statistical language models based on neural networks[J]. *Presentation at Google, Mountain View*, 2nd April, 2012.

LDCCNLP at IJCNLP-2017 Task 2: Dimensional Sentiment Analysis for Chinese Phrases Using Machine Learning

Peng Zhong[1], Jingbin Wang[1]

[1] College of Mathematics and Computer Science, Fuzhou University, Fuzhou, P.R. China

Abstract

Sentiment analysis on Chinese text has intensively studied. The basic task for related research is to construct an affective lexicon and thereby predict emotional scores of different levels. However, finite lexicon resources make it difficult to effectively and automatically distinguish between various types of sentiment information in Chinese texts. This IJCNLP2017-Task2 competition seeks to automatically calculate Valence and Arousal ratings within the hierarchies of vocabulary and phrases in Chinese. We introduce a regression methodology to automatically recognize continuous emotional values, and incorporate a word embedding technique. In our system, the MAE predictive values of Valence and Arousal were 0.811 and 0.996, respectively, for the sentiment dimension prediction of words in Chinese. In phrase prediction, the corresponding results were 0.822 and 0.489, ranking sixth among all teams.

1 Introduction

Emotional analysis is a technique of mining and identifying potential emotional information in texts. Such techniques can allow for the automatic analysis of public opinion to help guide government policy making, can help firms improve products and services in response to customer feedback, and can help improve medical treatment through automatically identifying emotional labels in patients' medical records.

In general, affective states can be described in two ways: categorical representation and dimensional representation. (Calvo and D'Mello, 2010). Many studies have examined sentiment classification (Jiang et al., 2011; Boni et al., 2015). The categorical analysis represents affective states as several discrete class, such as positive and negative (Ekman, 1992). However, the categorical representation can't express the fine-grained intensity of emotion. Therefore, dimensional representation has emerged as an important topic in sentiment analysis emerge for application in different fields (Li and Hovy, 2014; Preotiuc-Pietro, 2015; Choudhury, 2012; Wang et al., 2016a; 2016b; Yu et al., 2016a). The dimensional representation can represent any affective state as a point in a continuous multi-dimensional space. In linguistic theory, sentiment can be represented as a point in a bi-dimensional space defined in terms of Valence (the degree of pleasant and unpleasant) and Arousal (the degree of exciting and calm) (Russell, 1980). The resulting space is called VA space.

Dimensional sentiment analysis has attracted widespread attention for tasks involving natural language processing. The dimensional affective lexicon has been widely used in dimensional sentiment analysis, such as in CVAW (Yu et al., 2016b), ANEW (Bradley and Lang, 1999) and so on. Given the limited availability of affective lexicons, especially for Chinese, the aim of the IJCNLP 2017 task 2 is to automatic identify VA ratings of word-level and phrase-level in Chinese. This paper presents a system that uses word embeddings (Mikolov et al., 2013a; 2013b; Pennington et al., 2014; Yu et al., 2017) to represent the Chinese word and phase as

Proceedings of the 8th International Joint Conference on Natural Language Processing, Shared Tasks, pages 84–88,
Taipei, Taiwan, November 27 – December 1, 2017. ©2017 AFNLP

input, and uses the regression method to fit the valence and arousal ratings (Brereton and Lloyd, 2010).

The rest of this paper is organized as follows. Section 2 presents the method used to train the word vectors of the traditional Chinese corpus. Section 3 describes the evaluation methods and results. Section 4 presents conclusions.

2   PROPOSED METHOD

2.1   Data Collection

The task of this competition is based on the prediction of traditional Chinese texts. The domain and dimension of the corpus will affect the quality of the word vector (Lai et al., 2016). Therefore，for this task, we collected two kinds of corpus for the construction of a traditional Chinese corpus:

1. Chinese Wikipedia Dumps

The Wikipedia Extractor tool is used to extract articles from Wikipedia text. After removing punctuation, OpenCC is used to convert all remaining text into Traditional Chinese.

2. Taiwan Commercial Times

To obtain a richer traditional Chinese text, we used crawler programs to obtain news content on the webpages of the Taiwan Commercial Times. text is obtained with the scale of 0.65G in total after cleaning up punctuations and non-Chinese content.

After obtaining the traditional Chinese corpus, the two pieces of corpora are merged, scaling 1.6G. We then used the CKIP word segmentation system to segment the text to produce a traditional Chinese corpus containing 767,103 words.

2.2   Word Vector Training

After constructing the Chinese corpus, we needed to transform the words into numerical vectors usable by the machine learning regression algorithm. Word embedding techniques can represent words as continuous low-dimensional vectors which contain the semantic and syntactic information of words. The semantic similarity between words can be obtained by calculating the distance between vectors. We use two methods to train two types of word vectors.

Word embeddings can be obtained by using a neural network to train the language model (Xu and Rudnicky, 2000). Using the relationship between word contexts, we can obtain the feature output of the hidden layer in the process of word prediction. Google's Word2Vec tool is based on this principle, and we can use it to train different dimensions of the word vector.

Words that always appear together are semantically similar, and their meaning may be reflected by co-occurrence context (Chen and You, 2002). Through matrix co-occurrence, we can also train low-dimensional word vectors with semantic similarity. We use the Glove tool (Pennington et al., 2014) to train this kind of co-occurrence based word vector. For each type of word vector, we will train five dimension vectors, with dimensions of 100, 150, 200, 250 and 300.

2.3   Model

For each subtask, we use five regression models in machine learning to carry out experiment: Ridge Regression, K Nearest Neighbors (KNN), Decision Trees(DT), Support Vector Regression (SVR), and AdaBoost. These models are implemented by scikit-learn.

3   Experiments and Evaluation

3.1   Dataset

The Shared Task2 contains two subtasks: namely VA rating prediction of words and phrases in Chinese.

The training set of the word VA ratings prediction task 2,802 emotion words with valence-arousal ratings in the CVAW2.0 affective lexicons (Yu et al., 2016) provided by the organizer. In the prediction task of the VA rating of the phrases, the training set contains 2250 phrases, VA ratings also annotated. The contest test set consists of 750 words and 750 phrases that are not annotated with VA ratings.

3.2   Evaluation metrics.

Performance was evaluated by comparing the difference between the predicted values and the corresponding actual values in the test set. The IJCNLP 2017 Task 4 published results for all participants using both mean absolute error (MAE) and Pearson correlation coefficient (PCC).

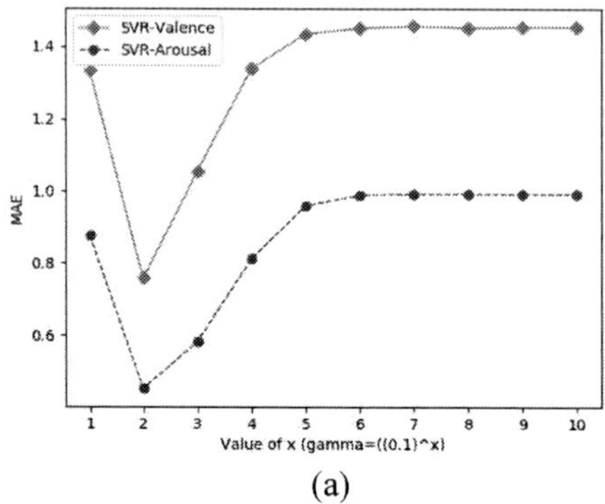
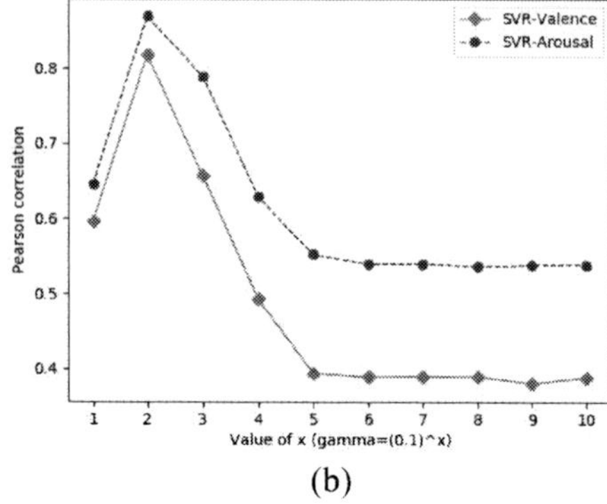

(a)   (b)

Figure 1: Parameter gamma selection for support vector regression methods, evaluated on the development set of Chinese phase using MAE and PCC.

$$MAE = \frac{1}{n}\sum_{i=1}^{n}\left|A_i - P_i\right|$$

$$PCC = \frac{1}{n-1}\sum_{i=1}^{n}\left(\frac{A_i - \overline{A}}{\sigma_A}\right)\left(\frac{P_i - \overline{P}}{\sigma_P}\right)$$

where A_i is the actual value, P_i is the predicted value, n is the number of test samples, $\overline{A}$ and $\overline{P}$ respectively denote the arithmetic mean of A and P, and σ is the standard deviation. The MAE measures the error rate and the Pearson correlation coefficient shows the correlation between the actual value and predicted result.

3.3 Implementation details

For the two sub-tasks, we divided the experiment into two parts.

In the word prediction task, we use word vectors of different dimensions and different types obtained from training mentioned above to convert the words in the training set into corresponding word vectors. An n-dimensional random vector is generated as corresponding token with the value for each dimension within the range of -0.25 and +0.25, given that the word doesn't belong to the realm of our corpus, where n represents current word embedding dimension.

For the phrase predicting task, such steps are executed, follow these steps: First, with CKIP system phrases are divided into words, with a maximum of three words per phrase. Then we translate each word in phrases into corresponding word vector, the conversion method used here identical to the transformation process of the word task; finally, each phrase is embodied by phrase vectors of 3*n with feature vectors of all words preserved; for a phrase comprised of less than 3 words, 0 is used to fill the vacant values of phrase vectors.

Before each experiment, we disrupted the training set and performed 5-fold validation to adjust and record the parameters of each model based on the cross-validation results.

Different model parameters affect the performance of the regression algorithm. In each subtask, we adjust the model parameters based on the performance of forecast results with evaluation matrice.

The following is an example of parameter adjustment process for the SRV algorithm with phrase VA prediction task based on the 300-dimensional word vector produced by the Glove, in which we use the MAE and Pearson correlation coefficients to recognize the prediction performance. First, the kernel function of appropriate SRV algorithm is selected by predicting the result of crossing validation sets. After the comparison, we use rbf kernel function. Then, the value of the gamma parameter of the rbf kernel is adjusted again by the result of 5-fold cross validation.

In Fig. 1(a), the point x on the abscissa is an integer ranging from 1 to 10, representing the change in the value of gamma, and the value of gamma is equal to the x power of 0.1. The ordinate is the MAE evaluation result from different gamma values with the SVR algorithm. It can be seen from Fig. 1 that when x = 2, that is, gamma 0.01, the model has the best MAE value for Valence and Arousal prediction of the phrase.

Figure 1(b) shows the influence of different gamma values over the Pearson correlation coefficients of the predicted results. When gamma is 0.01, the coefficient value for Valence and Arousal prediction results reaches highest. Results.

For the two sub-tasks, we use the Word2Vec and GloVe word vector with 100, 150, 200, 250, and 300 dimensions to compare the effect of the regression model. The following figure shows the results of the phrase prediction task.

Figure 2 evaluates the prediction results of the

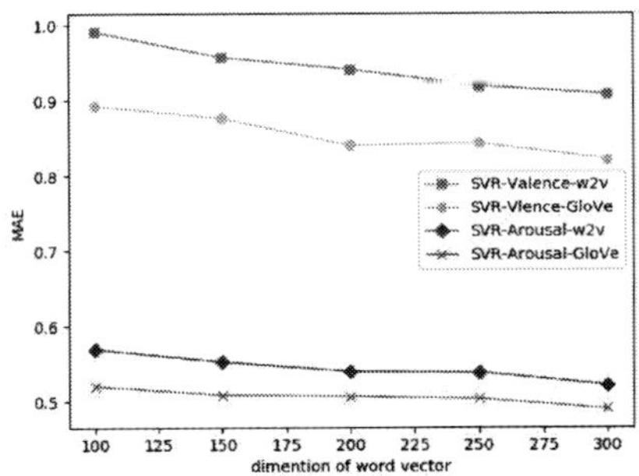

Figure 2: Selection of the dimension and type of word vector.

phrase test set using the SVR regression model. The abscissa represents the number of word vector dimensions from 100 to 300. For each dimension, we perform experiments on the word vector trained by Word2Vec (Mikolov et al., 2013a; Mikolov et al., 2013b) and GloVe (Pennington et al., 2014). The ordinate is the MAE evaluation value of the test set prediction results for specific model.

1) As the number of word vector dimensions increases, the predictive result is getting better, both for the Word2Vec word vector and the GloVe word vector, the same outcome seen for richer features of word vectors. Experiments show that the same conclusion can be drawn from comparing the predictions of words and phrases in the other proposed regression models.

2) The word vectors based on word concurrence matrix trained by GloVe is better than that of Word2Vec related to word contexts in VA rating

prediction task for phrases. However, in word pre-

Word	Valence		Arousal	
	MAE	PCC	MAE	PCC
KNN	1.219	0.521	1.235	0.346
DT	1.372	0.407	1.385	0.181
SVR	**0.811**	**0.769**	**0.996**	**0.479**
AdaBoot	0.934	0.696	1.091	0.364
Ridge	0.857	0.754	1.056	0.451

Phase	Valence		Arousal	
	MAE	PCC	MAE	PCC
KNN	0.916	0.632	0.605	0.743
DT	1.092	0.495	0.821	0.543
SVR	**0.822**	**0.762**	**0.489**	**0.828**
AdaBoot	1.035	0.723	0.622	0.744
Ridge	1.779	0.322	1.019	0.481

Table 1: The best predictions for each model in word and phrase prediction tasks

diction tasks, using Word2Vec to train the word vector performs better than GloVe.

Table 1 summarizes the best predictive results for each model in the two subtasks. The best results for predictions of words and phrases are obtained using the SVR regression models.

4   Conclusions

To automatically identify the valence-arousal ratings for lexicon augmentation, this paper presents a machine learning regression model to predict valence-arousal ratings of Chinese words and phrases. We use the word embeddings to produce the word vector for the lexicon vocabulary. Experiments on both Chinese words and phrases show that the proposed method provides good predictive results. The SVR method outperformed other regression methods. Future work will focus on further improving predicative performance. The modifier can be considered as the characteristic of Chinese phase for the predictive result.

References

Mohammad Al Boni, Keira Zhou, Hongning Wang, and Matthew S. Gerber. 2015. Model adaptation for personalized opinion analysis. In *Proceedings of the 53rd*

Annual Meeting of the Association for Computational Linguistics and the 7th International Joint Conference on Natural Language Processing (ACL/IJCNLP-15), pages 769–774.

Margaret M. Bradley and Peter J. Lang. 1999. Affective norms for English words (ANEW): Instruction manual and affective ratings. Technical Report C-1, Univerity of Florida, Gainesville, FL.

R. G. Brereton and G. R. Lloyd. 2010. Support vector machines for classification and regression. *Analyst*, 135(2):230–267.

R. A. Calvo and Sidney. D'Mello. 2010. Affect detection: An interdisciplinary review of models, methods, and their applications. *IEEE Trans. Affective Computing*, 1(1): 18-37.

Keh Jiann Chen and Jia Ming You. 2002. A study on word similarity using context vector models. *Computational Linguistics and Chinese Language Processing*, 7(2):37–58.

Munmun De Choudhury, Scott Counts, and Michael Gamon. 2012. Not all moods are created equal! Exploring human emotional states in social media. In *Sixth international AAAI conference on weblogs and social media*, pages 66–73.

Paul Ekman. 1992. An argument for basic emotions. *Cognition and Emotion*, 6(3-4), 169-200.

Long Jiang, Mo Yu, Ming Zhou, Xiaohua Liu, and Tiejun Zhao. 2011. Target-dependent twitter sentiment classification. In *Proceedings of the 49th Annual Meeting of the Association for Computational Linguistics: Human Language Technologies (ACL-11)*, pages 151–160.

Siwei Lai, Kang Liu, Shizhu He, and Jun Zhao. 2016. How to generate a good word embedding. *IEEE Intelligent Systems*, 31(6):5–14.

Jiwei Li and Eduard Hovy. 2014. Sentiment Analysis on the People's Daily. In *Proc. of the 2014 Conference on Empirical Methods in Natural Language Processing (EMNLP-14)*, pages 467–476.

Tomas Mikolov, Kai Chen, Greg Corrado, and Jeffrey Dean. 2013a. Efficient estimation of word representations in vector space. *Computer Science*.

Tomas Mikolov, Ilya Sutskever, Kai Chen, Greg Corrado, and Jeffrey Dean. 2013b. Distributed representations of words and phrases and their compositionality. *Advances in Neural Information Processing Systems*, 26:3111–3119.

Jeffrey Pennington, Richard Socher, and Christopher Manning. 2014. Glove: Global vectors for word representation. In *Proc. of the 2014 Conference on Empirical Methods in Natural Language Processing (EMNLP-14)*, pages 1532–1543.

Daniel Preotiuc-Pietro, Johannes Eichstaedt, Gregory Park, Maarten Sap, Laura Smith, Victoria Tobolsky, H. Andrew Schwartz, and Lyle Ungar. 2015. The role of personality, age, and gender in tweeting about mental illness. In *Proc. of the Workshop on Computational Linguistics and Clinical Psychology: From Linguistic Signal To Clinical Reality*, pages 21–30.

James A Russell. 1980. A circumplex model of affect. *Journal of Personality and Social Psychology*, 39(6):1161–1178.

Jin Wang, Liang-Chih Yu, K. Robert Lai, and Xuejie Zhang. 2016a. Community-based weighted graph model for valence-arousal prediction of affective words. *IEEE/ACM Transactions on Audio Speech and Language Processing*, 24(11):1957–1968.

Jin Wang, Liang-Chih Yu, K. Robert Lai, and Xuejie Zhang. 2016b. Dimensional sentiment analysis using a regional CNN-LSTM model. In *Proc. of the 54th Annual Meeting of the Association for Computational Linguistics (ACL-16)*, pages 225-230, 2016.

Wei Xu, Alexander I Rudnicky. 2000. Can artificial neural networks learn language models? In *The Proceedings of the Sixth International Conference on Spoken Language Processing*, pages 202–205.

Liang-Chih Yu, Lung-Hao Lee, and Kam-Fai Wong. 2016a. Overview of the IALP 2016 shared task on dimensional sentiment analysis for Chinese words, in *Proc. of the 20th International Conference on Asian Language Processing (IALP-16)*, pages 156-160.

Liang-Chih Yu, Lung-Hao Lee, Shuai Hao, Jin Wang, Yunchao He, Jun Hu, K. Robert Lai, and Xuejie Zhang. 2016b. Building Chinese affective resources in valence-arousal dimensions. In *Proceedings of the 15th Annual Conference of the North American Chapter of the Association for Computational Linguistics: Human Language Technologies (NAACL/HLT-16)*, pages 540-545.

Liang-Chih Yu, Jin Wang, K. Robert Lai, Xue-jie Zhang. 2017. Refining word embeddings for sentiment analysis. In *Proc. of the 2017 Conference on Empirical Methods in Natural Language Processing (EMNLP-17)*, pages 545–550.

CKIP at IJCNLP-2017 Task 2: Neural Valence-Arousal Prediction for Phrases

Peng-Hsuan Li
CSIE, National Taiwan University
No. 1, Sec. 4, Roosevelt Rd.
Taipei 10617, Taiwan
jacobvsdanniel@gmail.com

Wei-Yun Ma
IIS, Academia Sinica
No. 128, Sec. 2, Academia Rd.
Taipei 11529, Taiwan
ma@iis.sinica.edu.tw

Hsin-Yang Wang
IIS, Academia Sinica
No. 128, Sec. 2, Academia Rd.
Taipei 11529, Taiwan
whyntut@gmail.com

Abstract

CKIP takes part in solving the Dimensional Sentiment Analysis for Chinese Phrases (DSAP) share task of IJCNLP 2017. This task calls for systems that can predict the valence and the arousal of Chinese phrases, which are real values between 1 and 9. To achieve this, functions mapping Chinese character sequences to real numbers are built by regression techniques. In addition, the CKIP phrase Valence-Arousal (VA) predictor depends on knowledge of modifier words and head words. This includes the types of known modifier words, VA of head words, and distributional semantics of both these words. The predictor took the second place out of 13 teams on phrase VA prediction, with 0.444 MAE and 0.935 PCC on valence, and 0.395 MAE and 0.904 PCC on arousal.

1 Introduction

Sentiment analysis can be a useful tool in understanding public opinions for items of various subjects, such as movies, hotels, and political figures, from unstructured texts. The problem is often defined in two different ways: one that assigns texts to discrete categories, and the other that seeks to get every sample a real value for each dimension (Calvo and Mac Kim, 2013).

For the Dimensional Sentiment Analysis for Chinese Phrases (DSAP) share task of IJCNLP 2017, two dimensions are used to capture the emotions people put in phrases: *valence*, which captures the positive-negative polarity of phrases, and

Type	Count	VA Label
Negation Word	4	No
Modal Word	6	No
Degree Word	42	No
Head Word	2802	Yes
Phrase	2250	Yes

Table 1: Training data statistics for DSAP.

arousal, which represents the degree of excitement. The values of both dimensions are limited to a closed interval between 1 and 9, where 1 represents most negative for valence and calmest for arousal.

The DSAP shared task calls for systems that automatically predict VA for Chinese phrases to overcome the scarcity of labeled Chinese phrases and words. Lists of words for different types of modifiers are provided. This includes negation words like 不 and 沒有, modal words like 本來 and 應該, and degree words like 有點 and 更加. In addition, some head words with VA annotations are also provided (Yu et al., 2016). Finally, a training data of VA-annotated phrases with their modifier types, e.g. (deg_neg, 稍微不小心), are provided. Table 1 shows the statistics of the training data.

However, besides predicting VA for phrases of which the VA of the head words are known, a seemingly separate task of predicting the VA of unseen words is also required for the competition. Hence, effectively, multiple predictors were built to solve the 4 different problems: phrase valence, phrase arousal, word valence, and word arousal.

Proceedings of the 8th International Joint Conference on Natural Language Processing, Shared Tasks, pages 89–94,
Taipei, Taiwan, November 27 – December 1, 2017. ©2017 AFNLP

Hyper-parameter	Trial Range	Final Setting	
		Valence	Arousal
C	$10^{-3}, 10^{-2}, 10^{-1}, 10^{0}, 10^{1}, 10^{2}, 10^{3}$	10^{1}	10^{1}
ϵ	$10^{-4}, 10^{-3}, 10^{-2}, 10^{-1}, 10^{0}, 10^{1}, 10^{2}, 10^{3}$	10^{-2}	10^{-1}
γ	$10^{-5}, 10^{-4}, 10^{-3}, 10^{-2}, 10^{-1}, 10^{0}, 10^{1}, 10^{2}, 10^{3}, 954^{-1}$	10^{-2}	954^{-1}

Table 2: Grid search hyper-parameters for SVR-RBF.

2 Phrase VA Predictors

Two predictors are constructed and trained similarly for the phrase valence problem and phrase arousal problem. The predictors can be separated into two stages: one that acquires an embedding for a given phrase, and the other that performs the mapping to VA values based on regression analyses.

2.1 Word Segmentation

The first step is to segment a phrase into words. One general way of doing this is to use a popular existing Chinese word segmentation system (Ma and Chen, 2004). However, to best utilize the given knowledge about modifiers and head words with known VA, we developed a simple longest-match segmentation system which uses given data files to make its decision.

For each phrase that are given as a sequence of characters, we first try to match trailing characters to a head word with known VA. Then iteratively leading characters are matched with known modifier words, resulting in a segmented phrase with a sequence of types of its modifiers. For the training data, this matching scheme successfully segments most phrases with correct modifier sequences. The two exceptions are documented below.

First, for the phrase 不是, no head word with known VA can be found. One general solution to this situation is to use word VA predictors to generate the VA of its head word (either 不是 or 是). However, since this phrase is actually not a good sentiment-expressing phrase, we think it is better to simply exclude it from the training data.

The other exception is a set of phrases that ends in 不爽, e.g. 十分不爽. Although both 爽 and 不爽 are words with known VA, 不爽 should be preferred in resolving the segmentation ambiguity according to our longest match principle. However, the resulting modifier type sequence (degree) of (十分,不爽) would be different from the provided (degree,negation) of (十分,不,爽). Recognizing

both segmentation can be correct, we choose to split 不 and 爽 as this reduces data sparsity.

2.2 Phrase Features

Having acquired the correct segmentation of phrases, the next question is then how a phrase embedding should be generated for this specific problem. This includes how word embeddings are generated, and how they are combined into phrase embeddings. In addition, some other phrase features that are useful for the problem should be concatenated to these embeddings.

Due to the sparsity of labeled Chinese phrases and words for sentiment analysis, we use unsupervised word embeddings without further tuning. The corpus on which we compute the distributional semantics of Chinese words comes from both the Chinese Gigaword corpus (Graff and Chen, 2003) and the Sinica Corpus (Chen et al., 1996). The former contains over 735 million Chinese characters from the Central News Agency of Taiwan, and the latter contains over 17 million Chinese characters from documents of balanced topics. We use the GloVe algorithm (Pennington et al., 2014) to obtain 300-dimensional word embeddings from a union of these corpora. The resulting 517,015 embeddings cover all words in the training phrases.

To combine word embeddings of phrases to phrase embeddings, we notice the sparsity of available phrase and hence take a simple approach. Observing all given phrases are a compound of one to two modifier words and one head word, we append the word embeddings of the modifier words of a phrase to the word embedding of its head word. With zero paddings to the phrases with only one modifier word, 900-dimensional phrase embeddings are acquired for all phrases.

Finally, two additional features are concatenated to these embeddings. The first is a 2-dimensional VA vector of the head word of each phrase. The second is a 52-dimensional vector indicating which of the 52 modifiers exist in each phrase. As a result, a 954-dimensional feature vector is composed for every phrase.

2.3 Regression Models

We deploy a series of regression models to gradually approach the problem from the most generalizable models to the most powerful ones, including ridge regression, Support Vector Regression with RBF kernels (SVR-RBF), and multi-layered feed-forward Neural Networks (NN).

The ridge regression is an L2-regularized linear model which is the simplest and fastest because the optimization has an analytical solution. The SVR-RBF adds a non-linear feature transformation before a linear tube regression, leaving many hyper-parameters to be decided but still guaranteeing global optimum for each set of hyper-parameter values. Finally, NN-flavored models are so powerful that every real-valued functions with close-interval domains can be approximated as good as required. However, there is not a guaranteed selection of training schedules of parameters to reach the global optimum.

We acknowledge the sparsity of the labeled data of this task as well as the difficulties in analyzing the non-linear relationships between features and targets of many natural language tasks. Hence, all these models are explored and searched for good hyper-parameters to give an empirical comparison and a suggestion of the best model.

3 Word VA Predictors

As described by Wang and Ma (2016), three predictors are constructed to solve the dimensional sentiment analysis problem for Chinese words.

3.1 E-HowNet-Based Predictor

The first word VA predictor is based on E-HowNet, an expert-built ontology containing the definitions of and relations between about 90 thousand Chinese words. With the knowledge of the sets of synonyms (synsets), the VA of unlabeled words can be predicted by its synonyms of which VA are known.

If multiple labeled synonyms exist for an unlabeled word, the known VA are averaged to give a single prediction. However, if no labeled synonyms of a word can be found, the predictor would fail to predict its VA.

3.2 Word Embedding-Based Predictor

The second predictor relies on distributional semantics of words to determine their similarity. For every unlabeled word, top 10 similar words with known VA are selected, and their VA are averaged as the prediction.

The predictor gains from the fact that most words have pre-trained word embeddings, and hence seldom fails. However, the root cause of failure, the sparsity of labeled words, is not resolved. While the E-HowNet-based predictor gives better results by enforcing synonymity, the embedding-based predictor traded performance for coverage by considering all labeled words in selecting the most similar ones. As a result, the VA of 惡夢 (nightmare) might be used for 美夢 (good dream) because its word embedding is the closest among all labeled words. Averaging the VA of the 10 most similar words other than selecting the most similar one as the prediction somehow alleviates this problem.

3.3 Character-Based Predictor

To enhance the performance of word arousal predictions, a third predictor based on individual characters to propagate labeled arousal is built. The heuristics is that, for many words or even phrases in Chinese, the semantics of their characters contributes strongly to the semantics of the whole. This holds especially when the composing characters are synonyms or near synonyms, e.g. 踊 (leap) and 躍 (jump) for 踊躍 (enthusiastic). Although the contribution is poetic, we could leverage that the words containing similar characters might have similar arousal levels, e.g. 活躍 (active) and 踊躍.

Specifically, the arousal of a character is computed as the average arousal of the labeled words that contains it. Then the arousal of a testing word is predicted as the average arousal of its composing characters which have arousal computed.

4 Experiments

4.1 Phrase Validation Data

The hyper-parameter values of phrase VA predictor models are selected by their performance on the validation set, and the two top-performing predictors are submitted to be evaluated on the testing set. However, as there are only 2250 labeled phrases, 5-fold cross validation is used to gain more reliable evaluations.

Model	Valence MAE	Valence PCC	Arousal MAE	Arousal PCC
Head Word	1.535	0.432	0.794	0.667
Modifier Multiplication	0.522	0.924	0.572	0.836
Ridge	0.967	0.718	0.419	0.898
SVR-RBF	0.408	0.949	0.371	0.919
NN-(750,600,600,450)	**0.334**	**0.966**	**0.361**	**0.922**

Table 3: Cross validation results on training phrases.

Model	Valence MAE	Valence PCC	Arousal MAE	Arousal PCC
Official Linear Baseline	1.051	0.610	0.607	0.730
CKIP-Run1	0.492	0.921	0.382	0.908
CKIP-Run2	0.444	0.935	0.395	0.904
THU_NGN-Run1	0.349	0.960	0.389	0.909
THU_NGN-Run2	**0.345**	**0.961**	**0.385**	**0.911**

Table 4: Testing results of DSAP best submissions.

Specifically, the 2249 segmented phrases, excluding 不是, are randomly shuffled and the first 5 sets of 449 phrases are used as validation samples in turn. All models then share the same 5-fold split of training data.

In addition, we do not group phrases with the same head words, so for example, 也許喜歡, 本來喜歡, and 可能喜歡 might be in different splits. This simulates the fact that unseen phrases might have the same head words as some labeled phrases. However, this could also suffer from overfitting due to data sparsity.

4.2 Baseline Models

Two explainable models are tested to serve as the baseline for the Chinese phrase VA task. The first one, head word model, predicts the VA of a phrase by that of its head word. The second, modifier-multiplication model, multiplies trainable scalar weights of known modifiers to the head word VA (Equation 1 and Equation 2).

$$v_p = 5 + (v_h - 5) \prod_{m \in M} w_m^v \qquad (1)$$

$$a_p = 1 + (a_h - 1) \prod_{m \in M} w_m^a \qquad (2)$$

p is the testing phrase, h is the head word of p, and M is the set of modifiers of p. v stands for valence, a stands for arousal, and w stands for the trainable weights of each modifier.

The modifier-multiplication model centers head word valence around the median 5, which is presumably the neutrality of opinion polarity. On the other hand, head word arousal are centered around 1, assuming it stands for no excitement. Note that the models degenerate to the head word baseline when all modifier weights default to 1.

Table 3 shows the validation results of the baseline models as well as other models. It can be seen that the multiplication model serves as a strong and explainable baseline.

4.3 Phrase VA Models

Ridge

The ridge regression model has one hyper-parameter: the regularization weight. However, we leave it to be decided by a leave-one-out cross validation of the training split. This gives a non-parametric ridge regression model. As shown in Table 3, it performs worse than the strong baseline on valence but better on arousal.

SVR-RBF

The SVR-RBF model has three hyper-parameters: the error parameter C, the tube parameter ϵ, and the RBF kernel parameter γ. Table 2 shows the trial range of our grid search and the selected best set of values. This non-linear model brings a significant improvement.

NN

Our feed-forward neural networks have a fix L2-regularzation weight of 1. However, we set the possible number of hidden layers to include 1 to 4, and possible dimensions for each layer to include 150, 300, 450, 600, and 750. With a constraint that a layer cannot have a higher dimension

SVR-RBF	Valence MAE	Valence PCC	Arousal MAE	Arousal PCC
h, m, va, mod	0.41	0.95	0.37	**0.92**
m, va, mod	**0.36**	**0.96**	**0.36**	**0.92**
va, mod	0.45	0.93	0.40	0.90
va	1.34	0.44	0.73	0.67
mod	1.31	0.35	0.71	0.66
NN-(300,300,300)	**Valence MAE**	**Valence PCC**	**Arousal MAE**	**Arousal PCC**
h, m, va, mod	**0.34**	**0.97**	**0.36**	**0.92**
m, va, mod	0.37	0.96	0.38	0.91

Table 5: Feature analysis results by cross validation. h stands for the 300d head word embedding, m stands for the 600d modifier embeddings, va stands for the 2d head word VA, and mod stands for the 52d modifier existence vector.

than its previous layer, this yields a total of 125 permutations of network shapes, which will easily explode were a few more dimensions and layers added. Table 3 shows the best configuration, which surpasses other simpler models.

4.4 Phrase VA Test Results

The DSAP shared task releases 750 phrases as the testing set. These phrases have neither VA labels nor modifier information. We use the approaches described in Section 2.1 and Section 2.2 to segment the testing phrases and obtain their 954-dimensional feature vectors.

We submitted the predictions of SVR-RBF and NN, the second and the best performing model in cross validation, as CKIP-Run1 and CKIP-Run2. Our NN model turns out to be one of the best phrase VA predictors, second only to the submissions of team THU_NGN. Table 4 shows these results as well as the official baseline performance of a linear model on word embeddings.

4.5 Phrase VA Feature Analysis

We perform an ablation analysis to shed light on the contributions of each features that lead to highly correlated outputs to the ground truth labels. Table 5 shows the results on cross validation using decreasingly less features. It turns out that just the head word VA plus the information of modifier existence is enough to make highly correlated deductions of phrase VA (above 0.9 PCC), but no single one of them would do. In addition, the contribution of head word embeddings seems to be weak.

4.6 Word VA Test Results

As in the Dimensional Sentiment Analysis of Chinese Words (DSAW) shared task of IALP 2016, An ensemble of the three predictors, the E-HowNet-based, the embedding-based, and the character-based, is used to generate the final submission of testing results. A simple 5:5 ensemble between the E-HowNet-based predictor and the embedding-based predictor (before adding the character-based predictor for arousal) turns out to be one of the best predictors, second only to the submissions of team THU_NGN and team AL_I_NLP. Specifically, 0.602 MAE and 0.858 PCC are achieved for word valence, and 0.949 MAE and 0.576 PCC are achieved for word arousal.

5 Conclusion

We have demonstrated the approaches behind the submissions of team CKIP on the DSAP shared task, and the results on the testing set shows that they are suitable for the task. For the prediction of the valence and the arousal of Chinese phrases, our feature analysis indicates that the non-linear relations between the VA of the head word and the information of modifier appearances are enough to produce highly correlated results to the ground truth. For the prediction of the valence and the arousal of Chinese words, the E-HowNet ontology shows its usefulness again.

The approaches as a whole achieve compelling results for future takes on Chinese sentiment analysis problems, which are expected to be more sophisticated and toward real-world applications.

References

Rafael A Calvo and Sunghwan Mac Kim. 2013. Emotions in Text: Dimensional and Categorical Models. *Computational Intelligence*, 29(3):527–543.

Keh-Jiann Chen, Chu-Ren Huang, Li-Ping Chang, and Hui-Li Hsu. 1996. Sinica Corpus: Design Methodology for Balanced Corpora. *Language*, 167:176.

David Graff and Ke Chen. 2003. Chinese Gigaword LDC2003T09. *Philadelphia: Linguistic Data Consortium*.

Wei-Yun Ma and Keh-Jiann Chen. 2004. Design of CKIP Chinese Word Segmentation System. *International Journal of Asian Language Processing*, 14(3):235–249.

Jeffrey Pennington, Richard Socher, and Christopher D. Manning. 2014. Glove: Global Vectors for Word Representation. In *EMNLP*, volume 14, pages 1532–1543.

Hsin-Yang Wang and Wei-Yun Ma. 2016. CKIP Valence-Arousal Predictor for IALP 2016 Shared Task. In *International Conference on Asian Language Processing*, pages 164–167.

Liang-Chih Yu, Lung-Hao Lee, Shuai Hao, Jin Wang, Yunchao He, Jun Hu, K. Robert Lai, and Xuejie Zhang. 2016. Building Chinese Affective Resources in Valence-Arousal Dimensions. In *Proceedings of the 2016 Conference of the North American Chapter of the Association for Computational Linguistics: Human Language Technologies*, pages 540–545, San Diego, California. Association for Computational Linguistics.

CIAL at IJCNLP-2017 Task 2: An Ensemble Valence-Arousal Analysis System for Chinese Words and Phrases

Zheng-Wen Lin
ISA, National Tsing
Hua University, Taiwan
victorlin12345@gmail.com

Yung-Chun Chang
Graduate Institute of Data Science,
Taipei Medical University, Taiwan
changyc@tmu.edu.tw

Chen-Ann Wang
ISA, National Tsing
Hua University, Taiwan
openan7@gmail.com

Yu-Lun Hsieh
IIS, Academia Sinica, Taiwan
morphe@iis.sinica.edu.tw

Wen-Lian Hsu
IIS, Academia Sinica, Taiwan
hsu@iis.sinica.edu.tw

Abstract

Sentiment lexicon is very helpful in dimensional sentiment applications. Because of countless Chinese words, developing a method to predict unseen Chinese words is required. The proposed method can handle both words and phrases by using an ADVWeight List for word prediction, which in turn improves our performance at phrase level. The evaluation results demonstrate that our system is effective in dimensional sentiment analysis for Chinese phrases. The Mean Absolute Error (MAE) and Pearson's Correlation Coefficient (PCC) for Valence are 0.723 and 0.835, respectively, and those for Arousal are 0.914 and 0.756, respectively.

1 Introduction

Due to the vigorous development of social media in recent years, more and more user-generated sentiment data have been shared on the Web. It is a useful means to understand the opinion of the masses, which is a major issue for businesses. However, they exist in the forms of comments in a live webcast, opinion sites, or social media, and often contain considerable amount of noise. Such characteristics pose obstacles to those who intend to collect this type of information efficiently. It is the reason why opinion mining has recently become a topic of interest in both academia and business institutions. Sentiment analysis is a type of opinion mining where affective states are represented categorically or by multi-dimensional continuous values (Yu et al., 2015). The categorical approach aims at classifying the sentiment into polarity classes (such as positive, neutral, and negative,) or Ekman's six basic emotions, *i.e.*, anger, happiness, fear, sadness, disgust, and surprise (Ek-

man, 1992). This approach is extensively studied because it can provide a desirable outcome, which is an overall evaluation of the sentiment in the material that is being analyzed. For instance, a popular form of media in recent years is live webcasting. This kind of applications usually provide viewers with the ability to comment immediately while the stream is live. Categorical sentiment analysis can immediately classify each response as either positive or negative, thus helping the host to quickly summarize every period of their broadcast.

On the other hand, the dimensional approach represents affective states as continuous numerical values in multiple dimensions, such as valence-arousal space (Markus and Kitayama, 1991), as shown in Fig. 1. The valence represents the de-

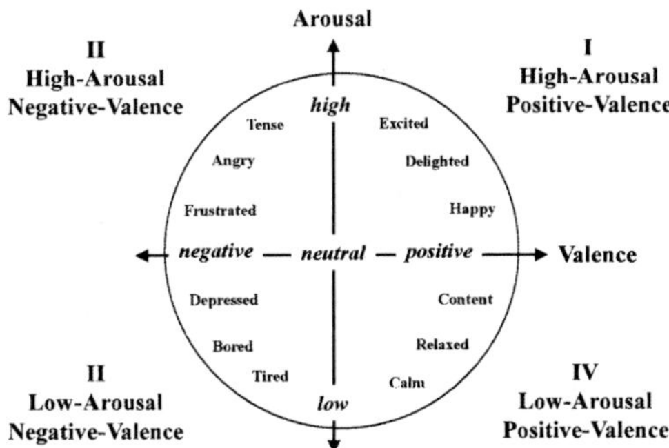

Figure 1: Two-dimensional valence-arousal space.

gree of pleasant and unpleasant (*i.e.*, positive and negative) feelings, while the arousal represents the degree of excitement. According to the two-dimensional representation, any affective state can be represented as a point in the valence-arousal space by determining the degrees of valence and arousal of given words (Wei et al., 2011; Yu et al., 2015) or texts (Kim et al., 2010). Dimen-

Proceedings of the 8th International Joint Conference on Natural Language Processing, Shared Tasks, pages 95–99,
Taipei, Taiwan, November 27 – December 1, 2017. ©2017 AFNLP

sional sentiment analysis is an increasingly active research field with potential applications including antisocial behavior detection (Munezero et al., 2011) and mood analysis (De Choudhury et al., 2012).

In light of this, the objective of the Dimensional Sentiment Analysis for Chinese Words (DSAW) shared task at the 21th International Conference on Asian Language Processing is to automatically acquire the valence-arousal ratings of Chinese affective words and phrases for compiling Chinese valence-arousal lexicons. The expected output of this task is to predict a real-valued score from 1 to 9 for both valence and arousal dimensions of the given 750 test words and phrases. The score indicates the degree from most negative to most positive for valence, and from most calm to most excited for arousal. The performance is evaluated by calculating mean absolute error and Pearson correlation coefficient between predicted and human-annotated reference scores for two dimensions separately. Participants are required to predict a valence-arousal score for each word, and each phrase.

In order to tackle this problem at the word level, we propose a hybrid approach that integrates valence extension and word embedding-based model with cos similarity to predict valence dimensions. Word embedding-based model with SVM and regression to predict arousal dimensions. At phrase level, we use our ADVWeight List extracted from training sets and our word level method to predict both valence and arousal.

The remainder of this paper is organized as follows. The proposed method is in Section 2. In Section 3, we evaluate performance and compare it with other methods. Finally, some conclusions are listed in Section 4.

2 Method

This study takes 2,802 single words in CVAW 2.0 (Yu et al., 2016) and 2,250 multi-word phrases, both annotated with valence-arousal ratings, as training material. At word level, we use E-HowNet (Chen et al., 2005), a system that is designed for the purpose of automatic semantic composition and decomposition, to extract synonyms of the words from CVAW 2.0, and expand it to 19,611 words with valence-arousal ratings, called WVA. Fig. 2 illustrates the proposed framework. In order to cope with the problem of unknown

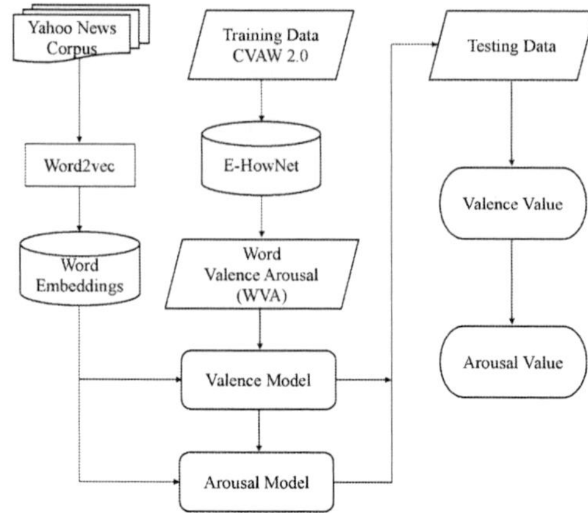

Figure 2: Process of Word Emotional dimension model construction.

words, we separate words in WVA into 4,184 characters with valence-arousal ratings, called CVA. The valence-arousal score of the unknown word can be obtained by averaging the matched CVA. Moreover, previous research suggested that it is possible to improve the performance by aggregating the results of a number of valence-arousal methods (Yu et al., 2015). Thus, we use two sets of methods for the prediction of valence: (1) prediction based on WVA and CVA, and (2) a kNN valence prediction method. The results of these two methods are averaged as the final valence score.

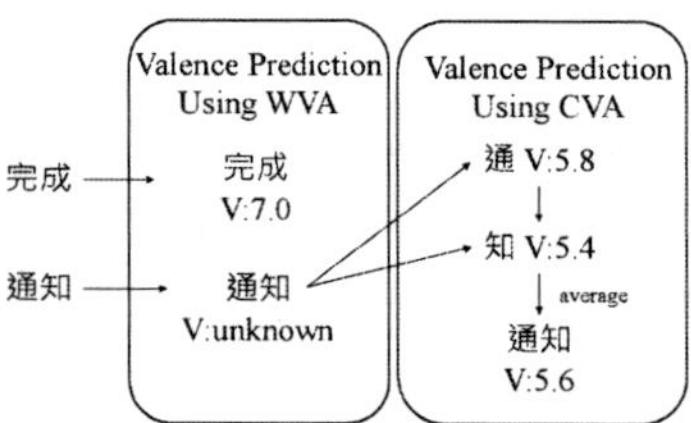

Figure 3: Word Valence prediction method based on WVA and CVA.

First, we describe the prediction of valence values. As shown in Fig. 3, the "完成" of the test data exists in the WVA, so we can directly obtain its valence value of 7.0. However, another word "通知" does not exist in the WVA, so we search in CVA and calculate a valence value of 5.6. Additionally, we propose another prediction method of the valence value, as shown in Fig. 4, based on kNN. We begin by computing the similarity between words using word embeddings(Mikolov et al., 2013). Then, 10 most similar words are selected and their scores calculated by Eq. 1.

$$\text{Valence}_{\text{KNN}} = \frac{\sum_{i=1}^{x} N_x}{X} \tag{1}$$

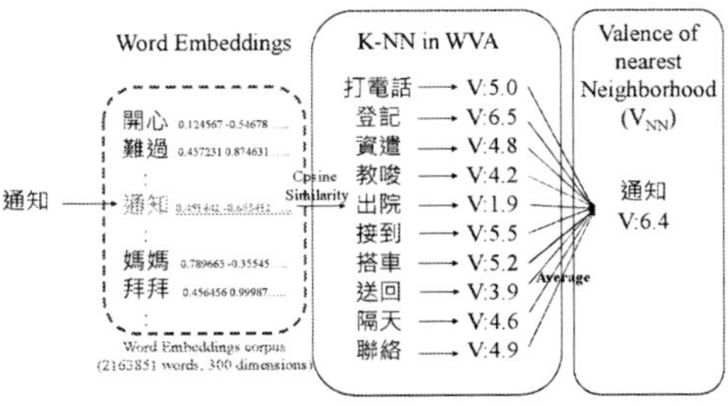

Figure 4: Word valence prediction method based on kNN.

As for the arousal prediction, we propose two methods: (1) linear regression, and (2) support vector regression (SVR) which averages linear regression and SVM predictions as the final arousal score. As shown in Fig. 6, this study considers the linear regression equation in each range according to the valence-arousal value of words in WVA. According to our observation of the data, valence values are generally distributed in the value of 3-7. In order to boost learning of different ranges of data, we distribute them in to two categories. For example, the work "殺害" has a valence value of 1.6. By our design, it will be distributed to categories with valance value of 1 and 2. When the linear regression training is finished, we can predict the corresponding arousal score according to the valence value of the word. As for the SVR-based approach, we first train 300-dimensional word embeddings for all words in WVA using online Chinese news corpus[1]. As shown in Fig. 6, L is the label of the sample, and Dim represents the dimension of the features. We then predict the value of arousal through SVR. Finally, we aggregate the arousal scores predicted by these two methods by taking an average. We observe that the values obtained by linear regression are convergent, while the SVR values are more divergent. So, averaging of the two values can overcome the shortcomings of these methods.

At phrase level, we first experiment with using the proposed word-level model to predict the va-

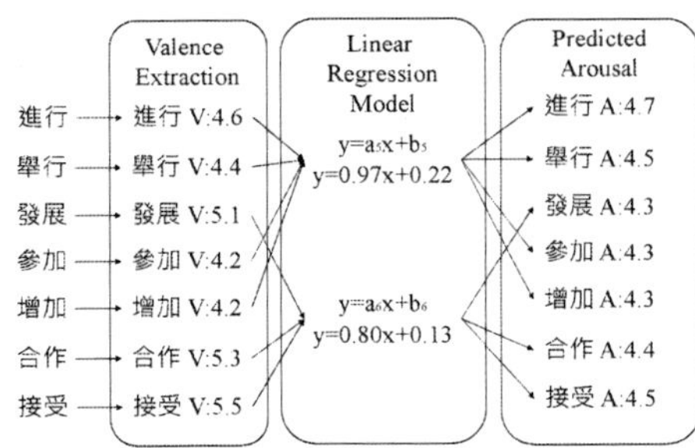

Figure 5: Arousal prediction method based on linear regression.

lence and arousal values. Unfortunately, the results are not satisfactory. We then explore the possibility to incorporate linguistic knowledge into the model. Structurally, phrases can be split into the adverb (ADV) and the adjective (ADJ). An adverb is a word that modifies an adjective in a phrase. For instance, "開心" (happy) with a preceding "非常 (very)" becomes "非常開心 (very happy)," which we consider has an increased degree of happiness. Following this line of thought, we explore ADVs as weighting factors for ADJs. The ADVList and ADVWeight List are extracted from 2,250 multi-word phrases. We employ them to split phrases into ADV and ADJ parts. Subsequently, the valence and arousal values of an ADJ is determined by the word-level prediction model, while those of the ADV is used as an offset. An illustration of our phrase-level prediction process is in Fig. 7.

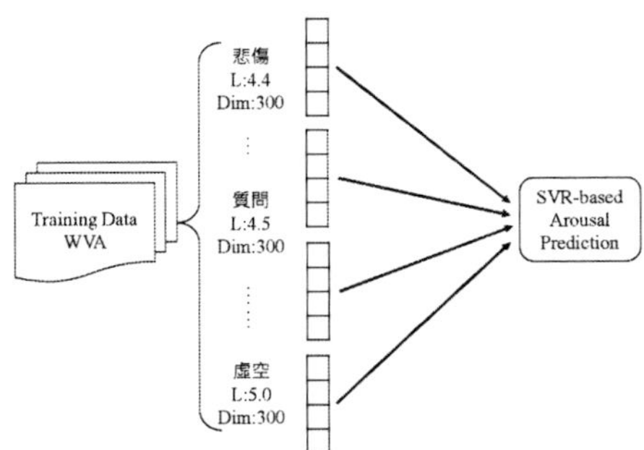

Figure 6: Arousal prediction method based on support vector regression (SVR).

As shown in Fig. 7, in order to obtain the weight of the ADV word "最," we need to use ADVList to split phrases that contain "最" into the format of "[ADV] [ADJ]." Then, our word prediction

---

[1]Collected from Yahoo News between years 2007–2017.

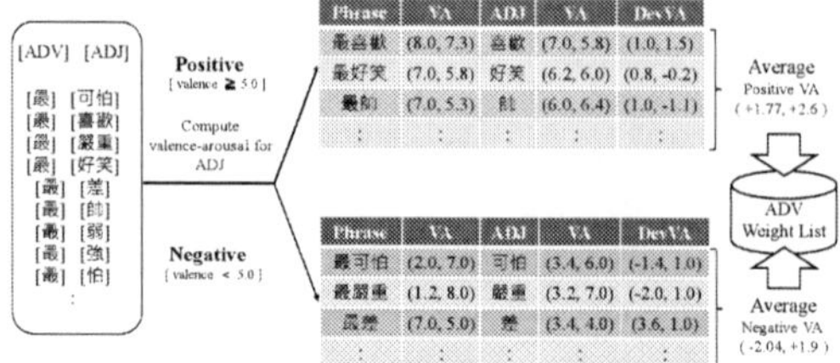

Figure 7: ADV Weight List construction.

model is used to obtain valence (VA) value of the ADJ part. It will be deducted from the VA of the corresponding phrases, and then the remainders are averaged to become the final ADV weight of the word "最". That is, ADVWeight(最) $=$ mean($VA_{Phrase} - VA_{ADJ}$). Most importantly, we hypothesize that ADVs have different effects on phrases with different ADJs, namely, those with valence values ≥ 5.0 and < 5.0. Thus, we have to consider them separately. In the end, there will be four weights for the ADV "最": Positive valence offset, Positive arousal offset, Negative valence offset, and Negative arousal offset.

3 Experiments

We utilize the test data in DSAP_TestW_Input, which contains 750 samples, for performance evaluation. The metrics used are mean absolute error (Mean Absolute Error) and Pearson Correlation Coefficient ($P < 0.01$). In this shared task, valence and arousal values are evaluated separately.

Table 1 shows the results of valence's performance evaluation, V_{WVA} is the result of WVA alone, and V_{CVA} is the result of CVA. V_{WCVA} is the combination of WVA and CVA of the forecast results. V_{kNN} is a valence prediction method based on kNN. V_{WVAE} is in WVA through word embeddings to find 10 neighbors, and take the average. Through the comparison of performance, we found that V_{WCVA} and V_{WVAE} obtained good results with MAEs being 0.527 and 0.508, respectively, and the PCCs are 0.816 and 0.824. These results suggest that they are highly relevant, so we try to combine the two methods (namely, V_{mixed}.) The final MAE and PCC were 0.496 and 0.845, which is the best-performing method.

Table 2 shows the performance of arousal for different regression methods. $R_{Polyfit}$ and R_{Linear} use Polyfit Regression and Linear Regression to predict arousal, while R_{WVA} is based on linear regression. In addition, S_{CVAW} and S_{WVA} use non-corpusated SVR models. R_{WVA} achieved an outstanding performance of an MAE of 0.939, but was the worst performer in PCC; S_{WVA} was slightly inferior to R_{WVA} in MAE, but was superior in PCC with a value of 0.427. Notably, the values predicted by S_{WVA} are evenly distributed and are more similar to the actual answers, so we try to combine the two methods (RS) to achieve a performance of 0.858 and 0.474 on MAE and PCC, achieving the most outstanding results.

Table 1: Valence method performance.

	V_{WVA}	V_{CVA}	V_{WCVA}	V_{kNN}	V_{WVAE}	V_{mixed}
MAE_V	0.701	0.616	0.527	0.778	0.508	0.496
PCC_V	0.831	0.795	0.816	0.728	0.824	0.845

Table 2: Arousal method performance.

	$R_{Polyfit}$	R_{Linear}	R_{WVA}	S_{CVAW}	S_{WVA}	RS
MAE_A	1.043	0.953	0.939	1.281	1.003	0.858
PCC_A	0.294	0.296	-0.003	0.367	0.471	0.474

Table 3: Average word-level score and rank of runs 1 and 2 from the participating teams.

Team	V_{MAE}	V_{PCC}	A_{MAE}	A_{PCC}	Rank
AL_I_NLP	0.546	0.8915	0.855	0.6725	1
THU_NGN	0.5595	0.8825	0.9022	0.6545	2
NCTU-NTUT	0.6355	0.844	0.946	0.5545	4
CKIP	0.6335	0.8565	1.041	0.5725	4.5
MainiwayAI	0.7105	0.798	1.0085	0.5305	5.5
CIAL	0.644	0.8515	1.0375	0.4245	6.5
XMUT	0.946	0.701	1.036	0.451	7.5
CASIA	0.725	0.803	1.036	0.451	7.5
Baseline	0.984	0.643	1.031	0.456	8.6
FZU-NLP	1.015	0.645	1.1155	0.4125	10.75
SAM	1.098	0.639	1.027	0.378	10.75
NCYU	1.0785	0.654	1.166	0.415	11.25
NTOU	0.987	0.622	1.1235	0.2565	12.25
NLPSA	1.054	0.5825	1.207	0.351	13.25

Table 3 lists the averaged word-level score and rank of runs 1 and 2 from the participating teams. The Rank column in Table 3 represents the averaged rank of each team. The best-performing team, AL_I_NLP, obtained 0.546 in V_{MAE}, 0.8915 in V_{PCC}, 0.855 in A_{MAE}, and 0.6725 in A_{PCC}. Our method (CIAL) only rank in the middle.

Table 4 lists the averaged phrase-level score and rank of runs 1 and 2 from the participating teams. The Rank column in Table 4 represents the averaged rank of each team. The best-performing team, THU_NGN, obtained 0.347 in

Table 4: Average phrase-level score and rank of runs 1 and 2 from the participating teams.

Team	V_{MAE}	V_{PCC}	A_{MAE}	A_{PCC}	Rank
THU_NGN	0.347	0.9605	0.387	0.91	1
CKIP	0.468	0.928	0.3885	0.906	2.75
NTOU	0.4625	0.9195	0.4305	0.876	3.25
NCTU-NTUT	0.4535	0.9295	0.5025	0.8395	3.5
AL_I_NLP	0.5285	0.9005	0.465	0.8545	4.5
MainiwayAI	0.5945	0.8675	0.539	0.803	6
NLPSA	0.699	0.8235	0.6325	0.7295	7.75
FZU-NLP	0.869	0.697	0.5477	0.785	8
SAM	0.96	0.669	0.722	0.704	10
CIAL	0.9375	0.741	1.255	0.521	11
NCYU	1.105	0.6975	0.768	0.668	11
Baseline	1.051	0.61	0.61	0.61	11
CASIA	1.008	0.598	0.816	0.683	11.5
XMUT	1.723	0.064	1.163	0.084	13.75

V_{MAE}, 0.9695 in V_{PCC}, 0.387 in A_{MAE}, and 0.91 in A_{PCC}. Our method (CIAL) surpasses baseline.

4 Conclusion

The system we developed for DSAW integrates E-HowNet and word embeddings with K-Nearest Neighbors in valence dimension. Support vector regression and linear regression in arousal dimensions. The evaluation results show that the system performance outperforms previous work, but only achieves mediocre performance in this competition. Since the method we used for arousal prediction is still very straightforward, addressing the improvement of its performance should be our target for future research of dimensional sentiment analysis.

Acknowledgments

We are grateful for the constructive comments from three anonymous reviewers. This work was supported by grant MOST106-3114-E-001-002 and MOST105-2221-E-001-008-MY3 from the Ministry of Science and Technology, Taiwan.

References

Keh-Jiann Chen, Shu-Ling Huang, Yueh-Yin Shih, and Yi-Jun Chen. 2005. Extended-HowNet – a representational framework for concepts. In *Proceedings of OntoLex 2005 - Ontologies and Lexical Resources IJCNLP-05 Workshop*.

Munmun De Choudhury, Scott Counts, and Michael Gamon. 2012. Not all moods are created equal! exploring human emotional states in social media. In *Sixth international AAAI conference on weblogs and social media*.

Paul Ekman. 1992. An argument for basic emotions. *Cognition & emotion* 6(3-4):169–200.

Sunghwan Mac Kim, Alessandro Valitutti, and Rafael A Calvo. 2010. Evaluation of unsupervised emotion models to textual affect recognition. In *Proceedings of the NAACL HLT 2010 Workshop on Computational Approaches to Analysis and Generation of Emotion in Text*. Association for Computational Linguistics, pages 62–70.

Hazel R Markus and Shinobu Kitayama. 1991. Culture and the self: Implications for cognition, emotion, and motivation. *Psychological review* 98(2):224.

Tomas Mikolov, Ilya Sutskever, Kai Chen, Greg S Corrado, and Jeff Dean. 2013. Distributed representations of words and phrases and their compositionality. In *Advances in neural information processing systems*. pages 3111–3119.

Myriam Munezero, Tuomo Kakkonen, and Calkin S Montero. 2011. Towards automatic detection of antisocial behavior from texts. *Sentiment Analysis where AI meets Psychology (SAAIP)* page 20.

Wen-Li Wei, Chung-Hsien Wu, and Jen-Chun Lin. 2011. A regression approach to affective rating of chinese words from anew. *Affective Computing and Intelligent Interaction* pages 121–131.

Liang-Chih Yu, Lung-Hao Lee, Shuai Hao, Jin Wang, Yunchao He, Jun Hu, K Robert Lai, and Xue-jie Zhang. 2016. Building chinese affective resources in valence-arousal dimensions. In *NAACL/HLT-16*. pages 540–545.

Liang-Chih Yu, Jin Wang, K Robert Lai, and Xue-jie Zhang. 2015. Predicting valence-arousal ratings of words using a weighted graph method. In *ACL (2)*. pages 788–793.

Alibaba at IJCNLP-2017 Task 2: A Boosted Deep System for Dimensional Sentiment Analysis of Chinese Phrases

Xin Zhou and **Jian Wang** and **Xu Xie** and **Changlong Sun** and **Luo Si**
{eric.zx,eric.wj,Xu.Xie,luo.si}@alibaba-inc.com
changlong.scl@taobao.com

Abstract

This paper introduces Team Alibabas systems participating IJCNLP 2017 shared task No. 2 Dimensional Sentiment Analysis for Chinese Phrases (DSAP). The systems mainly utilize a multi-layer neural networks, with multiple features input such as word embedding, part-of-speech-tagging (POST), word clustering, prefix type, character embedding, cross sentiment input, and AdaBoost method for model training. For word level task our best run achieved MAE 0.545 (ranked 2nd), PCC 0.892 (ranked 2nd) in valence prediction and MAE 0.857 (ranked 1st), PCC 0.678 (ranked 2nd) in arousal prediction. For average performance of word and phrase task we achieved MAE 0.5355 (ranked 3rd), PCC 0.8965 (ranked 3rd) in valence prediction and MAE 0.661 (ranked 3rd), PCC 0.766 (ranked 2nd) in arousal prediction. In the final our submitted system achieved 2nd in mean rank.

1 Introduction

The task is to predict the affective states of a given (traditional) Chinese word in a continuous numerical value (score from 1 to 9) in the two-dimensional valence-arousal (V-A) space (Yu et al., 2016), indicating the degree from most negative to most positive for valence, and from most calm to most excited for arousal, which is the same as 2016s task. And in addition, predict the affective states of a given (traditional) Chinese phrase in the same V-A space. A human-tagged training data set containing 2802 words and 2250 phrases is used as the training set, another set of 750 words and 750 phrases is used as testing set. The result is measured by Mean Absolute Error (MAE) and Pearson Correlation Coefficient (PCC) respectively.

This paper aims to present an introduction to Team Alibabas systems: data resources, feature engineering, model construction, and evaluation.

2 Chinese Corpus for Model Training

We have used the following text corpus with gratefulness for the openness of knowledge sharing.

1. Chinese Wikipedia dump with time stamp of 2017-07-20. There are over 1.3 million articles. Download link is at `https://dumps.wikimedia.org/zhwiki/20170720/`

2. Several forums dump (hot, boy-girl, movie, etc) from Taiwan online discussion board `https://www.ptt.cc/bbs`. There are around 70,000 articles. In addition to the main body, there are also 10 to 20 user comments in each article.

3. Liberty News Times articles from 2016-01-01 to 2017-08-15. We have used several sub-boards include Focus, Politics, Society, Local, Movie and Sports. There are around 100,000 articles.

All corpus is normalized to simplified Chinese characters before input into word embedding training. And after some evaluation only the first two sets of corpus are used to train the final model for V-A prediction.

Proceedings of the 8th International Joint Conference on Natural Language Processing, Shared Tasks, pages 100–104,
Taipei, Taiwan, November 27 – December 1, 2017. ©2017 AFNLP

3 Word Embedding

Although in the final model there are multiple features input, it is worthwhile describing word embedding in more details, because first, it has been a widely used representation of Chinese sentiment and semantic aspects recently, and second, it is also the input for other feature engineering. In our work, we have tried the following methods for word embedding in word V-A modeling.

- word2vec

  We have used open source python toolkit Gensim (Khosrovian et al., 2008) package. Skip-gram (Mikolov et al., 2013) methods are explored.

  These CWE models are trained with window size of 5, 15 iterations, 5 negative examples, minimum word count of 10, Skip-Gram (Mikolov et al., 2013) with starting learning rate of 0.025 , the output word vectors are of 300 dimensions.

- GloVe

  GloVe (Pennington et al., 2014) is an unsupervised learning algorithm for obtaining vector representations for words.

  The GloVe model is trained with window size of 8, minimum word count of 5 and maximum iteration of 20, the output word vectors are of 300 dimensions.

- Character-enhanced word embedding (CWE)

  Character-enhanced word embedding (Chen et al., 2015) (CWE) leverage composing characters to model the semantic meaning of word which shows effectiveness.

  The model setting is same as that of word2vec.

- cw2vec

  Cw2vec (Cao et al., 2017) proposes a stroke n-gram method for better handling of Chinese characters than Roman alphabets. An analogy to FastText (Bojanowski et al., 2016) that use sub-word information to enrich word embedding can help understand the method: in Chinese characters stroke n-gram is used as sub-word.

  The model setting is same as that of word2vec.

Different word embedding schemes are evaluated for both word and phrase level.

For phrase V-A modeling, word segmentation and average pooling are performed, and then word2vec is used to output word embedding.

4 Feature Engineering

In this section other more complex features are in addition to word embedding will be introduced.

For word level modeling

- CE: Average pooling of character embedding with 300 dimensions. The character embedding is trained with cw2vec as in section 3.

- CLU: Cluster feature of word. We use K-means to obtain 300 clusters with the word embedding trained with cw2vec as in section 3 and then represent the word cluster by one hot vector of 300 dimensions.

- POS: Part-of-speech-tagging (POST) of words containing verb, adverb, adjective, noun.

- VA: Words valence value used in arousal model training, and vice versa. The feature is represented by a one-dimension vector normalized to 1.

- POL: The polarity of word in NTUSD sentiment lexicon dictionary. The polarity of word is either positive of negative. The NTUSD sentiment dictionary is available at http://academiasinicanlplab. github.io/

For phrase level modeling

- TYPE: The prefix word of each phrase contains degree word (DEG),negative (NEG) word and modal word (MOD). As a result the prefix type is categorized into DEG / DEG-NEG /NEG-DEG / MOD-DEG / NEG / MOD-NEG / MOD. For example the type of "DEG-NEG" means the phase has a prefix with a degree word followed by a negative word. There are 7 prefix types, so this feature is represented by one hot vector of 7 dimensions.

- TAG: Word type feature. There are 4 types of words in the phrase - degree word (DEG), negative word (NEG), modal word (MOD), sentiment word (SEN), so each word type can be represented by a one hot vector of 4 dimensions. Finally the TAG feature is represented by a concatenation of word type vector.

- CE: Same as word level

5 Model Construction

Inspired by (Du and Zhang, 2016) in submitted system, boosted neural network is used. Adaptive-Boosting (AdaBoosting) (Freund et al., 1996; Drucker, 1997) is used as boosting algorithm and there are 30 base regression models as most.

Neural network is used as base regression model with relu (Glorot et al., 2011) as activation function and Adam (Kingma and Ba, 2014) as its training algorithm and a constant learning rate of 0.001. For word V-A modeling the neural network is with 5 hidden layers and each layer is with 100/100/50/50/20 neurons. For phrase V-A modeling a one-layer neutral of 100 neurons in size network is used.

6 Evaluation

Evaluation is conducted locally by mean value of 5 rounds of 10 folds cross validation on training data, each round has constant and unique random seed.

6.1 Word level task

For word level we evaluate the performance of different word embedding methods and then we fix the word embedding type and evaluate different features.All manual features are converted to one hot vector or dense vector as a part of the input layer of neural network in addition to embedding features.

Word embedding comparison

Different embedding methods in section 3 are evaluated with boosted neural network, and we only report skip-gram schema in word2vec, CWE and cw2vec.

In Table 1, cw2vec outperforms all and CWE is slightly better than word2vec. Maybe we don't obtain the best hyper parameter so that GloVe gets worst performance.

Feature comparison

Different features in section 4 are evaluated in this part. WE denotes word embedding feature and other symbol are as listed in section 4.

Embeddings	Valence		Arousal	
	MAE	PCC	MAE	PCC
GloVe	0.605	0.809	1.241	0.618
word2vec	0.531	0.896	0.739	0.718
CWE	0.527	0.899	0.731	0.728
cw2vec	0.493	0.911	0.722	0.733

Table 1: Embedding comparison for word level

Features	Valence		Arousal	
	MAE	PCC	MAE	PCC
WE	0.493	0.911	0.722	0.733
WE+POS	0.491	0.913	0.723	0.734
WE+CE	0.460	0.924	0.683	0.768
WE+VA	0.495	0.908	0.723	0.726
WE+CE+POS	0.460	0.924	0.682	0.770
WE+CE+POL	0.437	0.932	0.677	0.773
WE+CE+POS+POL	0.435	0.933	0.675	0.773
WE+CE+POS+POL+CLU	0.413	0.938	0.567	0.840

Table 2: Feature comparison for word level

In Table 2, we can see CE (character embedding feature) and CLU(cluster feature) improve performance significantly. SEN (polarity feature) benefits valence prediction over arousal prediction, while POS feature and VA feature improve model performance slightly.

6.2 Phrase level task

For phrase level we also evaluate different pooling approaches besides the comparisons in word level task.

Embedding comparison

For phrase level experiment, phrase are segmented into words and use average pooling of word embedding to denote the phrase.

In Table 3 different from word level experiment word2vec achieves the best performance and GloVe under-performs other methods. Cw2vec is slightly better than CWE.

Embedding pooling comparison

As word2vec is fixed we evaluate the maximum pooling and average pooling. Table 4 shows average pooling is obviously better than maximum pooling as expected.

Features comparison

Now we have fixed the the embedding method

Embeddings	Valence		Arousal	
	MAE	PCC	MAE	PCC
GloVe	0.551	0.866	0.879	0.612
word2vec	0.462	0.937	0.434	0.883
CWE	0.479	0.929	0.439	0.88
cw2vec	0.475	0.934	0.438	0.881

Table 3: Embedding comparison for phrase level

Pooling	Valence		Arousal	
	MAE	PCC	MAE	PCC
average pooling	0.462	0.937	0.434	0.883
max pooling	0.590	0.897	0.610	0.851

Table 4: Pooling comparison for phrase level

Embeddings	Valence		Arousal	
	MAE	PCC	MAE	PCC
AWE	0.462	0.938	0.434	0.883
AWE+CE	0.463	0.937	0.434	0.884
AWE+POL	0.434	0.945	0.436	0.884
AWE+TAG	0.427	0.945	0.398	0.901
AWE+TYPE	0.416	0.948	0.396	0.903
AWE+TAG+POL	0.393	0.953	0.398	0.901
AWE+TYPE+POL	0.192	0.988	0.224	0.967

Table 5: Feature comparison for phrase level

to word2vec and average pooling is used. In this part AWE denotes average pooling of word embeddings, CE denotes average pooling of character embeddings. POL is a concatenation of one hot vector in words of phrase segmentation and padding 0 upto the longest length, so is TAG. Other features are described in section 4.

Table 5 presents the result that CE (character embedding feature) doesn't achieves positive result while TAG and TYPE and POL achieve extremely good performance. From the experiment we figure out the prefix type and polarity feature contains rich information for this task.

In the final submission for word level task, we use all features above. Run2 is an average boosted neural network applied with word embedding features on cw2vec and CWE while Run1 is generated on cw2vec alone. For phrase level task AWE, TYPE and POL are the best features used in Run1 and Run2. Run1 and Run2 use the same features and method with different random initial parameters for boosted neural network.

7 Conclusion

This system paper demonstrates Alibabas system for Dimensional Sentiment Analysis of Chinese Words and Phrases. We use boosted neural network as model for both word and phrase task. For word task cw2vec word embedding, average character embedding, cluster feature and polarity are identified as the best features. For phrase task word2vec word embedding, prefix type and polarity are identified as the best features. In the final test set we achieved MAE 0.545, PCC 0.892 in word valence estimation and MAE 0.857, PCC 0.678 in word arousal estimation and achieved MAE 0.526, PCC 0.901 in phrase valence estimation and MAE 0.465, PCC 0.854 in phrase arousal estimation. For average performance of word and phrase task we achieved MAE 0.5355(3rd), PCC 0.8965(3rd) in valence prediction and MAE 0.661(3rd), PCC 0.766(2nd) in arousal prediction. Our final submitted system achieved 2nd place in mean rank.

References

Piotr Bojanowski, Edouard Grave, Armand Joulin, and Tomas Mikolov. 2016. Enriching word vectors with subword information. *arXiv preprint arXiv:1607.04606*.

Shaosheng Cao, Wei Lu, Jun Zhou, and Xiaolong Li. 2017. Investigating chinese word embeddings based on stroke information.

Xinxiong Chen, Lei Xu, Zhiyuan Liu, Maosong Sun, and Huan-Bo Luan. 2015. Joint learning of character and word embeddings. In *IJCAI*, pages 1236–1242.

Harris Drucker. 1997. Improving regressors using boosting techniques. In *ICML*, volume 97, pages 107–115.

Steven Du and Xi Zhang. 2016. Aicyber's system for ialp 2016 shared task: Character-enhanced word vectors and boosted neural networks. In *Asian Language Processing (IALP), 2016 International Conference on*, pages 161–163. IEEE.

Yoav Freund, Robert E Schapire, et al. 1996. Experiments with a new boosting algorithm. In *Icml*, volume 96, pages 148–156.

Xavier Glorot, Antoine Bordes, and Yoshua Bengio. 2011. Deep sparse rectifier neural networks. In *Proceedings of the Fourteenth International Conference on Artificial Intelligence and Statistics*, pages 315–323.

Keyvan Khosrovian, Dietmar Pfahl, and Vahid Garousi. 2008. Gensim 2.0: a customizable process simulation model for software process evaluation. *Making Globally Distributed Software Development a Success Story*, pages 294–306.

Diederik Kingma and Jimmy Ba. 2014. Adam: A method for stochastic optimization. *arXiv preprint arXiv:1412.6980*.

Tomas Mikolov, Ilya Sutskever, Kai Chen, Greg S Corrado, and Jeff Dean. 2013. Distributed representations of words and phrases and their compositionality. In *Advances in neural information processing systems*, pages 3111–3119.

Jeffrey Pennington, Richard Socher, and Christopher Manning. 2014. Glove: Global vectors for word representation. In *Proceedings of the 2014 conference on empirical methods in natural language processing (EMNLP)*, pages 1532–1543.

Liang-Chih Yu, Lung-Hao Lee, Shuai Hao, Jin Wang, Yunchao He, Jun Hu, K Robert Lai, and Xue-jie Zhang. 2016. Building chinese affective resources in valence-arousal dimensions. In *HLT-NAACL*, pages 540–545.

NLPSA at IJCNLP-2017 Task 2:
Imagine Scenario: Leveraging Supportive Images for Dimensional Sentiment Analysis

Szu-Min Chen, Zi-Yuan Chen, Lun-Wei Ku
Academia Sinica
128 Academia Road, Section2
Nankang, Taipei 11529, Taiwan
{b02902026, b02902017}@ntu.edu.tw
lwku@iis.sinica.edu.tw

Abstract

Categorical sentiment classification has drawn much attention in the field of NLP, while less work has been conducted for dimensional sentiment analysis (DSA). Recent works for DSA utilize either word embedding, knowledge base features, or bilingual language resources. In this paper, we propose our model for IJCNLP 2017 Dimensional Sentiment Analysis for Chinese Phrases shared task. Our model incorporates word embedding as well as image features, attempting to simulate human's imaging behavior toward sentiment analysis. Though the performance is not comparable to others in the end, we conduct several experiments with possible reasons discussed, and analyze the drawbacks of our model.

1 Introduction

Dimensional Sentiment prediction is a subcategory of sentiment analysis. Traditionally, the goal of the sentiment classification task is either binary, mostly positive and negative, or categorical, such as happy, angry, and sad(Pang et al., 2002; Rosenthal et al., 2017). Instead of categorizing different emotions to a fixed number of classes, the dimensional approach projects each emotion to valence-arousal (VA) space. Valence indicates the level of pleasant and unpleasant, while arousal shows the level of excitement and calm. This methodology has drawn more attention recently since the valence-arousal space is continuous comparing to the discrete classes used previously, so it implies the better capability to describe the emotion, while better benefiting downstream model for further application.

In this paper we propose our model participating in the IJCNLP 2017 dimensional sentiment analysis shared task in which participants are asked to predict the numerical valence-arousal on words and phrases. For details of the shared task, 2,802 words are given for training and 750 words are for testing; 2,250 and 750 phrases are provided in the phrase track, for training and testing respectively. Phrases are composed by at least one of the degree, negation or modal with a word. Degree stands the level for the feeling, negation means the negative of the feeling, and modal represents the frequency of the feeling. Examples can be found in Table 2. And the type of modifier of each phrase is given, as shown in Table 3. The predict result is evaluated by the organizer with the mean absolute error (MAE) and the Pearson correlation coefficient (PCC) (Pearson, 1895) as metrics.

Recent approaches tackling the VA prediction problem on word and phrase includes neural-network based method and graphical-based method, with detail described in Section 3. However, the former suffers from the insufficient data, especially data in Chinese, while the latter heavily utilizes pretrained word-embedding which mostly capture syntactic features of words but not semantic features.

We therefore consider the way how human will determine sentiment of given words or phrases. In our experience, humans imagine the scene when they are given such word or phrase. For example, when humans heard the word "欣喜若狂"(ecstatic), they will think of acclamation, laughter on faces, and other positive scenes, as shown in Figure 1. These imaginations can be regarded as contexts of the word "欣喜若狂"(ecstatic), which helps humans decide the degree of positive/negative and exciting/calm of the word.

Considering the data inadequacy of annotated

Proceedings of the 8th International Joint Conference on Natural Language Processing, Shared Tasks, pages 105–111,
Taipei, Taiwan, November 27 – December 1, 2017. ©2017 AFNLP

Figure 1: The example of scene that people may imagine with the word "欣喜若狂"(ecstatic). These images are directly downloaded from the Internet.

Word		
Word	Valence	Arousal
成功(success)	8.2	6.6
暗殺(assassinate)	1.8	6
狂喜(ecstatic)	8.6	8.8
Phrase		
Phrase	Valence	Arousal
最爲出色(most excellent)	8.056	6.288
極度失望(very disappoint)	1.63	7.244
略爲放鬆(little relaxing)	6.2	1.2

Table 1: Examples of word and phrase training instances.

VA corpus and the behavior of human, we proposed a model that takes the word as well as the images related to that word, which are directly downloaded from internet, as input. The key idea is to leverage the huge amount of information on the Internet and the feature extraction ability of convolution neural network to overcome the small size of annotated datas, and also balance the importance of word embedding with respect to the view from model.

The rest of this paper is organized as following: Section 2 overviews the shared task,related works are reviews in Section 3, Section 4 illustrates our valence-arousal prediction with image model, Section 5 is for the experiment and the result,the experimental results are discussed and analyzed in Section 6, and Section 7 concludes the paper with future works.

2 Related Work

There are several different methods toward the VA prediction task, some researches about the valence arousal prediction on paragraphs are conducted (Wang et al., 2016b; Nicolaou et al., 2011), while

degree	negation	modal
十分(really)	不能(cannot)	也許(maybe)
稍微(little)	沒(no)	本來(originally)
超級(very)	沒有(no)	應該(perhaps)

Table 2: Examples of degree, negation, modifier in phrase

modifier's type	phrase
deg	異常驚人
neg_deg	沒有太驚訝
mod_neg	本來不支持

Table 3: Examples of types of modifiers and corresponding phrases. "deg", "neg", "mod" stand for "degree", "negation", "modal" respectively. Besides, the "_" symbol denotes combinations of modifiers in order. The three phrases in second column represent "extraordinarily surprising", "not too surprised", and "was not supported originally" in English, respectively.

in this work, our goal is to directly predict the values of valence and arousal on words and phrases only. Thus, we will discuss those works which utilize the words and some kinds of auxiliary information, like the translation from English to Chinese or word tag from Wordnet, but do not incorporate the context information, like a sentence annotated with VA score. Also, we will briefly cover some works corresponding to image sentiment classification.

2.1 Graph-Based Approach

In the work of (Yu et al., 2015), the objective is to predict the V and A score for each single word. The method proposed is a weighted graph model, each vertex is a vector representation of a word, and the edge is weighted by the cosine similarity between two words. The unseen words use the neighboring seed words' labeled scores, which weighted by the similarity, to update themselves' score. This can be considered an iterative process and will loop until converge, and since the similarity is calculated based on word embedding, it is critical that the word embedding used in training can indeed represent the relationship between word with respect to sentiment. In the work of (Wang et al., 2016a), they try to deal with the task by purposing a community-based method. They define a *Modularity* term which can be viewed as the difference between the sum of all similarities between words within a community C, and the sum of all similarities between words in C and all the other words that not belongs to C. The training step is to maximize the modularity term with respect to all communities. After convergence they treat each community as a new graph and predict unseen words' rating from their neighbors. A main drawback of graph-based method is that they almost depend solely on the information provided by word embedding which contain inadequate semantic features, thus make the model cannot be interpreted intuitively.

2.2 Linear-Regression Approach

Besides graphical model, some of the other works use linear regression to deal with the problem as in (Wei et al., 2011) and (Wang et al., 2015). Both of the works use English corpus (ANEW) as source domain and transform the rating to the Chinese words. The former work first cluster both English and Chinese work into several groups based on the SUMO concept in WordNet, then for each different cluster they use a linear regression model to predict Chinese words' VA score based on the corresponding English words. The latter work use a variation of linear regression, where a datapoint will be locally weighted by its neighbors' VA score. Also we found that the interrelationship between valence and arousal ratings is considered in this work, and they use quadratic polynominal function to model the relationship and use it as the regression features.

2.3 Image Sentiment Classification

Though object or facial detection of image has made lots of progress in recent years, we notice that, as far as we know, only few works try to deal with sentiment classification in image domain. Reasons might be the lack of annotated data and the difficulty of this task, which need to determine the emotion by taking all the information in the picture into consideration, such as the facial expressions or color tone of the picture that related to some higher-level abstract concept, rather than merely find some specific objects. The work in (You et al., 2015) train a convolution neural network model on a weakly-labeled (where labels are machine generated) Flicker dataset. It uses a progressive training method which first makes prediction then selects a subset with higher prediction confidence in term of probability in the training data, then use them to further fine-tuned the model. The experiment was also be conducted that

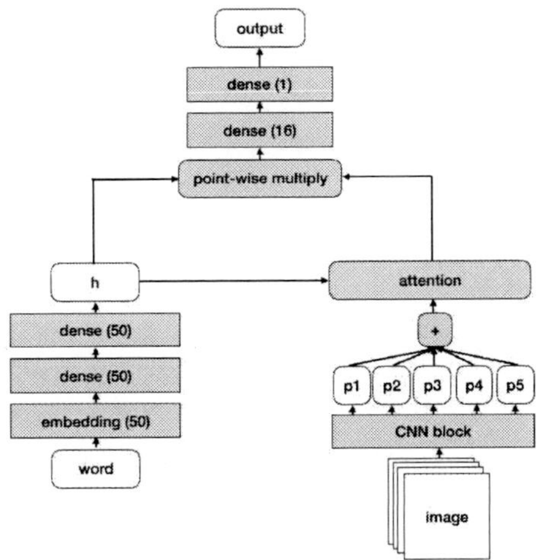

Figure 2: Model for dimensional sentiment analysis

transfer the model from Flicker dataset to Twitter and yield promising performance, thus we think convolution neural net indeed can extract some sentiment features.

3 Dimensional Sentiment Analysis by Image

This section introduces the model architecture. Section 4.1 propose our model for word track, and Section 4.2 illustrates our model for phrase track. Settings of hyperparameters are defined in Section 6.1.

3.1 Word-Level

The model we proposed is in figure 2. For each word in training set, we will choose five images gathered from the internet as input as well as that word. The model has two separate parts for processing two different kinds of input.

3.1.1 Image Processing

The right part of the model is for processing images. There are six convolution layers totally, while each two layers can be viewed as a block since they have same filter sizes and filter numbers. At the end of each block there is a max-pooling layer. After the CNN there is a fully-connected layer used to extract the features from images. Then we use another dense layer to generate a scalar, which indicates the polarity of the word, from each of five vectors. The scalars are denoted as $P_j \in \mathbb{R}^k$, where k is the dimension of word embedding, $j \in \{0, 1, 2, 3, 4\}$ means the jth image

3.1.2 Word Processing

The left part of the model is used to process word information. We use Glove as pretrained word embedding and freeze the weight during training phase. Then we use two fully connected layers, by which we hope to extract sentiment features from original word embedding, the output can be viewed as sentiment word vector, denoted as h_i.

3.1.3 Integration of word and images

After processing two kinds of inputs, we apply the attention mechanism on five polarity scalars with respect to the sentiment word vectors. The calculation of attention weights can be written as

$$e_{i,j} = \tanh\left(W_a h_i + W_b P_{ij} + b\right) \tag{1}$$

$$a_{i,j} = \frac{exp\left(e_{i,j}\right)}{\sum_{j'=0}^{4} exp\left(e_{i,j'}\right)} \tag{2}$$

where $W_a \in \mathbb{R}^{1 \times k}, W_b \in \mathbb{R}^{1 \times k}, b \in \mathbb{R}$ are learned by the model during training. After the calculation of the attention weight, we perform element-wise multiplication on the polarity vectors obtained from images.

$$c_i = \sum_{j'=0}^{4} a_{i,j'} P_i \tag{3}$$

Obtaining the weighted polarity vector c_i, we then perform element-wise multiplication on sentiment word vector and the output vector of attention mechanism to calculate

$$h_i' = c_i \otimes h_i \tag{4}$$

Since the images are collected from the Internet, we have no guarantee about the qualities of the images. Some images, in consequence, might be useless or even have negative effect for the model to predict valence or arousal score. The attention mechanism above gives our model the capacity to determine how importance each image is with respect to reflecting the sentiment. For example, it can give lower attention weight to images regarded as irrelevant to the proceeding words, then

using less feature from the images in final prediction stage.

The last part of the model is a fully-connected layer with $sigmoid$ activation function, of which output is a real-value prediction.

3.2 Phrase

We model a phrase as a word with modifiers, thus we add several layers to deal with modifiers explicitly and leave other parts of model unchanged.

Since the modifiers' types are given, an intuitive method to process phrase is to multiply the representation of those modifiers and word. The reason is that the modifiers will change the meaning and/or intensity of a word, which can be explained as the alteration of a vector in word embedding space.

A concrete example is to represent a negation, we could multiply -1 on it. Multiplying -1 makes opposite direction of any vectors, so it gives the opposite meaning of word vectors. Note that since we are using same embedding for modifiers and words, they are in the same embedding space. So the direct multiplication of the modifier embedding and the word embedding is achievable and reasonable.

Given a phrase, we first split it into degree, negation, modal and word, while a matrix fulled with one is used if such modifier does not exist. A same pretrained word embedding is used to process them to the same embedding space. With the embedding, a dense regression is performed on the degree embedding, negation embedding, and the modal embedding, while a different dense regression is used for the word embedding. In the end, we multiply the vectors to get the representation of phrase.

With the same process attention mechanism performed on images, we then multiply the representation of phrase we obtain above with the polarity from images. Then a fully-connected neural network and a $sigmoid$ function is used to compute the final output.

4 Experiment

In this section, we describe the setting of model we use on shared task. Furthermore, we conduct two additional experiment as below, to analyze the behavior of our model.

1. Using different numbers of images for each word and comparing the performance.

Submit	Valence MAE	Valence PCC	Arousal MAE	Arousal PCC
Word Level				
Run1	1.108 (22)	0.561 (22)	1.207 (23)	0.351 (22)
Run2	1 (19)	0.604 (22)	1.207 (23)	0.351 (22)
Phrase Level				
Run1	0.709 (14)	0.818 (15)	0.632 (16)	0.732 (16)
Run2	0.689 (13)	0.829 (14)	0.633 (17)	0.727 (17)

Table 4: Result of IJCNLP 2017 dimensional sentiment analysis shared task. Rank among all submission is shown in the bracket.

2. Comparing the model with the other neural-network based model which does not incorporate the image information

4.1 Model Settings

In the word-level experiment, we use 50-dimension GloVe which trained on Chinese Gigaword Corpus as pretrained word embedding, 3 CNN blocks use 16, 32, 64 as filter numbers respectively and 3x3 as kernel size. Following the CNN we use a fully-connected layer with 200 hidden units. On the other side of the model, a two layers dense with hidden size 50 is used for regression. In the end, there is a dense layer with hidden size 16 for final computation.

About training, we use mean squared error as our loss function, mini-batch with size 16, and use Nadam(Dozat, 2016) for optimization, learning rate is initialized to 0.005 and 0.004 scheduled decay. Dropout layers (Srivastava et al., 2014) with dropout rate 0.3 and batch normalization mechanism (Ioffe and Szegedy, 2015) are inserted after each CNN block, while early-stopping being used with monitoring the behavior of validation mean absolute error since it is the metric used in shared task. We shuffle and partition the data to train on 2661 instances and validation on 141 instances. Hoping to lower the variance in the training data, we manually divide the VA rating with 10 and multiply it back to original scale after prediction. At each epoch we save the best model with respect to validation mean absolute error and use it to evaluate the current Pearson Correlation Coefficient.

Only slightly different settings are applied to phrase-level experiment. There are two regressions for modifiers and words, each with hidden size 50, and there is no batch normalization mechanism after each CNN block. After shuffle and the same partition strategy, we have 2025 training instances and 225 validation instances. In the end,

Figure 3: Most of images show no relevance to the corresponding word and phrase.

a same methodology to prevent high variance is adapted.

We submit two runs to the system. In the second run we fine-tuned the hyper-parameter of the phrase model and we use over-sampling to train the word model since we find there are few instances with extreme ratings. So for those data-points whose ratings are very large (> 7) or small (< 3), we replicate them two times in training set.

4.2 Additional Experiment

The details of two additional experiments are introduced as following.

Using different numbers of images Motivation of our first experiment is that the images we used in our models are automatically downloaded from the Internet, and we have no guarantee about relevance between images and corresponding words or phrases. Therefore we try different numbers of images for training, trying to implicitly control the degree our model relies on image information.

Comparing to an FFNN model To evaluate the usefulness of images, we also implement a feed-forward neural network (FFNN) containing two hidden layers that directly takes word embedding as input and output the valence or arousal rating of each word.

number of images	Valence MAE	Valence PCC	Arousal MAE	Arousal PCC
5 images	0.618(1.15)	0.838(0.55)	0.845(1.15)	0.54(0.37)
4 images	0.718(1.07)	0.74(0.59)	0.811(1.054)	0.60(0.39)
3 images	0.792(1.01)	0.75(0.60)	0.868(1.072)	0.57(0.37)
2 images	0.679(1.06)	0.82(0.53)	0.826(1.063)	0.53(0.35)

Table 5: The relationship between number of images and performance in validation set, while the value in the bracket denotes the performance on testing set.

Model	Valence MAE	Valence PCC	Arousal MAE	Arousal PCC
FFNN	0.746(1.108)	0.79(0.57)	0.780(1.13)	0.58(0.35)
Our model	0.618(1.15)	0.838(0.55)	0.845(1.15)	0.54(0.37)

Table 6: Two model's behavior on the validation and testing set, our model using 5 images as input.

5 Results & Discussion

Results of shared task The shared task results of word- and phrase-track are showed in Table 4. The rank of each team is decided by the average of rank considering each metric, which is shown between brackets. In word-level, our models show relatively unsatisfactory performance among other teams, with rank 17.5/24 in first run and 17/24 in second run. We discover that the testing result is significantly worse than training and validation, and since the distribution of VA ratings in training and testing are similar after analysis, the possible reason is that the training set is too small for model that it's ability of generalize to unseen data is weak.

Result of phrase-level is better than that of word-level. We think the reason is that when our model encounter different phrase with some or all the same modifiers, the same modifiers can stand as a reference. This reference helps our model preciously update its representation of the different part of the phrase, which results in better performance.

Using different numbers of images The experiment result is shown in Table 6. We find that there is no obvious difference of the performance no matter how many images we utilize. By looking to Figure 4, the fourth row shows that the model is able to attend relevant images, but in second row, all the images are irrelevant so the model doesn't know what to do and give all the image and word embedding same attention weights. This indicates that the attention mechanism is not mature enough to ignore the useless images. The lack of training data is one reason and the quality of images also largely affects the model.

Comparing to an FFNN model The result is shown in Table 7. According to this experiment, we notice that though FFNN model is quite unstable and the mean absolute error varies over multiple training phases, the model with image perform only slightly better than FFNN, sometimes even worse.After some investigation we conclude that this result is due to the poor relevance between images and words. So we further analyze the image data.

Quality of images We manually check lots of images and find that a considerable portion of the images crawled from internet are very irrelevant to the corresponding word and thus have negative effect, as shown in Figure 3. We use Google search due to the lack of image dataset with Chinese label. However, since the Google image search will consider the relation between a query and the paragraph that co-occur with each image, so we might download lots of images have little or no relevance to the word, and since many words in the dataset have abstract meaning, e.g. happy or sad, rather than just represent an object, e.g. table or cat, so it is much harder to get the images which represent the words accurately. For example, the first two images of the word ”生育”(fertility) is appeared in article discusses the fertility policy of Nazi Germany, while the images of the word ”誠實”(honesty) are some images and posters of the movie ”Gone Girl”. ”誠實”(honesty) is indeed relevant to the plot of the movie ”Gone Girl”, but the images of that movie are useless to our model. These pictures can serve as a distraction to the model rather than provide useful information.

Possible solutions Since the result of the shared task is unsatisfactory to us, we're going to point

Figure 4: The attention heat map of words and images shows that it cannot attend on words only, while often attend on irrelevant images.

out some problems and propose some possible solution. For the severe problem of image mentioned above, maybe we can use some image dataset with English label such as ImageNet since it is much bigger, then translate the Chinese word to English to obtain corresponding pictures and using Google search for auxiliary. Another reason should account for the bad performance is the lack of training data, it is hard to train a large network by using less than three thousand instances. To tackle this problem we can also incorporate English corpus with VA ratings to pretrain our model, or train a network for sentiment classifier first and transfer the weight to initialize our model.

6 Conclusion

In this paper, we propose a novel approach to tackle the dimensional sentiment analysis by incorporating information from images, a resource that, as far as we know, hasn't been used in this domain. Although the result isn't promising enough, we conduct several experiments and some feasible solutions are proposed, hoping to better utilize our model.

References

Timothy Dozat. 2016. Incorporating nesterov momentum into adam.

Sergey Ioffe and Christian Szegedy. 2015. Batch normalization: Accelerating deep network training by reducing internal covariate shift. In *International Conference on Machine Learning*, pages 448–456.

Mihalis A Nicolaou, Hatice Gunes, and Maja Pantic. 2011. Continuous prediction of spontaneous affect from multiple cues and modalities in valence-arousal space. *IEEE Transactions on Affective Computing*, 2(2):92–105.

Bo Pang, Lillian Lee, and Shivakumar Vaithyanathan. 2002. Thumbs up?: sentiment classification using machine learning techniques. In *Proceedings of the ACL-02 conference on Empirical methods in natural language processing-Volume 10*, pages 79–86. Association for Computational Linguistics.

Karl Pearson. 1895. Note on regression and inheritance in the case of two parents. *Proceedings of the Royal Society of London*, 58:240–242.

Sara Rosenthal, Noura Farra, and Preslav Nakov. 2017. Semeval-2017 task 4: Sentiment analysis in twitter. In *Proceedings of the 11th International Workshop on Semantic Evaluation (SemEval-2017)*, pages 502–518.

Nitish Srivastava, Geoffrey E Hinton, Alex Krizhevsky, Ilya Sutskever, and Ruslan Salakhutdinov. 2014. Dropout: a simple way to prevent neural networks from overfitting. *Journal of machine learning research*, 15(1):1929–1958.

Jin Wang, Liang-Chih Yu, K Robert Lai, and Xue-jie Zhang. 2015. A locally weighted method to improve linear regression for lexical-based valence-arousal prediction. In *Affective Computing and Intelligent Interaction (ACII), 2015 International Conference on*, pages 415–420. IEEE.

Jin Wang, Liang-Chih Yu, K Robert Lai, and Xuejie Zhang. 2016a. Community-based weighted graph model for valence-arousal prediction of affective words. *IEEE/ACM Transactions on Audio, Speech, and Language Processing*, 24(11):1957–1968.

Jin Wang, Liang-Chih Yu, K Robert Lai, and Xuejie Zhang. 2016b. Dimensional sentiment analysis using a regional cnn-lstm model.

Wen-Li Wei, Chung-Hsien Wu, and Jen-Chun Lin. 2011. A regression approach to affective rating of chinese words from anew. *Affective Computing and Intelligent Interaction*, pages 121–131.

Quanzeng You, Jiebo Luo, Hailin Jin, and Jianchao Yang. 2015. Robust image sentiment analysis using progressively trained and domain transferred deep networks. In *AAAI*, pages 381–388.

Liang-Chih Yu, Jin Wang, K Robert Lai, and Xue-jie Zhang. 2015. Predicting valence-arousal ratings of words using a weighted graph method. In *ACL (2)*, pages 788–793.

NCYU at IJCNLP-2017 Task 2: Dimensional Sentiment Analysis for Chinese Phrases using Vector Representations

Jui-Feng Yeh*, Jian-Cheng Tsai, Bo-Wei Wu, Tai-You Kuang

Department of Computer Science & Information Engineering,
National Chia-Yi University,
Chiayi city, Taiwan (R.O.C.)
{ralph, s1033027, s1032881, s1050470}@mail.ncyu.edu.tw

Abstract

This paper presents two vector representations proposed by National Chiayi University (NCYU) about phrased-based sentiment detection which was used to compete in dimensional sentiment analysis for Chinese phrases (DSACP) at IJCNLP 2017. The vector-based sentiment phrase-like unit analysis models are proposed in this article. E-HowNet-based clustering is used to obtain the values of valence and arousal for sentiment words first. An out-of-vocabulary function is also defined in this article to measure the dimensional emotion values for unknown words. For predicting the corresponding values of sentiment phrase-like unit, a vector-based approach is proposed here. According to the experimental results, we can find the proposed approach is efficacious.

1 Introduction

As we known, humanity is composed of rationality and sensibility. In the latest decays, the computational thinking based-on logical inference has been mature than that based on perceptual ones. However, the computation technologies cannot be practical perfectly in real life without perceptual sensibility indeed. Consequently, affective computing is one of the most essential trends in artificial intelligence in the near future. Nowadays, logic inference has been developed and practiced in the real-life in latest decays. Actually, no emotional expression makes the intelligent systems and robots to act like machine, but not human. The goal of affective computing is to compute the issues related to, arises from, or deliberately influences emotions. Only rational interpretation without human-like emotion cannot express the full meaning and intension in human-machine interactions.

As increasing of the number of the network users, the on-line social computing has more and more popular. Therefore, the detection of the user in cyber space is more and more desired (Pang and Lee, 2008). Considering of the data styles, the two major ones are image and text in social media such as Facebook, Twitter, LinkedIn, Pinterest, Instagram and Snapchat. Actually, the emotion sates of the users are detected from their post information (Rosenthal et al., 2015). Hao et al. (2015) proposed that the sentiment is analyzed by the complex network. They also used sentiment modes network which built by the sentiment dictionary for sentiment analysis. The method of building sentiment modes network is converted the abstract posts into sentiment fragments by sentiment dictionary and coarse graining to build the sentiment modes. However, to detect the affective information from the image-based data such as picture is still one of the open questions. We plan to classify the emotion from the text data at this time. Due to the symbolic representation of text, the new computing technologies usually applied in treating the problems in natural language first. From the psychological constructionist views, emotions are experienced when affective stated are made meaningful as specific instances of the emotion categories (Lindquis et al., 2016). Lindquis et al. also proposed a think: putting words into feelings and putting feelings into words. From this view point, we can sure that lan-

Proceedings of the 8th International Joint Conference on Natural Language Processing, Shared Tasks, pages 112–117,
Taipei, Taiwan, November 27 – December 1, 2017. ©2017 AFNLP

guage is corrected with emotion. Therefore, the emotional element embedded in natural language is one of important works about affective computing in the near future.

This paper is organized as follows. Section 2 describes the related works; affective computing and the description about the emotion categories and dimensional valence-arousal space are illustrated. Section 3 the proposed method of vector-based approach is presented with derivation of mathematical formulas. In Section 4, we analyze the performance in experimental results of the proposed approach. Finally, Section 5 will draw the conclusion of this paper.

2   Related Works

Since affective computing is a new trend in computer science, considerable quantity researches are invested within the latest twenty years. As we known, the aim of the affective computing is to obtain and provide the functionality of human-like sensibility, the real-life data is important for system building.

Affective computing means the technologies computes that related to, arises from and deliberately influences emotions. The goal of affective computing is to recognize, express, and generate emotions from environment. Instead on rational computing only, the systems are desired to act like human. Since Turing test, computer scientists have much effort on artificial intelligence especially in detecting, percept and express emotion. Therefore, social rules extended to machine in several media type. For example, computer vision technology can be applied to detect the emotional facial expression. Combined with audio and speech, a multimodal agent with emotional interaction functions can be developed and practically applied in real environment. Enabling communication of emotion is an attracting in human-machine interactions. *"The question is not whether intelligent machines can have any emotions, but whether machines can be intelligent without any emotions."* said by Marvin Minsky. It is trying to make computer with the capability to deal with the emotional issues in human machine interactions.

About recognition of emotion/sentiment, the goal is to classify the type and degree of emotion that is displayed by users. First, we can divide the emotion classification into two kinds: discrete categories and dimensional models. The former means the emotion classes are discrete and with different constructs. The latter denotes that emotions should be described as continuous value regression in dimensional basis in groups.

Due to the alteration of word usage, Li et al. (2017) pointed out the importance of partition sentence correctly which influence the meaning of the sentiment. The article proposed a method is according the enhanced mutual information (EMI) score of new word user-invented to get the new words. EMI score of the words represent the possibility it is a new words, it the higher the more possible. Similarly, new sentiment word detection is still one of essential issues for affective computing. Herein, Huang et al. (2014) found the sentiment word and polarity prediction of new sentiment word is one of the main contributions of this paper. They used the likelihood ratio test (LRT) method which can quantify the degree of association to find the new words and the method produce the framework is fully unsupervised. Moreover, the polarity prediction of sentiment word is benefit for classification of sentiment Words and sentiment analysis.

Word embedding for sentiment classification is one of main steams (Tang et al., 2014; Yao and Li, 2016). Wang et al. (2016b) adopted the deep learning method, CNN-LSTM, to deal with the sentiment analysis problems. Wang et al. (2016) adopted the deep learning method, CNN-LSTM, to deal with the sentiment analysis problems. Yao and Li (2016) presented the method which finding the feature vector of special word in context is by word2vec. In addition, the paper proposes a new idea which is using the feature vector represent the words' sentiment polarity. Yet, this idea remains more and more research to prove because their corpus in a particular context is limited. Yeh et al. (2016) adopted the linear regression for the values about valence and arousal of Chinese words. Mellem et al. (2016) invested a sentence processing in anterior superior temporal cortex shows a social-emotional bias.

3   Vector Representations and   Estimation

The term "sentiment phrase-like unit" is defined as a constitution that is composed of a head word and modifier words. Herein, the head word must be a sentiment word. The modifier can be empty, or degree and negation words. An example is illustrated in the Figure 1. After word segmentation and parsing, a parse tree is obtained. We can find that sentiment word is "喜歡(like)" and two modifiers "不(dis)" and "很(very)" in this sentence. According to the previous definition, three "Sentiment phrase-like unit", "喜歡(like)," 不喜歡(dis-like), "很不喜歡(dis-like very much)" are extracted here.

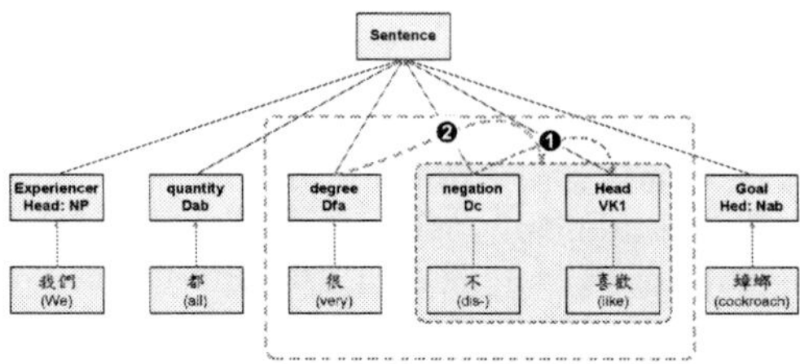

Figure 1: An example for sentiment phrase-like unit in a parse tree of the Chinese sentence "我們很不喜歡蟑螂(We all dis-like cockroach very much). "

Since the sentiment phrase-like unit is essential for affective computing, the question which has been touched from time to time but not explored is how to provide the values of the sentiment phrase-like unit automatically in valence and arousal. Thus, we will describe the process of building a Chinese emotional dictionary with valence-arousal values and the way of how to predict the valence-arousal values of the phrases based on the values of emotional words. In the part of building our dictionary, we used up to four ontologies, E-HowNet, ANTUSD, SentiWordNet 3.0 and CVAW as knowledge bases. In the part of predicting the valence-arousal values of the phrases, we used the CVAP ontology as our training data to train the influence degree value of degree and negative adverb.

The knowledge bases used in the proposed method are illustrated as follows. E-HowNet is a frame-based and extended from HowNet. The purpose of E-HowNet is that makes the concept of the real world can be written in a way that the computer can read. It includes the element, basic concept element, related function and additional symbol. We used these relations of E-HowNet to classify the training words, as shown in Figure 2. The ANTUSD contains 27,370 words and collects handbook noted of word for a long time. It includes NTUSD, NTCIR MOAT task dataset, Chinese Opinion Treebank, AciBiMA, CopeOpi and E-HowNet.SentiWordNet 3.0 is a lexical resource publicly available for research purposes and explicitly devised for supporting sentiment analysis and opinion mining applications. It is also the result of automatically annotating all WordNet synsets according to their degrees of positivity, negativity, and neutrality. The sentiment scores of SentiWordNet 3.0 are ranging from 0 to 1 including 0 and 1.The CVAW which contains 1,653 words noted with valence-arousal ratings built by Chinese valence-arousal resources. It contains seven attributes which is the number, Valence_Mean, Valence_SD, Arousal_Mean, Arousal_SD and Frequency in sequence. The valence-arousal ratings of CVAW are scored a value between 0 and 9.The CVAP contains 2,251 pharses which classified as six types including degree, degree_negative, mod, mod_degree, negative and negative_degree that annotated with valence-arousal ratings. The valence-arousal ratings of CVAP are scored a value between 0 and 9.

For building a lexical-based sentiment word set, an E-HowNet-based clustering is used here. The word of included relation was defined in the E-HowNet ontology. We cluster the words by using level definition of E-HowNet and let the words of synsets are clustered a group. Every group of synsets are corresponded to a hypernym. At the

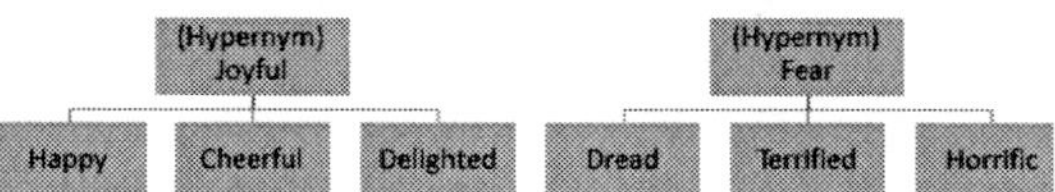

Figure 2: An example of the words in same synset and the same hypernym.

end, the group of hypernym is formed by gathered the words of CVAW gathered, as shown in Figure 2. By using the hypernym, we can get more the emotional words of classified in the same synset. And then, we can expand the words of the dictionary when we used the more hypernym to get more synsets. Based the all above ontology, we convert the valence-arousal values of our dictionary from the valence-arousal values of words. The function of calculate the words is used our dictionary to find the valence-arousal values of words and if the word is build in our dictionary by ANTUSD ontology, we used OOV function to predict the arousal values because the all values of the words are neutral. If the words do not exist in our dictionary, we still can predict the values by the OOV function which is in the next section.

The Sentiment phrase-like unit is composed of the degree adverb, negative adverb and the emotional words. If we want to predict the value, we can start from the value of the words. The valence and arousal value of words can be obtained by the above function and the degree and negative adverb can be acquired from training data, so we used as follow formula to achieve goals:

$$E_v' = D_V * (E_v - C) + C, E_v \in Valence \qquad (1)$$

and

$$E_a' = D_A * (E_a - C) + C, E_a \in Arousal \qquad (2)$$

where E_v and E_a denote the original value of valence and arousal and E_v' and E_a' represent the value after calculating. C is center value of the valence and arousal and D_V、D_A is a real-number show the degree and negative adverb influence how much the degree of the word value. As the Formula, we believe the modified mood is not the addition result of the composed of words so we used the multiplication to show that. The reason why we need to subtract the C from the E_v、E_a is the subtracted value represent the degree of original emotion and we used that to predict can get the closer emotion value. Additionally, a function for out of vocabulary is defined here. OOV is the abbreviation of the Out of vocabulary and the timing of use is a word cannot be calculated by above function that word does not be found in our dictionary. By OOV function, we can solve the problem which the word does not exist in our dictionary and the formula is as follows.

$$X = \frac{\sum_{Seq_n=1}^{n} \frac{\sum_{i=1}^{N} x_i}{N}}{Seq_n}, X \in Valence \qquad (3)$$

and

$$Y = \frac{\sum_{Seq_n=1}^{n} \frac{\sum_{i=1}^{N} y_i}{N}}{Seq_n}, Y \in Arousal \qquad (4)$$

The OOV function is used to predict valence-arousal value of the undefined words by defined word in our dictionary. We get the average valence-arousal value of each character separately and add the all values to gain the average as the valence-arousal value of the undefined words. Although the OOV function is mainly to solve the above problem, we have also designed a function in it which is support the calculation of phrases. In order to solve the tough which the calculation of phrase may go wrong because the phrase is not consist by only a degree adverb, a negative adverb and a word, we decided adding the function of again searching the adverb and again calculating assume the adverb was found in OOV to let the result of phrase calculation better.

4   Experimental Results

For evaluating for the proposed approach, a system was developed. The data preparation, metric and results are illustrated as following sections. Based on Chinese valence-arousal words 2.0 (CVAW 2.0) developed by (Yu et al. 2016), we have the adjustment set defined in (Yeh et al. 2016). According to the definitions, we proposed two vector-based approaches for predicting for the values of the valence and arousal. Since the test corpus consists 750 word-level and 750 phrases-like level sentiment units. We need the data structure to simultaneously represent the valence-arousal value and the degree of the emotion, the float scores are used here. For a given input test pattern either in word level or phrase-like level, we can get the float scores from 1 to 9 for both valence and arousal which is the mainly dimensional representation about the extent of the emotion from most negative to most positive for valence and from most calm to most excited for arousal. The input and output formats are "word/ phrase_id, word/phrase", and "word/ phrase_id, vallence_value, arousal_value" separately. The following is an example of the input and output, the part of word is :認真(earnest), 寬恕(forgive), and 說服(convince) and the part of phrase is:十分不滿(very dissatisfied), 很可怕(very scary), and 十分壯觀(very spectacular). The word input are "1001, 認真," "1002, 寬恕," and "1003, 說服" and the phrase input are "2001, 十分不滿," "2002, 很可怕," and "2003, 十分壯觀." The word output are "1001, 7.0, 5.0," "1002, 6.2, 4.6," and "1003, 5.2, 3.6." The corresponding phrase output are "2001, 2.256, 7.444," "2002, 2.500, 7.000," and "2003, 7.722, 7.138." There are totally 750 testing instances of test data including word and phrase level units as described previously. The performance is assessed by censoring the difference between machine-predicted ratings and human-annotated which valence and arousal are treated independently. The metrics are the same as those were used in IALP 2016 including Mean Absolute Error (MAE) and Pearson correlation coefficient (PCC). The corresponding formulates are illustrated as the eq. (3) and (4).

$$MAE = \frac{1}{n}\sum_{i=1}^{n} |A_i - P_i| \qquad (5)$$

and

$$r = \frac{1}{n-1}\sum_{i=1}^{n}\left(\frac{A_i - \bar{A}}{\sigma_A}\right)\left(\frac{P_i - \bar{P}}{\sigma_P}\right), \qquad (6)$$

where A_i denotes the human-annotated ratings and P_i denotes the machine-predicted ratings. n is the number of test samples, $\bar{A}$ and $\bar{P}$ respectively denote the arithmetic mean of A and P, and σ is the standard deviation.

According to the above function, we predict the valence-arousal values with the test data and the results are displayed on the dimension graph as Figure 3, Figure 4, Figure 5, and Figure 6. X-axis and Y-axis represents valence and arousal individually. We performed the experiment 2 times by two different proposed approaches to predict the valence-arousal values for the input test patterns. First way is just using OOV function and second way is using above all functions. From the observations, we can get total 1,500 results of valence-arousal values which there are 750 respectively belong to word and phrase and scale to the emotional space.

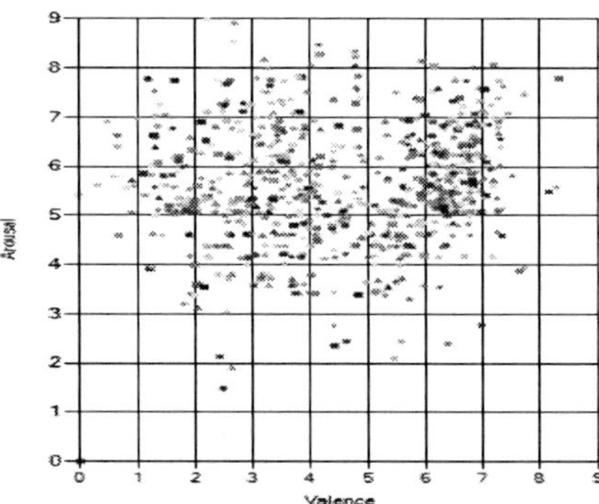

Figure 3: The result of NCYU-Run1's phrase

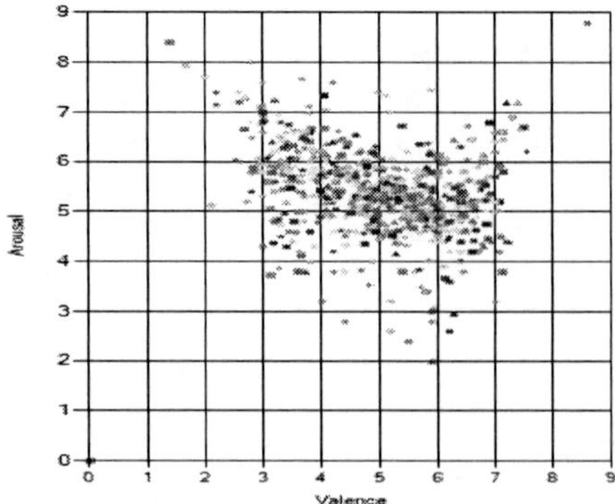

Figure 4: The result of NCYU-Run1's word

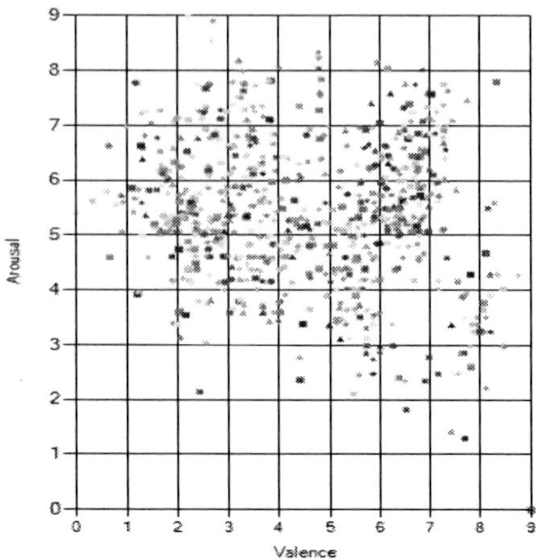

Figure 5: The result of NCYU-Run2's phrase

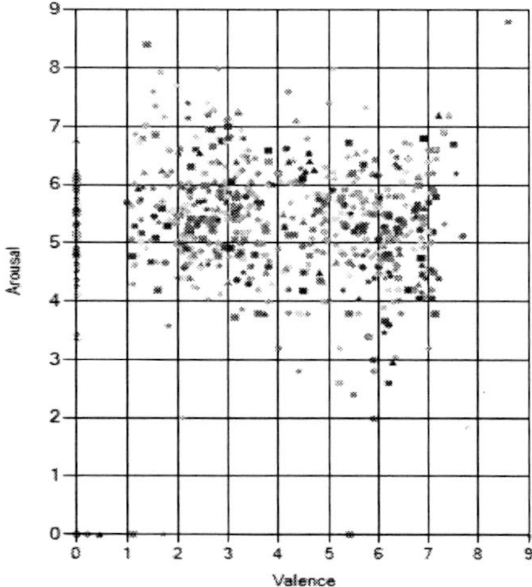

Figure 6: The result of NCYU-Run2's word

Considering of the baseline system, the experimental results about the proposed approaches are shown in following Table 1, Table 2, and Table 3. Table 1 and Table 2 shows the results of analyzed the valence and arousal in MAE and PCC. We can find the performance of the proposed approaches is near to that of baseline system. These results shows that the proposed method is able to provide a correct automatically labeling. From Table 3, we can find that the similar condition appears in mean rank.

Submission	Valence MAE (rank)	Valence PCC (rank)
NCYU-Run1	0.9785 (19)	0.685 (19)
Baseline	1.0175 (20)	0.6265 (22)
NCYU-Run2	1.2050 (23)	0.6665 (20)

Table 1: The results of analyzed the valence in averaging performance.

Submission	Arousal MAE (rank)	Arousal PCC (rank)
Baseline	0.819 (14)	0.593 (13)
NCYU-Run1	0.945 (20)	0.549 (16)
NCYU-Run2	0.989 (22)	0.534 (21)

Table 2: The result of analyzed the arousal in averaging performance

Submission	Mean Rank
Baseline	17.25
NCYU-Run1	18.5
NCYU-Run2	21.5

Table 3: The mean rank of averaging performance

5 Conclusions

A vector-based approach containing the E-HowNet-based clustering and OOV function for sentiment phrase-like unit is proposed in this paper. Since the dimensional affective representation is increasing, a valence-arousal space is reasonable. According the structure of sentiment phrase-like unit that contains the emotion word as head-word and negation and degree words as modifiers is defined. Applied the proposed method, we can observe that the proposed approach is workable and efficient.

References

Hao, X., An, H., Zhang, L., Li, H., and Wei, G. 2015. Sentiment Diffusion of Public Opinions about Hot Events: Based on Complex Network. *PloS one*, 10(10), e0140027.

Huang, M., Ye, B., Wang, Y., Chen, H., Cheng, J., and Zhu, X. 2014. New Word Detection for Sentiment Analysis. In *ACL (1)* : 531-541.

Li, W., Guo, K., Shi, Y., Zhu, L., & Zheng, Y. 2017. Improved New Word Detection Method Used in Tourism Field. *Procedia Computer Science*, 108: 1251-1260.

Lindquist, K., Gendron, M., Satpute, A. B., & Lindquist, K. 2016. Language and emotion. In *Handbook of emotions*. The Guilford Press New York, NY.

Mellem, M. S., Jasmin, K. M., Peng, C., & Martin, A. 2016. Sentence processing in anterior superior temporal cortex shows a social-emotional bias. Neuropsychologia, 89: 217-224.

Pang, B. and Lee L. 2008. Opinion Mining and Sentiment Analysis. *Foundations and Trends in Information Retrieval*, 2(1-2):1–135.

Rosenthal S., Nakov P., Kiritchenko S., Mohammad Saif M, Alan Ritter, and Veselin Stoyanov. 2015. Semeval-2015 Task 10: Sentiment Analysis in Twitter. In *Proceedings of the 9th International Workshop on Semantic Evaluation*, SemEval: 451–463.

Tang, D., Wei, F., Yang, N., Zhou, M., Liu, T., & Qin, B. 2014. Learning Sentiment-Specific Word Embedding for Twitter Sentiment Classification. In *ACL (1)* : 1555-1565.

Wang, J., Yu, L. C., Lai, K. R., & Zhang, X. 2016. August). Dimensional sentiment analysis using a regional CNN-LSTM model. In ACL 2016— *Proceedings of the 54th Annual Meeting of the Association for Computational Linguistics*. Berlin, Germany 2: 225-230.

Yao, Y., & Li, G. 2016. Context-aware Sentiment Word Identification: sentiword2vec. arXiv preprint arXiv:1612.03769.

Yeh, J. F., Kuang, T. Y., Huang, Y. J., & Wu, M. R. 2016. Dimensional sentiment analysis in valence-arousal for Chinese words by linear regression. In *Proceedings of International Conference on Asian Language Processing (IALP)*, 2016:328-331

Yu L. C., Lee L.-H., Hao S., Wang J., He Y., Hu J., Lai K. Robert, and Zhang X.. 2016. Building Chinese affective resources in valence-arousal dimensions. In *Proceedings of NAACL/HLT-16*: 540-545.

MainiwayAI at IJCNLP-2017 Task 2: Ensembles of Deep Architectures for Valence-Arousal Prediction

Yassine Benajiba   **Jin Sun**   **Yong Zhang**   **Zhiliang Weng**   **Or Biran**

Mainiway AI Lab

`{yassine,jin.sun,yong.zhang,zhiliang.weng,or.biran}@mainiway.com`

Abstract

This paper introduces Mainiway AI Labs submitted system for the IJCNLP 2017 shared task on Dimensional Sentiment Analysis of Chinese Phrases (DSAP), and related experiments. Our approach consists of deep neural networks with various architectures, and our best system is a voted ensemble of networks. We achieve a Mean Absolute Error of 0.64 in valence prediction and 0.68 in arousal prediction on the test set, both placing us as the 5th ranked team in the competition.

1 Introduction

While traditional sentiment analysis is concerned with discrete polarity classes, the dimensional approach has recently drawn considerable attention as a way of modeling sentiment more accurately. In this framework, affective states are represented as points in a multi-dimensional continuous space, such as the Valence-Arousal (VA) space described by Russell (1980), and shown in Figure 1.

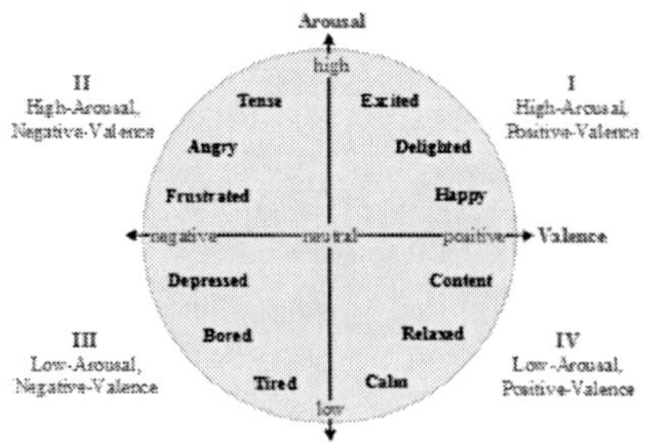

Figure 1: The two-dimensional Valence-Arousal space.

The DSAP shared task at IJCNLP 2017 is the second task related to Chinese sentiment analy-sis in the VA space, the first being the Dimensional Sentiment Analysis of Chinese Words at IALP 2016 (Yu et al., 2016a)(Yu et al., 2016b). The evaluation metrics in DSAP, as in the previous competition, are the Mean Absolute Error (MAE) and the Pearson Correlation Coefficient (PCC).

In contrast to the IALP task, where the test set consisted of single words only, the DSAP test set contains both single words and multi-word phrases. The variable length of the input adds a technical complexity to the typical modern approach to this task, which relies on an artificial neural network applied to the input in an embedding space, as phrase-level representations present many difficulties and are an ongoing area of research.

This paper presents our method of acquiring embedded representations, the various network architectures we utilize in the final system and our ensemble method, along with pre-competition experiments. In addition, we discuss the results of experiments with a nearest neighbor-based smoothing approach that was not included in the final system but provided interesting and valuable insight.

2 Models and Embeddings

This section describes several deep neural network architectures used in our experiments as well as the embedded word representation we use as input to the networks.

2.1 Embeddings

Word embeddings - continuous vector representations of textual units such as words or characters - are a standard approach for representing semantics. One popular option is *word2vec*, which generates embeddings for single words using either the CBOW or the skip-gram model (Mikolov et al., 2013). A more powerful approach is that

Proceedings of the 8th International Joint Conference on Natural Language Processing, Shared Tasks, pages 118–123,
Taipei, Taiwan, November 27 – December 1, 2017. ©2017 AFNLP

of *fastText*,[1] a tool for generating embeddings at the word or character level (Bojanowski et al., 2017). Like *word2vec*, *fastText* uses either the CBOW or the skip-gram model to learn embeddings from a text corpus. The difference between the two is illustrated in Figure 2; in this paper, we use character-level embeddings of 300 dimensions trained on Chinese Wikipedia with *fastText* using the skip-gram model.

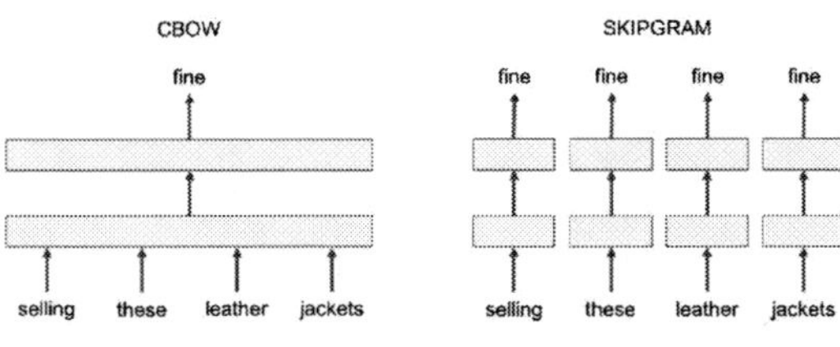

Figure 2: CBOW and skip-gram training architectures

The input to the neural network (described in the next section) is the embedding space representation of the text input. In the case of unseen words or phrases, the representation is constructed by *fastText* from its constituent character n-grams.

2.2 Network architecture

We treat the prediction of valence and arousal values as two regression tasks, and use a deep neural network to represent them. As the competition rules allow two separate runs, we chose two of these architectures as our final systems; in this section, we describe several architectures and ideas from which we made our choices. Section 3 describes the experimental results for these options, as well as the two systems that participated in the competition.

In all variations described below, the input layer is a 300-dimensional embedding space and the output layer is a single output. The hidden layers are all dense, with ReLU for the activation function and Adam for the optimization algorithm, with a batch size of 135 and no dropout. The loss function is the Mean Squared Error (MSE).

Using these base parameters, we first experiment with varying the number of hidden layers. Using a *rectangle* architecture, where all hidden layers consist of 300 fully connected neurons, we

---

[1] https://github.com/facebookresearch/fastText

experimented with zero, three, and six hidden layers.

In addition to the rectangle architecture, we also tried an *hourglass* architecture with six hidden layers where the dimensionalities of the hidden layers (after the 300-dimensional input layer) are 225, 175, 100, 175, 225 and 300. The idea here is to compact the semantic information of the embeddings into a lower-dimensional sentiment information as it passes through the network, alleviating overfitting. This is conceptually similar to the intuition behind Auto Encoders.

Finally, we leverage both architectures using an ensemble method which averages the predictions of both models. To generalize from a two-model ensemble, we define a $2n$-model ensemble which averages between the predictions of $2n$ models, n rectangular (R) and n hourglass (H):

$$y = \frac{\lambda \sum_{i-1}^{n} R_i(x) + (1 - \lambda) \sum_{i=1}^{n} H_i(x)}{n}$$

Where λ is a tunable weight hyperparameter which in this work we keep at 0.5. This adds a final layer to the model, illustrated for 20 models in Figure 3. The ensemble approach reduces the variance of the results and increase the accuracy of individual predictions.

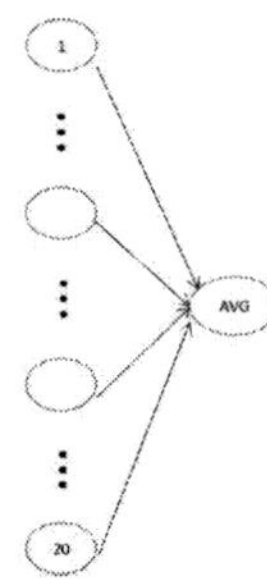

Figure 3: A final layer averaging 20 model predictions

3 Experimental Results and Task Results

This section describes the experiments we conducted with the variants described in the previous section as well as the final selected systems and their performance in the competition.

In addition to our architecture variants, we include two baselines to put these results in context: a linear classifier baseline, and a single-layer Boosted Neural Network (BNN), an architecture

Model	Layers (dense)
Rectangle, no hidden layers	[300; 1]
Rectangle, 3 hidden layers	[300; 300, 300, 300; 1]
Rectangle, 6 hidden layers	[300; 300, 300, 300, 300, 300, 300; 1]
Hourglass, 6 hidden layers	[300; 225, 175, 100, 175, 225, 300; 1]
Ensemble, $n = 1$	Ensemble of Rectangle(6) and Hourglass(6)
Ensemble, $n = 10$	Ensemble of Rectangle(6) $\times 10$ and Hourglass(6) $\times 10$

Table 1: Model architectures

Model	CVAW				CVAP			
	Valence		Arousal		Valence		Arousal	
	MAE	PCC	MAE	PCC	MAE	PCC	MAE	PCC
Linear	0.740	0.805	0.877	0.593	1.044	0.657	0.579	0.785
BNN	0.633	0.856	0.762	0.690	0.706	0.848	0.505	0.844
Rectangle, no hidden layers	0.697	0.829	0.838	0.638	0.659	0.864	0.521	0.840
Rectangle, 3 hidden layers	0.577	0.869	0.787	0.670	0.491	0.913	0.465	0.867
Rectangle, 6 hidden layers	0.585	0.854	0.816	0.634	**0.452**	**0.909**	0.488	0.850
Hourglass, 6 hidden layers	0.580	0.863	0.793	0.663	0.502	0.907	0.471	0.861
Ensemble, $n = 1$	0.557	0.878	0.771	0.679	0.487	0.912	0.459	0.870
Ensemble, $n = 10$	**0.531**	**0.887**	**0.740**	**0.707**	0.461	0.922	**0.448**	**0.876**

Table 2: Experimental results

that was popular at the IALP 2016 task (Du and Zhang, 2016). The architectures of the different variants are listed in detail in Table 1.

The results are shown in Table 2, highlighted by best MAE. The first thing to notice is that all deep architectures (three and six hidden layers) perform significantly better than the baseline and the BNN; that result validated our intuition that predicting a sentiment output from a semantic-space input requires multiple transformative layers.

Clearly, the $n = 10$ ensemble model has the best performance overall. The 6-hidden-layer rectangle model achieves better performance in Valence on CVAP, however. We therefore chose these two models as our two systems for the competition: the rectangular model with 6 hidden layers for Run 1, and the $n = 10$ ensemble model for Run 2. The architectures of these models are illustrated further in Figure 4 and Figure 5 for Run 1 and Run 2, respectively.

Note that while the same architecture was used in each run for both valence and arousal, the model was trained separately for each of the two tasks, using the training data provided for the competition.

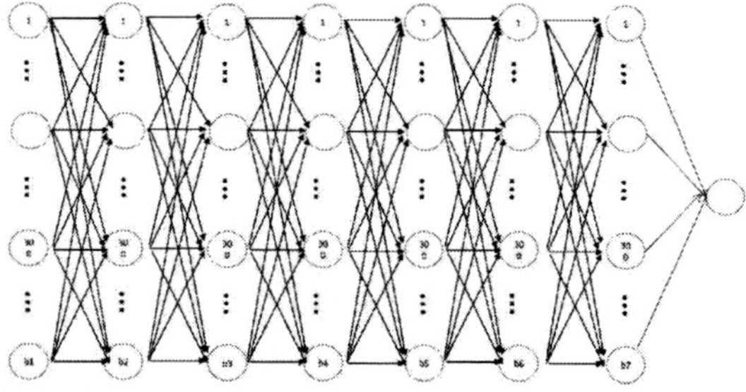

Figure 4: Run 1 architecture diagram

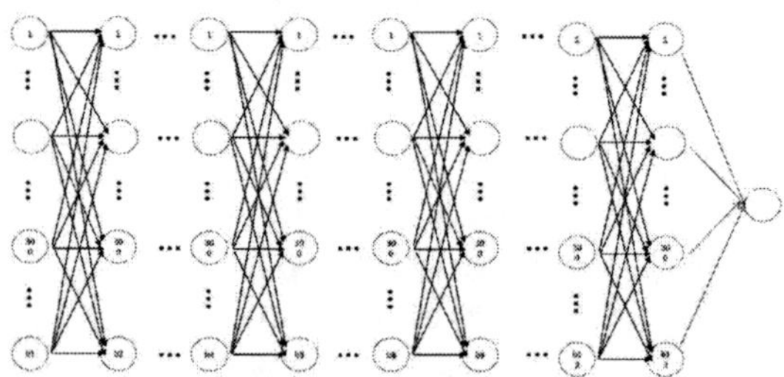

Figure 5: Run 2 architecture diagram

Submission	Valence				Arousal				Mean
	MAE	Rank	PCC	Rank	MAE	Rank	PCC	Rank	Rank
THU_NGN-Run2	0.427	1	0.9345	1	0.6245	1	0.7985	1	1
THU_NGN-Run1	0.4795	2	0.9085	2	0.6645	4	0.766	3	2.75
AL_I_NLP-Run2	0.5355	3	0.8965	3	0.661	3	0.766	2	2.75
AL_I_NLP-Run1	0.539	4	0.8955	4	0.659	2	0.761	4	3.5
CKIP-Run1	0.547	7	0.8895	6	0.6655	5	0.742	5	5.75
NCTU-NTUT-Run1	0.543	5	0.887	7	0.72	6	0.695	8	6.5
NCTU-NTUT-Run2	0.546	6	0.8865	8	0.7285	7	0.699	7	7
CKIP-Run2	0.5545	8	0.895	5	0.764	10	0.7365	6	7.25
MainiwayAI-Run2	**0.6415**	**9**	**0.837**	**10**	**0.7545**	**9**	**0.6825**	**9**	**9.25**
MainiwayAI-Run1	**0.6635**	**10**	**0.8285**	**11**	**0.793**	**13**	**0.651**	**11**	**11.25**
FZU-NLP-Run1	0.8165	14	0.7655	13	0.7425	8	0.6535	10	11.25
NTOU-Run2	0.757	13	0.7365	15	0.7775	12	0.61	12	13
CIAL-Run1	0.6835	11	0.844	9	0.9765	21	0.5895	14	13.75
NTOU-Run1	0.6925	12	0.805	12	0.7765	11	0.5225	22	14.25
CASIA-Run1	0.8665	16	0.7005	17	0.9425	19	0.5555	15	16.75
NLPSA-Run2	0.8445	15	0.7165	16	0.92	17	0.539	20	17
Baseline	**1.0175**	**20**	**0.6265**	**22**	**0.819**	**14**	**0.593**	**13**	**17.25**
NLPSA-Run1	0.9085	18	0.6895	18	0.9195	16	0.5415	18	17.5
NCYU-Run1	0.9785	19	0.685	19	0.945	20	0.549	16	18.5
SAM-Run1	1.029	21	0.654	21	0.8745	15	0.541	19	19
CIAL-Run2	0.898	17	0.7485	14	1.316	24	0.356	23	19.5
FZU-NLP-Run2	1.0675	22	0.5765	23	0.92	18	0.544	17	20
NCYU-Run2	1.205	23	0.6665	20	0.989	22	0.534	21	21.5
XMUT-Run1	1.3345	24	0.3825	24	1.0995	23	0.2675	24	23.75

Table 3: task results.

3.1 Task Results

The final competition results are shown in Table 3, with our system highlighted. The ensemble approach of Run 2 achieved higher results than the rectangular network of Run 1, which is consistent with our experimental results. Compared to other participants, we ranked fifth out of the 13 participating teams, with the Tsinghua and Alibaba teams coming first and second, respectively. The Run 2 system retained a very consistent rank of 9-10 across all task / dataset combinations.

4 Nearest Neighbor Experiments

The major drawback of embeddings when we are modeling a sentiment-related problem is that words of opposite polarities obtain very similar embeddings since they occur in similar contexts. The experiments we report in the previous sections show our research work to build a robust statistical model for valence and arousal despite this limitation of the embeddings. As we have shown, significantly good results can be obtained by using a deep network of dense layers.

We have experimented with a different idea that we would like to discuss separately in this section since we did not include it in the runs we submitted to the shared task. This idea consists of enriching the *fastText* embeddings with additional dimensions that indicate the valence/arousal values

of the immediate semantic neighborhood in which the word we want to score is encountered. The steps that we take to infer these new dimensions can be described as follows:

1. $w \leftarrow$ word we want to score

2. $v \leftarrow$ fastText embedding of w

3. $nnList \leftarrow$ list of N nearest neighbors of v in the training set

4. $sortedNnList \leftarrow$ sort $nnList$ from lowest to highest value of valence/arousal score

As specified in the algorithm, the sorting is performed according to the score. Consequently, we obtain a different embedding for valence and arousal since both the order and the values of the new dimensions are different. Also, it is important to note that, the main reason behind sorting the scores of the nearest neighbors is to give a semantic consistency to the newly added features. By doing so, we make sure that the neural network that is going to perform the regression finds in these new dimensions an indication of the distribution of valence/arousal values in the immediate semantic neighborhood of the word we want to score. Sorting the nearest neighbors according to distance does not allow to achieve this semantic consistency of the dimensions.

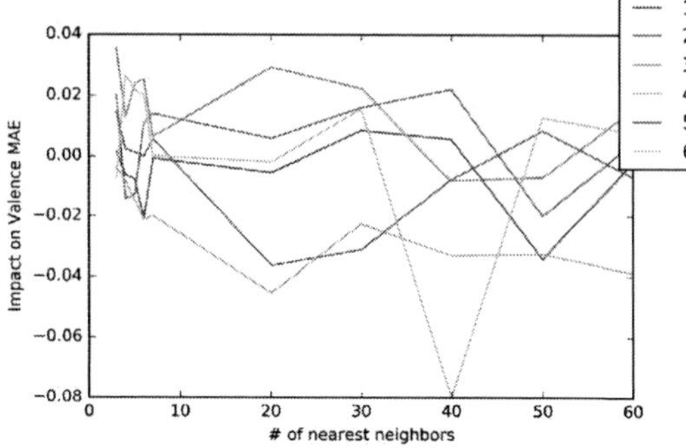

Figure 6: Impact on Valence MAE for neural networks of different depths after adding N nearest neighbor features

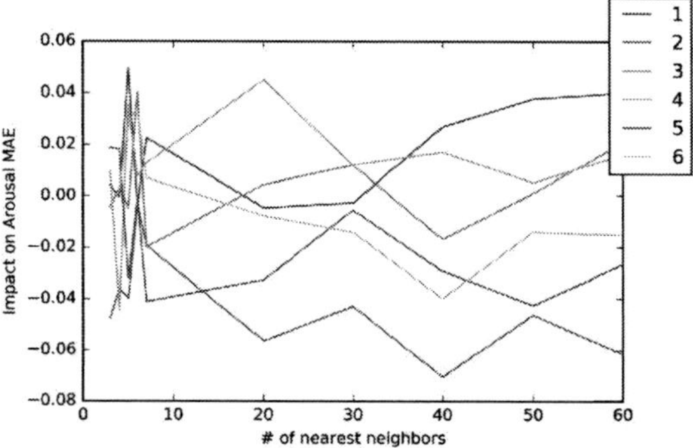

Figure 7: Impact on Arousal MAE for neural networks of different depths after adding N nearest neighbor features

Figures 6 and 7 show the obtained results.

The figures show the impact of adding the new features discussed in this section with difference values of N for neural networks with different layers. The general trend for both valence and arousal is that there an inflection point before and after which the new features either hurt or don't significantly help the results. We can also see however that for arousal the impact of the new features is significant even when N has a value between 3 and 7. Whereas for valence, we can only see a significant impact when the value of N is above 20.

This means that there is no clear correlation between the semantic neighborhood and the valence/arousal score, yet the situation is seemingly different between valence and arousal at the detailed level. For this reason, we wanted to go one step further in our analysis to shed more light on the relationship between the Euclidean distance (which we use to find the nearest neighbors) and the valence/arousal score. This is important specially because the learning machine needed infor-

mation from less neighbors and ended up benefiting more from them for arousal scoring than valence.

In order to be able to visualize and try to interpret this relationship the difference between the score of a word from the mean score of its semantic neighborhood, i.e. we compute the histogram of the z-score of the words score with respect to the distribution of their semantic neighborhood. Figures 8 and 9 show these histograms for valence and arousal, respectively.

The two histograms clearly show that whereas the arousal distribution is similar to a Gaussian distribution centered around 0, the valence distribution looks more like a mixture of two Gaussians one centered around 5 and the other around -5. In other words, the arousal score of a word is more often than not the average arousal score of its immediate neighbors. This explains why in our experiments the nearest neighbor features were very helpful. For valence, however, the score of a word is very often at a standard deviation distance of -5 or 5 from the mean. We believe, this could be the main reason why it was harder for the neural network to use the semantic neighborhood information more efficiently in the case of valence.

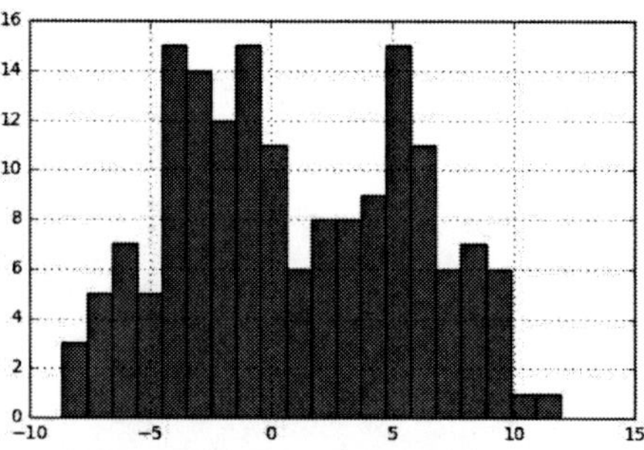

Figure 8: Histogram of Valence Z-score in the immediate Semantic Neighborhood

Finally, we would like to mention that the main reason we didn't include these new features in our final run is because the final MAE is better when we use deep networks with fastText features only.

5 Conclusion and Future Work

In this paper we describe our participation in DSAP 2017 shared task. We describe the various neural networks we explored. We also describe how we use ensemble methods to improve

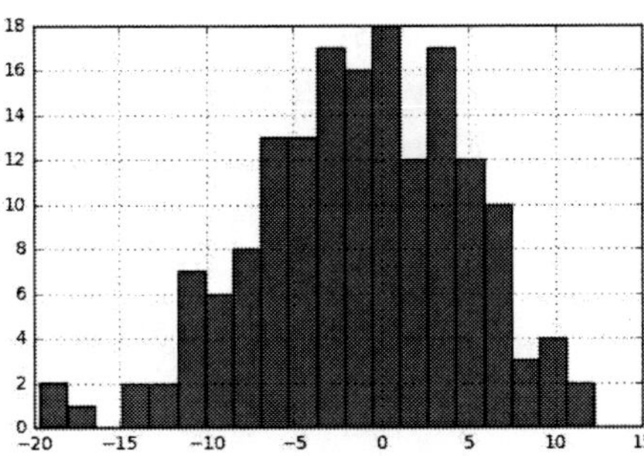

Figure 9: Histogram of Arousal Z-score in the immediate Semantic Neighborhood

the performance. In the latter, each classifier is trained independently with fine tuned layer parameters and we combine them by voting (averaging the scores).

In this work, we use character n-gram based word embedding with the help of *fastText*, hence the performance is limited by the embedding itself. We report our analysis of the relationship between the semantic neighborhood of a word and its valence/arousal score. In the future, we would extend our work to use sub-character components (radicals/strokes/components) learning in together with word embeddings to improve the performance further.

References

Piotr Bojanowski, Edouard Grave, Armand Joulin, and Tomas Mikolov. 2017. Enriching word vectors with subword information. *Transactions of the Association for Computational Linguistics* 5:135–146.

Steven Du and Xi Zhang. 2016. Aicyber's system for IALP 2016 shared task: Character-enhanced word vectors and boosted neural networks. In *2016 International Conference on Asian Language Processing, IALP 2016, Tainan, Taiwan, November 21-23, 2016.* pages 161–163.

Tomas Mikolov, Ilya Sutskever, Kai Chen, Greg S Corrado, and Jeff Dean. 2013. Distributed representations of words and phrases and their compositionality. In C. J. C. Burges, L. Bottou, M. Welling, Z. Ghahramani, and K. Q. Weinberger, editors, *Advances in Neural Information Processing Systems 26*, pages 3111–3119.

J.A. Russell. 1980. A circumplex model of affect. *Journal of personality and social psychology* 39(6):1161–1178.

Liang-Chih Yu, Lung-Hao Lee, Shuai Hao, Jin Wang, Yunchao He, Jun Hu, K. Robert Lai, and Xuejie Zhang. 2016a. Building chinese affective resources in valence-arousal dimensions. In *Proceedings of the 2016 Conference of the North American Chapter of the Association for Computational Linguistics: Human Language Technologies*. San Diego, California, pages 540–545.

Liang-Chih Yu, Lung-Hao Lee, and Kam-Fai Wong. 2016b. Overview of the IALP 2016 shared task on dimensional sentiment analysis for chinese words. In *2016 International Conference on Asian Language Processing, IALP*. Tainan, Taiwan, pages 156–160.

NCTU-NTUT at IJCNLP-2017 Task 2:
Deep Phrase Embedding using Bi-LSTMs for Valence-Arousal Ratings Prediction of Chinese Phrases

Yen-Hsuan Lee, Han-Yun Yeh and Yih-Ru Wang
Department of Electrical Engineering,
National Chiao Tung University
Hsinchu, Taiwan, ROC
yhl0305.cm05g@g2.nctu.edu.tw
henry034.cm05g@g2.nctu.edu.tw
yrwang@mail.nctu.edu.tw

Yuan-Fu Liao
Department of Electronic Engineering,
National Taipei University of Technology
Taipei, Taiwan, ROC
yfliao@ntut.edu.tw

Abstract

In this paper, a deep phrase embedding approach using bi-directional long short-term memory (Bi-LSTM) neural networks is proposed to predict the valence-arousal ratings of Chinese phrases. It adopts a Chinese word segmentation frontend, a local order-aware word-, a global phrase-embedding representations and a deep regression neural network (DRNN) model. The performance of the proposed method was benchmarked on the IJCNLP 2017 shared task 2. According the official evaluation results, our system achieved mean rank 6.5 among all 24 submissions.

1 Introduction

Recently, sentiment analysis has been approached from many different views. Among them, the two-dimensional valence-arousal space (Yu, et al., 2016) (as in Fig. 1) is promising. In this framework, the valence dimension describes the degree to which an emotion is pleasant or unpleasant, and the arousal dimension describes the degree to which an emotion is associated with high or low energy.

To promote this framework to Chinese language, a series of dimensional sentiment analysis shared tasks (Yu, et al., 2016) had been established since 2016. This paper reports our entry to the second one, i.e., the IJCNLP 2017 Shared Task: Dimensional Sentiment Analysis for Chinese Phrases[1].

Different from previous round, this year's task takes the ratings of phrases into considered. Unlike words, phrases usually have adverbs that could modify or even turn over the sentiment words in different degrees. For example, the word "爽" by itself describes a person in a pleasure mood. And the phrase "好 爽" means the man is feeling so good. But the phrase "不 爽" in fact indicates that person is unhappy. Moreover, the order of words is critical. Comparing the two phrases "完全 不 同意" and "不 完全 同意", the first one means "totally disagree", but the latter one to some extent represents "agree".

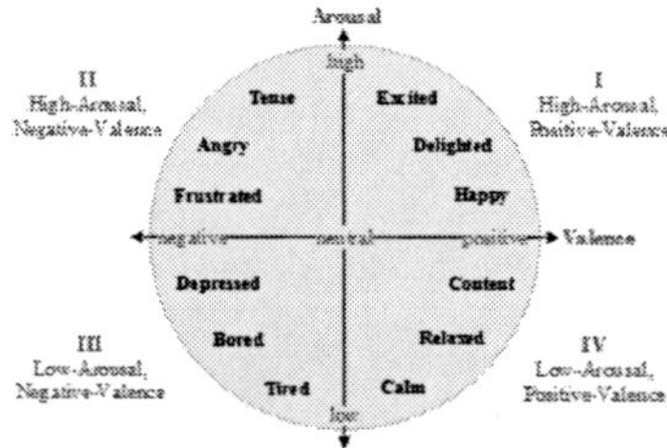

Figure 1: The two-dimensional valence-arousal (VA) space (from [1]).

In order to handle both the modifiers and word order issues, we refresh our previous model (Chou, et al., 2016) and proposed a new deep phrase embedding approach in this paper. The main idea is to build both a local order-aware word- and a recurrent neural network (RNN)-based phrase-embedding representations. To this end, a VA prediction system as shown in Fig. 2 is

---

[1] http://nlp.innobic.yzu.edu.tw/tasks/dsa_p/

Proceedings of the 8th International Joint Conference on Natural Language Processing, Shared Tasks, pages 124–129,
Taipei, Taiwan, November 27 – December 1, 2017. ©2017 AFNLP

proposed. It adopts a Chinese word segmentation frontend, a local order-aware Word2Vec, a Bi-LSTM Phrase2Vec and a DRNN module.

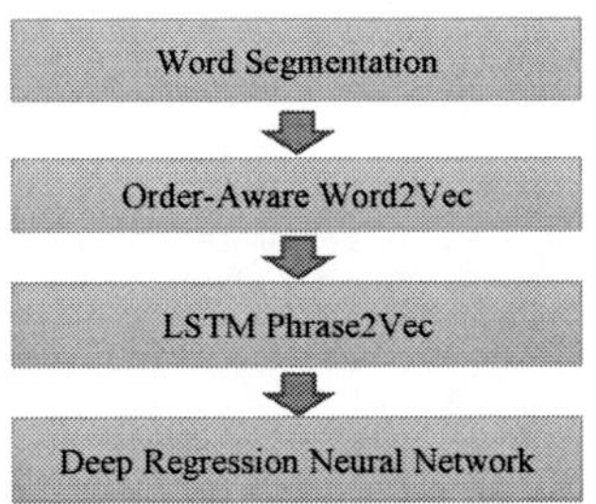

Figure 2: The Block Diagram of the proposed VA ratings prediction of Chinese Phrases approach.

It is worth mentioning that, the purpose of this study is not only to build an effective VA ratings prediction of Chinese phrases system but also to test the performance of our condition random field (CRF)-based Chinese parser (Wang and Liao, 2012). Because a good Chinese word segmentation frontend plays an important role in the success of this task.

2 The Proposed VA Prediction System

The procedures to build the proposed VA ratings system are shown in Fig. 3. First of all, a CRF-based Chinese parser is applied for word segmentation. Then an order-aware Word2Vec and a Phrase2Vec model are trained. Finally, a regression model is adopted to predict the VA ratings of Chinese phrases using the extracted phrase embeddings.

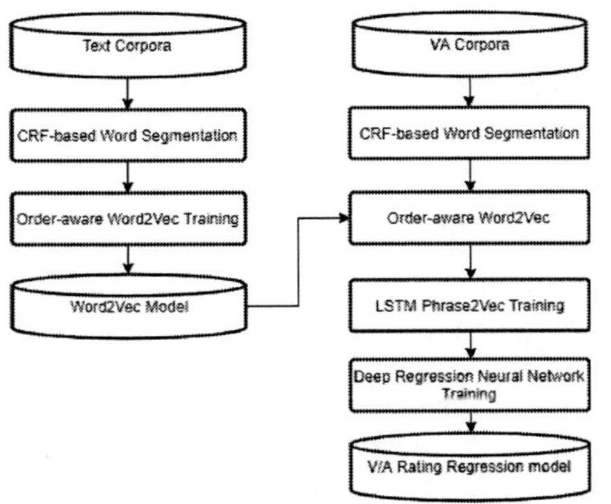

Figure 3: The procedure flowchart to build the proposed system for VA ratings prediction of Chinese phrases.

In the following subsections, four major system modules will be described in more detail including the (1) CRF-based Chinese parser, (2) order-aware Word2Vec, (3) Bi-LSTM Phrase2Vec and (4) DRNN models.

2.1 Chinese Word Segmentation

Our Chinese word segmentation frontend is a CRF-based parser as shown in Fig. 4. There are three main modules in this system, including (1) text normalization, (2) word segmentation and (3) part of speech (POS) tagging. The whole system was trained using error-corrected version of Sinica Balanced Corpus ver. 4.0^2.

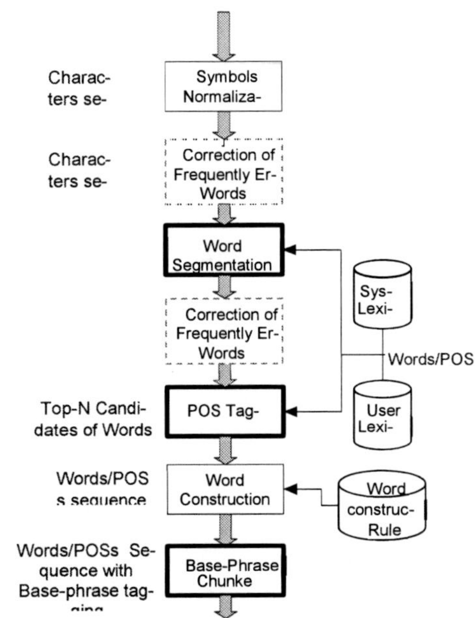

Figure 4: The schematic diagram of the CRF-based Chinese parser.

2.2 Order-Aware Word2Vec

Word to vector (Word2Vec) algorithms (Mikolov, et al., 2013), such as Skip-gram and continuous bag of words (CBOW), are widely used in natural language processing tasks. However, Skip-gram and CBOW only consider the context words but ignore their positions in a phrase. The Consequence is that they cannot deal well with the word order issue.

---

2 http://www.aclclp.org.tw/use_asbc.php

To solve this problem, we adopted a modified version of the Continuous Window (CWindow) and Structured Skip-gram approaches proposed by Wang (2015) to preserve the order cues, i.e., the 2-Bag-of-Words (2-BOW) and 2-Skip-gram methods as shown in Fig. 5.

Unlike conventional CBOW and Skip-gram models, 2-BOW and 2-Skip-gram take two contextual bags of words (before and after the target word) into consideration and use two separate projection matrices to preserve the word order information. By this way, order-aware word embedding representations could be generated.

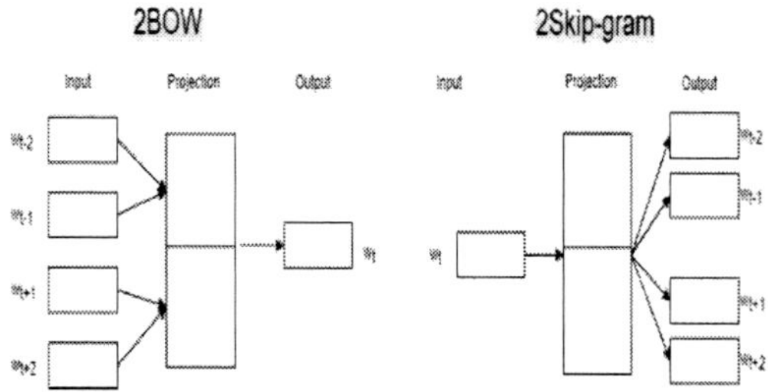

Figure 5: The architectures of the 2-BOW (left) and 2-Skip-gram (right) models.

2.3 Bi-LSTM-based Phrase2Vec

The other difficulty is that the length of phrases is variable. To deal with this problem, the many-to-one LSTM-based (Sepp and Schmidhuber) Phrase2Vec model as shown in Fig. 6 is proposed here.

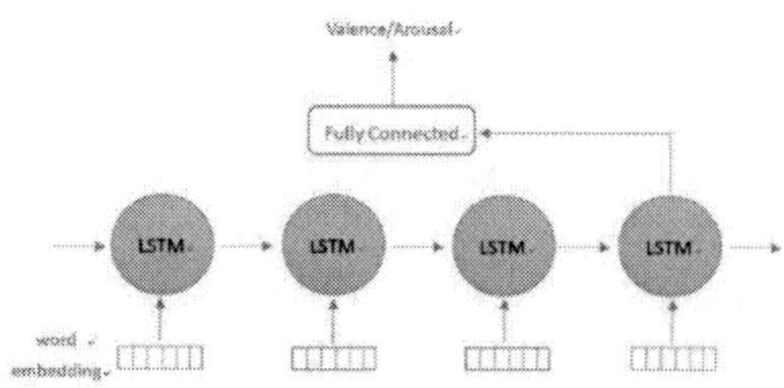

Figure 6: The architecture of the many-to-one LSTM-based Phrase2Vec model.

This is a sequence-to-sequence approach. Each word in a phrase is fed into the LSTM one-by-one at different time step and the last LSTM state vector is treated as the embedding representation of the whole phrase. Using this model, phrases with different numbers of words could all be successfully processed in the same way.

Moreover, a Bi-LSTM-based (Schuster and Paliwal) Phrase2Vec model (as shown in Fig. 7) is also introduced in this paper. The purpose is to explore the word order cues in both the forward and backward directions.

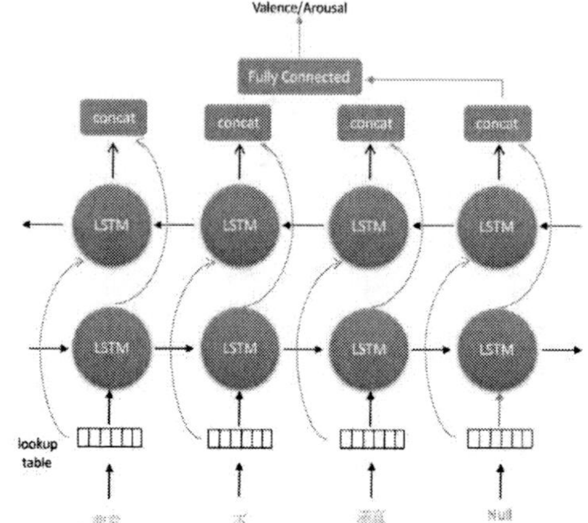

Figure 7: The architecture of the bi-directional LSTM-based Phrase2Vec model.

2.4 Deep Regression Neural Network

Finally, a fully connected feedforward network as shown in Fig. 8 is applied as a non-linear regression model to predict the VA ratings of Chinese phrases.

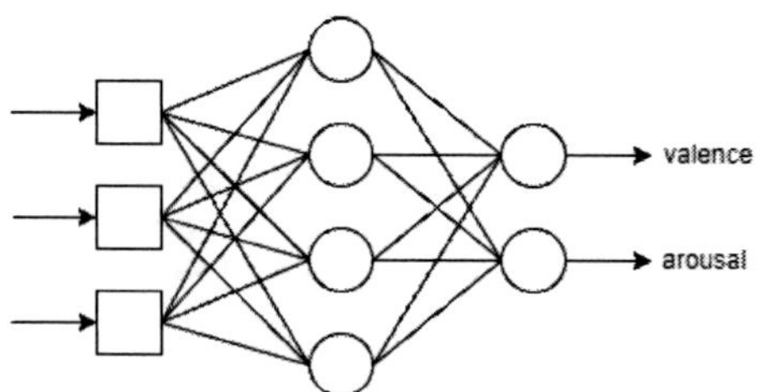

Figure 8: The deep regression neural network for VA ratings prediction of Chinese phrases.

3 Sentiment Analysis Experiments

To benchmark the proposed methods, several preliminary experiments were first conducted to find the optimal model configurations. Then two sets of VA ratings prediction results generated by the best models were submitted for official evaluation.

In the following subsections, the performance of different model combinations will be described in detail.

3.1 Experimental Settings

3.1.1 Text Corpora for Word Embeddings

In this paper, the Skip-gram, CBOW, 2-Skip-gram and 2-BOW models were all trained using the same set of text corpora including (1) LDC Chinese Gigaword Second Edition[3], (2) Sinica Balanced Corpus ver. 4.0, (3) CIRB0303[4], (Chinese Information Retrieval Benchmark, version 3.03), (4) Taiwan Panorama Magazine[5], (5) TCC300[6] and (6) Wikipedia (ZH_TW version).

They were then utilized to project every Chinese word into a high dimensional vector space for further VA analysis.

3.1.2 VA Corpora

The Chinese Valence-Arousal Words 2.0 (CVAW 2.0) and Chinese Valence-Arousal Phrase (CVAP) databases provided by IJCNLP-2017 shared task were divided into a training and a test subsets and used in all the following experiments. Among them, CVAW 2.0 consists of 2,802 affective words and CVAP has 2,250 multi-words phrases. They are all annotated with valence-arousal ratings by hand. In all the following experiments, 10% of CVAW 2.0 and CVAP data are used for validation.

3.1.3 Official Evaluation Metrics

Two evaluation metrics were adopted by the IJCNLP-2017 shared task. The first one is the mean absolute error (MAE, as defined in Eq. (1), lower is better).

$$MAE = \frac{1}{n}\sum_{i=1}^{n}|A_i - P_i| \qquad \ldots\ldots (1)$$

Here A_i denotes the VA ratings ground-truths annotated by human, P_i is automatically predicted VA rating values, n is the number of test samples.

Another one is the Pearson correlation coefficient (PCC, as shown in Eq. (2), higher is better)

$$PCC = \frac{1}{n-1}\sum_{i=1}^{n}(\frac{A_i - \overline{A}}{\sigma_A})(\frac{P_i - \overline{P}}{\sigma_P}) \ \ldots\ldots (2)$$

Here $\{\overline{A}, \sigma_A\}$ and $\{\overline{P}, \sigma_P\}$ represent the means and the standard deviations of the human-annotated and machine predicted VA ratings, respectively.

3.2 Preliminary Experimental Results

3.2.1 Different Word Embedding Models

Since the performance of sentiment analysis highly depends on the quality of word embeddings, five different word embedding models including: Skip-gram, CBOW, 2-Skip-gram, 2-CBOW and 2-Skip-gram+2-CBOW were first tested using the same variable input length LSTM (vLSTM) Phrase2Vec backend. In all the experiments, cross validation approach was used to train and test the models. And the window size was all fixed at 15.

Table 1 shows the performances of different Word2Vec models. It was found that 2-Skip-gram+2-BOW and 2-BOW approaches with 300-dimensional embedding vectors achieved the best prediction results for words and phrases, respectively.

Table 1: Performance (MAE) comparison of VA ratings prediction of Chinese words and phrases on different Word2Vec models.

Word	Dimension		
	200	250	300
Skip-gram	0.8275	0.845	0.836
CBOW	0.819	0.8165	0.8205
2-Skip-gram	0.839	0.843	0.8185
2-BOW	0.8085	0.8035	0.8615
2-Skip-gram+2-BOW	0.8035	0.812	**0.783**

Phrase	Dimension		
	200	250	300
Skip-gram	0.541	0.5105	0.491
CBOW	0.4075	0.4055	0.4025
2-Skip-gram	0.4965	0.46	0.458
2-BOW	0.4335	0.4105	**0.3965**
2-Skip-gram+2-BOW	0.397	0.4005	0.407

3.2.2 Different LSTM Structures

Four types of LSTM models were then trained using the same cross validation approaches, including:

- Fixed length LSTM (LSTM): the input sequence was word-padded to the same length.
- Variable length LSTM (vLSTM): The length input sequence is dynamic without word-padding.
- Bi-directional LSTM (Bi-LSTM): Fixed input length but with bi-directional LSTM model.

[3] https://catalog.ldc.upenn.edu/LDC2005T14
[4] http://www.aclclp.org.tw/use_cir.php
[5] https://www.taiwan-panorama.com/en
[6] http://www.aclclp.org.tw/use_mat.php#tcc300edu

- Variable length bi-directional LSTM (vBi-LSTM): Dynamic sequence length plus the bi-directional LSTM model.

Table 2 reports the performance of different LSTM models (all with the 2-Skip-gram+2BOW with 300-dimension word embeddings frontend). The results indicate that, in general, the variable input length LSTM models work better than the fixed ones.

Table 2: Performance (MAE) comparison of VA ratings prediction of Chinese words and phrases on different LSTM models.

Word	Valence	Arousal	Average
LSTM	0.64	0.954	0.797
vLSTM	0.625	0.982	0.8035
Bi-LSTM	**0.622**	0.961	0.7915
vBi-LSTM	0.638	**0.928**	**0.783**
Phrase	Valence	Arousal	Average
LSTM	0.377	0.415	0.396
vLSTM	**0.364**	0.418	**0.391**
Bi-LSTM	0.387	**0.402**	0.3945
vBi-LSTM	0.388	0.426	0.407

3.3 Official Evaluation Results

Based on the results of the preliminary experiments, two runs (NCTU+NTUT run1 and run2) were submitted to ICJNLP2017 shared task for official benchmark. Both run1 and run2 adopted the 2-Skip-gram+2-BOW model with 300-dimension word embeddings plus the variable input length LSTM models. The only difference is that run1 used the vLSTM and run2 adopted the vBi-LSTM model, respectively.

Table 3 and 4 shows the official evaluation results of our two submissions. The performance of the run1 and run2 are all promising (with only a marginal difference between these two models).

Table 3: Official MAE evaluation results of the NCTU+NTUT's submissions (Run1 and Run2).

Word	Valence	Arousal	Average
Run1	**0.632**	0.952	0.792
Run2	0.639	**0.94**	**0.7895**
Phrase	Valence	Arousal	Average
Run1	0.454	**0.488**	**0.471**
Run2	**0.453**	0.517	0.485

Table 4: Official PCC evaluation results of the NCTU+NTUT's submissions (Run1 and Run2).

Word	Valence	Arousal	Average
Run1	**0.846**	0.543	0.6945
Run2	0.842	**0.566**	**0.704**
Phrase	Valence	Arousal	Average
Run1	0.928	**0.847**	**0.8875**
Run2	**0.931**	0.832	0.8815

4   Conclusions

In this paper, we had proposed and evaluated various order-aware embedding representations in both word- and phrase-levels. It is found that the order-aware Word2Vec and LSTM-based Phrase2Vec all could improve the performance of VA ratings prediction of Chinese phrases. In brief, our system achieved mean rank 6.5 among in total 24 submissions in the official ICJNLP2017 shared task evaluation. Finally, the latest version of our Chinese parser is available on-line at http://parser.speech.cm.nctu.edu.tw/.

Acknowledgments

This work was supported by the Ministry of Science and Technology, Taiwan with contract 105-2221-E-027-119, 105-2221-E-009-142-MY2 and 106-2221-E-027-128.

References

Liang-Chih Yu, Lung-Hao Lee, Shuai Hao, Jin Wang, Yunchao He, Jun Hu, K. Robert Lai, and Xuejie Zhang. 2016a. Building Chinese affective resources in valence-arousal dimensions. In *NAACL/HLT*, pages 540-545.

Liang-Chih Yu, Lung-Hao Lee and Kam-Fai Wong. 2016b. Overview of the IALP 2016 shared task on dimensional sentiment analysis for Chinese words. In *IALP*, pages 156-160.

Wei-Chieh Chou, Chin-Kui Lin, Yih-Ru Wang, Yuan-Fu Liao. 2016. Evaluation of weighted graph and neural network models on predicting the valence-arousal ratings of Chinese words. In *IALP* pages 168-171.

Yih-Ru Wang and Yuan-Fu Liao. 2012. A Conditional Random Field-based Traditional Chinese Base-Phrase Parser for SIGHAN Bake-off 2012 Evaluation. In *CLP 2012*. pages 231.

Tomas Mikolov, Ilya Sutskever, Kai Chen, Greg S Corrado, and Jeff Dean. 2013. Distributed representations of words and phrases and their compositionality. In *Advances in Neural Information Processing Systems*, pages 3111–3119.

Ling Wang, Chris Dyer, Alan Black and Isabel Trancoso. 2015. Two/Too Simple Adaptations of Word2Vec for Syntax Problems. In *HLT-NAACL*.

Hochreiter Sepp and Jürgen Schmidhuber. 1997. Long short-term memory. In *Neural computation 9.8*, pages 1735-1780.

Mike Schuster and Kuldip K. Paliwal. 1997. Bidirectional recurrent neural networks. In *IEEE Transactions on Signal Processing* 45.11. pages 2673-2681

NTOUA at IJCNLP-2017 Task 2:
Predicting Sentiment Scores of Chinese Words and Phrases

Chuan-Jie Lin and Hao-Tsung Chang
Department of Computer Science and Engineering
National Taiwan Ocean University
Keelung, Taiwan ROC.
{cjlin, htchang.cse}@ntou.edu.tw

Abstract

This paper describes the approaches of sentimental score prediction in the NTOU DSA system participating in DSAP this year. The modules to predict scores for words are adapted from our system last year. The approach to predict scores for phrases is keyword-based machine learning method. The performance of our system is good in predicting scores of phrases.

1 Introduction

The task of Dimensional Sentiment Analysis for Chinese Phrases (DSAP), a shared task held in IJCNLP 2017, focuses on predicting valence and arousal scores of Chinese words and phrases. It is the second evaluation project of sentiment score prediction in word level (Yu *et al.*, 2016b), but the first task in phrase level.

The valence of a word or phrase represents the degree of pleasant and unpleasant (or positive and negative) feelings. For example, "happy" is a positive word and "sad" is negative.

The arousal of a word or phrase represents the degree of excitement and calm. For example, "surprise" is more excited and "tired" is calmer.

Valence and arousal can be used to define a space where the features denote dimensions (Russell 1980; Kim *et al.*, 2010; Malandrakis *et al.*, 2011; Wei *et al.*, 2011; Calvo and Kim, 2013; Paltoglou *et al.*, 2013; Yu *et al.*, 2015; Wang *et al.*, 2016). These two dimensions are independent. There are positive-excited words like "delighted", positive-calm words like "relaxed", negative-excited words like "angry", and negative-calm words like "bored".

The applications of sentiment analysis include antisocial behavior detection (Munezero *et al.*, 2011), mood analysis (Choudhury *et al.*, 2012) and product review ranking (Ren and Nickerson, 2014).

It was our second attempt of sentiment rating prediction in word level. We simply chose the best two systems developed during DSAW in 2016 (Yu *et al.*, 2016a),

which are described in Section 2. For phrases, we proposed a simple keyword-based machine learning method as described in Section 3.

2 Predicting by Co-Occurrence

This year, we experimented two simple methods to predict sentiment scores of words. One method focuses on predicting valence scores and the other on arousal scores. Both systems use co-occurrence information from Google Web 1T 5-grams[1] (Google N-grams for short hereafter).

To illustrate our method, we first define two functions of co-occurrence scores between a target word t and a context word w. The **right co-occurrence frequency** $coFreqR(t, w, n)$ is the frequency of the n-gram $a_1a_2...a_n$ where $a_1 = t$ and $a_n = w$. The **left co-occurrence frequency** $coFreqL(t, w, n)$ is the frequency of the n-gram $a_1a_2...a_n$ where $a_1 = w$ and $a_n = t$. Note that we only used bigram to 5-gram data, therefore $2 \leq n \leq 5$.

2.1 Co-Occurrence with Sentiment Words

The first system predicts sentiment scores of a target word by its co-occurrence with other sentiment words. All sentiment words provided in the DSAW training data are considered as the "context words" in the $coFreq()$ functions. Two kinds of features are defined as follows.

The **right co-occurrence sentiment features** sf_{nR} of a target word t is the average of

$$sentiScore(w) \times \log(coFreqR(t, w, n))$$

for all the sentiment words w whose $coFreqR(t, w, n)$ values are positive, where $sentiScore(w)$ is either the valence or arousal score of w.

Similarly, the **left co-occurrence sentiment features** sf_{nL} of a target word t is the average of $sentiScore(w) \times \log(coFreqL(t, w, n))$ for all the sentiment words w whose $coFreqL(t, w, n)$ values are positive. Given that $2 \leq n \leq 5$, totally four right co-occurrence sentiment features and four left co-occurrence sentiment features are defined.

---

[1] https://catalog.ldc.upenn.edu/LDC2006T13

Proceedings of the 8th International Joint Conference on Natural Language Processing, Shared Tasks, pages 130–133,
Taipei, Taiwan, November 27 – December 1, 2017. ©2017 AFNLP

2.2 Co-Occurrence with Degree Adverbs

The second system predicts sentiment scores of a target word by its co-occurrence with degree adverbs such as "非常" (very) and "有點" (a little). We collected a set of degree adverbs from Tongyici Cilin, a dictionary about Chinese synonyms. These degree adverbs are considered as the "context words" in the $coFreq()$ functions. Two kinds of features are defined as follows.

The *right co-occurrence degree features df_{nR}* of a target word t is the average of $\log(coFreqR(t, d, n))$ for all the degree adverbs d whose $coFreqR(t, d, n)$ values are positive. Similarly, the *left co-occurrence degree features df_{nL}* of a target word t is the average of $\log(coFreqL(t, d, n))$ for all the degree adverbs d whose $coFreqL(t, d, n)$ values are positive. Given that $2 \leq n \leq 5$, totally four right co-occurrence degree features and four left co-occurrence degree features are defined.

3 Sentiment Changing by Adverbs

This is the first evaluation project of sentiment score prediction in phrase level. The "phrases" used this year have the same pattern: [RB | MD]⁺ JJ, where JJ is an adjective, preceded by one or more adverbs (RB) or modals (MD). It is interesting to see how an adverb or modal word can change the sentiment score of an adjective.

There are two types of adverbs seen in the test data this year: negation words (NEG) and adverbs of degree (DEG). A negation word such as "不" (not) often alters a sentiment score into its opposite direction in some degree, while an adverb of degree such as "非常" (very) often enhance a sentiment score along its original direction.

However, the effect of modal words (MOD) such as "應該" (should) or "可能" (might) is less predictable. Maybe they would change the sentiment degrees toward the neutral point.

These adverbs and modal words can be compound as well. There are 4 combinations seen in the training data:

- DEG_NEG: such as "完全 不 怕" (totally not afraid)
- MOD_DEG: such as "可能 很 怕" (might-be very afraid)
- MOD_NEG: such as "可能 不 怕" (might not be-afraid)
- NEG_DEG: such as "不 太 怕" (not very afraid)

Based on the adverbs or modal words detected before an adjective, we proposed two different methods to predict sentiment scores of phrases, as described in Sections 3.2 and 3.3. Before that, we will explain how we decide the preceding adverb combinations.

3.1 Adverb-Combination Detection

As we know that the phrases are written in the pattern of [RB | MD]⁺ JJ, we use the following recursive grammars to detect the preceding adverbs and modal words.

sentiPhrase := [RB | MD] sentiPhrase
sentiPhrase := [RB | MD] JJ

When parsing a phrase P, if it can be divided into an adverb (or modal) with an adjective (which appears in the dictionary), the division is accepted and the parsing is finished. Otherwise, if P can be divided into A+B where A is an adverb (or modal), B will be further parsed with the same grammars.

For example, the phrase "很難過" (very sad) is divided into "很" (very) and "難過" (sad), because "很" (very) is known as an adverb and "難過" (sad) is an adjective collected in the sentiment dictionary.

For another example, the phrase "沒有太難過" (not too sad) is divided into "沒有" (not) and "太難過" (too sad). Because "太難過" (too sad) is not a word, it is further divided into "太" (too) and "難過" (sad).

Note that the process can be repeated as many times as necessary with no limitation, so are our proposed methods. The longest combination found in the test data has only two words.

3.2 Phrase-Level Features

3.2.1 Deciding Core-Adjective Feature Values

The first two features we used are the valence and arousal scores of the core adjective. In the training process, only those training examples whose core adjectives can be also be found in the DSAW training set (which means their sentiment scores are correct) are used. In the testing process, if we do not know the sentiment scores of the core adjective, we will use our DSAW system to predict their scores in advance.

Note that both valence and arousal scores of the core adjective are used together, no matter when it is predicting the valence score or arousal score of a phrase.

3.2.2 Adverb-Combination Feature

The third feature we used is the adverb combination detected in front of the core adjective. We inserted underscores between adverbs, such as "應該_沒有_太", "沒有_太", or "沒有" if only one adverb is found.

In another experiment, we only take the leftmost adverb as the feature value, which method is described in Section 3.3.2.

3.3 Phrase-Level Sentiment Prediction

We proposed two different systems to predict sentiment scores of phrases. The two systems worked on similar features but different procedures.

3.3.1 Predicting by Adverb-Combinations

The first system took the whole phrase of preceding adverbs and modal words as the third feature. Some examples of feature values are given here, where the first column depicts the phrases and the second the feature values:

更加小心　　更加, 4.6, 6

稍微不小心　稍微_不, 4.6, 6

稍微不痛　　稍微_不, 3, 6.2

In the first two examples, the core adjective is "小心" (careful) whose valence score is 4.6 and arousal score is 6, and the core adjective in the third example is "痛" (hurtful) whose valence score is 3 and arousal score is 6.2.

As mentioned in Section 3.2.1, if the sentiment scores of a core adjective is unknown (i.e. not found in the training data), its score will be predicted by DSAW system first in the testing process, or this example will be discarded during the training process.

3.3.2 Predicting by Single Adverbs

The second system only took the leading adverb or modal word as the third feature.

In the training process, these two sets of phrases were chosen as training data:

- Phrases in the pattern of [RB | MD] JJ whose core adjectives appear in the DSAW training set.
- Phrases in the pattern of [RB | MD] AA where AA is a phrase that appears in the DSAP training set.

In these two sets, the sentiment scores of the core adjectives or phrases are accurate thus can be used as feature values. There are two examples:

超級可愛　　超級, 7, 6.2

超級不安全　超級, 3.444, 5

In the first example, the core adjective is "可愛" (cute), and the DSAW training data provides its valence score as 7 and arousal score as 6.2. In the second example, the core phrase is "不安全" (not safe), and the DSAP training data provides its valence score as 3.444 and arousal score as 5.

In the testing process, a given phrase is first divided into an adverb (or modal word) and a core phrase. If the sentiment scores of this core phrase can be found in the training data, the given phrase can be predicted directly.

If the sentiment scores of the core phrase are unknown, these scores should be predicted in advance, either by DSAP system or DSAW system. For example, to predict the phrase "超級不可恨", it is divided into "超級" + "不" + "可恨" first. The sentiment scores of the adjective "可恨" (hateful) is predicted by our DSAW system. And then the phrase "不" + "可恨" (not hateful) is predicted by our DSAP system with the just-predicted sentiment scores of "可恨" as feature values. Finally, the phrase "超級" + "不" + "可恨" (extremely not hateful) is predicted by our DSAP system by the sentiment scores of "不可恨" as feature values.

4 Run Submission and Evaluation Results

Two runs were submitted to the IJCLCLP 2017 Shared Task: Dimensional Sentiment Analysis for Chinese Phrases as requested by the organizers. Their strategies to train DSAW (for predicting words) and DSAP (for predicting phrases) modules are described as follows.

- NTOUA1: the DSAW module was trained by using co-occurrence sentiment features, and the DSAP was using trained by adverb-combination features.
- NTOUA2: the DSAW module was trained by using co-occurrence degree features; the DSAP was trained by using single-adverb features, and its prediction process was recursive as described in Section 3.3.2.

Both systems were trained by the random forest algorithm, a machine learning method. This method performed the best during our training process.

Table 1 lists the evaluation results of our submitted runs. Results were evaluated on (1) words (2) phrases (3) all about valence and arousal scores, respectively, in the metrics of mean absolute error (MAE) and Pearson correlation coefficient (PCC). The ranks of our systems among all the submitted systems are also depicted.

Table 1. Performance of NTOU Runs in DSAP 2017

Task & Metric (rank)	NTOUA1	NTOUA2
Word, Valence, MAE	0.913(15)	1.061(19)
Word, Valence, PCC	0.700(16)	0.544(22)
Word, Arousal, MAE	1.133(17)	1.114(16)
Word, Arousal, PCC	0.163(23)	0.350(21)
Phrase, Valence, MAE	0.472(7)	0.453(4)
Phrase, Valence, PCC	0.910(8)	0.929(5)
Phrase, Arousal, MAE	0.420(5)	0.441(6)
Phrase, Arousal, PCC	0.882(5)	0.870(6)
All, Valence, MAE	0.692(12)	0.757(13)
All, Valence, PCC	0.805(12)	0.737(15)
All, Arousal, MAE	0.777(11)	0.778(12)
All, Arousal, PCC	0.523(22)	0.610(12)
All, Rank	14.25	13

Both our DSAP modules perform very well in predicting sentiment scores of phrases (best ranked at Top 4).

There may not be significant difference between the two DSAP methods.

Simple adverb features are very effective. It also means that the sentiment score of the core adjective is the most critical information in sentiment prediction. This year, all the accurate sentiment scores of core adjectives can be found in the training data.

Unfortunately, neither of our DSAW modules achieved good performance in the formal test. We should greatly improve our DSAW module in the future.

5   Conclusion

This paper proposed two approaches to predict valence and arousal scores of Chinese words and two approaches for scores of Chinese phrases.

Before predicting a Chinese phrase, its leading adverbs or modal words are detected in advance. Its sentiment score can be predicted either by considering the whole set of leading adverbs, or recursively decided by single leading adverbs. The results show that this strategy achieves rather good performance.

Since the key to successfully predict sentiment scores of phrases is still a good DSAW system, we will study more about DSAW in the future.

References

Rafael Calvo, and Sunghwan Mac Kim. 2013. "Emotions in text: dimensional and categorical models," *Computational Intelligence*, 29(3): 527-543.

Munmun De Choudhury, Scott Counts, and Michael Gamon. 2012. "Not all moods are created equal! Exploring human emotional states in social media," *Proceedings of ICWSM-12*, 66-73.

Sunghwan Mac Kim, Alessandro Valitutti, and Rafael Calvo. 2010. "Evaluation of unsupervised emotion models to textual affect recognition," *Proceedings of the NAACL HLT 2010 Workshop on Computational Approaches to Analysis and Generation of Emotion in Text*, 62-70.

Su-Chu Lin, Shu-Ling Huang, You-Shan Chung, and Keh-Jiann Chen. 2013. "The lexical knowledge and semantic representation of E-HowNet," *Contemporary Linguistics*, 15(2): 177-194.

Nikos Malandrakis, Alexandros Potamianos, Elias Iosif, and Shrikanth Narayanan. 2011. "Kernel models for affective lexicon creation," *Proceedings of INTERSPEECH-11*, 2977-2980.

Myriam Munezero, Tuomo Kakkonen, and Calkin Montero. 2011. "Towards automatic detection of antisocial behavior from texts," *Proceedings of the Workshop on Sentiment Analysis where AI meets Psychology (SAAIP) at IJCNLP-11*, 20-27.

Georgios Paltoglou, Mathias Theunis, Arvid Kappas, and Mike Thelwall. 2013. "Predicting emotional responses to long informal text," *IEEE Transaction Affective Computing*, 4(1): 106-115.

Jie Ren and Jeffrey Nickerson. 2014. "Online review systems: How emotional language drives sales," *Proceedings of AMCIS-14*.

James Russell. 1980. "A circumplex model of affect," *Journal of Personality and Social Psychology*, 39(6): 1161-1178.

Jin Wang, Liang-Chih Yu, K. Robert Lai and Xuejie Zhang. 2016. "Community-based weighted graph model for valence-arousal prediction of affective words," *IEEE/ACM Transaction Audio, Speech and Language Processing*, 24(11): 1957-1968.

Wen-Li Wei, Chung-Hsien Wu, and Jen-Chun Lin. 2011. "A regression approach to affective rating of Chinese words from ANEW," *Proceedings of ACII-11*, 121-131.

Liang-Chih Yu, Jin Wang, Robert Lai and Xuejie Zhang. 2015. "Predicting valence-arousal ratings of words using a weighted graph method," *Proceedings of ACL/IJCNLP-15*, 788-793.

Liang-Chih Yu, Lung-Hao Lee, Shuai Hao, Jin Wang, Yunchao He, Jun Hu, K. Robert Lai, and Xuejie Zhang. 2016a. "Building Chinese affective resources in valence-arousal dimensions," *Proceedings of NAACL/HLT-16*, 540-545.

Liang-Chih Yu, Lung-Hao Lee and Kam-Fai Wong. 2016b. "Overview of the IALP 2016 shared task on dimensional sentiment analysis for Chinese words", *Proceedings of IALP-16*, 156-160.

CYUT at IJCNLP-2017 Task 3: System Report for Review Opinion Diversification

Shih-Hung Wu [1], Su-Yu Chang [2], and Liang-Pu Chen[3]
[1,2] Dept. of CSIE, Chaoyang University of Technology, Taichung, Taiwan (R.O.C)
[3]DSI, Institute for Information Industry, Taipei, Taiwan (R.O.C)

Abstract

Review Opinion Diversification (RevOpiD) 2017 is a shared task which is held in International Joint Conference on Natural Language Processing (IJCNLP). The shared task aims at selecting top-k reviews, as a summary, from a set of re-views. There are three subtasks in RevOpiD: helpfulness ranking, representativeness ranking, and exhaustive coverage ranking. This year, our team submitted runs by three models. We focus on ranking reviews based on the helpfulness of the reviews. In the first two models, we use linear regression with two different loss functions. First one is least squares, and second one is cross entropy. The third run is a random baseline. For both k=5 and k=10, our second model gets the best scores in the official evaluation metrics.

1 Introduction

This paper reports how our team participated the Review Opinion Diversification (RevOpiD) 2017[1] shared task held in International Joint Conference on Natural Language Processing (IJCNLP). The shared task aims at selecting top-k reviews from a set of Amazon online product reviews on three different aspects, which are corresponding to three subtasks in RevOpiD: helpfulness ranking, representativeness ranking, and exhaustive coverage ranking (Singh et al., 2017).

This year, for k=5 and k=10, our team submitted three runs each by three models. We focus on ranking reviews based on the helpfulness of the reviews. In the first two models, we use linear regression with two different loss functions. The third run is a random baseline.

The paper is organized as follows: Section 2 gives the basic thought of how we construct our system. Section 3 shows our system architecture. The result is discussed in section 4. The conclusion and future works is in section 5.

2 Methodology

Our system follows the general machine learning approach. 1. Prepare the training data, 2. Find the proper features, 3. Train a model, and 4. Evaluate the result.

After observing the training data a little bit, we found that there are many reviews with zero vote (e.g. helpful[0/0]), which means there is no one voting this review at all. We cannot tell whether the review is not helpful, so that nobody voted, or the review is too new so people had no opportunity to vote it before the data was gathered. Therefore, we decide to filter out all the reviews with zero vote in the training set. The data preprocessing helps to get a better training result on training set. The zero vote data cause a lot of training error, since the zero vote data will make a regression system to give very low weights on all features.

Our system used two kinds of features: the length of a review, and the numbers of words with certain part-of-speech (POS) in the review; based on our experience on Chinese online review helpfulness prediction. In our previous works, we found that the distribution of certain part-of-speech (POS) will affect the ranking of opinion (Hsieh et al., 2014). Traditionally speaking, verbs, nouns, and adjectives are grouped as content words. The more content words are involved, the more informative, so the more helpful, the review is.

We chose the linear regression model this year. Many previous works have shown that linear regression model can be used to predict the helpfulness (Wu et al., 2017).

Our optimization goal is to rank the helpfulness according to the helpful votes. The problem has been studied by several previous works and shows promising result that text analysis results can help

---

[1] https://sites.google.com/itbhu.ac.in/revopid-2017

Proceedings of the 8th International Joint Conference on Natural Language Processing, Shared Tasks, pages 134–137,
Taipei, Taiwan, November 27 – December 1, 2017. ©2017 AFNLP

helpfulness prediction (Zeng and Wu. 2013)(Zeng et al., 2014).

3 System Architecture

3.1 Data Preprocessing

During the pre-processing, our system filtered out the reviews with zero vote. There are 3,619,981 reviews in the Training data. After filtering out the zero vote reviews, there are only 1,215,671 reviews remaining in our training set. There are 2,404,310 zero-vote-reviews, which occupies about 66% of the original training set.

3.2 Features

Our system used four features: the first one is the length of a review. The second to fourth ones are the numbers of verbs (VB), nouns (NN), and adjectives (JJ) in the review. The POS of words in review is tagged by the tagging function of a python toolkit NLTK (Loper and Bird, 2002). The tag set is defined as Penn treebank (Santorini, 1990), shown in Table 1. Actually there are other tags that also verbs (VBD, VBG, VBN, VBP, VBZ), nouns (NNS, NNP, NNPS), and adjectives (JJR, JJS). Due to the time limitation, we do not count them in in our system. We believed that the proportion of each POS tag in the reviews should be similar.

3.3 The Linear Regression Model A

To implement the linear regression in model A, we use the Python Scikit-learn (Pedregosa et al., 2011) In this linear regression module, the training data is standardized by the fit_transform() function, and the loss function is Least squares. The test data is then ranked according to the helpfulness prediction of the regression model.

3.4 The Linear Regression Model B

The second model is implemented with the Google TensorFlow toolkit (Allaire et al., 2016). The training data is not standardized. The linear regression formula is as follows:

$$\text{Hypothesis} = (W*X) + b \qquad (1)$$

where X is the input data matrix. The weights W and the bias b are randomly initialized. The learning rate is 0.01. The optimizer is GradientDescentOptimizer. The training_epochs is 10,000. The loss function is the reduce_mean function, which is the average cross entropy of each training batch. The model is then used as our second model. The test data is then ranked according to the helpfulness prediction of the regression model.

	Tag	Description
1	CC	Coordinating conjunction
2	CD	Cardinal number
3	DT	Determiner
4	EX	Existential *there*
5	FW	Foreign word
6	IN	Preposition or subordinating conjunction
7	JJ	Adjective
8	JJR	Adjective, comparative
9	JJS	Adjective, superlative
10	LS	List item marker
11	MD	Modal
12	NN	Noun, singular or mass
13	NNS	Noun, plural
14	NNP	Proper noun, singular
15	NNPS	Proper noun, plural
16	PDT	Predeterminer
17	POS	Possessive ending
18	PRP	Personal pronoun
19	PRP$	Possessive pronoun
20	RB	Adverb
21	RBR	Adverb, comparative
22	RBS	Adverb, superlative
23	RP	Particle
24	SYM	Symbol
25	TO	*to*
26	UH	Interjection
27	VB	Verb, base form
28	VBD	Verb, past tense
29	VBG	Verb, gerund or present participle
30	VBN	Verb, past participle
31	VBP	Verb, non-3rd person singular present
32	VBZ	Verb, 3rd person singular present
33	WDT	Wh-determiner
34	WP	Wh-pronoun
35	WP$	Possessive wh-pronoun
36	WRB	Wh-adverb

Table 1: part-of-speech tags used in the Penn Treebank

4 Experiments

4.1 The Data Set

Data set is provide by the task organizer. The training, development and test data have been extracted and annotated from Amazon SNAP Review Dataset. (He and McAuley, 2016)

	For sub-task A	For subtask B					For subtask C	
METRICS LIST:	mth	cos_d	cos	cpr	a-dcg	wt	unwt	recall
CYUT1_A_5	0.71	0.83	0.84	0.7	4.28	504.18	14.31	0.71
CYUT2_A_5	**0.84**	**0.87**	**0.88**	0.7	**5.22**	**575.58**	**17.67**	**0.83**
CYUT3_A_5 (random baseline)	0.7	0.79	0.81	0.07	3.53	408.58	11.04	0.66
FAAD1_A_5	0.78	0.86	0.87	0.49	4.27	494.03	14.04	0.76
FAAD2_A_5	0.78	0.85	0.86	0.52	4.34	495.35	14.34	0.75
FAAD3_A_5	0.78	0.84	0.85	0.51	4.11	486.51	13.35	0.72
JUNLP_A_5	0.8	0.83	0.85	0.46	4.05	475.54	13.12	0.74
JUNLP_B_5	0.7	0.86	0.87	0.71	4.98	556.94	16.9	0.81
BASE_R_B_5	0.64	0.84	0.84	0.74	4.53	533.41	15.33	0.73
JUNLP_C_5	0.53	0.8	0.81	0.3	3.58	390.44	10.94	0.67

Table 2: Official Run Results of RevOpiD 2017 for k=5

	For sub-task A	For subtask B					For subtask C	
METRICS LIST:	mth	cos_d	cos	cpr	a-dcg	wt	unwt	recall
CYUT1_A_10	0.76	0.9	0.92	0.7	5.22	1280.6	36.53	0.89
CYUT2_A_10	**0.86**	0.91	0.92	**0.76**	**6.06**	**1517.1**	**45.79**	**0.95**
CYUT3_A_10 (random baseline)	0.75	0.89	0.9	0.14	4.48	1135.9	30.29	0.88
FAAD1_A_10	0.81	0.92	0.93	0.61	5.18	1325.2	37.54	0.89
FAAD2_A_10	0.84	0.91	0.92	0.65	5.2	1318.8	37.8	0.9
FAAD3_A_10	0.83	0.92	0.94	0.65	5.16	1317.5	36.8	0.92
JUNLP_A_10	0.84	0.91	0.92	0.59	5.04	1301.4	36.21	0.92
JUNLP_B_10	0.75	0.9	0.91	0.68	5.71	1384.6	41.03	0.91
JUNLP_C_10	0.73	0.88	0.9	0.39	4.46	1045.6	28.93	0.85

Table 3: Official Run Results of RevOpiD 2017 for k=10

4.2 The Official Evaluation Results

The official evaluation results is shown in Table 2 and 3. Our three runs are denoted as CYUT#_A_k for k=5 and k=10, # for 1, 2, and 3. The metric abbreviations are as follows (Singh et al., 2017):

For subtask A:

mth: The fraction of reviews included with more than half votes in favor.

For subtask B:

cos_d: discounted cosine similarity
cos: Cosine Similarity
cpr: cumulative proportionality (Dang and Croft, 2012)
a-dcg: Alpha-DCG (Clarke et al., 2008)
wt: weighted relevance

For subtask C:

unwt: unweighted relevance
recall: The fraction of opinions/columns covered by the top k ranked list.

4.3 Discussion

For k=5, the second run (**CYUT2_A_5**) gets the highest scores in seven of the eight official evaluation metrics. For k=10, the second run (**CYUT2_A_10**) gets the highest scores in six of the eight official evaluation metrics. This study shows that optimization the helpfulness (Subtask A) with cross entropy can also help exhaustive coverage (Subtask C), and help representativeness (Subtask B).

5 Conclusions and Future Works

Our team participated the RevOpiD 2017, focused on ranking reviews based on the helpfulness of the reviews. However, the result shows that it can also help on the exhaustive coverage, and representativeness. Our second linear regression model gets the highest scores in the official evaluation metrics for both k=5 and k=10.

We chose the linear regression model this year. There are still other machine learning models could be used in the future, such as deep neural networks. In deep learning paradigm, it is possible to bypass the feature engineering efforts. That is, we do not need to worry about which features are more useful.

Acknowledgments

This study is conducted under the "Online and Offline integrated Smart Commerce Platform (4/4)" of the Institute for Information Industry which is subsidized by the Ministry of Economic Affairs of the Republic of China. This study is also supported by the Ministry of Science under the grant numbers MOST106-2221-E-324-021-MY2.

References

JJ Allaire, Dirk Eddelbuettel, Nick Golding, and Yuan Tang. 2016. tensorflow: R Interface to TensorFlow. https://github.com/rstudio/tensorflow

Charles L.A. Clarke, Maheedhar Kolla, Gordon V. Cormack, Olga Vechtomova, Azin Ashkan, Stefan Büttcher, and Ian MacKinnon. 2008. Novelty and diversity in information retrieval evaluation. In Proceedings of the 31st annual international ACM SIGIR conference on Research and development in information retrieval (SIGIR '08). ACM, New York, NY, USA, 659-666. DOI: http://dx.doi.org/10.1145/1390334.1390446

Van Dang and W. Bruce Croft. 2012. Diversity by proportionality: an election-based approach to search result diversification. In Proceedings of the 35th international ACM SIGIR conference on Research and development in information retrieval (SIGIR '12). ACM, New York, NY, USA, 65-74. DOI: https://doi.org/10.1145/2348283.2348296

Ruining He and Julian McAuley. 2016. Ups and Downs: Modeling the Visual Evolution of Fashion Trends with One-Class Collaborative Filtering. In Proceedings of the 25th International Conference on World Wide Web (WWW '16). International World Wide Web Conferences Steering Committee, Republic and Canton of Geneva, Switzerland, 507-517. DOI: https://doi.org/10.1145/2872427.2883037

Hsien-You Hsieh, Vitaly Klyuev, Qiangfu Zhao, Shih-Hung Wu. 2014. *SVR-based outlier detection and its application to hotel ranking.* In proceedings of IEEE 6th International Conference on Awareness Science and Technology (iCAST-2014), Paris, France.

Edward Loper and Steven Bird. 2002. NLTK: the Natural Language Toolkit. In Proceedings of the ACL-02 Workshop on Effective tools and methodologies for teaching natural language processing and computational linguistics - Volume 1 (ETMTNLP '02), Vol. 1. Association for Computational Linguistics, Stroudsburg, PA, USA, 63-70. DOI: https://doi.org/10.3115/1118108.1118117

Fabian Pedregosa, Gaël Varoquaux, Alexandre Gramfort, Vincent Michel, Bertrand Thirion, Olivier Grisel, Mathieu Blondel, Peter Prettenhofer, Ron Weiss, Vincent Dubourg, Jake Vanderplas, Alexandre Passos, David Cournapeau, Matthieu Brucher, Matthieu Perrot, Édouard Duchesnay. 2011. Scikit-learn: Machine Learning in Python. Journal of Machine Learning Research, 12(Oct): 2825–2830.

Beatrice Santorini. 1990. "Part-of-Speech Tagging Guidelines for the Penn Treebank Project (3rd Revision)", July.

Anil Kumar Singh, Avijit Thawani, Anubhav Gupta and Rajesh Kumar Mundotiya. Evaluating Opinion Summarization in Ranking. Proceedings of the 13th Asia Information Retrieval Societies Conference (AIRS 2017). Jeju island, Korea. November, 2017.

Anil Kumar Singh, Avijit Thawani, Mayank Panchal, Anubhav Gupta and Julian McAuley. Overview of the IJCNLP-2017 Shared Task on Review Opinion Diversification (RevOpiD-2017). In Proceedings of the IJCNLP-2017 Shared Tasks. Taipei, Taiwan. December, 2017.

Shih-Hung Wu, Yi-Hsiang Hsieh, Liang-Pu Chen, Ping-Che Yang, Liu Fanghuizhu. 2017. *Temporal Model of the Online Customer Review Helpfulness Prediction.* in Proceedings of the 2017 IEEE/ACM International Conference on Advances in Social Networks Analysis and Mining (ASONAM), Sydney, Australia, 31 July - 03 August.

Yi-Ching Zeng and Shih-Hung Wu. 2013. *Modeling the Helpful Opinion Mining of Online Consumer Reviews as a Three-class Classification Problem.* in Proceedings of the SocialNLP workshop, Nagoya, Japan, Oct. 14, 2013.

Yi-Ching Zeng, Tsun Ku, Shih-Hung Wu, Liang-Pu Chen, and Gwo-Dong Chen. 2014. *Modeling the Helpful Opinion Mining of Online Consumer Reviews as a Classification Problem,* International Journal of Computational Linguistics & Chinese Language Processing ,Vol. 19, No. 2, June.

JUNLP at IJCNLP-2017 Task 3: A Rank Prediction Model for Review Opinion Diversification

Monalisa Dey, Anupam Mondal, Dipankar Das
Jadavpur University, Kolkata, India
monalisa.dey.21@gmail.com,
anupam@sentic.net, ddas@cse.jdvu.ac.in

Abstract

IJCNLP-17 Review Opinion Diversification (RevOpiD-2017) task has been designed for ranking the top-k reviews of a product from a set of reviews, which assists in identifying a summarized output to express the opinion of the entire review set. The task is divided into three independent subtasks as subtask-A, subtask-B, and subtask-C. Each of these three subtasks selects the top-k reviews based on helpfulness, representativeness, and exhaustiveness of the opinions expressed in the review set individually. In order to develop the modules and predict the rank of reviews for all three subtasks, we have employed two well-known supervised classifiers namely, Naïve Bayes and Logistic Regression on the top of several extracted features such as the number of nouns, number of verbs, and number of sentiment words etc from the provided datasets. Finally, the organizers have helped to validate the predicted outputs for all three subtasks by using their evaluation metrics. The metrics provide the scores of list size 5 as (0.80 (mth)) for subtask-A, (0.86 (cos), 0.87 (cos_d), 0.71 (cpr), 4.98 (a-dcg), and 556.94 (wt)) for subtask B, and (10.94 (unwt) and 0.67 (recall)) for subtask C individually.

1 Introduction

Review opinion diversification shared task aims to produce top-k reviews for each product from a set of reviews, so that the selected top-k reviews act as a summary of all the opinions expressed in the reviews set. The three independent subtasks incorporate three different ways of selecting the top-k reviews, based on helpfulness, representativeness, and exhaustiveness of the opinions expressed in the review set. The helpfulness refers to the usefulness rating of reviews. Representativeness indicates the popular perspectives expressed in the corpus, whereas exhaustiveness shows the opinion based coverage of reviews of the products (Singh et al., b).

In order to rank and identify the top-k reviews for all the subtasks, we have designed three isolated modules using two well-known machine learning classifiers as Naïve Bayes and Logistic Regression on the top of our extracted features such as number of nouns, verbs, and sentiment etc.

These modules help to resolve the following challenges to identify the top-k reviews of products for the corpus, which is presented as a contribution of the paper.

A. Dataset collection for each subtasks: To the process, the organizers have provided two datasets as training and development [1].

B. Module building for all three subtasks: In order to build the prediction modules, we have extracted various features such as number of nouns, number of verbs, number of negation words, and sentiment etc. from the provided datasets. Thereafter, these features are applied on Naïve Bayes and Logistic Regression classifiers to learn and predict the score of reviews based on helpfulness, representativeness, and exhaustiveness. The predicted scores assist in identifying the top-k reviews of the products from the corpus.

C. Evaluation of the proposed module for all three subtasks: To evaluate, we have processed the test dataset provided by the organizers on the proposed modules and obtained the results for all the three subtasks individually. Thereafter, these results are applied on the evaluation metrics offered

---

[1] https://sites.google.com/itbhu.ac.in/revopid-2017/data

Proceedings of the 8th International Joint Conference on Natural Language Processing, Shared Tasks, pages 138–142,
Taipei, Taiwan, November 27 – December 1, 2017. ©2017 AFNLP

by the organizers to validate all the modules.

The proposed modules help to design various opinion-based diversification applications along with summarization (Krestel and Dokoohaki, 2011; Kacimi and Gamper, 2011; Krestel and Dokoohaki, 2015; Dey,). In the following sections, we have discussed the contribution of the paper as proposed modules and evaluation techniques in details.

2 Proposed Modules

In the present work, we have designed three modules to attempt subtasks A, B, and C according to the properties as usefulness, representativeness, and exhaustiveness. These modules help to identify the top-k reviews against their predicted rank. So, we have used two well-known classifiers namely Naïve Bayes and Logistic Regression in the presence of extracted features from the datasets. The features have been diversified based on the above-mentioned nature and type of the subtasks. The following subsections discuss the data collection, feature extraction, and module building steps in details.

2.1 Data Collection

A well defined dataset is very important to develop any information extraction system. To the process, the organizers provided three datasets namely development, training, and test, which they have collected from Amazon SNAP Review dataset. Thereafter, the organizers have annotated the development and test datasets. The annotated dataset sample of a review contains various features namely, ID of the reviewer, ID of the product, name of the reviewer, helpfulness rating of the review, review text, rating of the product, summary of the review, and time of the review. The development dataset is used for learning the three modules, whereas test dataset is applied for predicting and evaluating the top-k reviews of each product.

2.2 Subtasks Description and Feature Extraction

Subtask-A: Subtask-A aims to produce a ranked list of k reviews based on its predicted usefulness while simultaneously trying to reduce the redundancy among the ranked list.

In the given data, the usefulness rating feature is a user-collected field. We have observed from the development and training datasets that certain linguistic features play a major role in determining the usefulness of a review. Keeping this in mind, we have extracted various features namely, number of words, number of stop words, number of bi-grams, number of trigrams, and tf-idf from the datasets. In order to extract these features, we have written few python (python 2.7) scripts using various packages such as nltk [2].

Subtask-B: The subtask focuses on producing a ranked list of k reviews so as to maximize representativeness of the ranked list. The ranked list of reviews should summarize the opinions expressed in the reviews, both diverse and novel.

To achieve this, we have studied the dataset carefully and observed that the lexical features of the review are presented as an important part in identifying an ideal representation covering popular perspectives. Hence, we have used the features extracted for subtask-A along with three additional features namely, number of verbs, number of nouns, and number of adjectives from the datasets to prepare the final feature set for subtask-B. Number of nouns and verbs help to identify the important linguistic keywords from the reviews, whereas, number of adjectives assist in recognizing useful sentiment keywords.

Subtask-C: Subtask-C emphasizes on producing a ranked list so as to include the majority of opinions regarding the product. The correctness of the list is judged on the basis of how exhaustively the list covers all the opinions. It is to be noted that the ranked list should be the best in expressing all forms of opinions.

In order to achieve this objective, we have chosen to observe the sentiments expressed in each opinion. We have also perceived that both positive and negative opinions have to be included in order to increase the opinion coverage. Besides, linguistic features also take part in determining all forms of viewpoints. Keeping all these observations in mind, we have prepared the feature set by adding few sentiment features namely, number of sentiment words, number of negations, number of positive words, and number of negative words along with the mentioned linguistic features of subtask-B. The sentiment features have been extracted using SentiWordNet [3] and SenticNet [4] re-

---

[2] www.nltk.org/
[3] http://sentiwordnet.isti.cnr.it/s
[4] http://sentic.net/

sources (Esuli and Sebastiani, 2006; Cambria et al., 2016).

For example, the following review has been labeled with the sentiment features such as number of sentiment words (6), number of negations (2), number of positive words (5), and number of negative words (1).

"It arrived quickly, looks sturdy and doesn't take too much room in the trunk, but I haven't needed it yet, so only 4 stars."

2.3 Modules Building

In order to predict the rank for all the three subtasks, we have applied two conventional supervised machine learning classifiers viz. Naïve Bayes and Logistic Regression. These classifiers have been learned using the extracted features as mentioned in the previous subsections. Thereafter, to predict the final rank for the reviews of the products, we have used the test dataset provided by the organizers. To obtain a single predicted output as rank for each review, we have calculated the average of both of the models predicted scores. The following steps illustrate the overview of the modeling building parts.

Step-1: The development dataset supplied by the organizers has been processed with our written python scripts (python version 2.7) and few sentiment resources to extract various features such as number of nouns, number verbs, number of negation words, and sentiment words etc for all the subtasks.

Step-2: The extracted features are distributed into three segments based on the nature of the subtasks namely helpfulness, representativeness, and exhaustiveness.

Step-3: Thereafter, the segments are processed with the Naïve Bayes and Logistic Regression classifiers to develop all the three modules consequently.

Step-4: The test dataset provided by the organizers is applied on the proposed modules individually to predict the rank of reviews.

Step-5: The predicted ranks help to identify top-k (the value of k decided by the organizers as 5 and 10) reviews of each product from the dataset.

The following section describes the overall evaluation process for all the subtasks.

3 Evaluation

In order to evaluate the output of the proposed modules as top-*k* reviews from the given reviews set for all three subtasks, we have taken help of the organizers provided evaluation metrics (Singh et al., a). The metrics are presented for all the three subtasks. Subtask-A has been evaluated using more than half's (mth), whereas Subtask-B is validated through cosine similarity (cos), discounted cosine similarity (cos_d), cumulative proportionality (cpr), alpha-DCG (a-dcg), and weighted relevance (wt) metrics. On the other hand, unweighted relevance (unwt) and recall metrics are applied to evaluate Subtask-C. The following subsections are discussed about the output of the designed modules for each subtasks in details.

3.1 Validation of Subtask-A

The applied mth metric refers the fraction of reviews included with more than half votes in favour. Hence, they have calculated *Upvotes*, users who found the review helpful and *Downvotes*, users who didn't find the review helpful to find the favour as yes, no, and not counted. The total number of yes favours and combination of yes and no favours help to calculate the mth as shown in Equation 1.

$$mth = \frac{yes}{yes + no},\qquad(1)$$

where yes and no represent the total number of yes and no favours respectively.

The equation assists in measuring the mth score of our proposed module for two different files with list size 5 and list size 10 (Singh et al., b). Table 1 shows a comparative study between our module (JUNLP) and other modules of participants of this shared task.

3.2 Validation of Subtask-B

Subtask-B has been evaluated using five different metrics viz. cosine similarity (cos), discounted cosine similarity (cos_d), cumulative proportionality (cpr), alpha-DCG (a-dcg), and weighted relevance (wt) [5]. Table 2 and Table 3 indicate the mentioned metrics scores for our proposed module

---

[5] https://sites.google.com/itbhu.ac.in/revopid-201fsu7/evaluation

Participating Groups	List size 5	List size 10
CYUT1	0.71	0.76
CYUT2	0.84	0.86
CYUT3	0.70	0.75
JUNLP	**0.80**	**0.84**
FAAD1	0.78	0.81
FAAD2	0.78	0.84
FAAD3	0.78	0.83

Table 1: A comparative study between all participants of subtask-A of this shared task for two different files with list size 5 and 10.

and a comparative study between all the submitted module of this subtask.

Metrics	List size 5	List size 10
cos	0.86	0.90
cos_d	0.87	0.91
cpr	0.71	0.68
a-dcg	4.98	5.71
wt	556.94	1384.6

Table 2: The evaluation output of our proposed module (JUNLP) for subtask-B.

	JUNLP		BASE_R	
Metrics	List size 5	List size 10	List size 5	List size 10
cos	0.86	0.90	0.84	-
cos_d	0.87	0.91	0.84	-
cpr	0.71	0.68	0.74	-
a-dcg	4.98	5.71	4.53	-
wt	556.94	1384.6	533.41	-

Table 3: A comparative study between all the submitted modules for subtask-B of this shared task.

3.3 Validation of Subtask-C

Another two metrics as unweighted relevance (unwt) and recall are used to validate the output of subtask-C. Unweighted relevance indicates a discounted sum of number of opinions present in the ranked list, whereas recall is the fraction of the relevant opinions that are successfully retrieved by the ranking. The output of the proposed module for subtask-C is presented in Table 4.

Finally, we can conclude that our proposed modules provide noticeable scores for all three subtasks as compared to other participants.

Metrics	List size 5	List size 10
unwt	10.94	28.93
recall	0.67	0.85

Table 4: Evaluation output of our proposed module (JUNLP) for subtask-C.

4 Conclusion and Future Scopes

This paper presents a rank prediction model for review opinion diversification to IJCNLP-2017 RevOpiD shared task. The task is distributed into three subtasks viz. helpfulness, representativeness, and exhaustiveness based ranking of the product reviews. We have developed three isolated modules for the subtasks individually. Two well-known machine learning classifiers namely Naïve Bayes and Logistic Regression have been applied on the extracted features to design these modules. We are able to obtain noticeable outputs using evaluation metrics provided by the organizers for all the proposed modules. Finally, the paper presents comparative studies between all the submitted systems and our system for all the subtasks. In future, we will attempt to improve the accuracy of our proposed modules by incorporating more fine grained features.

References

Erik Cambria, Soujanya Poria, Rajiv Bajpai, and Björn W Schuller. 2016. Senticnet 4: A semantic resource for sentiment analysis based on conceptual primitives. In *COLING*, pages 2666–2677.

Monalisa Dey. Ntcir-12 mobileclick: Sense-based ranking and summarization of english queries.

Andrea Esuli and Fabrizio Sebastiani. 2006. Sentiwordnet: A publicly available lexical resource for opinion mining. In *Proceedings of LREC*, volume 6, pages 417–422. Citeseer.

Mouna Kacimi and Johann Gamper. 2011. Diversifying search results of controversial queries. In *Proceedings of the 20th ACM international conference on Information and knowledge management*, pages 93–98. ACM.

Ralf Krestel and Nima Dokoohaki. 2011. Diversifying product review rankings: Getting the full picture. In *Proceedings of the 2011 IEEE/WIC/ACM International Conferences on Web Intelligence and Intelligent Agent Technology-Volume 01*, pages 138–145. IEEE Computer Society.

Ralf Krestel and Nima Dokoohaki. 2015. Diversifying customer review rankings. *Neural Networks*, 66:36–45.

Anil Kumar Singh, Avijit Thawani, Anubhav Gupta, and Rajesh Kumar Mundotiya. Evaluating opinion summarization in ranking. In *Proceeding of the 13th Asia Information Retrieval Societies Conference (AIRS 2017)*, November.

Anil Kumar Singh, Avijit Thawani, Mayank Panchal, Anubhav Gupta, and Julian McAuley. Overview of the ijcnlp-2017 shared task on review opinion diversification (revopid-2017). In *Proceedings of the IJCNLP-2017 Shared Tasks*, December.

ALL-IN-1 at IJCNLP-2017 Task 4:
Short Text Classification with One Model for All Languages

Barbara Plank
Center for Language and Cognition
University of Groningen
`b.plank@rug.nl`

Abstract

We present ALL-IN-1, a simple model for
multilingual text classification that does
not require any parallel data. It is based on
a traditional Support Vector Machine classifier exploiting multilingual word embeddings and character n-grams. Our model
is simple, easily extendable yet very effective, overall ranking 1st (out of 12 teams)
in the IJCNLP 2017 shared task on customer feedback analysis in four languages:
English, French, Japanese and Spanish.

1 Introduction

Customer feedback analysis is the task of classifying short text messages into a set of predefined
labels (e.g., bug, request). It is an important step
towards effective customer support.

However, a real bottleneck for successful classification of customer feedback in a multilingual
environment is the limited transferability of such
models, i.e., typically each time a new language
is encountered a new model is built from scratch.
This is clearly impractical, as maintaining separate models is cumbersome, besides the fact that
existing annotations are simply not leveraged.

In this paper we present our submission to the
IJCNLP 2017 shared task on customer feedback
analysis, in which data from four languages was
available (English, French, Japanese and Spanish).
Our goal was to build a single system for all four
languages, and compare it to the traditional approach of creating separate systems for each language. We hypothesize that a single system is beneficial, as it can provide positive transfer, particularly for the languages for which less data is available. The contributions of this paper are:

- We propose a very simple multilingual model
  for four languages that overall ranks first (out

of 12 teams) in the IJCNLP 2017 shared task
on Customer Feedback Analysis.

- We show that a traditional model outperforms
  neural approaches in this low-data scenario.

- We show the effectiveness of a very simple
  approach to induce multilingual embeddings
  that does not require any parallel data.

- Our ALL-IN-1 model is particularly effective
  on languages for which little data is available.

- Finally, we compare our approach to automatic translation, showing that translation
  negatively impacts classification accuracy.

- To support reproducibility and follow-
  up work all code is available at:
  `https://github.com/bplank/`
  `ijcnlp2017-customer-feedback`

2 ALL-IN-1: One Model for All

Motivated by the goal to evaluate how good a single model for multiple languages fares, we decided to build a very simple model that can handle
any of the four languages. We aimed at an approach that does *not* require any language-specific
processing (beyond tokenization) nor requires any
parallel data. We set out to build a simple baseline,
which turned out to be surprisingly effective. Our
model is depicted in Figure 1.

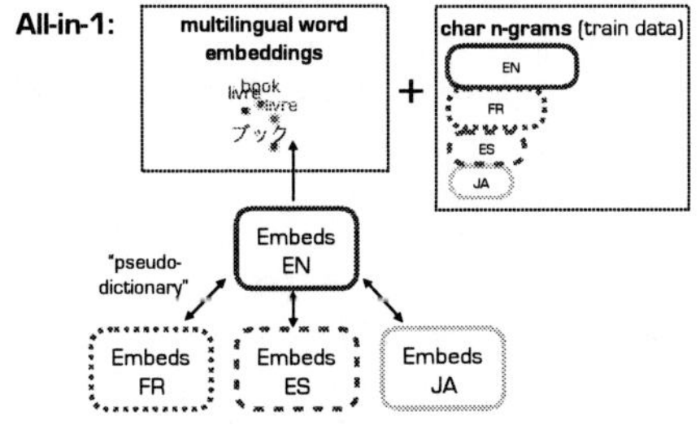

Figure 1: Overview of our ALL-IN-1 model.

Proceedings of the 8th International Joint Conference on Natural Language Processing, Shared Tasks, pages 143–148,
Taipei, Taiwan, November 27 – December 1, 2017. ©2017 AFNLP

Our key motivation is to provide a simple, general system as opposed to the usual ad-hoc setups one can expect in a multilingual shared task. So we rely on character n-grams, word embeddings, and a traditional classifier, motivated as follows.

First, character n-grams and traditional machine learning algorithms have proven successful for a variety of classification tasks, e.g., native language identification and language detection. In recent shared tasks simple traditional models outperformed deep neural approaches like CNNs or RNNs, e.g., (Medvedeva et al., 2017; Zampieri et al., 2017; Malmasi et al., 2017; Kulmizev et al., 2017). This motivated our choice of using a traditional model with character n-gram features.

Second, we build upon the recent success of multilingual embeddings. These are embedding spaces in which word types of different languages are embedded into the same high-dimensional space. Early approaches focus mainly on bilingual approaches, while recent research aims at mapping several languages into a single space. The body of literature is huge, but an excellent recent overview is given in Ruder (2017). We chose a very simple and recently proposed method that does not rely on any parallel data (Smith et al., 2017) and extend it to the multilingual case. In particular, the method falls under the broad umbrella of *monolingual mappings*. These approaches first train monolingual embeddings on large unlabeled corpora for the single languages. They then learn linear mappings between the monolingual embeddings to map them to the same space. The approach we apply here is particularly interesting as it does not require parallel data (parallel sentences/documents or dictionaries) and is readily applicable to off-the-shelf embeddings. In brief, the approach aims at learning a transformation in which word vector spaces are orthogonal (by applying SVD) and it leverages so-called "pseudo-dictionaries". That is, the method first finds the common word types in two embedding spaces, and uses those as pivots to learn to align the two spaces (cf. further details in Smith et al. (2017)).

3 Experimental Setup

In this section we first describe the IJCNLP 2017 shared task 4[1] including the data, the features, model and evaluation metrics.

---

[1]https://sites.google.com/view/customer-feedback-analysis/

	EN	ES	FR	JP
TRAIN	3066	1632	1951	1527
DEV	501	302	401	251
TEST	501	300	401	301

Table 1: Overview of the dataset (instances).

3.1 Task Description

The customer feedback analysis task (Liu et al., 2017) is a short text classification task. Given a customer feedback message, the goal is to detect the type of customer feedback. For each message, the organizers provided one or more labels. To give a more concrete idea of the data, the following are examples of the English dataset:

- "Still calls keep dropping with the new update" (*bug*)

- "Room was grubby, mold on windows frames." (complaint)

- "The new update is amazing." (*comment*)

- "Needs more control s and tricks.." (*request*)

- "Enjoy the sunshine!!" (*meaningless*)

3.2 Data

The data stems from a joint ADAPT-Microsoft project. An overview of the provided dataset is given in Table 1. Notice that the available amount of data differs per language.

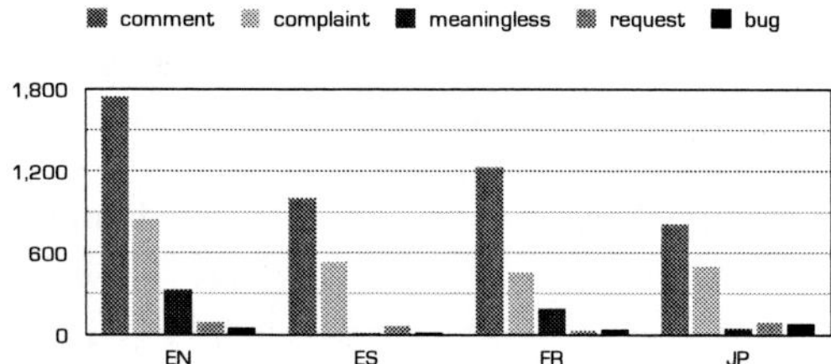

Figure 2: Distribution of the labels per language.

We treat the customer feedback analysis problem as a single-class classification task and actually ignore multi-label instances, as motivated next. The final label distribution for the data is given in Figure 2.

In initial investigations of the data we noticed that very few instances had multiple labels, e.g., "*comment,complaint*". In the English training data this amounted to ~4% of the data. We decided to ignore those additional labels (just picked the first in case of multiple labels) and treat the problem as a single-class classification problem. This was motivated by the fact that some labels were expected to be easily confused. Finally, there were some labels in the data that did not map to any of the labels in the task description (i.e., *'undetermined'*, *'undefined'*, *'nonsense'* and *'noneless'*, they were presumably typos) so we mapped them all to the *'meaningless'* label. This frames the task as a 5-class classification problem with the following classes:

- *bug,*
- *comment,*
- *complaint,*
- *meaningless* and
- *request.*

At test time the organizers additionally provided us with *translations* of the three language-specific test datasets back to English. These translations were obtained by Google translate. This allowed us to evaluate our English model on the translations, to gauge whether translation is a viable alternative to training a multilingual model.

3.3 Pre-processing

We perform two simple preprocessing steps. First of all, we tokenize all data using off-the-shelf tokenizers. We use `tinysegmenter`[2] for Japanese and the NLTK `TweetTokenizer` for all other languages. The Japanese segmenter was crucial to get sufficient coverage from the word embeddings later. No additional preprocessing is performed.

3.4 Multilingual Embeddings

Word embeddings for single languages are readily available, for example the Polyglot[3] or Facebook embeddings (Bojanowski et al., 2016), which were recently released.

In this work we start from the monolingual embeddings provided by the Polyglot project (Al-Rfou et al., 2013). We use the recently proposed approach based on SVD decomposition and a "pseudo-dictionary" (Smith et al., 2017) obtained from the monolingual embeddings to project embedding spaces. To extend their method from the

bilingual to the multilingual case, we apply pairwise projections by using English as pivot, similar in spirit to Ammar et al. (2016). We took English as our development language. We also experimented with using larger embeddings (Facebook embeddings; larger in the sense of both trained on more data and having higher dimensionality), however, results were comparable while training time increased, therefore we decided to stick to the smaller 64-dimensional Polyglot embeddings.

3.5 Model and Features

As classifier we use a traditional model, a Support Vector Machine (SVM) with linear kernel implemented in `scikit-learn` (Pedregosa et al., 2011). We tune the regularization parameter C on the English development set and keep the parameter fixed for the remaining experiments and all languages ($C = 10$).

We compared the SVM to `fastText` (Joulin et al., 2016). As we had expected `fastText` gave consistently lower performance, presumably because of the small amounts of training data. Therefore we did not further explore neural approaches.

Our features are character n-grams (3-10 grams, with binary tf-idf) and word embeddings. For the latter we use a simple continuous bag-of-word representation (Collobert et al., 2011) based on averaging and min-max scaling.

Additionally, we experimented with adding Part-Of-Speech (POS) tags to our model. However, to keep in line with our goal to build a *single system for all languages* we trained a single multilingual POS tagger by exploiting the projected multilingual embeddings. In particular, we trained a state-of-the-art bidirectional LSTM tagger (Plank et al., 2016)[4] that uses both word and character representations on the concatenation of language-specific data provided from the Universal Dependencies data (version 1.2 for En, Fr and Es and version 2.0 data for Japanese, as the latter was not available in free-form in the earlier version). The word embeddings module of the tagger is initialized with the multilingual embeddings. We investigated POS n-grams (1 to 3 grams) as additional features.

---

[2] `https://pypi.python.org/pypi/tinysegmenter`

[3] Despite their name the Polyglot embeddings are actually monolingual embeddings, but available for many languages.

[4] `https://github.com/bplank/bilstm-aux`

	EN	ES	FR	JP	AVG
MONOLINGUAL MODELS					
Embeds	50.6	82.0	66.5	65.1	66.05
Words (W)	66.1	86.9	73.2	73.6	74.95
Chars (C)	68.2	87.1	76.1	74.0	76.35
W+Chars (C)	65.9	87.7	75.7	74.0	75.82
C+Embeds‡	66.1	86.6	76.5	77.1	76.58
W+C+Embeds	65.9	87.8	75.6	76.8	76.52
BILINGUAL MODEL					
En+Es	67.6	86.6	–	–	–
En+Fr	66.6	–	77.8	–	–
En+Jp	66.7	–	–	77.9	–
MULTILINGUAL MODEL					
En+Es+Fr	68.3	87.0	77.9	–	–
ALL-IN-1‡	68.8	87.7	76.4	77.2	77.5
ALL-IN-1+POS	68.4	86.0	74.4	74.5	75.8

Table 2: Results on the development data, weighted F1. MONOLINGUAL: per-language model; MULTILINGUAL: ALL-IN-1 (with C+Embeds features trained on En+Es+Fr+Jp). ‡ indicates submitted systems.

	EN	ES	FR	JP	AVG
MONOLING	**68.6**	88.2	**76.1**	74.3	76.8
MULTILING	68.1	**88.7**	73.9	**76.7**	**76.9**
TRANSLATE	–	83.4	69.5	61.6	–

Table 3: Results on the test data, weighted F1. MONOLING: monolingual models. MULTILING: the multilingual ALL-IN-1 model. TRANS: translated targets to English and classified with EN model.

3.6 Evaluation

We decided to evaluate our model using weighted F1-score, i.e., the per-class F1 score is calculated and averaged by weighting each label by its support. Notice, since our setup deviates from the shared task setup (single-label versus multi-label classification), the final evaluation metric is different. We will report on weighted F1-score for the development and test set (with simple macro averaging), but use Exact-Accuracy and Micro F1 over all labels when presenting official results on the test sets. The latter two metrics were part of the official evaluation metrics. For details we refer the reader to the shared task overview paper (Liu et al., 2017).

4 Results

We first present results on the provided development set, then on the official evaluation test set.

4.1 Results on Development

First of all, we evaluated different feature representations. As shown in Table 2 character n-grams alone prove very effective, outperforming word n-grams and word embeddings alone. Overall simple character n-grams (C) in isolation are often more beneficial than word and character n-grams together, albeit for some languages results

are close. The best representation are character n-grams with word embeddings. This representation provides the basis for our multilingual model which relies on multilingual embeddings. The two officially submitted models both use character n-grams (3-10) and word embeddings. Our first official submission, MONOLINGUAL is the per-language trained model using this representation.

Next we investigated adding more languages to the model, by relying on the multilingual embeddings as bridge. For instance in Table 2, the model indicated as En+Es is a character and word embedding-based SVM trained using bilingual embeddings created by mapping the two monolingual embeddings onto the same space and using both the English and Spanish training material. As the results show, using multiple languages can improve over the in-language development performance of the character+embedding model. However, the bilingual models are still only able to handle pairs of languages. We therefore mapped all embeddings to a common space and train a single multilingual ALL-IN-1 model on the union of all training data. This is the second model that we submitted to the shared task. As we can see from the development data, on average the multilingual model shows promising, overall (macro average) outperforming the single language-specific models. However, the multilingual model does not consistently fare better than single models, for example on French a monolingual model would be more beneficial.

Adding POS tags did not help (cf. Table 2), actually dropped performance. We disregard this feature for the final official runs.

4.2 Test Performance

We trained the final models on the concatenation of TRAIN and DEV data. The results on the test set (using our internally used weighted F1 metric) are given in Table 3.

There are two take-away points from the main results: First, we see a positive transfer for languages with little data, i.e., the single multilingual model outperforms the language-specific models on the two languages (Spanish and Japanese) which have the least amount of training data. Overall results between the monolingual and multilingual model are close, but the advantage of our multilingual ALL-IN-1 approach is that it is a single model that can be applied to all four languages. Second, automatic translation harms, the performance of the EN model on the translated data is substantially lower than the respective in-language model. We could investigate this as the organizers provided us with translations of French, Spanish and Japanese back to English.

	EN	ES	FR	JP	AVG
Ours (MULTILING)	68.60	**88.63**	71.50	**75.00**	**76.04**
Ours (MONOLING)	68.80	88.29	**73.75**	73.33	75.93
YNU-HPP-glove†	**71.00**	–	–	–	–
FYZU-bilstmcnn	70.80	–	–	–	–
IITP-CNN/RNN	70.00	85.62	69.00	63.00	71.90
TJ-single-CNN†	67.40	–	–	–	
Baseline	48.80	77.26	54.75	56.67	59.37

Table 4: Final test set results (Exact accuracy) for top 5 teams (ranked by macro average accuracy). Rankings for micro F1 are similar, we refer to the shared task paper for details. Winning system per language in bold. †: no system description available at the time of writing this description paper.

Averaged over all languages our system ranked first, cf. Table 4 for the results of the top 5 submissions. The multilingual model reaches the overall best exact accuracy, for two languages training a in-language model would be slightly more beneficial at the cost of maintaining a separate model. The similarity-based baseline provided by the organizers[5] is considerably lower.

Our system was outperformed on English by three teams, most of which focused only on English. Unfortunately at the time of writing there is no system description available for most other top systems, so that we cannot say whether they used more English-specific features. From the system names of other teams we may infer that most teams used neural approaches, and they score

[5]"Using n-grams (n=1,2,3) to compute sentence similarity (which is normalized by the length of sentence). Use the tag(s) of the most similar sentence in training set as predicted tag(s) of a sentence in the test set."

	comm	compl	req	ml	bug
EN (MONOLING)	**82.3**	64.4	**60.0**	27.5	0
EN (MULTILING)	82.0	**65.0**	42.1	**28.6**	0
ES (MONOLING)	93.3	75.2	**72.7**	0	0
ES (MULTILING)	**93.5**	**76.2**	66.6	0	**66.6**
ES (TRANSLATE)	92.6	67.2	11.8	0	0
FR (MONOLING)	**86.4**	**65.6**	14.3	**47.6**	**54.5**
FR (MULTILING)	85.5	61.5	**16.6**	41.2	50.0
FR (TRANSLATE)	82.9	58.9	16.6	34.5	0
JP (MONOLING)	85.7	**67.8**	55.8	0	**50.0**
JP (MULTILING)	**87.0**	67.8	**65.2**	0	**50.0**
JP (TRANSLATE)	76.5	61.3	7.2	0	0

Table 5: Test set results (F1) per category (*comment (comm)*, *complaint (compl)*, *request (req)*, *meaningless (ml)* and *bug*), official evaluation.

worse than our SVM-based system.

The per-label breakdown of our systems on the official test data (using micro F1 as calculated by the organizers) is given in Table 5. Unsurprisingly less frequent labels are more difficult to predict.

5 Conclusions

We presented a simple model that can effectively handle multiple languages in a single system. The model is based on a traditional SVM, character n-grams and multilingual embeddings. The model ranked first in the shared task of customer feedback analysis, outperforming other approaches that mostly relied on deep neural networks.

There are two take-away messages of this work: 1) multilingual embeddings are very promising[6] to build single multilingual models; and 2) it is important to compare deep learning methods to simple traditional baselines; while deep approaches are undoubtedly very attractive (and fun!), we always deem it important to compare deep neural to traditional approaches, as the latter often turn out to be surprisingly effective. Doing so will add to the literature and help to shed more light on understanding why and when this is the case.

Acknowledgments

I would like to thank the organizers, in particular Chao-Hong Liu, for his quick replies. I also thank Rob van der Goot, Héctor Martínez Alonso and Malvina Nissim for valuable comments on earlier drafts of this paper.

[6]Our study is limited to using a single multilingual embedding method and craves for evaluating alternatives!

References

Rami Al-Rfou, Bryan Perozzi, and Steven Skiena. 2013. Polyglot: Distributed Word Representations for Multilingual NLP. In *CoNLL*.

Waleed Ammar, George Mulcaire, Yulia Tsvetkov, Guillaume Lample, Chris Dyer, and Noah A Smith. 2016. Massively Multilingual Word Embeddings. *arXiv preprint arXiv:1602.01925*.

Piotr Bojanowski, Edouard Grave, Armand Joulin, and Tomas Mikolov. 2016. Enriching word vectors with subword information. *arXiv preprint arXiv:1607.04606*.

Ronan Collobert, Jason Weston, Léon Bottou, Michael Karlen, Koray Kavukcuoglu, and Pavel Kuksa. 2011. Natural language processing (almost) from scratch. *Journal of Machine Learning Research*, 12(Aug):2493–2537.

Armand Joulin, Edouard Grave, Piotr Bojanowski, and Tomas Mikolov. 2016. Bag of tricks for efficient text classification. *arXiv preprint arXiv:1607.01759*.

Artur Kulmizev, Bo Blankers, Johannes Bjerva, Malvina Nissim, Gertjan van Noord, Barbara Plank, and Martijn Wieling. 2017. The power of character n-grams in native language identification. In *Proceedings of the 12th Workshop on Innovative Use of NLP for Building Educational Applications*, Copenhagen, Denmark. Association for Computational Linguistics.

Chao-Hong Liu, Yasufumi Moriya, Alberto Poncelas, Declan Groves, Akira Hayakawa, and Qun Liu. 2017. Introduction to ijcnlp 2017 shared task on customer feedback analysis. In *Proceedings of the 8th International Joint Conference on Natural Language Processing*, pages 1–7, Taipei, Taiwan. Association for Computational Linguistics.

Shervin Malmasi, Keelan Evanini, Aoife Cahill, Joel Tetreault, Robert Pugh, Christopher Hamill, Diane Napolitano, and Yao Qian. 2017. A report on the 2017 native language identification shared task. In *Proceedings of the 12th Workshop on Innovative Use of NLP for Building Educational Applications*, Copenhagen, Denmark. Association for Computational Linguistics.

Maria Medvedeva, Martin Kroon, and Barbara Plank. 2017. When sparse traditional models outperform dense neural networks: the curious case of discriminating between similar languages. In *Proceedings of the Fourth Workshop on NLP for Similar Languages, Varieties and Dialects (VarDial)*, Valencia, Spain. Association for Computational Linguistics.

F. Pedregosa, G. Varoquaux, A. Gramfort, V. Michel, B. Thirion, O. Grisel, M. Blondel, P. Prettenhofer, R. Weiss, V. Dubourg, J. Vanderplas, A. Passos, D. Cournapeau, M. Brucher, M. Perrot, and E. Duchesnay. 2011. Scikit-learn: Machine learning in Python. *Journal of Machine Learning Research*, 12:2825–2830.

Barbara Plank, Anders Søgaard, and Yoav Goldberg. 2016. Multilingual part-of-speech tagging with bidirectional long short-term memory models and auxiliary loss. In *Proceedings of the 54th Annual Meeting of the Association for Computational Linguistics (Volume 2: Short Papers)*, pages 412–418, Berlin, Germany. Association for Computational Linguistics.

Sebastian Ruder. 2017. A survey of cross-lingual embedding models. *CoRR*, abs/1706.04902.

Samuel L Smith, David HP Turban, Steven Hamblin, and Nils Y Hammerla. 2017. Offline bilingual word vectors, orthogonal transformations and the inverted softmax. *arXiv preprint arXiv:1702.03859*.

Marcos Zampieri, Shervin Malmasi, Nikola Ljubešić, Preslav Nakov, Ahmed Ali, Jörg Tiedemann, Yves Scherrer, and Noëmi Aepli. 2017. Findings of the vardial evaluation campaign 2017. In *Proceedings of the Fourth Workshop on NLP for Similar Languages, Varieties and Dialects (VarDial)*, Valencia, Spain. Association for Computational Linguistics.

SentiNLP at IJCNLP-2017 Task 4: Customer Feedback Analysis Using a Bi-LSTM-CNN Model

Shuying Lin[1,3,4], Huosheng Xie[1] Liang-Chih Yu[2,3] and K. Robert Lai[3,4]
[1]College of Mathematics and Computer Science, Fuzhou University, Fuzhou, P.R. China
[2]Department of Information Management, Yuan Ze University, Taiwan
[3]Innovation Center for Big Data and Digital Convergence, Yuan Ze University, Taiwan
[4]Department of Computer Science & Engineering, Yuan Ze University, Taiwan
Contact: lcyu@saturn.yzu.edu.tw

Abstract

Analysis of customer feedback helps improve customer service. Much online customer feedback takes the form of online reviews, but the tremendous volume of such data makes manual classification impractical, raising the need for automatic classification to allow analysis systems to identify meanings or intentions expressed by customers. The aim of shared Task 4 of IJCNLP 2017 is to classify customer feedback into six tags. We present a system that uses word embeddings to express features of the sentence in the corpus, using the neural network as the classifier to complete the shared task. The ensemble method is then used to obtain a final predictive result. The proposed method ranked first among twelve submissions in terms of micro-averaged F1 and second for accuracy.

1 Introduction

Software companies receive tremendous amounts of online customer feedback every day, including product comments, bug reports, new feature requests, response complaints, capacity concerns and so on. The effective classification of this customer feedback can provide a foundation for improved customer service, but the huge amounts of data make manual classification impractical, raising the need for automatic classification to accurately identify customer meanings or intentions.

Sentence classification is a fundamental task for natural language processing (Collobert et al., 2011).

The goal of this shared task is to classify the cross language customer feedback into six categories (comment, request, bug, complaint, meaningless, and undetermined). Each sentence will be assigned at least one tag. It can be treated as a multi-label classification problem.

In recent years, deep neural network models such as convolutional neural networks (CNN) (Cun et al., 1990), recurrent neural networks (RNN) (Goller and Kuchler, 1996), long short-term memory (LSTM) (Hochreiter and Schmidhuber, 1997), and their combinations (Wang et al., 2016) have achieved remarkable results in many NLP tasks, including sentence classification (Kim, 2014; Kalchbrenner et al., 2014), sentiment analysis (Irsoy and Cardie, 2014; Liu et al., 2015), sarcasm detection (Ghosh and Veale, 2016; Amir et al., 2016). The neural network models can automatically infer the features and can be used as a sentence classifier. The word embeddings (Mikolov et al., 2013a; 2013b; Pennington et al, 214; Yu et al., 2017) can provide word vector representation that captures semantic and syntactic information of words. The word vector is used to build the sentence matrix and then inject information into sentence classifier. The LSTM can provide the sentence sequence information in one direction. Forward and backward networks respectively capture past and future information. Therefore, we used the bi-directional LSTM for our model.

This paper presents a system to classify English customer feedback into six labels (comment, request, bug, complaint, meaningless, and undetermined). The system uses the word vector of the

Proceedings of the 8th International Joint Conference on Natural Language Processing, Shared Tasks, pages 149–154,
Taipei, Taiwan, November 27 – December 1, 2017. ©2017 AFNLP

sentence as input, and the neural network as the

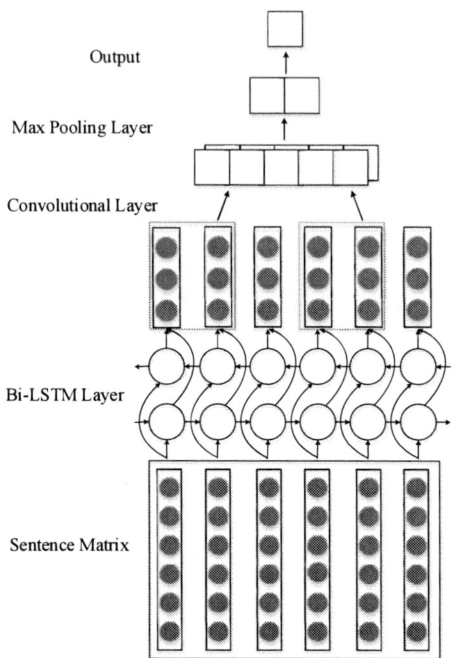

Figure 1: System architecture of the proposed bi-LSTM -CNN model.

classifier. The neural network uses the sentence matrix as input to classify the sentence into six labels. For multi-label classification, we construct a binary classifier for each label. The proposed model for sentence classification consists of two parts: a bi-directional LSTM and CNN. The bi-directional LSTM is used to capture the context of a sentence through sequential modeling. The sequence feature is used as the input for the CNN layer, which is then used to extract the most important feature to form the sentence representation. The logistic regression layer on the top is used to output the sentence labels.

The rest of this paper is organized as follows. Section 2 describes the model for sentence classification. Section 3 briefly introduces the ensemble method used in this paper. Section 4 reports experimental results and analysis. Section 5 presents conclusions and suggests directions for future work.

2 Model for Sentence Classification

The model aims to classify a sentence into six labels according to its sentence texts. Figure 1 shows the framework of the bi-directional LSTM-CNN model for sentence classification. In the input layer, the sentence is transformed into a sentence matrix based on the word vector. The word vectors of vocabulary words are trained from a large corpus using the Glove (Pennington et al., 2014) toolkit. The sentence matrix is fed into a forward LSTM network and a backward LSTM network. The representation sequence is then averaged over all timesteps and then concatenated to produce the final sequence representation. The sequence is the input of the CNN layer. The CNN extract the sequence feature information followed by logistic regression layer whose target is the class label for given sentence.

For a given corpus, we store the word vector in a look up matrix $M \in R^{d \times |V|}$, where $|V|$ is the vocabulary size of the given texts and d is the dimensionality of the word vector. For the sentence $S = \{s_1, s_2, ..., s_n\}$, n is the length of the sentence. Let $|V|$ denote the vocabulary of words, while d is the dimensionality of word vectors. The sentence matrix representation $X = \{x_1, x_2, ..., x_n\}$, x_i is the word vector of word s_i in accordance with the look up matrix M .

2.1 Recurrent Neural Network

To capture the relationship between the input sequences, we can use the RNN layer to transform word vector into the sentence feature representation.

Due to the vanishing gradients and exploding gradients problem (Pascanu et al., 2012), the LSTM (a certain type of RNN) is introduced for sequence modeling (Tang et al., 2015; Tai et al., 2015). The LSTM consists of three gates: input gate i, forget gate f and output gate o. The gate mechanisms work collaboratively to learn the long-term dependencies. At each time step t, the LSTM is calculated as follows:

$$i_t = \sigma(W_i x_t + U_i h_{t-1} + b_i)$$
$$f_t = \sigma(W_f x_t + U_f h_{t-1} + b_f)$$
$$g_t = \tanh(W_g x_t + U_g h_{t-1} + b_g)$$
$$o_t = \sigma(W_o x_t + U_o h_{t-1} + b_o) \qquad (1)$$
$$c_t = f_t * c_{t-1} + i_t * g_t$$
$$h_t = o_t * \tanh(c_t)$$

where x_t is the input from lower layer. h_{t-1} is the hidden state at time step t-1. The i_t , f_t , o_t are respectively called the *input, forget* and *output* gates. $W \in R^{\omega \times d}$ and $U \in R^{\omega \times d}$ are the weight matrices for different gates for input x_t and hidden state h_{t-1}. b denotes bias vectors. Here * is the element-wise multiplication, and the $\sigma(\cdot)$ and $\tanh(\cdot)$ are the element-wise activation function. The d can be the dimension of the word vector or the size of the hidden state in the lower layer.

A forward network and a backward network can respectively capture the past and future information. For sentence classification, it is beneficial to combine the past and future information in sequence modeling. Therefore, we use bi-directional LSTM to obtain the contextual information in sentence sequence modeling.

2.2 Convolutional Neural Network

The convolutional is used to extract n-gram features. We use a convolution filter $F \in R^{\omega \times d}$ to obtain the feature map $Y \in R^{n-\omega+1}$, The j-th element y_j is given by:

$$y_j = f\left(W \bullet x_{j:j+\omega-1} + b\right) \qquad (2)$$

where f is the Relu activation function, W is the weight matrix of convolution filter, b is a bias, ω is the length of the filter, and d is the dimension of the word vector. The convolutional layer uses multiple filters in parallel to obtain feature maps. It also can use convolutional filters of various length to extract different feature information.

The feature maps are fed into the max-pooling layer to obtain the most salient information to form the feature vector. The feature vector is useful for determining the output result.

3 Ensemble method

In statistics, ensemble methods use multiple learning algorithms to obtain better predictive performance (Maclin and Opitz, 1999; Rokach, 2010). In this paper, the ensemble methods use multiple results produced by the same NN-based method in different training times to obtain better predictive

Class	Training set	Development set
Comment	1758	276
Complaint	950	146
Meaningless	306	48
Request	103	19
Bug	72	20
Undetermined	22	3

Table 1: Data distributions of sentence labels in customer feedback: comment, complaint, meaningless, request, bug, and undetermined

performance. For multi-label classification, we make a variation of the voting rules in the ensemble method. The predictive outputs can be calculated in two steps: For each label, we assign the sentence to label i if the proportion of positive results in more than half of the total predictive result. After that, we assign it to label j with the most component predictions if the sentence was unannotated.

4 Experiments and Evaluation

Dataset. For the shared task on customer feedback analysis, several sentences of annotated and unannotated customer feedback in English were prepared, with a total of 3065 training texts, 500 development texts and 500 test texts. The training and development texts were annotated with six labels (comment, request, bug, complaint, meaningless, and undetermined). We evaluated the proposed bidirectional LSTM-CNN model by submitting the results of the test set to the IJCNLP 2017 Task 4 Customer Feedback Analysis. The distribution of the six labels shown in Table 1 indicates a data imbalance. Most of the data were assigned one of five class labels, and only a few were annotated as being undetermined. There are many pre-trained word vectors for English provided by word embeddings tool. We use the pre-trained word vectors trained on 840B tokens from common crawls and its dimensionality is 300 provided by Glove (Pennington et al., 2014) because of the high volume of the vocabulary. Word vectors are randomly initialized with uniform distribution sample if the word is not in the vocabulary of the pre-trained

	Micro- F1	Acc
Scores	0.7557	0.708
Rank	1	2

Table 2: Results of ensemble method for the best of the five results produced by the neural network model for IJCNLP-2017 Task 4.

word vectors.

Let Y be the vector representation of the label of the sentence. The labels $ls=\{\ l_1, l_2, l_3, l_4, l_5, l_6 \}$ and the sentence has multiple labels $\{l_1, l_2\}$. For each label, we use a binary classifier. Therefore, we can express the labels as: Y=(1, 1, 0, 0, 0, 0) to calculate the loss function through binary cross-entropy.

Experimental settings. The dataset containing the development set and training set is randomly shuffled and then re-divided for the 5-fold cross validation. The hyper-parameters of the neural network are chosen based on the performance on the development data. We obtain the final hyper-parameters by averaging the ten evaluation results of the development set in the 5-fold cross validation.

The epoch time is 10 to minimize the loss function. To avoid overfitting, we use the early stop mechanism and random dropout (rate of 0.25 or 0.5) (Srivastava et al., 2014). The nadam (Dozat, 2016) update rule is used to automatically tune the learning rate. The activation function in the top layer is a sigmoid function, which scales each label within a range 0 to 1. If the continuous result y_i is greater than 0.5, it is rounded up to 1, or set to 0 otherwise. The predicted result Y=(0, 0, 0, 0, 0, 0) for six labels is assigned to label i with the maximum value y_i of Y.

We first run experiments on CNN, LSTM and their combinations, including LSTM-CNN, CNN-LSTM, bi-LSTM and bi-LSTM-CNN. CNN1 and CNN2 have different hyper-parameters, a filter window of 3 with 256 feature maps in CNN1, and a filter window of 3 and 5 with 128 feature maps in CNN2.

We compare the results generated by the NN-based methods and select the best five results on

	NN-based		Ensemble	
	Micro-F1	Acc	Micro-F1	Acc
CNN1	0.7223	0.668	0.7342	0.682
CNN2	0.7383	0.694	0.7495	0.702
LSTM	0.5947	0.57	0.6425	0.618
LSTM-CNN	0.6931	0.658	0.7181	0.68
CNN-LSTM	0.7155	0.68	0.7332	0.69
Bi-LSTM	0.7417	0.7	0.7455	0.704
Bi-LSTM-CNN	0.7309	0.69	0.7557	0.708

Table 3: Comparative results of ensemble method with all NN-based methods for sentence classification.

the development set data in micro-averaged F1 to produce the ensemble result.

Evaluation metrics. IJCNLP 2017 Task 4 published the results for all participants assessed based on both accuracy and micro-averaged F1 measure. Given a binary classification, there are four basic outcomes: true positive (tp), true negative (tn), false positives (fp) and false negative (fn). The accuracy and F1 score (Powers, 2011) are evaluation measures B(tp, tn, fp, fn) used to evaluate the performance of a binary classification problem. Accuracy is the proportion of true results (both tp and tn) among the total test set. The micro-averaged F1 has a binary evaluation for its overall counts among all labels.

Results. A total of twelve teams participated in task 4. Table 2 shows the result of the ensemble method with the best of the five results produced by the bi-directional LSTM-CNN model. We obtain the best result by sorting the micro-averaged F1 for all labels. The ensemble result ranked first for micro-averaged F1 and second for accuracy.

Table 3 shows the best experimental results of ten runs for the neural network model for both accuracy and micro-averaged F1, along with rive runs for the ensemble method. We found that the ensemble method shows better performance, indicating that it can improve on all NN-based methods. The ensemble result in bi-LSTM-CNN achieves the best performance in all NN-based methods. The bi-LSTM yielded better performance without ensemble.

5 Conclusions

This study presents a neural network model to classify text-based customer feedback into six labels. We use the ensemble method to obtain the best of five results sorted by the micro-averaged F1. The use of the ensemble method can further improve performance in all NN-based methods. The bi-directional LSTM produces the sentence sequence feature, and the convolutional layer extracts the salient information from the sequence representation to classify the sentence into the multi-labels. Experimental results show that the bi-directional LSTM-CNN achieves best performance.

Future work will focus on exploring customer feedback in multiple languages and high-order correlations between labels should be taken into account to improve classification performance for both micro- and macro-averaged F1.

Acknowledgments

This work was supported by the Ministry of Science and Technology, Taiwan, ROC, under Grant No. MOST 105-2221-E-155-059-MY2 and MOST 105-2218-E-006-028.

References

Silvio Amir, Byron C. Wallace, Hao Lyu, Paula Carvalho, and Mario J. Silva. 2016. Modelling context with user embeddings for sarcasm detection in social media. In *Proc. of The 20th SIGNLL Conference on Computational Natural Language Learning*, pages 167–177.

Ronan Collobert, Jason Weston, Michael Karlen, Koray Kavukcuoglu, and Pavel Kuksa. 2011. Natural language processing (almost) from scratch. *Journal of Machine Learning Research*, 12(1):2493–2537.

Y. Le Cun, B. Boser, J. S. Denker, R. E. Howard, W. Habbard, L. D. Jackel, and D. Henderson. 1990. Handwritten digit recognition with a backpropagation network. In *Advances in Neural Information Processing Systems*, pages 396–404.

Timothy Dozat. 2016. Incorporating nesterov momentum into adam. In *ICLR 2016 workshop*, page 107.

Aniruddha Ghosh and Tony Veale. 2016. Fracking sarcasm using neural network. In *Proc. of the 7th Workshop on Computational Approaches to Subjectivity, Sentiment and Social Media Analysis (WASSA-16)*, pages 161-169.

C. Goller and A. Kuchler. 1996. Learning task-dependent distributed representations by backpropagation through structure. In *Proc. of the IEEE International Conference on Neural Networks (ICNN-96)*, pages 347–352.

Sepp Hochreiter and J¨urgen Schmidhuber. 1997. Long short-term memory. *Neural computation*, 9(8):1735–1780.

Ozan Irsoy and Claire Cardie. 2014. Opinion mining with deep recurrent neural networks. In *Proc. of the 2014 Conference on Empirical Methods in Natural Language Processing (EMNLP-14)*, pages 720–728.

Nal Kalchbrenner, Edward Grefenstette, and Phil Blunsom. 2014. A convolutional neural network for modelling sentences. *Eprint Arxiv*, 1.

Yoon Kim. 2014. Convolutional neural networks for sentence classification. *Eprint Arxiv.*

Pengfei Liu, Shafiq Joty, and Helen Meng. 2015. Fine-grained opinion mining with recurrent neural networks and word embeddings. In *Proc. of the 2015 Conference on Empirical Methods in Natural Language Processing (EMNLP-15)*, pages 1433–1443.

R. Maclin and D. Opitz. 1999. Popular ensemble methods: An empirical study. *Journal of Artificial Intelligence Research*, 11:169–198.

Tomas Mikolov, Kai Chen, Greg Corrado, and Jeffrey Dean. 2013a. Efficient estimation of word representations in vector space. *Computer Science.*

Tomas Mikolov, Ilya Sutskever, Kai Chen, Greg Corrado, and Jeffrey Dean. 2013b. Distributed representations of words and phrases and their compositionality. *Advances in Neural Information Processing Systems*, 26:3111–3119.

Razvan Pascanu, Tomas Mikolov, and Yoshua Bengio. 2012. On the difficulty of training recurrent neural networks. *Computer Science*, 52(3):III–1310.

Jeffrey Pennington, Richard Socher, and Christopher Manning. 2014. Glove: Global vectors for word representation. In *Proc. of the 2014 Conference on Empirical Methods in Natural Language Processing (EMNLP-14)*, pages 1532– 1543.

David M W Powers. 2011. Evaluation: From precision, recall and f-factor to roc, informedness, markedness & correlation. *Journal of Machine Learning Technologies*, 2:2229–3981.

Lior Rokach. 2010. *Ensemble-based classifiers*. Kluwer cademic Publishers.

Nitish Srivastava, Geoffrey Hinton, Alex Krizhevsky, Ilya Sutskever, and Ruslan Salakhutdinov. 2014. Dropout: a simple way to prevent neural networks from overfitting. *Journal of Machine Learning Research*, 15(1):1929–1958.

Kai Sheng Tai, Richard Socher, and Christopher D. Manning. 2015. Improved semantic representations from tree-structured long short-term memory networks. In *Proceedings of the 53rd Annual Meeting of the Association for Computational Linguistics and the 7th International Joint Conference on Natural Language Processing (ACL/IJCNLP-15)*, pages 1556–1566.

Duyu Tang, Bing Qin, and Ting Liu. 2015. Document modeling with gated recurrent neural network for sentiment classification. In *Proc. of the 2015 Conference on Empirical Methods in Natural Language Processing (EMNLP-15)*, pages 1422–1432.

Jin Wang, Liang-Chih Yu, K. Robert Lai, and Xuejie Zhang. 2016. Dimensional sentiment analysis using a regional CNN-LSTM model. In *Proc. of the 54th Annual Meeting of the Association for Computational Linguistics (ACL-16)*, pages 225-230.

Liang-Chih Yu, Jin Wang, K. Robert Lai, and Xue-jie Zhang. 2017. Refining word embeddings for sentiment analysis. In *Proc. of the 2017 Conference on Empirical Methods in Natural Language Processing (EMNLP-17)*, pages 545–550.

IIIT-H at IJCNLP-2017 Task 4: Customer Feedback Analysis using Machine Learning and Neural Network Approaches

Prathyusha Danda[1]
IIIT-Hyderabad
Hyderabad, India
500032

Pruthwik Mishra[1]
IIIT-Hyderabad
Hyderabad, India
500032

Silpa Kanneganti[2]
i.am+ LLC.
Bangalore, India
560071

Soujanya Lanka[3]
i.am+ LLC.
37 Mapex building
Singapore - 577177

Abstract

The IJCNLP 2017 shared task on Customer Feedback Analysis focuses on classifying customer feedback into one of a predefined set of categories or classes. In this paper, we describe our approach to this problem and the results on four languages, i.e. English, French, Japanese and Spanish. Our system implemented a bidirectional LSTM(Graves and Schmidhuber, 2005) using pre-trained glove(Pennington et al., 2014) and fastText(Joulin et al., 2016) embeddings, and SVM (Cortes and Vapnik, 1995) with TF-IDF vectors for classifying the feedback data which is described in the later sections. We also tried different machine learning techniques and compared the results in this paper. Out of the 12 participating teams, our systems obtained 0.65, 0.86, 0.70 and 0.56 exact accuracy score in English, Spanish, French and Japanese respectively. We observed that our systems perform better than the baseline systems in three languages while we match the baseline accuracy for Japanese on our submitted systems. We noticed significant improvements in Japanese in later experiments, matching the highest performing system that was submitted in the shared task, which we will discuss in this paper.

1 Introduction

Customer feedback analysis is a dominant problem, to the extent that there are companies whose principal purpose is to categorize feedback data. Classification of customer feedback would help companies gain a better perspective on the views of the customer. Comprehending customer feedback not only helps to understand the customer pulse better, but also to reply with an appropriate response. Hence, many companies understandably want an automated customer feedback analysis system. A major hurdle while doing this is dealing with the multilingual environment that is existent in most of the countries.

Considering the above points, the aim of the IJCNLP shared task on Customer Feedback Analysis is to classify real world customer feedback reviews into pre-defined set of classes. The goal is to achieve this by using data driven techniques in machine learning, which will help automate the classification process. The customer feedback are extracted, from Microsoft Office customers, in four languages, i.e. English, French, Spanish and Japanese. Since, there is no universal categorization for customer feedback, a set of six classes which would be applicable to all the entire set irrespective of the language they belong to, are created. These six classes are *comment, request, bug, complaint, meaningless* and *undetermined*. Each feedback was tagged with one or more classes. The task was to use this annotated data and build a model using supervised techniques. The model should be able to categorize a given review in one of the four aforementioned languages, into one or more of the classes.

We used bi-directional LSTMs (Graves and Schmidhuber, 2005) for the classification task at hand. We also used simple Naive Bayes classifier and SVM models as separate alternate approaches to achieve the intended goal. We found that the accuracy of the SVM model was almost on par with the bi-directional LSTM for English. We used glove pre-trained embeddings[1] (Pennington et al., 2014) for English while for the rest

---

[1]we used Common Crawl corpus with 840B tokens, 2.2M vocab, case-sensitive, 300-dimensional vectors available on https://nlp.stanford.edu/projects/glove/

155

Proceedings of the 8th International Joint Conference on Natural Language Processing, Shared Tasks, pages 155–160,
Taipei, Taiwan, November 27 – December 1, 2017. ©2017 AFNLP

of the languages we used fastText[2] (Joulin et al., 2016) embeddings. The SVM model with TF-IDF as features performed better for French data compared to the bi-directional LSTM with fastText word embeddings. For Japanese and Spanish language data, bi-directional LSTM with fastText models have performed better compared to the SVM with TF-df models respectively. Both these models made use of fastText word embeddings of those particular languages. The Naive Bayes with TF-IDF (McCallum et al., 1998) models on all four languages gave lesser accuracies compared to the SVM (Cortes and Vapnik, 1995) and bi-LSTM models.

This paper is organized as the following - section 2 explains the related work and section 3 details about the corpus. Different approaches employed are explained in the subsequent sections. Results constitutes sections 5 and Error Analysis & Observation are presented in section 6. We conclude our paper with the Conclusion & Future Work section.

2   Related Work

(Bentley and Batra, 2016) dealt with Microsoft Office users feedback, on which they applied various machine learning techniques. They implemented classification techniques on labeled data and applied clustering approaches for unlabeled data. They had reported 0.5667 recall and 0.7656 precision on English data using logistic regression in a one-versus-rest setting. The text was lemmatized, stop words were removed and POS tags and named entities were tagged in the pre-processing stage. They used n-grams up to 3 in a bag-of-words approach along with non-text features such as star rating, sentiment and the categorization that an agent gave to the feedback, from the pre-defined Agent Taxonomy. Another key point of this particular model is that the users have scope to label the already predicted data, thus making re-building and re-predicting feasible with newer and larger data, which can increase the precision of the model.

The 2017 GermEval task (Wojatzki et al., 2017) has been designed to extract opinions from the customer feedback on the services offered by a German public train operator Deutsche Bahn. The shared task included 4 subtasks - relevance predic-tion, document polarity identification, aspect and category identification, target opinion extraction. SVM (Cortes and Vapnik, 1995) and CRF (Lafferty et al., 2001) have been used to create baseline models[3].

Sentiment analysis on customer feedback data by (Gamon, 2004) using linear SVM for classification had yielded satisfying results. They used feedback items from a Global Support Services survey and a Knowledge Base survey. Satisfaction scores were on a scale from 1(not satisfied) to 4 (very satisfied). Each feedback was given one of these 4 scores. They used surface level features like n-grams as well as linguistic features like POS tagging. All the features were represented in a binary form (present or not present) except for the length of sentence. Feature reduction was done based on log likelihood ratio. F1 measure of 74.62 was reported for 1 versus 4 classification and 58.14 for 1 and 2 grouped together versus 3 and 4 grouped together, both using top 2k features.

3   Corpus Details

The statistics of the corpus used for this task is detailed in Table 1. A few examples extracted from the training set are given below:-

- The sentence "Some are fairly easy, but I definitely get stuck." is tagged as a "comment".

- The sentence "The only thing that wasn't that perfect was the internet connection." is labeled as "comment, complaint".

- "All offered drinks and food at the restaurants and bars are too expensive." is a sentence with tag "complaint".

4   Approach

Many machine learning algorithms rely heavily on features designed by domain experts which makes the labeling task cost inefficient. So we have not used any language specific features like part-of-speech tag, morph features, dependency labels etc. for the task. We describe our approaches in the following subsections.

4.1   Machine Learning Approaches

We used Support Vector Machines (SVM), logistic regression(Log-Reg), k-Nearest Neighbor(k=3, 5 for our experiments) and Gaussian Naive

[2]https://github.com/facebookresearch/fastText/blob/master/pretrained-vectors.md

[3]https://github.com/uhh-lt/GermEval2017-Baseline

Lang	Type	#Tokens-Case-Sensitive	#Tokens-Lowercase
English	Train	5449	4674
	Dev	1848	1663
	Test	1788	1589
Spanish	Train	3524	3119
	Dev	1043	933
	Test	1109	1015
French	Train	3930	3515
	Dev	1454	1332
	Test	1407	1306
Japanese	Train	1651	1648
	Dev	282	281
	Test	320	320

Table 1: Corpus Statistics for the Shared Task

Lang	Tag	Model	MicroAvg
English	bug	bi-LSTM	**0.19**
		SVM	-1.0
	comment	bi-LSTM	**0.81**
		SVM	0.80
	complaint	bi-LSTM	**0.63**
		SVM	0.62
	meaningless	bi-LSTM	**0.40**
		SVM	0.25
	request	bi-LSTM	0.13
		SVM	**0.29**
	undetermined	bi-LSTM	**-1.0**
		SVM	**-1.0**
Spanish	bug	bi-LSTM	**-1.0**
		SVM	**-1.0**
	comment	bi-LSTM	**0.92**
		SVM	**0.92**
	complaint	bi-LSTM	**0.75**
		SVM	0.68
	meaningless	bi-LSTM	**-1.0**
		SVM	**-1.0**
	request	bi-LSTM	0.50
		SVM	**0.53**
French	bug	bi-LSTM	0.17
		SVM	**0.22**
	comment	bi-LSTM	0.80
		SVM	**0.84**
	complaint	bi-LSTM	**0.61**
		SVM	**0.61**
	meaningless	bi-LSTM	**0.44**
		SVM	0.36
	request	bi-LSTM	**0.15**
		SVM	-1.0
	undetermined	bi-LSTM	**-1.0**
		SVM	**-1.0**

Table 2: Results on Test Data for English, Spanish and French using SVM with fastText features

Tag	MicroAvg
bug	0.4
comment	0.86
complaint	0.74
request	0.44
undetermined	-1.0

Table 3: Updated Test Results for Japanese. SVM model here used unigram-bigram tf-idf vectors as features

Bayes(NB) using sklearn library (Pedregosa et al., 2011). In the ML approaches, we used TF-IDF (Sparck Jones, 1972) vectors for the words(uni)[4] present in the training corpus. We also experimented with TF-IDF vectors for bigrams(bi) and trigrams(tri). Sklearn uses count vectorizers to convert text input into a collection of tokens. It gives the flexibility of including higher n-grams in the vocabulary. This can prove to be helpful in the classification task. We used sklearn linear SVM library with the settings mentioned in Table 9. We employed the one-versus-one strategy for the classification task. We implemented Naive Bayes where all the features are assumed to follow Gaussian distribution. We also created a logistic regression model with maximum iteration of 100 and tolerance level of 0.0001.

4.2 Neural Networks

We implemented mainly two neural network models - bi-directional LSTM(bi-LSTM) (Graves and Schmidhuber, 2005), multi-layer perceptron (MLP) (Sparck Jones, 1972) using (Chollet et al., 2015). The accuracies of these models are reported in the subsequent sections. These neural network models used word embeddings as features. Glove embeddings were used for English and fastText embedding for other three languages. For encoding a sequence, bidirectional LSTM uses contextual information in both the directions - past and future word vectors. This enables them to have a better semantic representation of any sequential data. The maximum length of the sample was set to 100. We used word embeddings of size 300 for all the languages. For MLP, we used a single hidden layer of 300 nodes. The sentences which have more than 100 tokens would be truncated and only the first 100 tokens take part in the learning. Adam optimizer (Kingma and Ba, 2014) was used for learning with default learning rate of 0.001 and categorical cross-entropy loss function.

5 Results

The experimental results on the development and test data for different languages are shown in Tables 2-9. The highest performing system measures are marked in bold. From the tables 4, 6 and 7, it can be seen that SVM with a linear kernel and TF-IDF features outperforms all other machine learn-

---

[4]All the keywords written in parenthesis are later used in the tables.

Lang	Model	Features	Exact-Accuracy	Partial-Accuracy	Macro-Average	Micro-Average
English	SVM	uni	0.67	0.67	**0.35**	0.68
		uni-bi	0.67	0.67	0.34	0.68
		uni-bi-tri	**0.68**	**0.68**	**0.35**	**0.69**
		glove-vectors	0.57	0.57	**0.35**	0.59
	NB	uni	0.67	0.67	**0.35**	0.68
	3-NN	uni	0.55	0.55	0.25	0.55
	5-NN	uni	0.55	0.55	0.23	0.56
	Log-Reg	uni	0.66	0.66	0.24	0.67
Spanish	SVM	uni	**0.90**	**0.90**	0.46	**0.89**
		uni-bi	0.82	0.82	0.27	0.82
		uni-bi-tri	0.82	0.82	0.27	0.82
	NB	uni	0.77	0.77	0.32	0.77
	3-NN	uni	0.84	0.84	**0.57**	0.84
	5-NN	uni	0.85	0.85	0.55	0.85
	Log-Reg	uni	0.88	0.88	0.32	0.88
French	SVM	uni	0.74	0.74	**0.36**	0.76
		uni-bi	0.60	0.60	0.16	0.62
		uni-bi-tri	0.60	0.60	0.16	0.62
	NB	uni	0.52	0.52	0.30	0.63
	3-NN	uni	0.64	0.64	0.30	0.66
	5-NN	uni	0.61	0.61	0.26	0.64
	Log-Reg	uni	**0.88**	**0.88**	0.32	**0.88**
Japanese	SVM	uni	0.70	0.70	0.59	0.72
		uni-bi	0.73	0.73	0.62	0.75
		uni-bi-tri	**0.74**	**0.74**	**0.65**	**0.77**
	NB	uni	0.38	0.39	0.31	0.44
	Log-Reg	uni	0.68	0.68	0.45	0.70

Table 4: Results on Development Data for English, Spanish, French and Japanese using ML Approaches. Updated models used for Japanese

Language	Model	Features	Exact Accuracy	Micro-Average	Partial Accuracy	Macro-Average
English	MLP	glove	0.63	0.63	0.36	0.65
	SVM	fastText	0.57	0.57	0.35	0.59
	bi-LSTM	glove	**0.65**	**0.66**	**0.45**	**0.68**
Spanish	MLP	fastText	0.81	0.81	0.32	0.81
	SVM	fastText	0.76	0.76	0.36	0.76
	bi-LSTM	fastText	**0.86**	**0.86**	**0.42**	**0.86**
French	MLP	fastText	0.66	0.66	0.33	0.69
	SVM	fastText	0.60	0.60	0.27	0.64
	bi-LSTM	fastText	**0.71**	**0.71**	**0.38**	**0.74**
Japanese	MLP	fastText	0.57	0.57	0.30	0.57
	SVM	uni	**0.60**	**0.60**	0.47	**0.60**

Table 5: Results on Development Data Using Neural Networks. SVM model here uses fastText vectors as features for English, Spanish and French, where as character unigrams for Japanese. Updated models used for Japanese

Language	Model	Exact Accuracy	Partial Accuracy	Micro-Average	Macro-Average
English	bi-LSTM	**0.65**	0.65	**0.68**	**0.36**
	SVM	**0.65**	**0.66**	**0.68**	0.34
Spanish	bi-LSTM	**0.86**	**0.86**	**0.86**	0.44
	SVM	0.85	0.85	0.85	**0.45**
French	bi-LSTM	0.65	0.65	0.69	**0.38**
	SVM	**0.70**	**0.70**	**0.72**	**0.38**
Japanese	bi-LSTM	**0.56**	**0.57**	**0.56**	**0.28**
	SVM	**0.56**	0.56	**0.56**	0.26

Table 6: Test Results; using older Japanese models. SVM model here uses TF-IDF vectors as features

Lang	Model	Features	Exact-Accuracy	Partial-Accuracy	Macro-Average	Micro-Average
Japanese	SVM	uni	0.74	0.74	**0.52**	0.75
		uni-bi	**0.76**	**0.76**	**0.52**	**0.77**
		uni-bi-tri	0.75	0.75	0.51	0.76
	Log-Reg	uni	0.67	0.70	0.45	0.70

Table 7: Updated Test Results for Japanese

Parameter	Value
Loss	Squared Hinge Loss
Penalty	L2
Iterations	1000
Tolerance	0.0001

Table 8: SVM Parameters

Class Pairs	#Common Words
Complaint Comment	1155
Meaningless Comment	657
Complaint Meaningless	584
Comment,Complaint Comment	514

Table 9: Class Distribution of Overlapping English Training Data

ing techniques. Naive Bayes' classifier relying on the maximum likelihood estimates performed poor across languages. K-nearest neighbor algorithm which depends on the vector representation of feedback and the euclidean distance from other vectors also did not perform reliably which is evident from the tables. From Table-5, we observed that bidirectional-LSTMs outperformed MLP and SVM when word vectors were considered as features. Bi-LSTMs represent a sequence better than the other two which in-turn increases the classification accuracy.

6 Error Analysis & Observation

A major observation in the data is that many words overlapped between different classes. The maximum overlap is observed between comment and complaints and this contributes to many false positives. The meaningless tag adds to the confusion, as these sentences have a huge overlap with comment and complaint classes. As the "undetermined" tag was not present in the training data, the system was unable to predict it. The labels which are combinations of two atomic labels are also contentious ones. For example: the label "comment, complaint" gets confused with "comment" as well as "complaint". The partial accuracy metric captures this whether one label is matched when the true label consists of two labels. The top four overlapping classes for English are shown in the Table 9. The statistics were got on English data as it had the maximum training samples. Examples of test errors-

- For the sentences "Lunch, they forgot one meal.", the system wrongly predicts the tag as "comment" while the correct label corresponds to "complaint".

- The sentence "This editor is good, but could still use some Hot needed improvements!" is tagged as "comment, complaint". Our system could only predict it as "comment".

The bi-LSTMs outperform MLPs as MLPs d not take any positional information into account. We also experimented with POS tags as features but we found that they do not offer any advantage in neural networks, instead they introduce additional noise to the data. The frequent classes exhibit better classification accuracy, as the model can classify them with high confidence. The accuracy was high for Spanish because it had relatively few labels compared to other languages. But the rare classes with low occurrence in the training data are ambiguous and difficult to classify correctly. Japanese was different compared to the rest of the three languages because of its agglutinative nature. Segmentation is a major challenge for Japanese language. So instead of tokenizing words with white spaces, we considered characters as tokens and obtained significant improvements in development and test data. For the improvements in the Japanese system, we used unigram TF-IDF vectors for SVM. No external tools were used for Japanese text segmentation. Our submitted Japanese system used whitespace-separated word vectors for SVM and bi-LSTM.

7 Conclusion & Future Work

In this paper, we showed that machine learning approaches and neural networks could achieve comparable accuracy to the systems relying on hand-crafted features. The bi-directional LSTMs also performed reasonably well with limited amount of data.

In the future, we intend to use character embeddings along with the word embeddings to get better representation of a sentence. This will also help in getting a representation for out-of-vocabulary(OOV) words. We can explore multilingual embeddings where words in one language can be mapped to its equivalent in another language. This can also help improve the classification accuracy. We intend to include some linguistic regularization (Qian et al., 2016) while learning the bi-LSTM to take advantage of intensifiers, negative words, positive words and other cue words.

Acknowledgements

We thank Vandan Mujadia and Pranav Dhakras for their valuable inputs and feedback for us on the paper.

References

Michael Bentley and Soumya Batra. 2016. Giving voice to office customers: Best practices in how office handles verbatim text feedback. In *Big Data (Big Data), 2016 IEEE International Conference on*, pages 3826–3832. IEEE.

François Chollet et al. 2015. Keras. `https://github.com/fchollet/keras`.

Corinna Cortes and Vladimir Vapnik. 1995. Support vector machine. *Machine learning*, 20(3):273–297.

Michael Gamon. 2004. Sentiment classification on customer feedback data: noisy data, large feature vectors, and the role of linguistic analysis. In *Proceedings of the 20th international conference on Computational Linguistics*, page 841. Association for Computational Linguistics.

Alex Graves and Jürgen Schmidhuber. 2005. Framewise phoneme classification with bidirectional lstm and other neural network architectures. *Neural Networks*, 18(5):602–610.

Armand Joulin, Edouard Grave, Piotr Bojanowski, and Tomas Mikolov. 2016. Bag of tricks for efficient text classification. *arXiv preprint arXiv:1607.01759*.

Diederik Kingma and Jimmy Ba. 2014. Adam: A method for stochastic optimization. *arXiv preprint arXiv:1412.6980*.

John Lafferty, Andrew McCallum, and Fernando CN Pereira. 2001. Conditional random fields: Probabilistic models for segmenting and labeling sequence data. *Proceedings of the 18th International Conference on Machine Learning, ICML-2001*, pages 282–289.

Andrew McCallum, Kamal Nigam, et al. 1998. A comparison of event models for naive bayes text classification. In *AAAI-98 workshop on learning for text categorization*, volume 752, pages 41–48. Madison, WI.

Fabian Pedregosa, Gaël Varoquaux, Alexandre Gramfort, Vincent Michel, Bertrand Thirion, Olivier Grisel, Mathieu Blondel, Peter Prettenhofer, Ron Weiss, Vincent Dubourg, Jake Vanderplas, Alexandre Passos, David Cournapeau, Matthieu Brucher, Matthieu Perrot, and Édouard Duchesnay. 2011. Scikit-learn: Machine learning in python. *J. Mach. Learn. Res.*, 12:2825–2830.

Jeffrey Pennington, Richard Socher, and Christopher Manning. 2014. Glove: Global vectors for word representation. In *Proceedings of the 2014 conference on empirical methods in natural language processing (EMNLP)*, pages 1532–1543.

Qiao Qian, Minlie Huang, and Xiaoyan Zhu. 2016. Linguistically regularized lstms for sentiment classification. *arXiv preprint arXiv:1611.03949*.

Karen Sparck Jones. 1972. A statistical interpretation of term specificity and its application in retrieval. *Journal of documentation*, 28(1):11–21.

Michael Wojatzki, Eugen Ruppert, Sarah Holschneider, Torsten Zesch, and Chris Biemann. 2017. Germeval 2017: Shared task on aspect-based sentiment in social media customer feedback. In *Proceedings of the GSCL GermEval Shared Task on Aspect-based Sentiment in Social Media Customer Feedback*.

ADAPT at IJCNLP-2017 Task 4: A Multinomial Naive Bayes Classification Approach for Customer Feedback Analysis task

Pintu Lohar, Koel Dutta Chowdhury, Haithem Afli, Mohammed Hasanuzzaman and Andy Way

ADAPT Centre
School of Computing
Dublin City University
Dublin, Ireland

`{FirstName.LastName}@adaptcentre.ie`

Abstract

In this age of the digital economy, promoting organisations attempt their best to engage the customers in the feedback provisioning process. With the assistance of customer insights, an organisation can develop a better product and provide a better service to its customer. In this paper, we analyse the real world samples of customer feedback from Microsoft Office customers in four languages, i.e., English, French, Spanish and Japanese and conclude a five-plus-one-classes categorisation (comment, request, bug, complaint, meaningless and undetermined) for meaning classification. The task is to determine what class(es) the customer feedback sentences should be annotated as in four languages. We propose following approaches to accomplish this task: (i) a multinomial naive bayes (MNB) approach for multi-label classification, (ii) MNB with one-vs-rest classifier approach, and (iii) the combination of the multilabel classification-based and the sentiment classification-based approach. Our best system produces F-scores of 0.67, 0.83, 0.72 and 0.7 for English, Spanish, French and Japanese, respectively. The results are competitive to the best ones for all languages and secure 3rd and 5th position for Japanese and French, respectively, among all submitted systems.

1 Introduction

With the rapid development of the Internet, the generation of online content has been near exponential during the last few years. A snapshot of the amount of online content generated per minute is shown in Figure 1. One of the items (shown by

Figure 1: Statistics of UGC generated per minute[2]

an arrow) in this figure shows that a huge amount of money ($750k$) is spent online per minute. Such an activity of the Internet users reflects how they are very much involved in online shopping. Due to this reason, industry sectors nowadays are more inclined to make use of online business development. For example, the big multinational companies (e.g., *Microsoft*[3], *Ebay*[4], *Amazon*[5] etc.) advertise and sell products via Internet. In response to this, customers frequently post product reviews on various websites in different languages. It is very important to understand the customers' behaviour because it provides marketers and business owners with insight that they can use to improve their business, products and overall cus-

---

[2] *Created by Lori Lewis, Vice President, Social Media - Cumulus Media/Westwood One*
[3] `https://www.microsoft.com/`
[4] `https://www.ebay.com/`
[5] `https://www.amazon.com/`

Proceedings of the 8th International Joint Conference on Natural Language Processing, Shared Tasks, pages 161–169,
Taipei, Taiwan, November 27 – December 1, 2017. ©2017 AFNLP

tomer experience. The present work is based on a joint ADAPT[6]-Microsoft research project, where the representative real world samples of customer feedback are extracted from Microsoft Office customers in four languages, i.e. English, French, Spanish and Japanese and concluded a five-plus-one-classes categorisation (comment, request, bug, complaint, meaningless and undetermined) for meaning classification. They prepared this corpus in order to provide an open resource for international customer feedback analysis. The task is to develop a system in order to find out which one among the provided six classes a customer feedback sentence belongs to. According to the criteria of classification, each feedback sentence must have at least one tag assigned to it. The sentence can also be annotated with multiple tags. We propose following three approaches to accomplish the task of feedback categorisation:

(i) the multinomial naive bayes (MNB) approach for multi-label classification,

(ii) the MNB with one-vs-rest classifier approach, and

(iii) the combination of the multilabel classification and the sentiment classification-based approach.

For sentiment classification, we use an automatic sentiment analysis tool (see Section 4.3). The experimental results show that the MNB with one-vs-rest classifier alone is sufficient enough to produce competitive results and hence becomes our best system among all the three approaches. Our system secures 3rd and 5th positions for Japanese and French, respectively.

The remainder of this paper is organised as follows. In Section 2, we provide a brief history of works in this field. Section 3 describe the process of customer feedback analysis along with some examples provided in this shared task. We provide a detailed description of the experiments in Section 4. The results are discussed in Section 5. Finally, we conclude and point out some possible future works in Section 6.

2   Related work

There is a number of research works done in the area of feedback analysis. For example, Bent-

---

ley and Batra (2016) implement the Office Customer Voice system that combines classification, on-demand clustering and other machine learning techniques with a rich web user interface. They use this approach to solve the problem of finding the signal in the feedback posted by the Microsoft office users. The work in Potharaju et al. (2013) presents NetSieve, a problem inference system that aims to automatically analyse ticket text written in natural language to infer the problem symptoms, troubleshooting activities, and resolution actions. In Nasr et al. (2014), they contribute to the literature on Transformative Service Research and customer feedback management by studying the overlooked area of positive customer feedback impact on the well-being of service entities. Wu et al. (2015) perform following three steps for understanding the customer reviews: (i) collectively using multiple machine learning algorithms to pre-process review classification, (ii) selecting the reviews on which all machine learning algorithms cannot agree and assign them to humans to process, and (iii) the results from machine learning and crowd-sourcing are aggregated to be the final analysis results. The work in Morales-Ramirez et al. (2015) presents a user feedback ontology specified in ontoUML (Guizzardi (2005)). They focus on online feedback given by the users upon their experience in using a software service or application. Dalal and Zaveri (2014) propose an opinion mining system that can be used for both binary and fine-grained sentiment classifications of user reviews. Their technique extends the feature-based classification approach to incorporate the effect of various linguistic hedges by using fuzzy functions to emulate the effect of modifiers, concentrators, and dilators. The work presented in Hu and Liu (2004) aims at mining and summarising all the customer reviews of a product. They only mine the features of the product on which the customers have expressed their opinions and whether the opinions are positive or negative. Their task is performed in three steps: (i) mining product features that have been commented on by customers, (ii) identifying opinion sentences in each review and deciding whether each opinion sentence is positive or negative, and (iii) finally summarizing the results.

Customer feedback analysis has a strong interconnection with sentiment analysis as the feedback is essentially the customers' reactions to-

---

さらにインスタでの写真の縮小まで出来なくなりました	bug
設定しなおしても変わりません	complaint
早く直して下さい	request
4/28 相変わらず、たったひとりの人だけタグ付け出来ません	bug
編集で付けようとしても、どうしてもその人のだけ消えてしまう	bug, comment
La desinstalo definitivamente.	complaint
El taxista nos ha timado y ha hecho más del doble del trayecto.	complaint
Desde la última actualización, cuando voy a entrar nunca vuelve a cargar.	bug
La recomiendo para todos	comment
De resto, todo muy bueno.	comment

Figure 2: Some examples of Feedback sentences in Spanish and Japanese

wards the product they are using and hence conveys a specific sentiment (e.g., negative, neutral, positive etc.). The work in Fang and Zhan (2015) categorises sentiment polarity of the online product reviews collected from *Amazon.com* by performing the experiments for both sentence-level categorisation and review-level categorisation. Broß (2013) detect the individual product aspects reviewers have commented on and to decide whether the comments are rather positive or negative. They focus on the two main subtasks of aspect-oriented review mining: (i) identifying relevant product aspects, and (ii) determining and classifying expressions of sentiment. Gräbner et al. (2012) propose a system that performs the classification of customer reviews of hotels by means of a sentiment analysis. They elaborate on a process to extract a domain-specific lexicon of semantically relevant words based on a given corpus (Scharl et al. (2003); Pak and Paroubek (2010)). The resulting lexicon backs the sentiment analysis for generating a classification of the reviews.

3 Customer feedback analysis

Most app companies treat the contents of these reports as confidential materials and also regard things such as categorisation of customer feedback as business secrets. To the best of our knowledge, there are only few openly available categorisations from these app companies. One of them is the commonly used categorisation which could be found in many websites, i.e., the five-class Excellent-Good-Average-Fair-Poor

(SurveyMonkey[7]). The other one is a combined categorisation of sentiment and responsiveness, i.e. another five-class Positive-Neutral-Negative-Answered-Unanswered, used by an app company Freshdesk[8]. There are many other categorisations for customer feedback analysis, however, most of them are not publicly available (e.g., Clarabridge[9], Inmoment[10])

To provide an open resource for international customer feedback analysis, the organisers of the shared task of customer feedback analysis in IJCNLP-2017 prepared a corpus using their proposed five-class categorisation of meanings as annotation scheme. As mentioned earlier in Section 1, a feedback sentence must have at least one tag and can also be annotated with multiple tags. Figure 2 shows some feedback examples in Spanish and Japanese provided by the organisers of the shared task. These examples are taken directly from the shared task webpage[11]. We can see from these examples that each sentence is most likely to be assigned one tag but it is also possible to assign more than one tag in case of multiple possibilities. For example, one of the sentences in Japanese in Figure 2 is assigned two tags (*bug* and *comment*).

4 Experiments

Statistics of the whole data sets in all four languages (i.e., English, Spanish, French and

---

[7] https://www.surveymonkey.com/r/BHM_Survey
[8] https://freshdesk.com/
[9] http://www.clarabridge.com/
[10] https://www.inmoment.com/
[11] https://sites.google.com/view/customer-feedback-analysis/

Japanese) is shown in Table 1. In this paper, we

Language	Train	Dev	Test
English	3,065	500	500
Spanish	1,631	301	299
French	1,950	400	400
English	1,526	250	300

Table 1: Data statistics per language

propose three different approaches (see Section 4.1, 4.2 and 4.3) to analyse the customer feedback in English. For the other languages, we apply the method that produces the best output for English feedback. In addition to this, we also apply this method to the available translations of the Spanish, French and Japanese feedback into English (see Section 4.4).

4.1 MNB classification

MNB is a specific instance of a Naive Bayes classifier which uses a multinomial distribution[12] for each of the features instead of referring to conditional independence of each of the features in the model. In this classification method, the distribution is estimated by considering the generative Naive Bayes principle, which assumes that the features are multinomially distributed in order to compute the probability of the document for each label and keep the label maximizing probability. Assuming the feature probabilities $P(x_i|c_j)$ are independent given the class c and for a document d represented as features x_1, x_2, ..., x_n; the equation for MNB can be written as follows:

$$C_{NB} = \arg\max_{c \in C} P(c_j) \prod_{x \in X} P(x|c) \quad (1)$$

Applying MNB classifiers to text classification, the equation can be represented as:

$$C_{NB} = \arg\max_{c_j \in C} P(c_j) \prod_{i \in positions} P(x_i|c_j) \quad (2)$$

where, *positions ← all word positions in test document*

For this task, we initially applied MNB classification method to label the whole training dataset in a single step. Subsequently, we also performed iterative process which is discussed in detail in the following section.

---

[12]https://web.stanford.edu/class/cs124/lec/naivebayes.pdf

4.2 MNB with one-vs-rest approach

This approach is a variation of MNB classification that works as follows:

(i) We apply an iterative process of one-vs-rest classification method. As there are total of six different categories available (*comment, complaint, meaningless, request, bug* and *undetermined*), we select one of these categories as *one*-class and consider the remaining as the *rest*-class. For example, we may select *comment* as *one*-class and treat the remaining as *rest*-class. These two groups of feedback can be considered as *comment* and *non-comment* classes, respectively. We then perform the classification process between the *comment* and the *non-comment* categories.

(ii) Once the feedback sentences are labeled as *comment* and *non-comment* classes, we opt out the sentences tagged as *comment* class and consider the rest with two new group of classes (for example, *complaint* and *non-complaint*). This iterative process continues until all the feedback sentences are assigned tags.

Figure 3 shows the iterative MNB classification using one-vs-rest approach. In each step, we classify the sentences into two categories exactly in the same way as discussed in step (i) and step (ii) above. We group the feedback into two classes; namely *comment* and *non-comment*. The *non-comment* class consists of other five remaining categories; (i) *complaint*, (ii) *meaningless*, (iii) *request*, (iv) *bug*, and (v) *undetermined*. Those sentences which are assigned *comment* tag are opted out and the remaining are considered for the next iteration. The process continued until only two categories are left (*bug* and *undetermined*) for classification. However, we can also begin with any other feedback categories instead of *comment*. The reason behind selecting *comment* is that in the initial experiments, our system performed better in tagging the *comment* class as compared to the other ones. It is easier to tag the feedback sentences that belong to this class because the total number of *comment* feedback is much more than that of any other classes and hence the system learns a better model for this class. The same is true for the other classes (i.e., *complaint, meaning-*

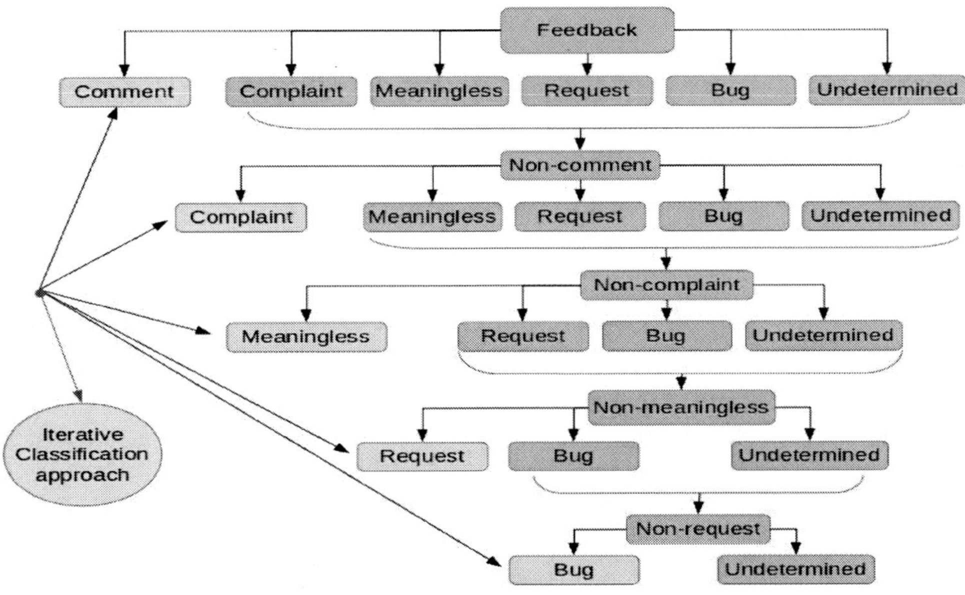

Figure 3: Iterative MNB classification with one-vs-rest approach

less, *request*, *bug* and *undetermined*) in the subsequent steps.

4.3 Multilabel classifier with sentiment classification

In addition to the approaches discussed in Section 4.1 and Section 4.2, we also apply sentiment classification approach and incorporate with the multilabel classification approach. We extract the sentiment scores (between 0 and 1, both inclusive) of all the feedback sentences using an automatic sentiment analysis tool (Afli et al., 2017), with 0 being extremely negative and 1 being extremely positive whereas any score close to 0.5 is considered to be neutral. Table 2 shows the observed sentiment range for different categories.

category	sentiment range
bug, complaint	0.2 to 0.6
meaningless, request	0.4 to 0.7
comment	0.4 to 0.9
undetermined	not fixed

Table 2: Sentiment range of Feedback categories

It is observed that some of the categories belong to overlapping ranges of sentiment scores. This observation implies that it is very difficult to identify a specific feedback category solely based on the sentiment scores due to the overlapping range of sentiment scores. However, it is visible in Table 2 that the *bug* and the *complaint* classes fall under the lower sentiment-score category. In contrast, *meaningless*, *request* and *comment* categories usually have higher sentiment scores, whereas the sentiment score for the *undetermined* category does not have any fixed range. Figure 4 shows the combination of multilabel classification and sentiment classification-based approach. Initially we filter out the *undetermined* and *meaningless* categories using the multilabel classification approach. The reasons behind performing this filtering are as follows: (i) the *undetermined* class has no fixed sentiment range, and (ii) the *meaningless* class has a specific sentiment range, but they are not related to customer feedback. This method works in following steps:

(i) Out of the six categories, *meaningless* and *undetermined* are filtered out using multilabel classification approach.

(ii) Sentiment scores are extracted for all the remaining feedback sentences.

(iii) Depending upon the sentiment scores, these feedback sentences are grouped into two different classes. For instance, if $score \geq 0.5$, the sentence is considered to be either *comment* or *request* class, and grouped together as *Comment_Request* category. In contrast,

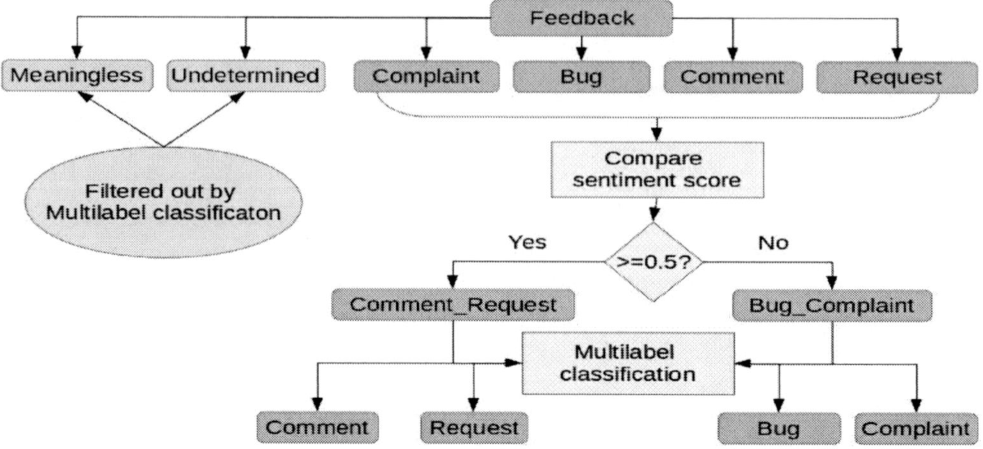

Figure 4: Machine learning combined with sentiment classification

if $score < 0.5$, it is treated as either *bug* or *complaint* class, and grouped together as *Bug_Complaint* category.

(iv) Finally, we apply multilabel classification to the *Comment_Request* category and identify each of *Comment* and *Request* classes. In a similar manner, each of *Bug* and *Complaint* classes are identified from the *Bug_Comment* group.

4.4 MNB for translated feedback

The translations of non-English (i.e., Spanish, French and Japanese) test data into English are also provided by the organisers. Since the translations of training data in these languages are not available, we train our classifier on English training data and then test it on the translations of Spanish, French and Japanese test data, respectively. Although our objective was to utilise the provided translations, this approach produces lower scores than other two approaches. The probable reason is that the trained model and the test data were originally in different languages.

5 Results

As the training and development data in English are larger than that of the other languages, we perform a series of different approaches (discussed in Section 4.1, Section 4.2 and Section 4.3) on English training data and applied the best approach to identify the feedback categories in other languages. These three approaches are termed as (i) MNB_all (for the MNB

classification), (ii) ML_SentClass (for the multilabel classifier with sentiment classification approach), and (iii) MNB_one-vs-rest (for the MNB with one-vs-rest approach). It can be seen from

Systems	Precision	Recall	F1 score
MNB_all	0.674	0.6493	0.6614
ML_SentClass	0.6687	0.6455	0.6569
MNB_one_vs_rest	**0.692**	**0.6667**	**0.6791**

Table 3: Three different methods for English data

the table that the best results are obtained by the "MNB_one_vs_rest" approach. For the other two approaches the scores obtained are relatively lower due to the fact that (i) in *MNB_all* approach (see Section 4.1 for details), we identify the tags for all categories in a single step which is relatively more difficult task as compared to the iterative approach, and (ii) in *ML_SentClass* system (see Section 4.3), it is difficult to distinguish between the feedback categories based on their sentiment scores as some of them have overlapping range of scores as shown in Table 2. Based on the above observations, we apply the "MNB_one_vs_rest" approach to the other languages. However, each of the above three systems performs more or less similar in predicting the feedback sentences per category. For more detailed analysis, we provide Table 4 that highlights the performance of one of our systems per feedback category.

It can be observed for Table 4 that our system produce the best results for the *comment* class. Two probable reasons for this can be as follows: (i) all the feedback sentences belonging

Tag	Oracle count	Predicted	Correct	Precision	Recall	F1 score
comment	285	261	214	0.8199	0.7508	0.7838
complaint	145	178	103	0.5786	0.7103	0.6377
bug	10	11	2	0.1818	0.2	0.1904
meaningless	62	27	11	0.4074	0.1774	0.2471
request	13	23	7	0.3043	0.5384	0.3888
undetermined	4	0	0	0	0	0

Table 4: System performance per feedback category using MNB_one_vs_rest approach

to the *comment* category contain positive words, and (ii) it is seen that the majority of the training data belongs to the *comment* class. It therefore becomes easier for the system to learn the model that can better identify a feedback under this category as compared to the other ones. In contrast, the other categories share much smaller portion of the whole training data and hence it becomes more difficult to correctly identify these tags by the models learned from these categories. However, our system fails to identify any tag under *undetermined* category as the training data for this category is too small to train a classifier model.

Table 5 provides the summary of the results for English feedback. A total of 53 systems was submitted and this table shows some of them. The ranking was performed in the decreasing order of F1 scores. A total of 12 teams participated in this shared task in 4 languages mentioned above. The team names are published as coded names starting from "TA" to "TJ" and end with language code name (e.g., "EN" for English). The full name of a submission is represented as "<TX>-<method_name>-<land_ID>" where X can be any letter from "A" to "J". All of our submitted systems start with "TK". For example, our best performing system (highlighted in bold letters in Table 5) is named as "TK-MNB_one_vs_rest-EN" where "'MNB_one_vs_rest" is the method name and "EN" is the language ID (English in this case). Most of the teams submitted multiple runs for all the 4 languages. As mentioned earlier, we conduct 3 different experiments and applied the best one to the other language data sets. In addition to this, we also test our system on the translations of Spanish, French and Japanese feedback sentences into English. Therefore, we submitted 3 systems for English and 2 systems for each of the other languages but as mentioned earlier in Section 4.4, the models learned from the English data produce lower score when tested on the translated

non-English test data into English. We therefore apply "MNB_one_vs_rest" method to the other languages. The performance of all the systems are evaluated using the precision, recall and F1 scores.

We can observe in Table 5 that out of the 53 submissions in English, our system (TK-MNB-one_vs_rest-EN) secures 18th position with 0.6791 of $F1$ score whereas the highest $F1$ score achieved is 0.7557 and the lowest is 0.4175. Table 6, 7 and 8 show the results for Spanish, French and Japanese, respectively. For French and Spanish test data, our system achieves 5th and 7th rank with the F1 scores of 0.8361 and 0.7268, respectively. The system performs best for the Japanese data in terms of ranking and secures the 3rd position. In overall, we can observe from the Table 5,6,7 and 8 that all the scores produced by our approach are relatively much closer to the highest scores than the lowest scores for all languages.

Rank	Systems	Precision	Recall	F1 score
1	TL-biLSTMCNN-EN	0.7485	0.7630	0.7557
2	TL-biCNN-EN	0.7383	0.7611	0.7495
...	...	...	...	...
18	**TK-MNB_one_vs_rest-EN**	**0.692**	**0.6667**	**0.6791**
19	TG-biLSTM-EN	0.6782	0.6782	0.6782
...	...	...	...	...
52	TB-M2-EN	0.4277	0.4277	0.4277
53	TB-M3-EN	0.4132	0.422	0.4175

Table 5: Results for English feedback sentences

Rank	Systems	Precision	Recall	F1 score
1	TA-M2-ES	0.8862	0.8862	0.8862
2	TA-M1-ES	0.8829	0.8829	0.8829
...	...	...	...	...
7	**TK-MNB_one_vs_rest-ES**	**0.8361**	**0.8361**	**0.8361**
8	TH-fastText-ES	0.8294	0.8294	0.8294
...	...	...	...	...
23	TF-NB-ES	0.5719	0.5719	0.5719
24	TF-SVM-ES	0.5719	0.5719	0.5719

Table 6: Results for Spanish feedback sentences

Finally, Table 9 highlights the summary of the overall results in all languages. It provides the

Rank	Systems	Precision	Recall	F1 score
1	TA-M1-FR	0.785	0.7476	0.7658
2	TC-CNN-FR-entrans	0.765	0.7286	0.7463
...	...	...	...	
5	**TK-MNB_one_vs_rest-FR**	0.745	0.7095	0.7268
6	TC-CNN-FR	0.735	0.7	0.7171
...	...	...	...	
26	TF-NN-FR	0.515	0.4905	0.5024
27	TF-ss_predtest-FR	0.4875	0.4643	0.4756

Table 7: Results for French feedback sentences

Rank	Systems	Precision	Recall	F1 score
1	TA-M2-JP	0.7912	0.7507	0.7704
2	TA-M1-JP	0.777	0.7348	0.7553
3	**TK-MNB_one_vs_rest-JP**	0.7167	0.6869	0.7015
...	...	...	...	...
10	TK-ML_Trans-JP	0.6224	0.5847	0.603
11	TH-CNN-JP	0.58	0.5559	0.5677
...	...	...	...	...
23	TF-LR-JP-entrans	0.5367	0.5144	0.5253
24	TF-LR-JP	0.3267	0.3131	0.3197

Table 8: Results for Japanese feedback sentences

Lang	No. of submission	Our rank	Highest score	Baseline score	Lowest score	Our score
JP	24	3	0.7704	0.5933	0.3197	0.7015
FR	27	5	0.7658	0.6026	0.4756	0.7268
ES	24	7	0.8862	0.7726	0.5719	0.8361
EN	53	18	0.7557	0.5393	0.4175	0.6791

Table 9: Summary of results for all languages

comparison among the highest score, the baseline scores (provided by the organisers), the lowest scores and the scores produced by our system. For all languages, our system performs better than the baseline and produces comparable results to the top ones. Our system secures 3rd and 5th rank for Japanese and French, respectively. In overall, the scores produced by our approach are competitive and relatively much closer to the highest scores than the lowest scores for all languages.

6 Conclusions and Future work

In this work, we presented different approaches based on (i) multinomial naive bayes algorithm, and (ii) a combination of multilabel classification and sentiment analysis technique to identify the tags of a collection of customer feedback in four languages. Initially we applied three different approaches for customer feedback-classification in English. We then selected one of these approaches that produced the highest scores and applied it to the other languages. In addition to this, we also tested our system on the translations of the feedback sentences (non-English feedback into English). Our system produced competitive re-

sults for all of the languages and secured 3rd and 5th rank for Japanese and French, respectively in terms of F1 score. However, all of the methodologies were not tested on non-English datasets. In future, we plan to apply them to the other languages in order to see the effects in the results. We will also extend our study on the frameworks using other efficient machine learning techniques to develop a new algorithm utilising the benefits of the sentiment analyser so that it can be effectively used in prediction.

Acknowledgments

This research is supported by Science Foundation Ireland in the ADAPT Centre (Grant 13/RC/2106) (www.adaptcentre.ie) at Dublin City University.

References

Haithem Afli, Sorcha McGuire, and Andy Way. 2017. Sentiment translation for low resourced languages: Experiments on irish general election tweets. In *Proceedings of the 18th International Conference on Computational Linguistics and Intelligent Text Processing*, Budapest, Hungary.

Michael Bentley and Soumya Batra. 2016. Giving voice to office customers: Best practices in how office handles verbatim text feedback. In *The fourth IEEE International Conference on Big Data*, pages 3826–3832, Washington DC, USA.

Jürgen Broß. 2013. *Aspect-Oriented Sentiment Analysis of Customer Reviews Using Distant Supervision Techniques*. Ph.D. thesis, Freie Universität Berlin, Berlin, Germany.

Mita K. Dalal and Mukesh A. Zaveri. 2014. Opinion mining from online user reviews using fuzzy linguistic hedges. *Applied Computational Intelligence and Soft Computing*, 2014:735942:1–735942:9.

Xing Fang and Justin Zhan. 2015. Sentiment analysis using product review data. *Journal of Big Data*, 2(1):5.

Dietmar Gräbner, Markus Zanker, Günther Fliedl, and Matthias Fuchs. 2012. Classification of customer reviews based on sentiment analysis. In *Proceedings of the International Conference on Information and Communication Technologies*, pages 460–470, Helsingborg, Sweden. Springer Vienna.

Giancarlo Guizzardi. 2005. *Ontological foundations for structural conceptual models*. Ph.D. thesis.

Minqing Hu and Bing Liu. 2004. Mining and summarizing customer reviews. In *Proceedings of the Tenth*

ACM SIGKDD International Conference on Knowledge Discovery and Data Mining, pages 168–177, Seattle, Washington, USA. ACM.

Itzel Morales-Ramirez, Anna Perini, and Renata S. S. Guizzardi. 2015. An ontology of online user feedback in software engineering. *Applied Ontology*, 10:297–330.

Linda Nasr, Jamie Burton, Thorsten Gruber, and Jan Kitshoff. 2014. Exploring the impact of customer feedback on the well-being of service entities: A tsr perspective. *Journal of Service Management*, 25(4):531–555.

Alexander Pak and Patrick Paroubek. 2010. Twitter as a corpus for sentiment analysis and opinion mining. In *Proceedings of the Seventh conference on International Language Resources and Evaluation*, pages 1320–1326, Valletta, Malta.

Rahul Potharaju, Navendu Jain, and Cristina Nita-Rotaru. 2013. Juggling the jigsaw: Towards automated problem inference from network trouble tickets. In *The 10th USENIX Symposium on Networked Systems Design and Implementation (NSDI)*, pages 127–141, Lombard, Illinois, USA.

Arno Scharl, Irene Pollach, and Christian Bauer. 2003. Determining the semantic orientation of web-based corpora. In *4th International Conference on Intelligent Data Engineering and Automated Learning*, Hong Kong, China.

Heting Wu, Hailong Sun, Yili Fang, Kefan Hu, Yongqing Xie, Yangqiu Song, and Xudong Liu. 2015. Combining machine learning and crowdsourcing for better understanding commodity reviews. In *Proceedings of the Twenty-Ninth AAAI Conference on Artificial Intelligence*, pages 4220–4221.

OhioState at IJCNLP-2017 Task 4: Exploring Neural Architectures for Multilingual Customer Feedback Analysis

Dushyanta Dhyani
The Ohio State University OH, USA
`dhyani.2@osu.edu`

Abstract

This paper describes our systems for IJC-NLP 2017 Shared Task on Customer Feedback Analysis. We experimented with simple neural architectures that gave competitive performance on certain tasks. This includes shallow CNN and Bi-Directional LSTM architectures with Facebook's Fasttext as a baseline model. Our best performing model was in the Top 5 systems using the Exact-Accuracy and Micro-Average-F1 metrics for the Spanish (85.28% for both) and French (70% and 73.17% respectively) task, and outperformed all the other models on comment (87.28%) and meaningless (51.85%) tags using Micro Average F1 by Tags metric for the French task.

1 Introduction

Customer Feedback Analysis (CFA) aims to analyze the feedback given by customers to various products/organizations. A primary component of CFA is to identify what the feedback is discussing so that further processing can be carried out appropriately. This requirement serves as a motivation for this shared task, which aims to classify user feedback in multiple languages into pre-defined categories and automate the process using machine learning methods for document classification.

2 Related Work

Document Classification is a well-studied problem in the NLP community with applications like sentiment analysis (Chen et al., 2016), language identification (Lui and Baldwin, 2012), email/document routing and even adverse drug reaction classification (Huynh et al., 2016). How-ever, the problem and various proposed solutions are highly domain and use-case specific. State of the art sentiment analysis models/architectures that perform well for news articles fail to perform well for Twitter sentiment analysis. Moreover, the Twitter sentiment analysis models have to be redesigned for tasks like target dependent sentiment analysis (Vo and Zhang, 2015). This shows that the type of models used for a particular domain depends a lot on the data and the granularity of the categories. Recent efforts (Kim, 2014; Zhang et al., 2015; Conneau et al., 2016; Yang et al., 2016; Joulin et al., 2016) show the applicability of a single (generally neural) model over a variety of datasets, showing their capability to model text classification tasks in a domain and language agnostic way.

3 Task Description

The goal of the shared task is: Given customer feedback in four languages (English, French, Spanish and Japanese) the participants should design systems that can classify customer feedback into pre-defined categories (comment, request, bug, complaint, meaningless and undetermined). Evaluation is done on per-language basis using a variety of metrics.

3.1 Dataset

The contest organizers provided customer feedback data in four languages. The size of train/dev/test samples for each of the sub task is shown in Table 1. About 5% of the samples across the data splits for English, French and Japanese task have multiple labels, while each sample in the Spanish task has only one label. For the data samples with a single label, the distribution was highly biased towards certain classes, with the comment and complaint categories covering 80%-95% across all data splits for each sub-task.

170

The contest organizers also provided a relatively larger corpus of unlabeled data. While this could be used in different ways like learning domain-specific word embeddings, we exclude it in our experiments.

Language	Train	Dev	Test
English(en)	3066	501	501
Spanish(es)	1632	302	300
French(fr)	1951	401	401
Japanese(jp)	1527	251	301
Total	8176	1455	1503

Table 1: Number of Training Samples for each sub-task

3.2 Evaluation

The contest organizers use 3 metrics to evaluate the submitted systems

- **Exact Accuracy**: All tags should be predicted correctly.

- **Micro-Average F1**: As discussed in (Manning et al., 2008), micro-average F1 gathers document level decisions across classes, thus giving more weight to large classes, which is the case across all the sub-tasks

- **Micro-Average by Tags**: Label specific micro-average F1.

4 Proposed Approach

Motivated by the success of a variety of architectures for document classification task, we use multiple methods for the given challenge. We used a recently released open source tool called Fasttext as our baseline. In addition to that, we used a commonly used CNN architecture and multiple LSTM based architectures. In this section we discuss various components of our systems.

4.1 Pre-processing

We used minimal text pre-processing by using in-built tokenizer's from TensorFlow (Abadi et al., 2015) and Keras (Chollet et al., 2015) across all our architectures. In addition to that, we applied some elementary text cleaning to the English data only, given our lack of understanding of other languages.

4.2 Models

4.2.1 fastText (OhioState-FastText)

Given its ease of use, we used the fastText (Joulin et al., 2016) tool[1] as our baseline model. At its core, fastText is a linear model with a few neat tricks to make the training fast and efficient. It takes individual word representations and averages them to get the representation of the given text. This representation is then passed through a softmax to get class distribution. Training is performed using Stochastic Gradient Descent to minimize the negative log-likelihood over all the classes. We used most of the default parameters as in the original tool. We, however, found that the model performs best on the dev set when the embedding dimension is set to 200 and the model is trained for 100 epochs. Since the size of training data and number of training labels were small, we used the softmax loss function (and not the hierarchical softmax and negative sampling methods) as training time was not a constraint.

4.3 Convolution Neural Networks (OhioState-CNN)

We also performed some basic experiments with CNN's given their applicability to text classification (Kim, 2014; Zhang et al., 2015; Conneau et al., 2016; Kalchbrenner et al., 2014) problems. We used a simplified version of the architecture from (Kim, 2014) as discussed here[2]. We set the word embedding size to 100 and trained the architecture for 10 epochs (after which it starts overfitting) . We used 128 filters of filter width 3,4 and 5 and added a dropout layer with retention probability of 0.5. We trained the model using Adam (Kingma and Ba, 2014) and the sigmoid cross entropy loss.

4.4 Bi-Directional LSTM

LSTM's have been shown to be extremely effective for learning representations for text, not only for sequence to sequence labeling tasks, but for general classification tasks (Yang et al., 2016) as well as language modeling (Li et al., 2015). We use Keras' ability to plug and play layers to experiment with a couple of architectures.

- **OhioState-biLSTM1** : A single layer Bi directional LSTM with an embedding layer

---

[1]We used the Python wrapper from pypi
[2]http://www.wildml.com/2015/12/implementing-a-cnn-for-text-classification-in-tensorflow/

	Sub-Tasks				
	EN		**ES**	**FR**	
Models	**EA**	**MAF**	**Both EA & MAF**	**EA**	**MAF**
OhioState-FastText	**63.4**	**65.36**	82.94	68	70.49
OhioState-CNN	54.20	56.13	81.27	65	67.8
OhioState-biLSTM1	61.2	63.79	82.61	**70**	**73.17**
OhioState-biLSTM2	61.6	63.98	**85.28**	68.5	71.71
OhioState-biLSTM3	62.8	64.97	79.93	65	67.56

Table 2: Performance of Various Models for Exact Accuracy (EA) and Micro-Average F1 (MAF) score

ES		**FR**			
Both EA & MAF		**EA**		**MAF**	
Plank-multilingual	88.63	Plank-monolingual	73.75	Plank-monolingual	76.59
Plank-monolingual	88.29	IITP-CNN-entrans	71.75	IITP-CNN-entrans	74.63
IIIT-H-biLSTM	86.29	Plank-multilingual	71.50	Plank-multilingual	74.39
IITP-RNN	85.62	**OhioState-biLSTM1**	70.00	**OhioState-biLSTM1**	73.17
OhioState-biLSTM2	85.28	IIIT-H-SVM	69.75	ADAPT-Run1	72.68

Table 3: Top-5 Performing systems for the Spanish and French Sub-Tasks

for the vocabulary and a dense layer with a sigmoid activation for the class labels. We also added a Dropout layer (with retention probability of 0.3) after the LSTM layer.

- **OhioState-biLSTM2** : We added a 1D Convolutional (with ReLU activation) and Max-Pooling layer after the word embedding layer which has shown to better represent n-gram like characteristics in text.

- **OhioState-biLSTM3** : We also added a Batch Normalization layer after the Convolution layer in the above architecture(though it decreased the performance)

Note that we did not make use of any pre-trained embeddings. We used the same training parameters for the 3 Bi-LSTM variants discussed above: Word embedding dimension, LSTM unit size and Batch Size were set to 64. We used the Adam (Kingma and Ba, 2014) optimizer with binary cross entropy loss.

A few points worth mentioning: While the CNN and Bi-LSTM architectures were trained in a multi-label setting, at prediction time, we only predict the label with the maximum score. Also, Japanese text in the corpus either has no or a single space and thus tokenization is not effective. So even though we achieve some (unconvincing) results for the Japanese task, we do not consider them as relevant to this sub-task which requires

more sub-word level treatment.

5 Results

We report the performance on 3 sub-tasks (leaving out Japanese for reasons previously discussed) for our models in Table 2 and comparison with systems designed by other teams in Table 3 using the exact accuracy and micro-average F1 metric.

While there is a considerable difference between our best performing system and the top systems for the English sub-task, we obtain competitive performance for the Spanish and French sub-tasks. Moreover, our LSTM based models outperform other systems for **comment and meaningless** category when evaluated using Micro Average by Tags metric for the French sub-task with an F-1 accuracy of 87.28% and 51.85% respectively. However, as shown in Table 4, our neural models failed to generalize to the infrequent labels as compared to a shallow model like fastText which is an expected behavior.

6 Conclusion

We propose some simple but effective neural architectures for customer feedback analysis. We show the effectiveness of LSTM based models for Text Classification in French and Spanish sub-tasks without any prior information like heavy pre-trained embeddings, thus making it easy to perform fast and effective hyper-parameter tuning and

Task	Comments	Complaint	Meaningless	Bug	Request
EN	BiLSTM2 (77.8)	BiLSTM1 (63.4)	fastText (48.3)	fastText (16.7)	fastText (53.9)
FR	**BiLSTM2 (87.3)**	BiLSTM1 (57.4)	**BiLSTM1 (51.9)**	fastText (20)	fastText (15.4)
ES	BiLSTM2 (92.6)	BiLSTM2 (68.9)	0	0	fastText (31.6)

Table 4: Our best performing models (F1) for each label of the English, French and Spanish sub-task (Scores in bold perform best amongst all submitted systems)

architecture exploration.

References

Martín Abadi, Ashish Agarwal, Paul Barham, Eugene Brevdo, Zhifeng Chen, Craig Citro, Greg S. Corrado, Andy Davis, Jeffrey Dean, Matthieu Devin, Sanjay Ghemawat, Ian Goodfellow, Andrew Harp, Geoffrey Irving, Michael Isard, Yangqing Jia, Rafal Jozefowicz, Lukasz Kaiser, Manjunath Kudlur, Josh Levenberg, Dan Mané, Rajat Monga, Sherry Moore, Derek Murray, Chris Olah, Mike Schuster, Jonathon Shlens, Benoit Steiner, Ilya Sutskever, Kunal Talwar, Paul Tucker, Vincent Vanhoucke, Vijay Vasudevan, Fernanda Viégas, Oriol Vinyals, Pete Warden, Martin Wattenberg, Martin Wicke, Yuan Yu, and Xiaoqiang Zheng. 2015. TensorFlow: Large-scale machine learning on heterogeneous systems. Software available from tensorflow.org.

Huimin Chen, Maosong Sun, Cunchao Tu, Yankai Lin, and Zhiyuan Liu. 2016. Neural sentiment classification with user and product attention. In *EMNLP*, pages 1650–1659.

François Chollet et al. 2015. Keras. https://github.com/fchollet/keras.

Alexis Conneau, Holger Schwenk, Loïc Barrault, and Yann Lecun. 2016. Very deep convolutional networks for natural language processing. *arXiv preprint arXiv:1606.01781*.

Trung Huynh, Yulan He, Alistair Willis, and Stefan Rüger. 2016. Adverse drug reaction classification with deep neural networks. In *Proceedings of COLING 2016, the 26th International Conference on Computational Linguistics: Technical Papers*, pages 877–887.

Armand Joulin, Edouard Grave, Piotr Bojanowski, and Tomas Mikolov. 2016. Bag of tricks for efficient text classification. *arXiv preprint arXiv:1607.01759*.

Nal Kalchbrenner, Edward Grefenstette, and Phil Blunsom. 2014. A convolutional neural network for modelling sentences. *arXiv preprint arXiv:1404.2188*.

Yoon Kim. 2014. Convolutional neural networks for sentence classification. *arXiv preprint arXiv:1408.5882*.

Diederik Kingma and Jimmy Ba. 2014. Adam: A method for stochastic optimization. *arXiv preprint arXiv:1412.6980*.

Jiwei Li, Minh-Thang Luong, and Dan Jurafsky. 2015. A hierarchical neural autoencoder for paragraphs and documents. *arXiv preprint arXiv:1506.01057*.

Marco Lui and Timothy Baldwin. 2012. langid. py: An off-the-shelf language identification tool. In *Proceedings of the ACL 2012 system demonstrations*, pages 25–30. Association for Computational Linguistics.

Christopher D. Manning, Prabhakar Raghavan, and Hinrich Schütze. 2008. *Introduction to Information Retrieval*. Cambridge University Press, New York, NY, USA.

Nitish Srivastava, Geoffrey E Hinton, Alex Krizhevsky, Ilya Sutskever, and Ruslan Salakhutdinov. 2014. Dropout: a simple way to prevent neural networks from overfitting. *Journal of machine learning research*, 15(1):1929–1958.

Duy-Tin Vo and Yue Zhang. 2015. Target-dependent twitter sentiment classification with rich automatic features. In *IJCAI*, pages 1347–1353.

Zichao Yang, Diyi Yang, Chris Dyer, Xiaodong He, Alexander J Smola, and Eduard H Hovy. 2016. Hierarchical attention networks for document classification. In *HLT-NAACL*, pages 1480–1489.

Xiang Zhang, Junbo Zhao, and Yann LeCun. 2015. Character-level convolutional networks for text classification. In *Advances in neural information processing systems*, pages 649–657.

YNU-HPCC at IJCNLP-2017 Task 4: Attention-based Bi-directional GRU Model for Customer Feedback Analysis Task of English

Nan Wang, Jin Wang and **Xuejie Zhang**
School of Information Science and Engineering
Yunnan University
Kunming, P.R. China
Contact:xjzhang@ynu.edu.cn

Abstract

This paper describes our submission to I-JCNLP 2017 shared task 4, for predicting the tags of unseen customer feedback sentences, such as comments, complaints, bugs, requests, and meaningless and undetermined statements. With the use of a neural network, a large number of deep learning methods have been developed, which perform very well on text classification. Our ensemble classification model is based on a bi-directional gated recurrent unit and an attention mechanism which shows a 3.8% improvement in classification accuracy. To enhance the model performance, we also compared it with several word-embedding models. The comparative results show that a combination of both word2vec and GloVe achieves the best performance.

1 Introduction

Understanding and being able to react to customer feedback is the most fundamental task in providing good customer service. The goal of task 4 of the custom feedback analysis of IJCNLP-2017 is to train classifiers for the detection of meaning in customer feedback provided in English, French, Spanish, and Japanese. This task can be considered a short-text classification task, which has recently become popular in many areas of natural language processing, including sentiment analysis, question answering, and dialog management. The feature representation of a short text is a key to classification, which is usually extracted as features based on uni-gram, bi-gram, n-gram, or other combination patterns of the bag-of-words (BoW) model.

Deep neural networks (Hinton and Salakhutdinov, 2006) and representation learning (Bengio et al., 2003) have recently brought new ideas to resolving the data sparsity problem, and various neural models for learning word representations have been proposed (Bengio et al., 2003; Collobert et al., 2011; Huang et al., 2012; Mikolov et al., 2013b). Mikolov et al. (2013b) showed that meaningful syntactic and semantic regularities can be captured in pre-trained word embedding. The embedding model measures the word relevance by simply using the cosine distance between two embedded vectors.

Using pre-trained word embedding, neural networks have achieved remarkable results, including a convolutional neural network (CNN) (Collobert et al., 2011) and recurrent neural network (RNN) (Mikolov et al., 2010). Furthermore, several advanced architectures such as long short-term memory (LSTM) (Hochreiter and Urgen Schmidhuber, 1997) and a gated recurrent unit (GRU) (Cho et al., 2014) have been proposed owing to their better ability to capture long-term dependencies. They are equipped with gates to balance the information flow from the previous and current time steps dynamically. In addition, neural processes involving attention have been extensively studied in the field of computational neuroscience (Itti et al., 1998; Desimone and Duncan, 1995). Recent studies have shown that attention mechanisms are flexible techniques, and that new changes can be used to create elegant and powerful solutions. Yang et al. (2016) introduced an attention mechanism using a single matrix and outputting a single vector. Instead of deriving a context vector in terms of the input, a summary is calculated by referring to the context vector learning as a model parameter. Raffel and Ellis (2015) proposed a feed-forward network model with an attention mechanism, which selects the most important element from each time step using learnable weights depending on the target. In addition, Parikh et al.

Proceedings of the 8th International Joint Conference on Natural Language Processing, Shared Tasks, pages 174–179,
Taipei, Taiwan, November 27 – December 1, 2017. ©2017 AFNLP

(2016) introduced an attention mechanism for two sentence matrices, which outputs a single vector, and built an alignment (similarity) matrix by multiplying learned vectors from each matrix, computing the context vectors from the alignment matrix, and mixing with the original signal.

In the present study, we used a uni-gram and bi-gram as features for a support vector machine (SVM) and naïve bayes as baseline methods. A deep learning method was also implemented for better text classification results. We created our model using a bi-directional gate recurrent unit (Bi-GRU) with an attention mechanism, and compared the results with different word-embedding models (word2vec, GloVe, and their concatenate modes). We found that our model using word2vec or GloVe slightly outperformed the baseline methods, whereas the ensemble model using both word2vec and GloVe achieved better performance in comparison to the other models.

2 Bi-GRUATT

Our model is based on a bidirectional GRU (Bahdanau et al., 2014) with an attention mechanism (Raffel and Ellis, 2015). GRU was designed to have more persistent memory, thereby making it easier to capture long-term dependencies than an RNN. Irsoy and Cardie (2014) showed that such a bi-directional deep neural network maintains two hidden layers, one for the left-to-right propagation, and the other for the right-to-left propagation. We chose the Bi-GRU model because it could obtain full information through two propagations. In addition, attention mechanisms allow for a more direct dependence between the states of the model at different points in time. In this section, our model is described using the following four steps: embedding, encoding, attending, and prediction. The model architecture is shown in Fig. 1.

Embedding. We took size L tokens of text as input, where L was the maximum length of all training texts. In this English training dataset, L is 117. In addition, every word in the text was embedded into a 300-dimensional vector through the pre-trained embedding model. For those words that cannot be recognized in the pre-trained model, the same dimensional vector of zeros was replaced. This was also used for padding out the sentence when it was shorter than L.

Mikolov et al. (2013a) proposed word2vec, which allows training on larger corpora, and

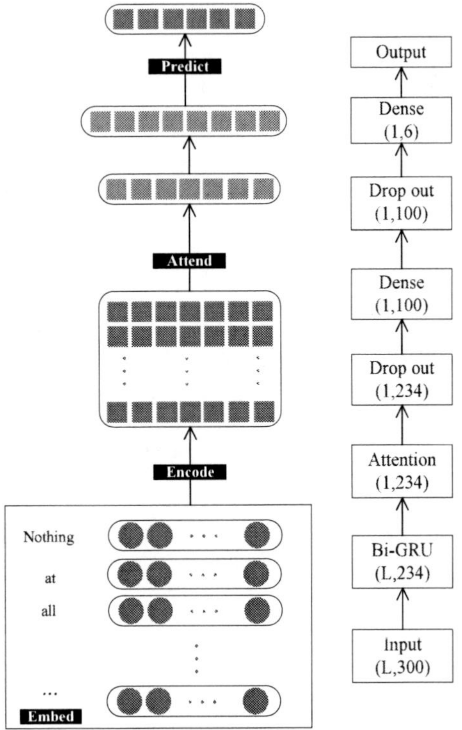

Figure 1: Architecture of Bi-GRUATT model. (the left-hand side ignores dropout layers which marked up on the right hand side, and L is the maximum length of all training texts.)

showed how semantic relationships emerge from such training. Pennington et al. (2014) proposed the GloVe approach, which maintains the semantic capacity of word2vec while introducing statistical information from a latent semantic analysis (LSA), which shows improvement in semantic and syntactic tasks. We tested word2vec and GloVe on pre-trained embedding models, and combined these two vectors, converted from each model, to a new 600-dimensional vector to obtain the advantages of both word2vec and GloVe.

Encoding. Through the given sequence of word vectors, the encoding step computes a representation of a sentence matrix, where each row represents the meaning of each token in the context of the rest of the sentence. We used a bi-directional GRU to summarize the contextual information from both directions of a sentence text, and obtained a full sentence matrix vector by concatenating the sentence matrix vector forward and backward at each time step. Similarly to the L-

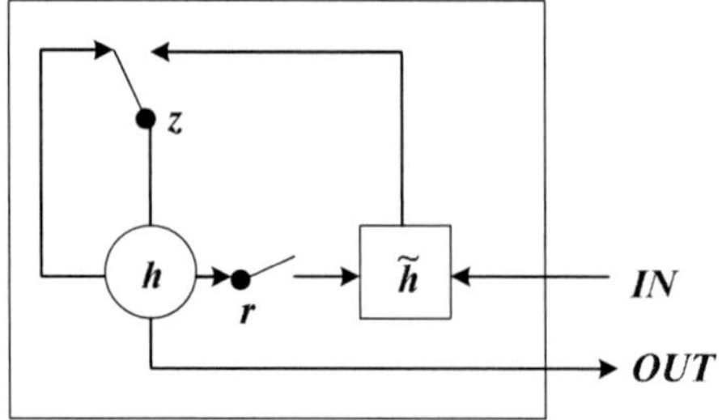

Figure 2: Illustration of gated recurrent units. (r and z are the reset and update gates, and h and $\tilde{h}$ are the activation and the candidate activation.)

	Train	Dev	Test
Comment	1758	276	285
Complaint	950	146	145
Request	103	19	13
Bug	72	20	10
Meaningless	306	48	62
Undefined	22	3	4
Total	**3065**	**500**	**500**

Table 1: Customer feedback classification of English dataset distribution of the shared task.

STM unit, the GRU has gating units that modulate the flow of information inside the unit, however, without having a separate memory cells (Chung et al., 2014). As is shown in Fig. 2. A GRU has two gates(a reset gate r, and an update gate z) rather than three gates in LSTM. Intuitively, the reset gate determines how to combine the new input with the previous memory, and the update gate defines how much of the previous memory to keep around. We ultized Bi-GRU instead of Bi-LSTM for its better performance on this task. For the activation function, softsign was used.

Attending. The attending step reduces the matrix representation generated by the encoding step into a single vector. The formula used by the attention mechanism to produce a single vector can be described as follows:

$$e_t = tanh(Wh_t) \tag{1}$$

$$\alpha_t = softmax(e_t) \tag{2}$$

$$c = \sum_{t}^{T} \alpha_t h_t \tag{3}$$

where h_t denotes the hidden state at each time step, and T is the total number of time steps in the input sequence. Vectors in hidden state sequence h_t are fed into the learnable function α_t to produce a probability vector α. Based on the weighting given by α, vector c is computed as the weighted average of h_t.

The characteristic advantage of an attention mechanism over other reduction operations is that the attention mechanism takes an auxiliary context vector as input. The context vector is crucial because it indicates which information to discard, and thus a summary vector is tailored to the network using it. The activation function of a dense layer during the attending step is tanh.

Prediction. After the text has been reduced to a single vector, we can learn the target representation as a class label, real value, or vector. The activation function of a dense layer during the prediction step is softmax.

3 Experiment

For comparison, we used SVM and Naïve Bayes models as the baseline methods to evaluate our system performance. The following subsections describe the baseline methods and the bidirectional GRU approach with an attention mechanism. We then tested the system results using different word embedding models individually and in combination.

3.1 Datasets

For this shared task, we got four languages (English, French, Spanish and Japanese) of customer feedback datasets. In this paper, only English datasets were used. The training data published by the organizers included sets of sentences annotated with six tags, comments, requests, bugs, complaints, and meaningless or undetermined statements. Each sentence has at least one tag assigned to it, and might be annotated with multiple tags. The distribution of all datasets is shown in Table 1. The total number is not equal to the sum of each category because several samples have multiple labels. We took these multi-labeled samples as separate samples with the same text and different labels.

For a better performance with deep learning, we additionally crawled user comments from the

Booking[1] and Amazon APP[2] websites, and trained the word2vec (Mikolov et al., 2013b) word-embedding model on about 26,148,855 tokens. GloVe (Pennington et al., 2014) was also used to develop the system using pre-trained word vector glove.840B.300d, which was trained on 840B tokens and is publicly available[3].

3.2 Implementation Details

The two baseline methods were implemented using scikit-learn (Pedregosa et al., 2011) in Python. Instead of a simple whitespace tokenizer, we used Unitok[4] as a full tokenizer because of its better performance. Baseline methods were used one-vs-all SVM method with linear kernel and multinomial Naïve Bayes method. All parameters were adjusted using a grid search function. We experimented with uni-gram and bi-gram separately, and in combination, using the word level as features.

We implemented our model using the Python Keras library with a TensorFlow backend. The recurrent dropout rate of the GRU was set to 0.2, and two other layers with dropout rates of 0.3 and 0.5 were added before the dense layer during the attending and prediction steps, respectively, to avoid overfitting of the system. The model was trained using rmsprop with a mini-batch size of 32 to minimize the loss of function of a categorical cross entropy.

We found that the provided training data were imbalanced. The smallest number of class samples was only 22, which accounts for 0.7% of the entire training dataset. The largest number of class samples was 1,758, which accounts for 54.7% of the training data. For this reason, an additional parameter sample weight was set for balancing the data. The loss was multiplied by the sample weight to improve the accuracy of a small number of classes.

Finally, the epoch was set to depend on an early stop, which relied on a validation set to determine when to stop the training. The epoch was fixed at around 20.

---

[1]https://www.booking.com/
[2]https://www.amazon.com/Best-SellersAppstoreAndroid/zgbs/mobile-apps/ref=zg_bs_nav_0
[3]https://nlp.stanford.edu/projects/glove/
[4]http://corpus.tools/wiki/Unitok

Methods	Acc	F1-Score	
		Micro	Macro
word2vec			
SVM	63.0	65.4	40.3
Naive Bayes	62.6	64.8	36.1
Bi-GRU (with weight)	61.2	62.2	41.2
Bi-GRUATT (no weight)	64.0	66.3	35.1
Bi-GRUATT (with weight)	**65.0**	**67.3**	**44.1**
GloVe			
Bi-GRUATT (no weight)	**71.0**	73.0	47.0
Bi-GRUATT (with weight)	64.0	66.1	47.7
word2vec+GloVe			
Bi-GRUATT (no weight)	**71.0**	**73.2**	48.8
Bi-GRUATT (with weight)	68.6	70.7	**49.9**

Table 2: Comparative results of methods with different word embedding.

3.3 Results

We validated the performance based on the development dataset, and used the same model weight on the test dataset to output the test results. For this shared task, the micro-average (Micro) and macro-average (Macro) were used in the evaluation along with the accuracy (Acc). The results of the baseline and our proposed models based on the word2vec embedding are shown in Table 2.

We found that using the combination of a unigam and bi-gram performed better than only a unigram or bi-gram individually for both the SVM and Naïve Bayes models. The attention mechanism enhanced 3-5% for the three evaluation indicators, and showed remarkable improvement with the parameter sample weight for the macro F1-score.

Different word-embedding models were employed in our experiment, the comparative results of which are also presented in Table 2. GloVe showed a clearly better performance over word2vec embedding, with a 7% improvement in accuracy owing to the training on larger corpora. Moreover, using the parameter sample weight to balance the training data, the model was trained to be biased toward small sample classes. As a result, the macro F1-score of Bi-GRUATT with the sample weight increased, whereas the micro F1-score decreased. And the combination of word2vec and glove achieved the best performance.

The model using word2vec and GloVe showed different performance on different tags. For example, as shown in Table 3, compared to Bi-GRUATT with weight of word2vec, F1-score of tags complaint, bug, meaningless increased 3-8% in the model with GloVe, however, decreased

Tags	Bi-GRUATT(with weight)		
	word2vec	GloVe	word2vec+GloVe
comment	79.0	76.0	80.5
complaint	61.5	64.8	63.0
bug	30.8	38.5	38.5
meaningless	48.5	54.4	54.5
request	42.9	37.5	57.1
undetermined	-1	-1	-1

Table 3: Comparative F1-score of each tag with different word embedding.

0.05-3% in tags comment and request. By combining word2vec and GloVe together, we not only got the higher score of their each tag, but also advanced the score of each tag.

The task attracted a total of 139 submissions of four languages from 12 teams. Our Bi-GRUATT model with a combination of word2vec and GloVe achieved the best result in terms of accuracy, and ranked sixth in micro F1-score, third in macro F1-score out of 56 submissions for the English language.

4   Conclusion and Future Work

In this paper, we presented our implemented solutions to IJCNLP task 4, with the goal of classifying six classes for customer feedback sentences of English. We promoted a bi-directional GRU with an attention mechanism, and presented two other baseline methods (SVM and Naïve Bayes) for comparison. The experiment results showed an improvement of around 8% when using the Bi-GRUATT model with GloVe and word2vec relative to the baseline methods; in addition, a sample weight parameter for imbalanced data achieved a good macro-average score, but with a decline in accuracy and micro-average score.

As future work, we will attempt a multi-label classification of this task, and test the performance of our model in other languages, such as Spanish, French, and Japanese.

Acknowledgments

This work was supported by the National Natural Science Foundation of China (NSFC) under Grant No.61702443 and No.61762091, and in part by Educational Commission of Yunnan Province of China under Grant No.2017ZZX030. The authors would like to thank the anonymous reviewers and the area chairs for their constructive comments.

References

Dzmitry Bahdanau, Kyunghyun Cho, and Yoshua Bengio. 2014. Neural Machine Translation by Jointly Learning to Align and Translate. *CoRR*, abs/1409.0473.

Yoshua Bengio, Réjean Ducharme, Pascal Vincent, and Christian Janvin. 2003. A Neural Probabilistic Language Model. *The Journal of Machine Learning Research*, 3:1137–1155.

Kyunghyun Cho, Bart van Merrienboer, Dzmitry Bahdanau, and Yoshua Bengio. 2014. On the properties of neural machine translation: Encoder-decoder approaches. In *SSST@EMNLP*, pages 103–111. Association for Computational Linguistics.

Junyoung Chung, Çaglar Gülçehre, KyungHyun Cho, and Yoshua Bengio. 2014. Empirical Evaluation of Gated Recurrent Neural Networks on Sequence Modeling. *CoRR*, abs/1412.3555.

Ronan Collobert, Jason Weston, Léon Bottou, Michael Karlen, Koray Kavukcuoglu, and Pavel Kuksa. 2011. Natural Language Processing (Almost) from Scratch. *Journal of Machine Learning Research*, 12:2493–2537.

Robert Desimone and John Duncan. 1995. Neural Mechanisms of Selective Visual Attention. *Annual Review of Neuroscience*, 18(1):193–222.

G. E. Hinton and R. R. Salakhutdinov. 2006. Reducing the Dimensionality of Data with Neural Networks. *Science*, 313(5786):504–507.

Sepp Hochreiter and J Urgen Schmidhuber. 1997. Long Short-Term Memory. *Neural Computation*, 9(8):1735–1780.

Eric H. Huang, Richard Socher, Christopher D. Manning, and Andrew Y. Ng. 2012. Improving word representations via global context and multiple word prototypes. In *ACL (1)*, pages 873–882. The Association for Computer Linguistics.

Ozan Irsoy and Claire Cardie. 2014. Opinion mining with deep recurrent neural networks. In *EMNLP*, pages 720–728. Association for Computational Linguistics.

Laurent Itti, Christof Koch, and Ernst Niebur. 1998. A model of saliency-based visual attention for rapid scene analysis. *IEEE Transactions on Pattern Analysis and Machine Intelligence*, 20(11):1254–1259.

Tomas Mikolov, Kai Chen, Greg Corrado, and Jeffrey Dean. 2013a. Efficient estimation of word representations in vector space. *CoRR*, abs/1301.3781.

Tomáš Mikolov, Martin Karafiát, Lukáš Burget, Jan Černocky̌, and Sanjeev Khudanpur. 2010. Recurrent Neural Network Based Language Model. In *Interspeech*, pages 1045–1048.

Tomas Mikolov, Wen-tau Yih, and Geoffrey Zweig. 2013b. Linguistic regularities in continuous space word representations. In *HLT-NAACL*, pages 746–751.

Ankur P. Parikh, Oscar Täckström, Dipanjan Das, and Jakob Uszkoreit. 2016. A Decomposable Attention Model for Natural Language Inference. In *EMNLP*, pages 2249–2255. The Association for Computational Linguistics.

Fabian Pedregosa, Gaël Varoquaux, Alexandre Gramfort, Vincent Michel, Bertrand Thirion, Olivier Grisel, Mathieu Blondel, Gilles Louppe, Peter Prettenhofer, Ron Weiss, Vincent Dubourg, Jake Vanderplas, Alexandre Passos, David Cournapeau, Matthieu Brucher, Matthieu Perrot, and Édouard Duchesnay. 2011. Scikit-learn: Machine Learning in Python. *Journal of Machine Learning Research*, 12:2825–2830.

Jeffrey Pennington, Richard Socher, and Christopher D Manning. 2014. Glove: Global vectors for word representation. In *EMNLP*, volume 14, pages 1532–1543.

Colin Raffel and Daniel P. W. Ellis. 2015. Feed-forward networks with attention can solve some long-term memory problems. *CoRR*, abs/1512.08756.

Zichao Yang, Diyi Yang, Chris Dyer, Xiaodong He, Alexander J. Smola, and Eduard H. Hovy. 2016. Hierarchical attention networks for document classification. In *HLT-NAACL*, pages 1480–1489. The Association for Computational Linguistics.

NITMZ-JU at IJCNLP-2017 Task 4: Customer Feedback Analysis

Somnath Banerjee
Jadavpur University, India

Partha Pakray
NIT Mizoram, India

Riyanka Manna and **Dipankar Das**
Jadavpur University, India

Alexander Gelbukh
Instituto Politécnico Nacional, Mexico

Abstract

In this paper, we describe a deep learning framework for analyzing the customer feedback as part of our participation in the shared task on Customer Feedback Analysis at the 8th International Joint Conference on Natural Language Processing (IJCNLP 2017). A Convolutional Neural Network (CNN) based deep neural network model was employed for the customer feedback task. The proposed system was evaluated on two languages, namely, English and French.

1 Introduction

Most of the companies provide their clients or customers provision to feedback in terms of register comments, complaints or suggestions in order to enhance service quality and the reputation of the company. Companies even provide toll free numbers for interactive communication where customers can speak with a service representative. Drastic change has been observed in customer feedback scenario after the advent of the computer. The use of computer has simplified the acquisition of information that is provided by customers. The use of Internet now allows companies to receive customer comments via electronic mail (email) and web page feedback techniques. Recently, a popular system is online dialogue interface where the service representatives interact with the customers live. Additionally, companies nowadays collect the customers feedback from various social media sites.

Understanding customer feedback is the most fundamental task to provide good customer services. The customer feedback is so valuable today that customer feedback analysis nowadays has become an industry on its own. A number of internet companies (also referred to as app companies) provide support to process and analyse the customer feedback for other companies. The business model for these app companies is to acquire customer feedback data from their clients and after analyzing the data using their internal tools these companies provide the reports to their clients periodically (Freshdesk, Nebula).

It is quite understandable that the reports which are generated by the app companies for their client are confidential materials. Also, the app companies keep the categorization of customer feedback as business secrets. However, three categorizations of customer feedback are openly available. The most commonly used categorization adopted by many website (SurveyMonkey[1]) is the five-class categorization, namely, *Excellent, Good, Average, Fair, Poor* (Yin et al., 2016). Another categorization, adopted by an app company Freshdesk, is also a five class classification which is a combined categorization of sentiment and responsiveness. The categorization includes the classes- *Positive, Neutral, Negative, Answered, Unanswered.* However, another app company called Sift adopted a seven-class classification which includes the classes- *Refund, Complaint, Pricing, Tech Support, Store Locator, Feedback, Warranty Info.* Although other categorizations for customer feedback analysis are present, most of them are not available publicly (Clarabridge, Inmoment[2], Equiniti[3]).

A common approach to text classification is to use Bag of Words (Harris, 1954), N-gram (Cavnar et al., 1994), and their term frequency-inverse document frequency (TF-IDF) (Sparck Jones, 1972) as features, and traditional models such as SVM

---

[1]https://www.surveymonkey.com
[2]http://www.inmoment.com/products/
[3]https://www.equiniticharter.com/services/complaints-management

Proceedings of the 8th International Joint Conference on Natural Language Processing, Shared Tasks, pages 180–183,
Taipei, Taiwan, November 27 – December 1, 2017. ©2017 AFNLP

(Joachims, 1998), Naive Bayes (McCallum et al., 1998) as classifiers. However, recently, many researchers (Collobert et al., 2011; Conneau et al., 2016; Kim, 2014; Zhang et al., 2015), using deep learning model, particularly the Convolutional Neural Networks. Our model is highly motivated by the CNN architecture described in (Collobert et al., 2011).

2   Task Description

In general perspective, this task is a classification problem. In a global multilingual environment, the two main challenges for international companies (such as Microsoft) to automatically detect the meanings of customer feedback are: i) no widely acknowledged classes for understanding the meanings for customer feedback, ii) the classification may not be applicable in multiple languages. The participants were provided real world samples of customer feedback from Microsoft Office customers in four languages (namely English, French, Spanish and Japanese) and a five-plus-one-classes categorization (namely *comment, request, bug, complaint, meaningless and undetermined*) for customer feedback meaning classification. A participant has to develop a system that can predict the class(es) for customer feedback sentences across four defined languages.

3   Dataset and Resources

The organizer of the customer feedback analysis provided the participants customer feedback sentences which were collected from Microsoft Office customers as part of the joint ADAPT-Microsoft research project. The sentences were annotated with six classes: comment, request, bug, complaint, meaningless, and undetermined. The dataset was provided in four languages, namely English, French, Spanish and Japanese. Each sentence has at least one tag assigned to it and may be annotated with multiple tags. We did not use any external resources as additional data, i.e., we used only the dataset which was provided for this task.

4   Proposed Architecture

The proposed model is inspired by the CNN architecture described in (Collobert et al., 2011). The proposed model for the customer feedback categorization is shown in Figure 1.

Pre-processing: We pre-processed the dataset provided for building the system. Initially, we removed the index from the data samples. In the provided dataset, a number of data samples were tagged with multiple classes. If a data sample was tagged with multiple tags, the data sample was modified. The following example shows the processing of a data sample tagged with two tags for training as a single tagged.
Original:
> *Renovations underway...dated.* ⇒ comment, complaint

After pre-processing:
> *Renovations underway...is dated.* ⇒ comment
> *Renovations underway...is dated.* ⇒ complaint

Embedding layer: Instead of using any pre-trained word embedding scheme, we have built a vocabulary table which is learnt from training data. The embedding layer works as a lookup table which maps vocabulary word indices into low-dimensional vector representations. The proposed architecture works for all the languages except Japanese because the Japanese sentences were not segmented.

Convolutional layer: This layer is the heart of the architecture. This layer made up of three 1D-Convolution layers. Each 1D-Convolution layer has kernel size equal to 3 and feature map equal to 128. During convolution operation filters are applied to extract the features. Then, max-pooling operation is applied to the feature map s to obtain the maximum value $s' = \max\{s\}$ for a particular filter. The objective of the max pooling is to capture the most important feature with the highest value for each feature map. Thus, one feature is extracted from one filter. However, the proposed architecture uses multiple filters with varying window sizes to obtain multiple features. We used the ReLU (Nair and Hinton, 2010) as our nonlinear activation function. .

Fully Connected layer: The max-pooling operation selects the best features from each convolutional kernel. Thus, all the resulting features which are selected from the max-pooling are combining in the fully-connected layer. The output of fully connected layer is passed to the output layer.

Output layer: The final layer (i.e., the output layer) made of 6 neurons as the customer feedback has 6 target classes. The output layer uses softmax as the nonlinear activation function.

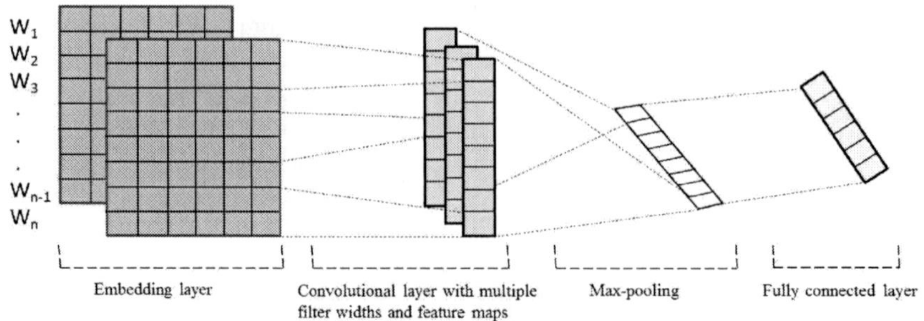

Figure 1: Model architecture

5 Results and Discussion

We have submitted the runs for English and French customer feedback. For English feedback, three runs were submitted. However, four runs were submitted for the customer feedback in French. In this shared task, for overall performance accuracy, macro-averaging and micro-averaging was used. The class specific performance was measured using precision, recall and F1-measure. For English, the best run achieved 0.388 in terms of accuracy. The evaluation is shown in Table 5. It is observed from Table 5 that the proposed model identified the 'comment' class more effectively than other classes. For English, the model did not identified the 'bug' and 'request' classes.

Overall performance			
Accuracy	0.388		
Macro-Avg	0.245895	0.204983	0.223583
Micro-Avg	0.427746	0.427746	0.427746
Class specific performance			
Tag	**Precision**	**Recall**	**F1-score**
comment	0.5549	0.6211	0.5861
complaint	0.2901	0.2621	0.2754
bug	0.0000	0.0000	NA
meaningless	0.1304	0.0968	0.1111
request	0.0000	0.0000	NA
undetermined	0.5000	0.2500	0.3333

Table 1: English Customer Feedback Evaluation

For French, we submitted 4 runs and the best run achieved 0.6675 in terms of accuracy. The macro-average and micro-average values were also satisfactory. The evaluation is shown in Table 2. It is observed from Table 2 that the proposed model performed the best for the 'complaint' class (F1-score: 0.8526). However, the model performed well on 'comment' (F1-score: 0.5455) and 'bug' (F1-score: 0.4717) classes. The model did not identified the 'meaningless', 'request' and 'undetermined' classes.

Overall performance			
Accuracy	0.6675		
Macro-Avg	0.303275	0.330574	0.316337
Micro-Avg	0.709443	0.697619	0.703481
Class specific performance			
Tag	**Precision**	**Recall**	**F1-score**
comment	0.5745	0.5192	0.5455
complaint	0.8664	0.8392	0.8526
bug	0.3788	0.6250	0.4717
meaningless	NA	NA	NA
request	0.0000	0.0000	NA
undetermined	0.0000	0.0000	NA

Table 2: French Customer Feedback Evaluation

During data pre-processing, we made the multiple tag data samples into single tagged. Therefore, for the same feedback text the system trained with two different tags. This created the ambiguity for the system. We believed that this ambiguity is the main reason for the decrease in performance of the proposed system.

6 Conclusions

We present this paper as part of our participation in the Customer Feedback Analysis shared task at IJCNLP. We proposed a CNN based deep learning framework for English and French. However, the proposed model performed well on French data than English data. Our embedding scheme did not work on Japanese as the sentences were not segmented. In future, we will employ Recurrent Neural Network to tackle the customer feedback analysis.

Acknowledgments

We would like to thank the organizers for organizing a wonderful research problem and giving opportunities for researchers to participate in it.

References

William B Cavnar, John M Trenkle, et al. 1994. N-gram-based text categorization. *Ann Arbor MI*, 48113(2):161–175.

Ronan Collobert, Jason Weston, Léon Bottou, Michael Karlen, Koray Kavukcuoglu, and Pavel Kuksa. 2011. Natural language processing (almost) from scratch. *Journal of Machine Learning Research*, 12(Aug):2493–2537.

Alexis Conneau, Holger Schwenk, Loïc Barrault, and Yann Lecun. 2016. Very deep convolutional networks for natural language processing. *arXiv preprint arXiv:1606.01781*.

Zellig S Harris. 1954. Distributional structure. *Word*, 10(2-3):146–162.

Thorsten Joachims. 1998. Text categorization with support vector machines: Learning with many relevant features. *Machine learning: ECML-98*, pages 137–142.

Yoon Kim. 2014. Convolutional neural networks for sentence classification. *arXiv preprint arXiv:1408.5882*.

Andrew McCallum, Kamal Nigam, et al. 1998. A comparison of event models for naive bayes text classification. In *AAAI-98 workshop on learning for text categorization*, volume 752, pages 41–48. Madison, WI.

Vinod Nair and Geoffrey E Hinton. 2010. Rectified linear units improve restricted boltzmann machines. In *Proceedings of the 27th international conference on machine learning (ICML-10)*, pages 807–814.

Karen Sparck Jones. 1972. A statistical interpretation of term specificity and its application in retrieval. *Journal of documentation*, 28(1):11–21.

Dawei Yin, Yuening Hu, Jiliang Tang, Tim Daly, Mianwei Zhou, Hua Ouyang, Jianhui Chen, Changsung Kang, Hongbo Deng, Chikashi Nobata, et al. 2016. Ranking relevance in yahoo search. In *Proceedings of the 22nd ACM SIGKDD International Conference on Knowledge Discovery and Data Mining*, pages 323–332. ACM.

Xiang Zhang, Junbo Zhao, and Yann LeCun. 2015. Character-level convolutional networks for text classification. In *Advances in neural information processing systems*, pages 649–657.

IITP at IJCNLP-2017 Task 4: Auto Analysis of Customer Feedback using CNN and GRU Network

Deepak Gupta*, Pabitra Lenka†, Harsimran Bedi*, Asif Ekbal*, Pushpak Bhattacharyya*

*Indian Institute of Technology Patna, India
†International Institute of Information Technology Bhubaneswar, India
*{deepak.pcs16, harsimran.mtcs16, asif, pb}@iitp.ac.in
†pabitra.lenka18@gmail.com

Abstract

Analyzing customer feedback is the best way to channelize the data into new marketing strategies that benefit entrepreneurs as well as customers. Therefore an automated system which can analyze the customer behavior is in great demand. Users may write feedbacks in any language, and hence mining appropriate information often becomes intractable. Especially in a traditional feature-based supervised model, it is difficult to build a generic system as one has to understand the concerned language for finding the relevant features. In order to overcome this, we propose deep Convolutional Neural Network (CNN) and Recurrent Neural Network (RNN) based approaches that do not require handcrafting of features. We evaluate these techniques for analyzing customer feedback sentences on four languages, namely English, French, Japanese and Spanish. Our empirical analysis shows that our models perform well in all the four languages on the setups of IJCNLP Shared Task on *Customer Feedback Analysis*. Our model achieved the second rank in French, with an accuracy of 71.75% and third ranks for all the other languages.

1 Introduction

Exploration and exploitation of customer feedbacks have become highly relevant and crucial for all the customer-centric business firms in today's world. Product manufacturers would like to know what their customers are liking or complaining about in order to improve their services or launch improved versions of products. Service providers would like to know how happy or unhappy a customer is with their service. According to a survey[1] 96% of unhappy customers do not complain but they advise 15% of their friends to not have any business dealings with the particular firm. With the huge amount of feedback data available, it is impossible to manually analyze each and every review. So there arises a need to automate this entire process to aid the business firms in customer feedback management.

A customer review analysis can be associated with its sentiment polarity ('positive', 'negative', 'neutral' and 'conflict') or with its interpretation ('request', 'comment', 'complaint'). There exists a significant number of works for sentiment classification (Pang et al., 2002; Glorot et al., 2011; Socher et al., 2013; Gupta et al., 2015; Deepak Gupta and Bhattacharyya, 2016), emotion classification (Yang et al., 2007; Li and Lu, 2009; Padgett and Cottrell, 1997) and customer review analysis (Yang and Fang, 2004; Mudambi and Schuff, 2010; Hu and Liu, 2004). However, the meaning of customer reviews (*request, complaint, comment* etc.) remains a relatively not much explored area of research.

Our present work deals with classifiyng a customer review into one of the six predefined categories. This can be trated as a document classification problem.

The classes are *comment, request, bug, complaint, meaningless* and *undetermined*. The feedback classification is performed across four different languages, namely English (**EN**), French (**FR**), Japanese (**JP**) and Spanish (**ES**). In Table 1 we depict few instances of customer feedbacks with their label(s) in different languages. One of critical issues in traditional supervised model is to come up with a good set of features that could be ef-

---

[1] https://goo.gl/8KVwBh

Proceedings of the 8th International Joint Conference on Natural Language Processing, Shared Tasks, pages 184–193,
Taipei, Taiwan, November 27 – December 1, 2017. ©2017 AFNLP

fective in solving the problem. Hence it is challenging to build a generic model that could perform reasonably well acoross different domains and languages. In recent times, the emergence of deep learning methods have inspired researchers to develop solutions that do not require careful feature engineering. Deep Convolutional Neural Network (CNN) and Recurrent Neural Network (RNN) are two very popular deep learning techniques that have been successfully used in solving many sentence and document classification (Kim, 2014; Xiao and Cho, 2016) problems. We aim at developing a generic model that can be used across different languages and platforms for customer feedback analysis.

The remainder of our paper is structured as follows: Section 2 offers the related literature survey for customer feedback analysis, where we discuss about the existing approaches. Section 3 describes our two proposed approaches, one based on CNN and the other based on amalgamation of RNN with CNN. Section 4 provides the detailed information about the data set used in the experiment and the experimental setup. Results, analysis and discussion are elucidated in Section 5. We put forward the future work and conclude the paper with Section 6. The source code of our system can be found here.[2]

2   Related Work

Analysis of customer feedback has been of significant interest to many companies over the years. Given the large amount of feedbacks available, interesting trends and opinions among the customers can be investigated for many purposes. In this section, we discuss the related literature in the analysis of customer feedbacks.

Bentley and Batra (2016) developed a Office customer voice (OCV) system that classifies customer feedback on Microsoft Office products into known issues. The classification algorithm is built on logistic regression classifiers of the Python scikit framework. They have also employed a custom clustering algorithm along with topic modeling to identify new issues from the feedback data. A domain specific approach described in (Potharaju et al., 2013) infers problems, activities and actions from network trouble tickets. The authors developed a domain specific knowledge base and an on-

tology model using pattern mining and statistical Natural Language Processing (NLP) and used it for the inference. Brun and Hagège (2013) offers a pattern to extract suggestions for improvements from user reviews. They combine linguistic knowledge with an opinion mining system to extract the suggestive expressions from a review. The presence of a suggestion indicates that the user is not completely satisfied with the product.

Over the years, many companies have developed feedback management systems to help other companies gain useful insight from the customer feedback data. Customer satisfaction survey done by Freshdesk [3] defines metrics for measuring customer satisfaction. They use a five class categorization ('positive', 'neutral', 'negative', 'answered' and 'unanswered'), thereby combining sentiment and responsiveness. Survey Monkey[4] also facilitates us to create survey forms and analyze them for customer satisfaction. It also uses a five-class categorization ('excellent', 'good', 'average', 'fair' and 'poor'), a commonly used rating mechanism. Customer Complaints Management[5] provides services and softwares to help business firms to manage and retain their customers. Identifying a category for customer feedback requires deep semantic analysis of the lexicons to identify the emotions expressed. Authors in (Asher et al., 2009) have provided detailed annotation guidelines for opinion expressions where each opinion lies in the four top level categories of *'Reporting', 'Judgement', 'Advise' and 'Sentiment'*. With the advent of deep learning, in recent years there has been a phenomenal growth in the use of neural network models for text analysis.Yin et al. (2016) have provided practical and effective comprehensive relevance solutions in Yahoo search engine. They have designed ranking functions, semantic matching features and query rewriting techniques for base relevance. Their network model incorporates a deep neural network and it is tested with the commercial Yahoo search engine.

In this shared task the organizers have introduced a customer feedback analysis model where the task is to classify a feedback into one of the six categories. In following section we describe our proposed deep learning based classification model

---

Feedback	Class(es)
nouveau bug : le rayon led anti yeux rouges se declanche intempestivement après avoir envoyé la photo !	bug
あと、タイムラインで他の人がお気に入りの記事を表示しないように設定できるようにしたい	request
Saw advertisements through an Internet travel booking site for hotel and zoo tickets in a package deal.	comment
La decoración en el hotel es excelente y las habitaciones tienen un toque chic.	comment
it is fast, but the controls are lousy, plus it keeps installing on my desktop shortcuts to place I don't want.	complaint
Mi pareja y yo hicimos una escapada romántica a Barcelona de cuatro días.	meaningless
Pour moi et avec modesties d'éloges, nero multimedia me rassure en ce sens que je peux:	undetermined
編集で付けようとしても、どうしてもその人のだけ消えてしまう	bug, comment

Table 1: Some instances of customer feedback in different languages annotated with their class(es)

for customer feedback analysis.

3 Network Architecture for Feedback Classification

In this section we describe our proposed neural network architecture for feedback classification. We propose two variants, the first one is convolution operation inspired CNN and the second one is the amalgamation of CNN with RNN.

3.1 Feedback classification using CNN

In this model a feedback sentence is subjected to CNN and the model predicts the most probable feedback class along with the confidence (probability) score. The model architecture is depicted in Fig 1. The input and output of the model are as follows:

INPUT: A feedback F, labeled with any of the six classes: (*comment, request, bug, complaint, meaningless,* and *undetermined*)

OUTPUT: Class(es) of the corresponding F

Our model uses similar network architectures used by Kim (2014) for performing the feedback classification task. We depict our model architecture in Figure 1. The architecture of a typical CNN is composed of a stack of distinct layers where each layer performs a specific function of transforming its input into a useful representation. A CNN comprises of *sentence representation*, one or more *convolutional layers* often interweaved with *pooling layer* (max-pooling being extremely popular), followed by *fully-connected layer* leading into a $softmax$ classifier. The components of CNN are described as follows:

3.1.1 Feedback Sentence Representation

As CNNs deal with fixed length inputs, we ensure that every input feedback sentence has the same length. To achieve this, input feedback sentences are padded according to the need. Each feedback sentence is padded to the maximum sentence length[6]. Padding of feedback sentences to the same length is useful because it allows us to efficiently batch our data while training. Let a feedback sentence F consisting of 'n' words be the input to our model such that $x = [x_1, x_2, \ldots x_n]$ where x_i is the ith word in the feedback sentence. Each token $x_i \in F$ is represented by its distributed representation $p_i \in R^k$ which is the k-dimensional word vector. The distributed representation p is looked up into the word embedding matrix W which is initialized either by a random process or by some pre-trained word embeddings like *Word2Vec* (Mikolov et al., 2013) or *GloVe* (Pennington et al., 2014). We then concatenate (row wise) the distributed representation p_i for every i^{th} token in the feedback F and build the feedback sentence representation matrix. The feedback sentence representation matrix $p_{1:n}$ can be represented as:

$$p_{1:n} = p_1 \oplus p_2 \oplus \cdots \oplus p_n \tag{1}$$

where $\oplus$ is the concatenation operator. Each row of the sentence representation matrix corresponds to the word vector representation of each token. The result of the embedding operation yields a 3-dimensional tensor.

3.1.2 Convolutional Layer

The convolutional layer is the core building block of a CNN. The common patterns (n-grams) in the training data are extracted by applying the convolution operation. These patterns are then passed to the next hidden layer to extract more complex patterns, or directly fed to a standard classifier (usually a $softmax$ layer) to output the final prediction. The convolution operation is performed on the feedback representation matrix *via* linear fil-

---

[6]maximum feedback sentence length: EN=116, FR=73, JP=7 and ES=92

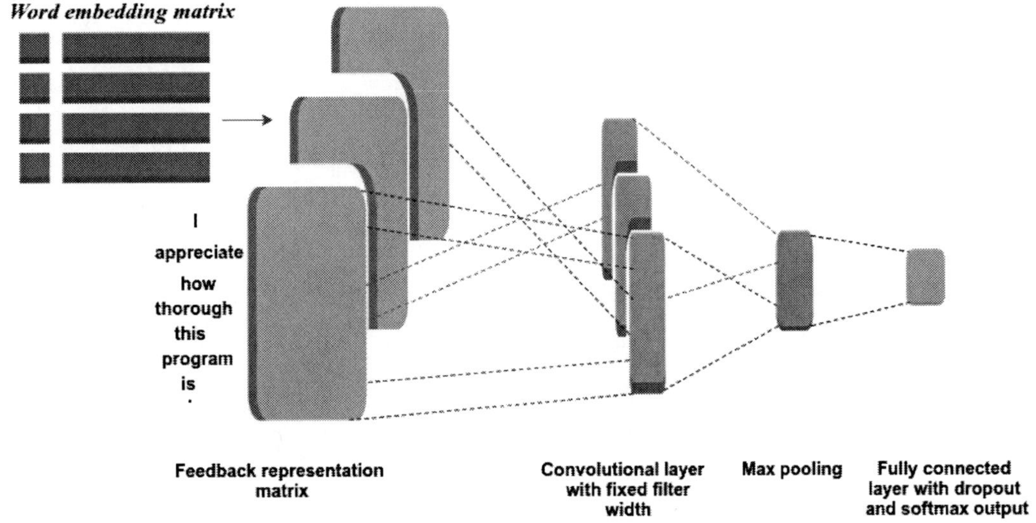

Figure 1: Convolution neural network based feedback classification model

ters (feature detectors). Owing to the inherent sequential structure of the text data, we use filters with fixed *width*. Then we simply vary the *height* of the filter, i.e. the number of adjacent rows (tokens) considered together. Here the *height* of the filter is the region size of the filter.

We consider a filter parameterized by the weight matrix w with a region size h. Thereafter we denote the feedback representation matrix by $S \in R^{n \times k}$, where k is the dimension of the word vector. The generated output $out_i \in R^{n-h+1}$ of the convolutional operator is obtained by repeatedly applying the filter on sub-matrices of S:

$$out_i = w \cdot S[i : i + h - 1], \qquad (2)$$

The sub-matrix of S from i^{th} row to $i + h - 1^{\text{th}}$ row is represented by $S[i : i + h - 1]$, where $i = 1 \dots n - h + 1$ and h is the height of the filter. A bias term $b \in R$ and an activation function f to each out_i is added which generates the *feature map* $c \in R^{n-h+1}$ for this filter where:

$$c_i = f(out_i + b) \qquad (3)$$

But the dimensions of the *feature map* produced by each filter will differ as a function of the number of words in the feedback sentence and the filter region size. Thus we apply a pooling function over each *feature map* to generate a vector of the fixed length.

3.1.3 Pooling Layer

The output of the convolutional layer is the input to the pooling layer. The primary utility of the pooling layer lies in progressively reducing the spatial dimensions of the intermediate representations. The operation performed by this layer is also called *down-sampling*, as there is a loss of information due to the reduction of dimensions. However, such a loss is beneficial for the network for two reasons:

1. Decreases the computational overhead of the network; and
2. Controls over-fitting.

The pooling layer takes a sliding window or a certain region that is moved in stride across the input which transforms the values into representative values. There are several pooling operations in practice such as *max pooling, min pooling, average pooling* and *dynamic pooling*. We have applied the *max pooling* operation (Collobert et al., 2011) on the feature map which transforms the representation by taking the maximum value from the values observable in the window. Max pooling has been favored over others due to its better performance. It also provides a form of translation invariance and robustness to position. However, Springenberg et al. (2014) have proposed to discard the pooling layer in the CNN architecture.

3.1.4 Fully-connected Layer

Fully-connected layers are typically used in the final stages of the CNN to connect to the output layer. It looks at what high level features most strongly correlate to a particular class. The features generated from the pooling layer p form the penultimate layer and are fed to a fully connected softmax layer to generate the classification. The $softmax$ classifier gives an intuitive output (normalized class probabilities) and also has a probabilistic interpretation. The output of the $softmax$ function is the probability distribution over tags (*comment, request, bug, complaint, meaningless,* and *undetermined*).

$$P(c = i | F, p, z) = softmax_i(p^{\mathrm{T}} w_i + z_i)$$
$$= \frac{e^{p^T w_i + z_i}}{\sum_{k=1}^{K} e^{p^T w_k + z_k}} \quad (4)$$

where z_k and w_k are the bias and weight vector of the kth labels.

3.2 Feedback Classification using CNN coupled with RNN

We propose a second method for feedback classification that combines both CNN and RNN. The typical architecture of these combinations is composed of a *convolutional feature extractor* applied on the input, then a *recurrent network* on top of the CNN's output, then an optional *fully connected layer* is added to RNN's output and finally fed into the *softmax layer*. We use convolutional layer as it learns to extract higher-level features that are invariant to local translation. By stacking up multiple convolutional layers, the network can extract higher-level, abstract, (locally) translation invariant features from the input sequence.

Apart from this advantage, it is noticed that several layers of convolution are required to capture long-term dependencies, due to the locality of the convolution and pooling. In order to capture long-term dependencies even when there is only a single layer present in the network, the recurrent layer comes handy. However, the recurrent layer increases the computational overhead due to its linearly growing computational complexity with respect to the length of the input sequence. So we have used a combination of convolutional and recurrent layers in a single model to ensure that it can capture long-term dependencies from the input more efficiently for the feedback classification task. Our model is similar to the one proposed

in Xiao and Cho (2016). They have used LSTM unit, however we have employed GRU (Cho et al., 2014).

$$\mathbf{z}_i = \sigma(\mathbf{W}_z c_i + \mathbf{V}_z \mathbf{h}_{i-1} + \mathbf{b}_z)$$
$$\mathbf{r}_i = \sigma(\mathbf{W}_r c_i + \mathbf{V}_r \mathbf{h}_{i-1} + \mathbf{b}_r)$$
$$\mathbf{c}_i = tanh(\mathbf{W} c_i + \mathbf{V}(\mathbf{r}_i \odot \mathbf{h}_{i-1}) + \mathbf{b})$$
$$\mathbf{h_i} = z_i \odot \mathbf{h}_{i-1} + (1 - \mathbf{z}_i) \odot \mathbf{c}_i$$

where $\mathbf{z}_i$, $\mathbf{r}_i$ and $\mathbf{c}_i$ are update gate, reset get and new memory content, respectively. c_i is the convolution output at time t. We take the last hidden states of both directions and concatenate them to form a fixed-dimensional vector, which are later fed into the next layer.

4 Datasets and Experimental Setup

4.1 Datasets

The data sets used in our experiments are provided by the organizers of the shared task on *Customer Feedback Analysis* of IJCNLP-2017. Data sets consist of representative real world samples of customer feedback from Microsoft Office customers in four languages, namely *English, French, Japanese* and *Spanish*. We obtain the English translations of test data of other three languages (*French, Japanese* and *Spanish*) which were translated using Google translate[7]. Each feedback in the data is annotated with one or multiple tags from the set of six tags (*comment, request, bug, complaint, meaningless* and *undetermined*). We show the dataset statistics for each language in Table 2.

4.2 Data Preprocessing

Some of the feedback sentences are annotated with multiple classes. Before feeding them to the network, we preprocessed the data by replicating the particular instance with all the possible classes.

4.3 Regularization

In order to prevent the model from over-fitting, we employed a dropout regularization (set to 50%) proposed by Srivastava et al. (2014) on the penultimate layer of the network. It "drops out" a random set of activations in the network. Dropout prevents feature co-adaptation by randomly setting some portion of hidden units to zero during the forward propagation when passing it to the softmax output layer in the end to perform classification. It also

---

[7]`https://translate.google.com/`

Language	Training							Development							Test						
	CO	CP	RQ	BG	ME	UD	Total	CO	CP	RQ	BG	ME	UD	Total	CO	CP	RQ	BG	ME	UD	Total
EN	1758	950	103	72	306	22	**3211**	276	146	19	20	48	3	**512**	285	145	13	10	62	4	**519**
ES	1003	536	69	14	9	0	**1631**	244	39	12	5	1	0	**301**	229	53	14	2	1	0	**299**
FR	1236	529	38	53	178	10	**2044**	256	112	6	8	36	1	**419**	255	104	11	8	40	2	**420**
JP	826	531	97	89	0	45	**1588**	142	73	22	18	0	9	**264**	170	94	26	14	0	9	**313**
Total	**4823**	**2546**	**307**	**228**	**493**	**77**	**8474**	**918**	**370**	**59**	**51**	**85**	**13**	**1496**	**939**	**396**	**64**	**34**	**103**	**15**	**1551**

Table 2: Data set statistics of all the languages. Notations used are defined as follows, **CO:** *comment*, **CP:** *complaint*, **RQ:** *request*, **BG:** *bug*, **ME:** *meaningless* and **UD:** *undetermined*,

forces the network to be redundant i.e. it should be able to provide the correct classification or output for a specific input even if some of the activations are dropped out.

4.4 Network Training and Hyper-parameters

We have applied the rectified linear units (ReLu) (Nair and Hinton, 2010) as the activation function in our experiment. We use the development data to fine-tune the hyper-parameters. In order to train the network, the stochastic gradient descent (SGD) over mini-batch is used and Backpropagation algorithm (Hecht-Nielsen, 1992) is used to compute the gradients in each learning iteration. We have not enforced L2 norm constraints on the weight vectors as Zhang and Wallace (2015) found that the constraints had a minimal effect on the end result. We have used cross-entropy loss as the loss function. The hyper-parameters of the best system in each language are listed in Table 6.

4.5 Experiments

We conduct experiments in two different ways: CNN based and CNN+RNN based. Further we perform the experiments with *original test data* and *English translated test data*. In each setting we experiment with all the four languages[8]. Through the experimental results we wanted to establish the fact that whether a simple machine translation would work or there is a need of native tools for the other languages. The following are the descriptions of our submission in the shared task.

1. **CNN:** The results obtained from the CNN model described in Section 3.1.

    (a) **With original test data:** We train the CNN model using the dataset provided for training and used the respective test data to obtain the results. This setting

of experiments are employed on all four languages (EN, FR, JP and ES).

    (b) **English translated test data:** We train the CNN model using the English training dataset and use the English translated test data of other languages (FR, JP and ES) to obtain the results.

2. **CNN+RNN:** The results obtained from the CNN+RNN model described in Section 3.2.

    (a) **With original test data:** Similar to CNN we train the CNN+RNN model using the dataset provided for training and use the respective test data to obtain the results. This setting of experiments are employed on all the four languages (EN, FR, JP and ES).

    (b) **English translated test data:** Again similar to CNN, we train the CNN+RNN model using the English training dataset and use the English translated test data of other languages (FR, JP and ES) for the evaluation.

We use the pre-trained Google word embedding[9] to initialize the word embedding matrix for English. The word embedding matrix for other three languages are initialized randomly[10].

5 Results and Discussions

We have submitted our results using both the models as discussed in Section 4.5. Table 3 summarizes the performance of both the models *with original test data*. Table 4 summarizes the performance of both the models on *English translated test data*. Table 7 shows the exact accuracy comparison with the models which achieve the best accuracy as compared to our model and also with the

---

[8]In the "English translated test data" setting, the experiments were performed with three languages (FR: French, JP: Japanese and ES: Spanish)

[9]https://code.google.com/archive/p/word2vec/

[10]due to some computational issues, we were unable to use pre-trained embeddings of other languages.

Language	Tags	CNN			CNN + RNN		
		Precision	Recall	F1-Score	Precision	Recall	F1-Score
Japanese	comment	0.564	0.965	0.711	0.569	0.994	0.724
Japanese	complaint	0.167	0.011	0.020	0.333	0.011	0.021
French	comment	0.789	0.867	0.826	0.785	0.886	0.832
French	complaint	0.630	0.558	0.592	0.603	0.452	0.516
French	request	−1	0	−1	1	0.091	0.167
French	meaningless	0.577	0.375	0.455	0.531	0.425	0.472
Spanish	comment	0.917	0.913	0.915	0.906	0.930	0.918
Spanish	complaint	0.597	0.755	0.667	0.656	0.755	0.702
Spanish	request	1	0.286	0.444	1	0.214	0.353
English	comment	0.826	0.818	0.822	0.713	0.775	0.743
English	complaint	0.611	0.738	0.669	0.538	0.593	0.564
English	request	1	0.077	0.143	0.625	0.385	0.476
English	meaningless	0.667	0.452	0.538	0.500	0.177	0.262

Table 3: Performance results of the model *with original test data* at the tags level. We did not provide the results of those tags which were not detected by our model.

Language	Tags	CNN			CNN + RNN		
		Precision	Recall	F1-Score	Precision	Recall	F1-Score
Japanese	comment	0.808	0.741	0.773	0.706	0.776	0.739
Japanese	complaint	0.571	0.766	0.655	0.552	0.511	0.530
Japanese	request	-1	0	-1	0.667	0.154	0.250
Japanese	bug	-1	0	-1	0.500	0.071	0.125
French	comment	0.837	0.863	0.849	0.766	0.875	0.817
French	complaint	0.679	0.692	0.686	0.651	0.538	0.589
French	request	1.000	0.091	0.167	-1	0	-1
French	meaningless	0.433	0.325	0.371	0.435	0.250	0.317
Spanish	comment	0.915	0.895	0.905	0.901	0.913	0.907
Spanish	complaint	0.636	0.792	0.706	0.603	0.660	0.631
Spanish	request	-1	0	-1	0.500	0.071	0.125

Table 4: Performance results of the model with *English translated test data* at the tags level. We did not provide the results of those tags which were not detected by our model.

baseline scores. Our systems easily predicted the true labels of sentences which had either positive connotation words like "great", "pleasant", "nice", "good", etc or negative connotation words like "not", "slow", "unable", "horrible", etc and classified them into *comment* and *complaint* classes respectively. The negative connotation words also appeared in the feedback sentences of *bug* class. But owing to the larger amount of training data in the *complaint* class as compared to the *bug* class, the negative connotation words appeared significantly in the *complaint* class. As a result, our systems had difficulty in predicting the true labels for the feedback sentences associated with the *bug* class. Our systems were unable to detect some

tags due to the class imbalance problem in the training as well as test data. The scores of our systems could have been much better, provided that we should have more labeled training data. The system performance can be improved by the language specific pre-trained word embeddings.

5.1 Error Analysis

We perform error analysis on the outputs of our best performing model. Our system failed to detect some of the true positive classes due to some inadequacy in the training data. Table 5 provides some examples (from different languages) where our system fails to detect the correct tags. We divide those inadequacy into three different cate-

Error Type	Language	Feedback	Reference	Predicted
Ambiguous	EN	Make a paid version so we don't have to deal with the ads	request	complaint
Ambiguous	ES	La verdad, ir, ir, no va mal.	comment	complaint
Ambiguous	FR	Une bouilloire et du thé et du café dans la chAmbiguousre (ainsi que sucre et lait). La salle de bain était grande.	comment	complaint
Ambiguous	JP	その後大浴場でサンセットを見てゆっくり入浴	comment	complaint
Missing Target Entity	EN	Work with any type of PDF	comment	meaningless
Missing Target Entity	ES	El agua salpicaba el suelo del baño.	complaint	comment
Missing Target Entity	FR	de la grosse arnaque !	complaint	meaningless
Missing Target Entity	JP	英語の勉強にもなりそう	comment	meaningless
Too short	EN	I gave up.	comment	complaint
Too short	ES	Decepcionante	complaint	meaningless
Too short	FR	Brunch en famille	meaningless	comment
Too short	JP	使えん	complaint	meaningless

Table 5: Some of the feedback instances from different languages where our model failed to predict the correct tags.

Parameter Name	EN	ES	FR	JP
Embeddings	Pre-trained	Random	Pre-trained	Pre-trained
Maximum epochs	100	200	100	100
Mini batch size	64	64	64	64
Number of filters	128	128	128	128
Filter window sizes	3,4,5	3,4,5	3,4,5	3,4,5
Dimensionality of word embedding	300	300	300	300
Dropout keep probability	0.5	0.5	0.5	0.5
Hidden unit size (CNN+RNN)	-	300	-	-

Table 6: Network hyper-parameters for the best system (ref: Table 7) in each language

	Accuracy		
Language	Best System	Our Best System	Best Baseline
EN	71.00%	70.00% (CNN)	48.80%
ES	88.63%	85.62% (CNN+RNN)	77.26%
FR	73.75%	71.75% (CNN-Trans)	54.75%
JP	75.00%	63.00% (CNN-Trans)	56.67%

Table 7: Performance comparison with the best system in the shared task and the best baselines (3-gram features based SVM classifier). **CNN-Trans**: CNN model with English translated test data

gories:

- **Ambiguous Feedback**: Ambiguous feedback sentences have several possible meanings or interpretations. Our system fails to comprehend such doubtful or uncertain nature of customer feedback.

- **Missing Target Entity in Feedback**: We found some feedback which were pretty straight without having a particular subject entitled to it. These type of feedback sentences fail to address about what is being referred to in the sentences. These sentences do not sound complete. Let's take an example : "Work with any type of PDF". It does not specify any comprehensive meaning. So the questions like "What will work?", "What is being talked about?" are bound to come up when the feedback sentences have an unstated subject. This, in turn, generates misclassification.

- **Too Short Feedback**: There are several shorter-length feedback sentences, which are generic and do not provide any good evidence. Sometimes, these type of feedback sentences fail to convey any proper meaning to the end user who deals with it. The systems also experience difficulty to correctly tag those feedback sentences.

6 Future Work and Conclusion

Convolutional neural networks (CNN) and recurrent neural networks (RNN) are architecturally two different ways of processing dimensioned and ordered data. These model the way the human visual cortex works, and has been shown to work incredibly well for natural language modeling and a number of other tasks. In our work, we extensively made use of CNN and RNN (GRU) to perform classification of customer feedback sentences into six different categories. Our proposed model performed well for all the languages. We have performed thorough error analysis to understand where our system fails. We believe that the performance can be improved by employing pre-trained word embeddings of the individual languages. Future work would focus on investigating appropriate deep learning method for classifying the short feedback sentences.

References

Nicholas Asher, Farah Benamara, and Yvette Yannick Mathieu. 2009. Appraisal of opinion expressions in discourse. *Lingvisticæ Investigationes*, 32(2):279–292.

Michael Bentley and Soumya Batra. 2016. Giving voice to office customers: Best practices in how office handles verbatim text feedback. *2016 IEEE International Conference on Big Data (Big Data)*, pages 3826–3832.

Caroline Brun and Caroline Hagège. 2013. Suggestion mining: Detecting suggestions for improvement in users' comments. *Research in Computing Science*, 70:199–209.

Kyunghyun Cho, Bart van Merrienboer, Caglar Gulcehre, Dzmitry Bahdanau, Fethi Bougares, Holger Schwenk, and Yoshua Bengio. 2014. Learning phrase representations using rnn encoder–decoder for statistical machine translation. In *Proceedings of the 2014 Conference on Empirical Methods in Natural Language Processing (EMNLP)*, pages 1724–1734, Doha, Qatar. Association for Computational Linguistics.

Ronan Collobert, Jason Weston, Léon Bottou, Michael Karlen, Koray Kavukcuoglu, and Pavel Kuksa. 2011. Natural language processing (almost) from scratch. *J. Mach. Learn. Res.*, 12:2493–2537.

Asif Ekbal Deepak Gupta, Ankit Lamba and Pushpak Bhattacharyya. 2016. Opinion mining in a code-mixed environment: A case study with government portals. In *International Conference on Natural Language Processing*, pages 249–258. NLP Association of India.

Xavier Glorot, Antoine Bordes, and Yoshua Bengio. 2011. Domain adaptation for large-scale sentiment classification: A deep learning approach. In *Proceedings of the 28th international conference on machine learning (ICML-11)*, pages 513–520.

Deepak Kumar Gupta, Kandula Srikanth Reddy, Asif Ekbal, et al. 2015. Pso-asent: Feature selection using particle swarm optimization for aspect based sentiment analysis. In *International Conference on Applications of Natural Language to Information Systems*, pages 220–233. Springer, Cham.

Robert Hecht-Nielsen. 1992. Neural networks for perception (vol. 2). chapter Theory of the Backpropagation Neural Network, pages 65–93. Harcourt Brace & Co., Orlando, FL, USA.

Minqing Hu and Bing Liu. 2004. Mining and summarizing customer reviews. In *Proceedings of the tenth ACM SIGKDD international conference on Knowledge discovery and data mining*, pages 168–177. ACM.

Yoon Kim. 2014. Convolutional neural networks for sentence classification. In *Proceedings of the 2014 Conference on Empirical Methods in Natural Language Processing (EMNLP)*, pages 1746–1751, Doha, Qatar. Association for Computational Linguistics.

Mu Li and Bao-Liang Lu. 2009. Emotion classification based on gamma-band eeg. In *Engineering in Medicine and Biology Society, 2009. EMBC 2009. Annual International Conference of the IEEE*, pages 1223–1226. IEEE.

Tomas Mikolov, Ilya Sutskever, Kai Chen, Greg S Corrado, and Jeff Dean. 2013. Distributed representations of words and phrases and their compositionality. In C. J. C. Burges, L. Bottou, M. Welling, Z. Ghahramani, and K. Q. Weinberger, editors, *Advances in Neural Information Processing Systems 26*, pages 3111–3119. Curran Associates, Inc.

Susan M Mudambi and David Schuff. 2010. What makes a helpful review? a study of customer reviews on amazon. com.

Vinod Nair and Geoffrey E. Hinton. 2010. Rectified linear units improve restricted boltzmann machines. In *Proceedings of the 27th International Conference on International Conference on Machine Learning*, ICML'10, pages 807–814, USA. Omnipress.

Curtis Padgett and Garrison W Cottrell. 1997. Representing face images for emotion classification. In *Advances in neural information processing systems*, pages 894–900.

Bo Pang, Lillian Lee, and Shivakumar Vaithyanathan. 2002. Thumbs up?: sentiment classification using machine learning techniques. In *Proceedings of the ACL-02 conference on Empirical methods in natural language processing-Volume 10*, pages 79–86. Association for Computational Linguistics.

Jeffrey Pennington, Richard Socher, and Christopher D. Manning. 2014. Glove: Global vectors for word representation. In *Empirical Methods in Natural Language Processing (EMNLP)*, pages 1532–1543.

Rahul Potharaju, Navendu Jain, and Cristina Nita-Rotaru. 2013. Juggling the jigsaw: Towards automated problem inference from network trouble tickets. In *Proceedings of the 10th USENIX Conference on Networked Systems Design and Implementation*, nsdi'13, pages 127–142, Berkeley, CA, USA. USENIX Association.

Richard Socher, Alex Perelygin, Jean Wu, Jason Chuang, Christopher D Manning, Andrew Ng, and Christopher Potts. 2013. Recursive deep models for semantic compositionality over a sentiment treebank. In *Proceedings of the 2013 conference on empirical methods in natural language processing*, pages 1631–1642.

Jost Tobias Springenberg, Alexey Dosovitskiy, Thomas Brox, and Martin A. Riedmiller. 2014. Striving for simplicity: The all convolutional net. *CoRR*, abs/1412.6806.

Nitish Srivastava, Geoffrey E Hinton, Alex Krizhevsky, Ilya Sutskever, and Ruslan Salakhutdinov. 2014. Dropout: a simple way to prevent neural networks from overfitting. *Journal of machine learning research*, 15(1):1929–1958.

Yijun Xiao and Kyunghyun Cho. 2016. Efficient character-level document classification by combining convolution and recurrent layers. *CoRR*, abs/1602.00367.

Changhua Yang, Kevin Hsin-Yih Lin, and Hsin-Hsi Chen. 2007. Emotion classification using web blog corpora. In *Web Intelligence, IEEE/WIC/ACM International Conference on*, pages 275–278. IEEE.

Zhilin Yang and Xiang Fang. 2004. Online service quality dimensions and their relationships with satisfaction: A content analysis of customer reviews of securities brokerage services. *International Journal of Service Industry Management*, 15(3):302–326.

Dawei Yin, Yuening Hu, Jiliang Tang, Tim Daly, Mianwei Zhou, Hua Ouyang, Jianhui Chen, Changsung Kang, Hongbo Deng, Chikashi Nobata, Jean-Marc Langlois, and Yi Chang. 2016. Ranking relevance in yahoo search. In *Proceedings of the 22Nd ACM SIGKDD International Conference on Knowledge Discovery and Data Mining*, KDD '16, pages 323–332, New York, NY, USA. ACM.

Ye Zhang and Byron C. Wallace. 2015. A sensitivity analysis of (and practitioners' guide to) convolutional neural networks for sentence classification. *CoRR*, abs/1510.03820.

YNUDLG at IJCNLP-2017 Task 5: A CNN-LSTM Model with Attention for Multi-choice Question Answering in Examinations

Min Wang, Qingxun Liu, Peng Ding, Yongbin Li, Xiaobing Zhou*

School of Information Science and Engineering,
Yunnan University, Yunnan, P.R. China
*Corresponding author, zhouxb.cn@gmail.com

Abstract

"Multi-choice Question Answering in Exams" is a typical question answering task, which aims to test how accurately the participants could answer the questions in exams. Most of the existing QA systems typically rely on handcrafted features and rules to conduct question understanding and/or answer ranking. In this paper, we perform convolutional neural networks (CNN) to learn the joint representations of question-answer pairs first, then use the joint representations as the inputs of the long short-term memory (LSTM) with attention to learn the answer sequence of a question for labeling the matching quality of each answer. All questions are restrained within the elementary and middle school level. We also incorporating external knowledge by training Word2Vec on Flashcards data, thus we get more compact embedding. Experimental results show that our method achieves better or comparable performance compared with the baseline system. The proposed approach achieves the accuracy of 0.39, 0.42 in English valid set, test set, respectively.

1 Introduction

Multi-choice question answering systems return the correct answer from four candidates to natural language questions. In recent years, a typical method is to model Question-Answer pairs and classify them (Severyn et al., 2016).

The nature of this way is to transform QA problem to classification problem. Some people tackle this directly by computing the cosine distance between question and answer (Feng et al., 2015; Santos et al., 2016). Besides, the development of largescale knowledge bases, such as FREEBASE (Bollacker et al., 2008), provides a rich resource to answer open domain questions. With the generative adversarial nets (Goodfellow, et al., 2014) emerging, it achieves higher performance in NLP or NLU. Neural generative question answering (Yin et al., 2015) is built on the encoder-decoder framework for sequence-to-sequence learning, and the architecture of this system holds the ability to enquire the knowledge-base, and is trained on a corpus of question-answer pairs.

Up to now, there are three mainstream methods for question answering tasks. The first one is based on sentiment contained in question-answer pairs (Zhou et al., 2015). The sentiment method learns to understand natural language questions by converting them into classification problem, 0/1 respectively represents negative or positive sentiment of the Q-A pairs, i.e., wrong answer or correct answer. The second approach uses information extraction techniques for open question answering (Yin et al., 2015; Yao and Van Durme, 2014; Bordes et al., 2014a; Bordes et al., 2014b; Yang et al,. 2015). This method retrieves a set of candidate answers from the knowledge-base, and then extract features from the question and their candidates to rank them. Yin (2015) enquires candidate answers from knowledge-base organized in the form of (subject, predicate, object) and then ranks the similarity between question and candidate answers, finally put out the answer sentence by a generator with

Proceedings of the 8th International Joint Conference on Natural Language Processing, Shared Tasks, pages 194–198,
Taipei, Taiwan, November 27 – December 1, 2017. ©2017 AFNLP

attention. And, the method proposed by Yao and Van Durme (2014) relies on rules and dependency parse results to extract handcrafted features for questions. Moreover, some methods (Bordes et al., 2014a; Bordes et al., 2014b) use the summation of question word embeddings to represent questions, which ignores word order information and cannot process complicated questions. The third way is correspondingly easy and directly computes the cosine distance between question and answer. Question and answer vectors are put into a hidden layer and then go through a CNN layer and maxpooling layer, finally computes the cosine distance between question and answer. This way doesn't use pre-trained word embeddings and can't accurately represent the relationship among words. Based on the above analyses, in this paper, we combine the first and second ways to model and train on large question answer datasets. Specifically, we transform this issue to classify question answer pairs negative or positive to judge the answer wrong or correct. Similar to the second way, we train word embeddings from external knowledge-base (KB), which creates a small, more compact embedding. Unlike some work or the baseline described retrieving related text from KB according to question or answer query, our system trains word embeddings on external KB and use CNN and LSTM model with attention mechanism to classify Q-A pairs. The model shares the same word embeddings trained by *word2vec*.

2 Data

We consider the question answer problem in Multi-choice as a sequence labeling task. All questions are restrained within the elementary and middle school level. The subjects of English subset contain biology, chemistry, physics, earth science and life science. We collect many question answer data based on the subjects including these five categories from Allen Institute for Artificial Intelligence (http://allenai.org/data.ht). Summary statistics of the datasets are listed in table 1.

Data	Num of Questions
SciQ	13,679
AI2	1,459
TQA	13,693
Aristo	20k
SS	46k
TrainSet	2,686
ValidSet	669

Table 1: Summary statistics for the datasets: Aristo and SS are used to train word embedding and the other used to train model. Number of questions stands for how many questions the dataset contains, each question has four candidate answers.

◆ **AI2 Science Questions v2**: 5,059 real science exam questions derived from a variety of regional and state science exams. The AI2 Science Questions dataset consists of questions used in student assessments in the United States across elementary and middle school grade levels. Each question is 4-way multiple choice format and may or may not include a diagram element.

◆ **Textbook Question Answering**: 1,076 textbook lessons, 26,260 questions, 6,229 images. Each lesson has a set of multiple choice questions that address concepts taught in that lesson. TQA has a total of 26,260 questions, in which 12,567 have accompanying diagrams. We just use the questions without diagrams from this dataset.

◆ **SciQ dataset**: 13,679 science questions with supporting sentences. The SciQ dataset contains 13,679 crowdsourced science exam questions about Physics, Chemistry, Biology, and other subjects. The questions are in multiple-choice format with 4 answer options each. For the majority of the questions, an additional paragraph with supporting evidence for the correct answer is provided.

◆ **Aristo MINI Corpus**: The Aristo Mini corpus contains 1,197,377 (very loosely science-relevant sentences drawn from public data). It provides simple science-relevant text that may be useful to help answer elementary science questions.

◆ **StudyStack Flashcards**: This content source is from StudyStack and manually organized in the form of question answer pairs. This gives us 400k flashcard records, questions followed by the correct answer. We use this and Aristo corpus to train the word embeddings.

3 System

This section explains the architecture of our deep learning model for modeling question-answer pairs and then to classify them. The system combines CNN with LSTM network, and the attention mechanism is also taken into account. First we put question and answer pairs into CNN network, and get question answer joint representations, then we input them into LSTM network, next we merge question and answer vectors by dot mode. Finally the softmax layer is applied to classify the joint representations.

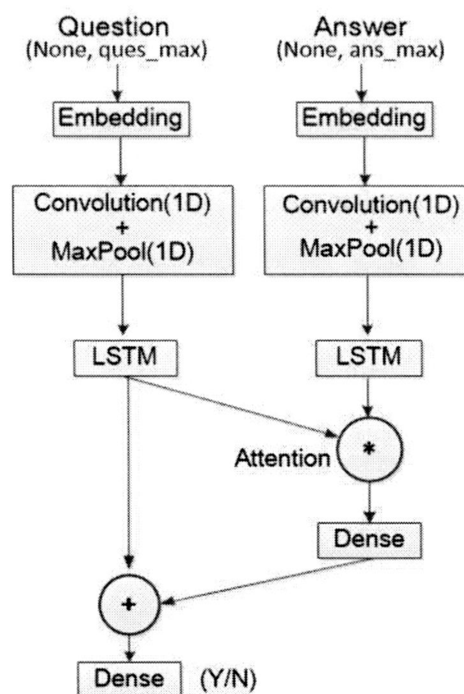

Figure 1: Our deep learning architecture for classifying question-answer pairs. The attention is developed by merging two LSTM output layers with the 'dot' mode.

3.1 CNN for QA Joint learning

The architecture of our CNN network for mapping sentences to feature vectors is shown in Fig.1. It is mainly inspired by the convolutional architectures used in (Blunsom et al., 2014; Kim, 2014; Aliaksei et al., 2016) for performing different sentence classification tasks. Different from the previous work, the goal of our distributional sentence model is to learn intermediate representations of questions and answers used to classify them into negative or positive. We use the following parameters: word embedding dimension is 300, sentence length is 64, kernel size is 5, number of filters is 32. In our model the input shape of the sentence (question or answer) is (None, 64), input this into embedding layer the shape changes to (None, 64, 300), next through

convolution computing, we get sentences shape (None, 60, 32). After pooling, we get (None, 30, 30) sentences vectors.

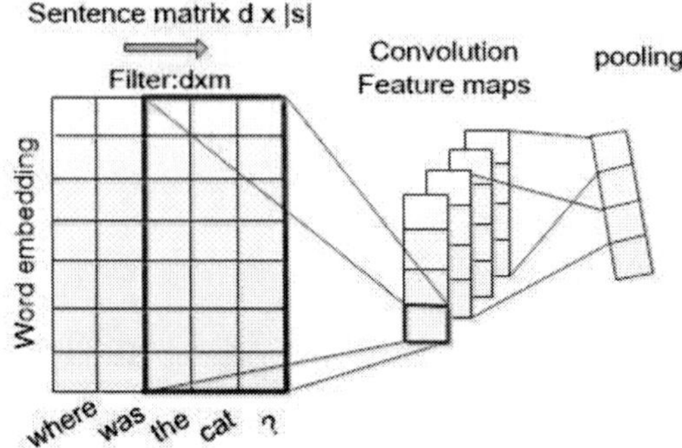

Figure 2: Our sentence model for mapping input sentences to their intermediate representations.

3.2 Combining LSTM and CNN for Ordinary Classification

Based on the joint representation of QA pairs, the LSTM layer of our model performs answer sequence learning to model semantic links between continuous answers. In Fig.1, unlike a conventional LSTM model which directly uses word embeddings as input, the proposed model takes outputs from a single layer CNN with maxpooling.

Due to the gradient vanishing problem, conventional RNNs are found difficult to be trained to exploit long-range dependencies. In order to mitigate this weak point in conventional RNNs, specially designed activation functions have been introduced. LSTM is one of the earliest attempts and still a popular option to tackle this problem. In the LSTM architecture, there are three gates (input i, forget f and output o), and a cell memory activation vector c. The vector formulas for recurrent hidden layer function H in this version of LSTM network are implemented as follows:

$$i_t = \sigma\left(W_{xi}x_t + W_{hi}h_{t-1} + b_i\right)$$

$$f_t = \sigma\left(W_{xi}x_t + W_{hi}h_{t-1} + b_f\right)$$

$$c_t = f_t c_{t-1} + i_t \tau\left(W_{xc}x_t + W_{hc}h_{t-1} + b_c\right)$$

$$o_t = \sigma\left(W_{xo}x_t + W_{ho}h_{t-1} + b_o\right)$$

$$h_t = o_t \theta\left(c_t\right)$$

where τ and θ are the cell input and cell output nonlinear activation functions which are stated as *tanh* in this paper.

3.3 Attention mechanism

Problem with RNNs in general is the vanishing gradient problem. While LSTMs address the problem, in QA contexts they can't characterize interaction between question and answer. The solution to this is attention mechanism, where the network is forced to look at certain parts of the context and ignore (in a relative sense) everything else. We just adopt a relatively easy way to accomplish this task.

The Keras merge layer provides a series of layer objects and methods for fusing two or more tensors. The Merge layer supports some predefined merge patterns, including sum, concat, mul, dot et al. Mode mul is to deal with the combined layer output to do a simple multiplication operation. Unlike mul, mode dot is used to tensor multiplication. One can use the dot_axis keyword parameter to specify the axis to be eliminated. For example, if the shapes of two tensors a and b are (batch_size,n), the output of dot is a tensor such as (batch_size, 1). We consider this as the attention vector in question and answer.

4 Experiment and Result analysis

We only participate in the English task, and this challenge employs the accuracy of a method on answering questions in test set as the metric, the accuracy is calculated as:

$$Accuracy = \frac{number\ of\ correct\ questions}{total\ number\ of\ questions}$$

As indicated in Table 2, the CNN-LSTM with attention model shows better experiment result than single CNN or LSTM. LSTM performs better than CNN, one reason may be when implementing convolution operation, there are much zeroes in sentences matrix after padding. Obviously, when adding attention mechanism, CNN and LSTM can obtain much improvements. In our experiment, we test two layer LSTMs with attention and CNN-LSTM with attention, this two models perform almost the same on valid set and test set, respectively. Finally, we choose the CNN-LSTM with attention model.

Model	Valid Acc	Test Acc
CNN	0.277	0.260
LSTM	0.286	0.292
CNN+Attention	0.301	0.283
LSTM+Attention	0.343	0.305
CNN-LSTM+Attention	0.396	0.422

Table 2: Overview of our result on the English Multi-choice question answering subset in examinations.

5 Conclusion and Future Work

In this paper, we present a question answer learning model, CNN-LSTM with attention for Multi-choice in examinations. This transformation from QA into classification problem is easy and clear. True question answer is complex, there is a need to take into account other features such similarity overlap words between questions and answers. The experiments provide strong evidence that distributed and joint representations are feasible in tackling QA problem. Experiment results demonstrate that our approach can learn the useful context from answering to improve the performance of Multi-choice question answer in exams, compared to baseline model. One of the reasons why our model performs well may be our training data is large and highly correlate to the valid set and test set.

In the future, we plan to explore the method using KB or other neural networks like generative adversarial networks (GAN), variational autoencoder (VAE) to model sentences and perform other NLP tasks.

Acknowledgments

This work was supported by the Natural Science Foundations of China under Grants No.61463050, No.61702443, No.61762091, the NSF of Yunnan Province under Grant No. 2015FB113, the Project of Innovative Research Team of Yunnan Province.

References

Severyn A, Moschitti A. 2016. Modeling Relational Information in Question-Answer Pairs with Convolutional Neural Networks. arXiv preprint arXiv:1604.01178.

Feng M, Xiang B, Glass M R, et al. 2015. Applying deep learning to answer selection: A study and an open task. In *IEEE Workshop on Automatic Speech Recognition and Understanding*, Pages 813-820.

Santos C D, Tan M, Xiang B, et al. 2016. Attentive Pooling Networks. arXiv preprint arXiv: 1602.03609.

Bollacker, K, Evans, C, Paritosh, P, et al. 2008. Freebase: a collaboratively created graph database for structuring human knowledge. In *International Conference on Management of Data*, pages 1247-1250.

Goodfellow I, Pouget-Abadie J, Mirza M, et al. 2014.Generative Adversarial Nets. In *Advances in Neural Information Processing Systems*, pages 2672-2680.

Yin J, Jiang X, Lu Z, et al. 2016. Neural Generative Question Answering. In *Proceedings of the Twenty-Fifth International Joint Conference on Artificial Intelligence*, pages 2972-2978.

Zhou X, Hu B, Chen Q, et al. 2015. Answer Sequence Learning with Neural Networks for AnswerSelection in Community Question Answering. arXiv preprint arXiv:1506.06490.

Yao X, Van Durme B. 2014. Information extraction over structured data: Question answering with freebase. In *Proceedings of the 52nd Annual Meeting of the Association for Computational Linguistics (Volume 1: Long Papers)*, pages 956-966. Association for Computational Linguistics.

Yao X, Berant J, Van Durme B. 2014. QA: Information Extraction or Semantic Parsing? In *Proceedings of the ACL 2014 Workshop on Semantic Parsing*, pages 82-86. Association for Computational Linguistics.

Bordes A, Chopra S, Weston J. 2014a. Question answering with subgraph embeddings. In *Proceedings of the 2014 Conference on Empirical Methods in Natural Language Processing (EMNLP)*, pages 615-620. Association for Computational Linguistics.

Bordes A, Weston J, Usunier N. 2014b. Open question answering with weakly supervised embedding models. In *Machine Learning and Knowledge Discovery in Databases—European Conference, ECML PKDD 2014, Nancy, France, September 15-19, 2014. Proceedings, Part I*, pages 165–180.

Yang Y, Yih W, Meek C. WikiQA: A Challenge Dataset for Open-Domain Question Answering. In *Proceedings of the 2015 Conference on Empirical Methods in Natural Language Processing*, pages 2013–2018.

Huang J, Zhou M, Yang D. 2007. Extracting chatbot knowledge from online discussion forums. In *Proceedings of the 20th international joint conference on artificial intelligence*, pages 423-428.

Ding S, Cong G, Lin C Y, et al. 2008. Using Conditional Random Fields to Extract Contexts and Answers of Questions from Online Forums. In *Proceedings of the Meeting of the Association for Computational Linguistics*, pages 710-718.

Wang B, Wang X, Sun C, et al. 2010. Modeling semantic relevance for question-answer pairs in web social communities. In *Proceedings of the 48th Annual Meeting of the Association for Computational Linguistics*, pages 1230-1238.

Yu L, Hermann K M, Blunsom P, et al. 2014. Deep Learning for Answer Sentence Selection. arXiv preprint arXiv:1412.1632.

Echihabi A, Marcu D. 2003. A noisy-channel approach to question answering. In *Proceedings of the 41st Annual Meeting on Association for Computational Linguistics-Volume 1*, pages 16-23. Association for Computational Linguistics.

Yang M C, Duan N, Zhou M, et al. 2014. Joint Relational Embeddings for Knowledge-based Question Answering. In *Conference on Empirical Methods in Natural Language Processing*, page 645-650. Association for Computational Linguistics.

Blunsom P, Grefenstette E, Kalchbrenner N. 2014. A convolutional neural network for modelling sentences. In *Proceedings of the 52nd Annual Meeting of the Association for Computational Linguistics*, pages 655-665.

Kim Y. 2014. Convolutional Neural Networks for Sentence Classification. In *Proceedings of the 2014 Conference on Empirical Methods in Natural Language Processing (EMNLP)*, pages 1746–1751.

ALS at IJCNLP-2017 Task 5: Answer Localization System for Multi-Choice Question Answering in Exams

Changliang Li[1], Cunliang Kong[1,2]
[1]Institute of Automation, Chinese Academy of Sciences
[2]Beijing Language and Culture University
changliang.li@ia.ac.cn, 201621198311@stu.blcu.edu.cn

Abstract

Multi-choice question answering in exams is a typical QA task. To accomplish this task, we present an answer localization method to locate answers shown in web pages, considering structural information and semantic information both. Using this method as basis, we analyze sentences and paragraphs appeared on web pages to get predictions. With this answer localization system, we get effective results on both validation dataset and test dataset.

1 Introduction

Multi-Choice Question Answering in Examinations is the 5th shared task in IJCNLP-2017, which aims to test how accurately system built by participants could answer the questions in exams. The dataset contains multiple choice questions from science and history curriculum, and is comprised of English part and Chinese part. In this work, we focus on the Chinese part.

We found that there are many web pages containing answers of the questions in dataset. To accomplish the task, we crawled these web pages and analyze answers appeared on them. When analyzing these pages, we need to compare sentences in the original dataset and sentences on web pages. There are many sentence pairs have the same meaning but with different forms. To process these sentences pairs, we use a localization method to locate the positions of sentences in web pages. We use edit distance of sentence pairs to represent structural similarities, and use cosine score of two vectors represented by a convolutional neural network (CNN) to represent semantic similarities. With merging these two scores together, we locate choices appeared on web pages.

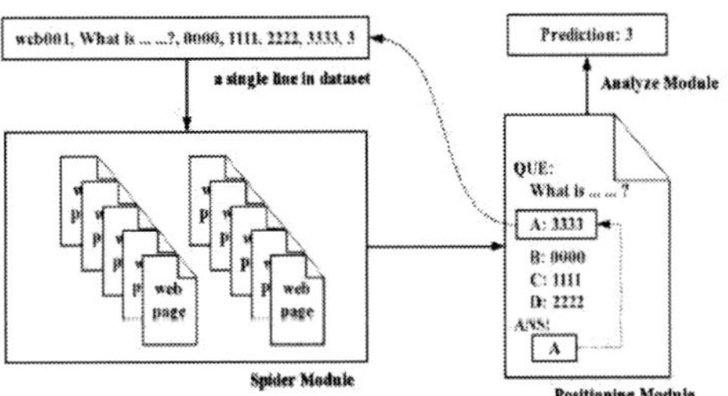

Figure 1: Overview of our system. Communication between modules is indicated by arrows.

Finally, we use the analyzed answer to find out the right choice.

This system can solve multi-choice question answering in exams as long as there are relevant web pages. The answer localization method used in the system can provide high robustness. The system is applicable to a variety of situations, even when choices on the web pages show different orders and different forms with choices in the original dataset.

The final accuracy score of our system on the test dataset is 58%, and on the validation dataset is 60%, while the baseline given by the organizer is 44.63%.

2 System Description

The system is comprised of three modules: spider module, positioning module and analysis module. Full system is as shown in figure 1. The following will describe these three parts separately.

Proceedings of the 8th International Joint Conference on Natural Language Processing, Shared Tasks, pages 199–202,
Taipei, Taiwan, November 27 – December 1, 2017. ©2017 AFNLP

2.1 Spider Module

To search related resources on the Internet, for each line in the dataset, we concatenate the question and choices as a query. After that, we use Baidu Search Engine to search relevant web pages with the query. We analyze and save web pages that relevant to each line as a single file with JavaScript Object Notation (JSON) format.

For line l in dataset, we have a question sentence q, choices c_i ($0 \leq i \leq 3$), and an answer a. And there are several web pages related to l, each of them is saved into two fields: QUE and ANS. Filed QUE contains the question and choices, and field ANS contains the answer shown on the web page.

2.2 Positioning Module

The positioning module is to select the fittest web page related to l, and position each choice shown on the web page.

Our target is to analyze predictions from field ANS of web pages. But the order of choices shown on web pages might be different from the order of choices shown in original dataset (as is shown in figure 1). Moreover, choices shown on web pages might have different forms, while they have the same meaning. There are various cases, we can cite some cases here as examples.

(1) Increasing or reducing words. The phrase 生物克隆 and the phrase 生物克隆技术 have the same meaning of *cloning technology*, but the latter has two more words than the former.

(2) Changing of word order. The phrase 种子的有无 means *have or not have seeds*, while the phrase 有无种子 has the same meaning.

(3) Synonyms. The phrase 产生二氧化碳 and the phrase 产生 CO_2 have the same meaning of *producing carbon dioxide* while 二氧化碳 and CO_2 are synonyms.

As we can see, it is necessary to solve the problem of orders and multiple forms. We use following steps to solve these problems.

Step 1, select the fittest web page. We use two strategies to choose the best one from several web pages.

(1) Field ANS should contains at least one character in 'A, B, C, D'.

(2) Field QUE should have the minimum edit distance ratio with the original question. The edit distance ratio of two strings a and b is defined as below.

$$r_e(a,b) = 1 - \frac{ED(a,b)}{\text{maxlen}(a,b)} \qquad (1)$$

where r_e is edit distance ratio, ED stands for edit distance.

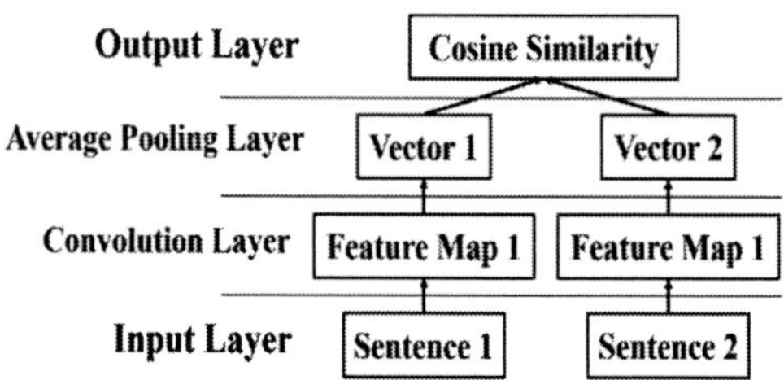

Figure 2: Convolutional architecture we used for computing semantic similarities.

Step 2, positioning each choice in field QUE.
(1) Computing structural similarities.
For c_i as the ith choice, we have a window size o_i defined as following:

$$o_i = len(c_i) + size \qquad (2)$$

where $size$ is an hyperparameter tuned using training dataset.

Getting o_i words from field QUE as a string s_t, where the first word of s_t is the tth word of field QUE, we use edit distance ratio to compute the structural similarity of c_i and s_t. i.e.:

$$sim_{i,t}^f = r_e(c_i, s_t) \qquad (3)$$

(2) Computing semantic similarities.
We use CNNs to represent the semantic information of c_i and s_t as two vectors v_i^c and v_t^s respectively. And we compute cosine score $sim_{i,t}^s$ of v_i^c and v_t^s as the semantic similarity of c_i and s_t.

In our implementation, we pad sentences to have the same length z, which is the max length of these sentences. As is shown in figure 2, there are four layers in the CNN model: input layer, convolution layer, average pooling layer and output layer. We now describe each in turn.

Input Layer. In each sentence, each word is represented as a d_0-dimensional precomputed word2vec (Mikolov et al. 2013) embedding. In this work, we set $d_0 = 30$. In this way, each sentence is represented as a matrix of dimension $d_0 \times z$.

Convolution layer. Let ω be the filter width, and $(v_0, v_1, \ldots, v_s)$ be the words of a sentence. We concatenate embeddings of $(v_{k-\omega+1}, \ldots, v_k)$ to be $c_k \in \mathbb{R}^{\omega \cdot d_0}$ ($\omega < k < z$). Then, we generate the representation $p_k \in \mathbb{R}^{d_1}$ for c_k using convolution weights $W \in \mathbb{R}^{d_1 \times \omega d_0}$ as follows:

$$p_k = f(W \cdot c_k + b) \tag{4}$$

where f is the activation function, $b \in \mathbb{R}^{d_1}$ is the bias.

Average pooling layer. There are several kinds of pooling commonly used to extract robust features from convolution, such as min pooling, max pooling and average pooling. In this work, we found average pooling showing the best result. This layer generates a pair of representation vectors for each of the two sentences. These two representations are then the basis for similarity computation.

Output layer. The last layer returns the output. In our work, we use cosine similarity of two representation vectors mentioned above as the output. i.e.:

$$sim_{i,t}^s = \frac{v_i^c \cdot v_t^s}{\|v_i^c\| \|v_t^s\|} \tag{5}$$

(3) Merging.

Merging structural similarity $sim_{i,t}^f$ and semantic similarity $sim_{i,t}^s$ together, we get the final similarity $sim_{i,t}$ of c_i and s_t.

$$sim_{i,t} = \alpha sim_{i,t}^f + (1 - \alpha)sim_{i,t}^s \tag{6}$$

where α is an hyperparameter tuned using train dataset.

To get the position of c_i in field QUE, we select the s_t that has biggest similarity with c_i. i.e.:

$$t^* = \text{argmax}(sim_{i,t}) \tag{7}$$

Finally, we get a tuple (i, t^*) that contains the order of a choice and its index in field QUE. Since there are four choices, we get a list L of four tuples.

Step 3, sorting the list and get the right order.

We sort the list L by the second element of tuples, and we assume the order after sorting is the order of choices appeared on the web page. i.e., the first tuple is the choice A, the second tuple is the choice B, and so on.

2.3 Analysis Module

In this module, we analyze the field ANS in saved web pages. In this way, we get the answer given by the web page such as A, B, C or D.

For ease of calculation, we use *0, 1, 2, 3* instead of A, B, C, D, so we get the result n ($0 \leq n \leq 3$).

To get the final result, we select the first element of the nth tuple in sorted list L as a^*. And a^* is the predicted answer of q.

3 Related Work

We got a lot of inspiration from others' work, they've given many shoulders on which this paper is standing.

Question answering has attracted lots of attention in recent years. Sukhbaatar et al. (2015) introduced a neural network with a recurrent attention model over a possibly large external memory, which is called end-to-end memory networks. After that, Kumar et al. (2015) introduced the dynamic memory network (DMN) which processes input sequences and questions, forms episodic memories, and generates relevant answers. Based on DMN, Xiong et al. (2016) proposed several improvements for memory and input modules, and introduced a novel input module for images in order to be able to answer visual questions. With rapid growth of knowledge bases (KBs) on the web and the development of neural network based (NN-based) methods, NN-based KB-QA has already achieved impressive results. Zhang et al. (2016) presented a neural attention-based model to represent the question with dynamic attention. Wang et al. (2016) have done a lot of valuable exploration of different attention methods in recurrent neural network (RNN) models.

Convolutional neural networks (CNNs) has been widely used in NLP fields in recent years, and yield effective results. Kalchbrenner et al. (2014) introduced a convolutional architecture dubbed the Dynamic Convolutional Neural Network (DCNN) for the semantic modeling of sentences. Kim (2014) used CNN for sentence classification, and achieved excellent results on multiple benchmarks. Yin et al. (2015) presented a general Attention Based Convolutional Neural Network (ABCNN) for modeling a pair of sentences, which can be applied to a wide variety of tasks. Hu et al. (2015) used CNN architectures for matching natural language sentences.

4 Experiment

The dataset we used is given by the organizer of IJCNLP-2017, shared task 5. The dataset totally contains 9080 lines in Chinese and is randomly divided into train, validation and test datasets, each line has the form like:

$$id, \text{``}q\text{''}, \text{``}c0\text{''}, \text{``}c1\text{''}, \text{``}c2\text{''}, \text{``}c3\text{''}, a$$

where id is the unique integer id for each question, q is the question text, $c0, c1, c2, c3$ is four choices respectively, and a is the correct answer which is only available for train dataset.

The dataset contains two subjects: biology and history. And detail statistics is showed as table 1.

	Train	Validation	Test	Total
Biology	2266	566	1699	4531
History	2275	568	1706	4549
Total	4541	1134	3405	9080

Table 1: Detail statistics of dataset.

We only use edit distance at first to collect choices on web pages with their similar choices in dataset as sentence pairs marked label '1'. Then we collect the same amount of sentence pairs which are not similar marked label '0'. With these sentence pairs, we set filter width ω in the convolutional architecture to be 3, and uses mean squared error loss function to train the CNN model.

After trained the convolutional architecture, we set hyperparameter $size$ in Eq. 2 as 5, α in Eq. 6 as 0.95. And the result of our system on test dataset is as shown in figure 3. As we can see, the answer

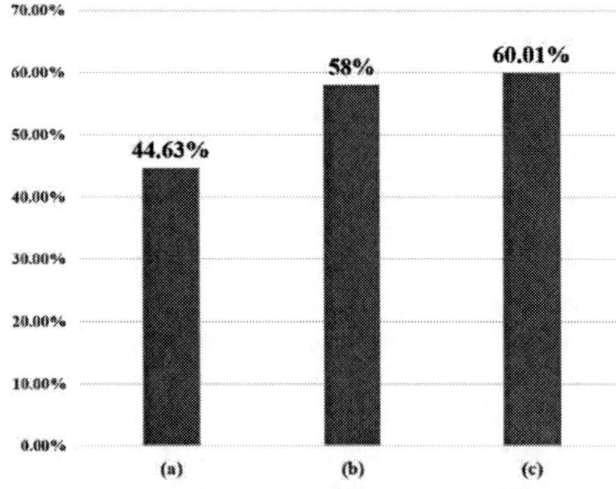

Figure 3: Comparing of system results. (a): The retrieval based method baseline. (b): The answer localization system on test dataset. (c): The answer localization system on validation dataset.

localization system performed well on both test dataset and validation dataset, while the accuracy on test dataset is 58%, on validation dataset is 60.01%.

5 Conclusion

This system uses an answer localization method of merging structural information and semantic information together, and uses this information to locate the correct answer appeared on web pages. The final results proved the effectiveness of the proposed method.

References

Yin, W., Schütze, H., Xiang, B., & Zhou, B. (2015). Abcnn: attention-based convolutional neural network for modeling sentence pairs. *Computer Science*.

Kalchbrenner, N., Grefenstette, E., & Blunsom, P. (2014). A convolutional neural network for modelling sentences. *Eprint Arxiv, 1*.

Hu, B., Lu, Z., Li, H., & Chen, Q. (2015). Convolutional neural network architectures for matching natural language sentences. *, 3*, 2042-2050.

Kim, Y. (2014). Convolutional neural networks for sentence classification. *Eprint Arxiv*.

Sukhbaatar, S., Szlam, A., Weston, J., & Fergus, R. (2015). End-to-end memory networks. *Computer Science*.

Kumar, A., Irsoy, O., Ondruska, P., Iyyer, M., Bradbury, J., & Gulrajani, I., et al. (2015). Ask me anything: dynamic memory networks for natural language processing. 1378-1387.

Xiong, C., Merity, S., & Socher, R. (2016). Dynamic memory networks for visual and textual question answering.

Mikolov, T., Sutskever, I., Chen, K., Corrado, G., & Dean, J. (2013). Distributed representations of words and phrases and their compositionality. *Advances in Neural Information Processing Systems,26*, 3111-3119.

Wang, B., Liu, K., & Zhao, J. (2016). Inner Attention based Recurrent Neural Networks for Answer Selection. *Meeting of the Association for Computational Linguistics* (pp.1288-1297).

Zhang, Y., Liu, K., He, S., Ji, G., Liu, Z., & Wu, H., et al. (2016). Question answering over knowledge base with neural attention combining global knowledge information.

MappSent at IJCNLP-2017 Task 5: A Textual Similarity Approach Applied to Multi-choice Question Answering in Examinations

Amir Hazem[1]   **Basma El Amal Boussaha**[1]   **Nicolas Hernandez**[1]

[1] LS2N - UMR CNRS 6004, Université de Nantes, France

{Amir.Hazem,Basma.Boussaha,Nicolas.Hernandez}@univ-nantes.fr

Abstract

In this paper we present MappSent, a textual similarity approach that we applied to the multi-choice question answering in exams shared task. MappSent has initially been proposed for question-to-question similarity (Hazem et al., 2017). In this work, we present the results of two adaptations of MappSent for the question answering task on the English dataset.

1 Introduction

Question-Answering is certainly one of the most challenging area of research of information retrieval (IR) and natural language processing (NLP) domains. If many investigations and countless approaches have been proposed so far, the developed systems still have difficulties to deal with text understanding. Mainly because of the complexity of the language in terms of lexical, semantic and pragmatic representations. However, with the boom of neural networks, various deep learning approaches ranging from a word level embedding representation (Bengio et al., 2003; Collobert and Weston, 2008; Mikolov et al., 2013; Pennington et al., 2014) to a longer textual level embedding representation such as phrases, sentences, paragraphs or documents (Socher et al., 2011; Mikolov et al., 2013; Le and Mikolov, 2014; Kalchbrenner et al., 2014; Kiros et al., 2015; Wieting et al., 2016; Arora et al., 2017) have been proposed and have shown promising results in many applications. Not to mention other more sophisticated approaches like recurrent neural networks (RNN) (Socher et al., 2011, 2014; Kiros et al., 2015), long short-term memory (LSTM) to capture long distance dependency (Tai et al., 2015) or convolutional neural networks (CNNs) (Kalchbrenner et al., 2014) to represent sentences.

Inspired by the new textual embedding representations (Wieting et al., 2016; Arora et al., 2017), we propose in this paper to adapt MappSent (Hazem et al., 2017) an approach that have initially been developed for question pairs similarity, to the task of multi-choice question answering in examinations. Two adaptations are proposed. The first one is a direct application of MappSent to question-answer pairs, while the second one can be seen as a pivot-based approach in which questions and answers are treated separately in two different sub-spaces. Then, the correct candidate is extracted by transitivity thanks to the similarity of test question-answering pairs regarding question-answering pairs of the training corpus. If the shared task provides datasets in two languages: Chinese and English, we only deal with English.

The remainder of this paper is organized as follows. Section 2 presents the multi-choice question answering in examination task and the provided training datasets. Section 3 describes MappSent, the textual similarity approach and its two adaptations to multi-choice question answering. Section 4 is devoted to the evaluation of the different approaches. Section 5 discusses the results and finally, Section 6 presents our conclusion.

2 Task and Resource Description

The task consists of a multi-choice question challenge. Given a question, four answers are provided and the purpose is to find the correct one among all of them. Answers can be words, values, phrases or sentences. The questions and their corresponding answers are of the elementary and middle school level extracted from science and history corpora. Two datasets are proposed: Chinese and English of five domains which are: *Biology*, *Chemistry*, *Physics*, *Earth Science* and *Life Science*. The size of the English dataset is 2686 questions for the

Proceedings of the 8th International Joint Conference on Natural Language Processing, Shared Tasks, pages 203–207,
Taipei, Taiwan, November 27 – December 1, 2017. ©2017 AFNLP

training set, 669 questions for the development set and 2012 for the test set. Hereafter an example extracted from the *Earth Science* domain:

- Most tsunami are caused by:
    1. (A) Earthquakes
    2. (B) Meteorites
    3. (C) Volcanic eruptions
    4. (D) Collisions of ships at sea

3 System Description

In order to understand the principle behind MappSent approach, it is important to introduce the task for which it has been designed. We first introduce the Question-to-Question similarity task of SemEval shared task [1], then we present MappSent, the approach that has been designed for this task and finally, we present its adaptation to the multi-choice question answering in examinations task.

3.1 Question-to-Question Similarity Task

In community question answering, the question-to-question similarity task (Task3, SubtaskB in SemEval) consists of reranking 10 related questions according to their similarity with respect to a given original question. Candidates are labeled as *PerfectMatch*, *Relevant* or *Irrelevant*. The training and development datasets consist of 317 original questions and 3,170 related questions[2]. The test sets of 2016 and 2017 respectively consist of 70 original/700 related questions and 88 original/880 related questions. The official evaluation measure towards which all systems were evaluated is the mean average precision (MAP) using the 10 ranked related questions. The experimental results of MappSent (Hazem et al., 2017) have shown the best results on SemEval (2016/2017) question-to-question similarity task over state-of-art approaches.

3.2 MappSent Approach

MappSent approach aims at providing a better representation of pairs of similar sentences, paragraphs and more generally, pieces of texts of any length. A prior condition is to have a training data set of annotated pairs of sentences. The main idea

is: given a set of similar sentences, the goal is to build a more discriminant and representative sentence embedding space. We first compute word embeddings of the entire corpus, then, each sentence is represented by an element-wise addition of its word embedding vectors. Finally, a mapping matrix is built using the SVD decomposition to project sentences in a new subspace. Similar sentences are moved closer thanks to a mapping matrix (Artetxe et al., 2016) learned from a training dataset containing annotated similar sentences. Basically, a set of similar sentence pairs is used as seed information to build the mapping matrix. The optimal mapping is computed by minimizing the Euclidean distance between the seed sentence pairs.

MappSent approach consists of the following steps:

1. We train a Skip-Gram [3] model using Gensim (Řehůřek and Sojka, 2010)[4] on a lemmatized training dataset.

2. Each training and test sentence is pre-processed. We remove stopwords and only keep nouns, verbs and adjectives while computing sentence embedding vectors and the mapping matrix. This step is not applied when learning word embeddings (cf.Step 1).

3. For each given pre-processed sentence, we build its embedding vector which is the element-wise addition of its words embedding vectors (Mikolov et al., 2013; Wieting et al., 2016; Arora et al., 2017). Unlike Arora et al. (2017) we do not use any weighting procedure while computing vectors embedding sum[5].

4. We build a mapping matrix where test sentences can be projected. We adapted Artetxe et al. (2016) approach in a monolingual scenario as follows:

    - To build the mapping matrix we need a mapping dictionary which contains similar sentence pairs.

---

[1] http://alt.qcri.org/semeval2017/task3/

[2] http://alt.qcri.org/semeval2016/task3/index.php?id=data-and-tools

[3] CBOW model had also been experienced but it turned out to give lower results while compared to the SkipGram model.

[4] To ensure the comparability of our experiments, we fixed the python hash function that is used to generate random initialization. By doing so, we are sure to obtain the same embeddings for a given configuration.

[5] We explored this direction without success.

- The mapping matrix is built by learning a linear transformation which minimizes the sum of squared Euclidean distances for the dictionary entries and using an orthogonality constraint to preserve the length normalization.

- While in the bilingual scenario, source words are projected in the target space by using the bilingual mapping matrix, in our case, original and related questions are both projected in a similar subspace using the monolingual sentence mapping matrix. This consists of our adaptation of the bilingual mapping.

5. Test sentences are projected in the new subspace thanks to the mapping matrix.

6. The cosine similarity is then used to measure the similarity between the projected test sentences.

3.3 MappSent Adaptation

Two ways of adapting MappSent to the question-answering task can be considered. The first approach illustrated in Figure 1 is to follow the same procedure as the question-to-question similarity task. This would consist on using annotated pairs of questions and there corresponding answers to build the mapping matrix. However, this approach may be counter-intuitive since answers are not similar to questions as opposed to the question-to-question similarity task where the strong hypothesis is the similarity between question pairs. Since the mapping matrix aims at representing sentences in a subspace based on a given criteria. One can assume that mapping pairs of questions and their correct answers in a new subspace as a plausible alternative. We denote this first adaptation by $MappSent_{QA}$.

The second approach illustrated in Figure 2 and denoted $MappSent_{QQAA}$ tends to keep the strong hypothesis of sentence pairs similarity. Hence, instead of building one mapping matrix to represent questions and answers, we built two mapping matrices, one that represent similar question pairs and the other one to represent similar answers pairs. Finally, for a given test question, we extract the most similar question in the training data. Then, we compute a Cosine similarity between its corresponding answer, and the four test candidates. We select as correct answer the test candidate with the highest similarity score.

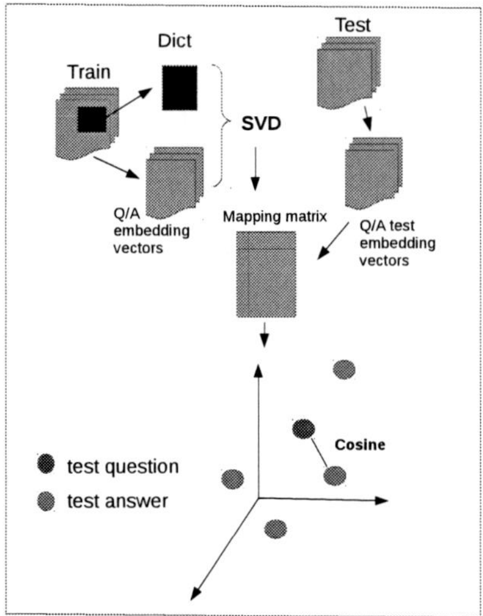

Figure 1: First adaptation: $MappSent_{QA}$

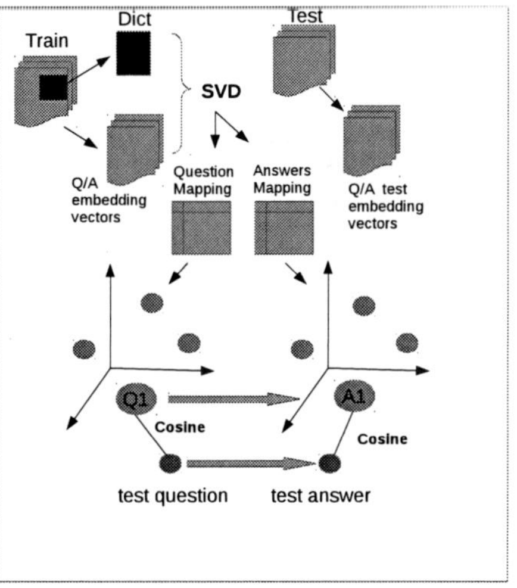

Figure 2: Second adaptation: $MappSent_{QQAA}$

3.4 Baseline

The baseline is a simple retrieval based approach which scores pairs of the question and each of its option as follows:

- concatenate a question with one of the candidate answers as a query

- use Lucene to search and extract relevant documents with the query

- score relevant documents by the similarity between the query and a given extracted document

- choose at most three highest scores to calculate the score of the pair of the question and the option

- output the pair with the highest score as the correct answer

4   Results

Method	Dev	Test
Baseline	29.45	-
$MappSent_{QA}$	33.3	29.5
$MappSent_{QQAA}$	**34.1**	**30.3**

Table 1: Results (Accuracy%) on IJCNLP 2017 shared task

Table 1 presents the results on the multi-choice question answering in examination task. We compare the two adaptations of MappSent approach that is: $MappSent_{QA}$ and $MappSent_{QQAA}$ to the baseline. We see that the two adaptations $MappSent_{QA}$ and $MappSent_{QQAA}$ outperform the baseline[6] on the development set. We see also that $MappSent_{QQAA}$ is slightly better than $MappSent_{QA}$ on both the development and the test sets. The best scores are 34.1% of accuracy on the development set and 30.1% of accuracy on the test set using $MappSent_{QQAA}$ approach.

5   Discussion

Several points have to be discussed regarding the obtained results of the two adaptations of MappSent. First, MappSent has been designed for question-to-question similarity. A direct application to question-answering pairs might be inappropriate. If the relations between similar question pairs are mainly lexical, semantics, reformulations, duplicates or near duplicates. Question-answering pairs are of a more complex relation nature, which can be pragmatic, rhetorical, elaboration, explanation, etc. This might explain the difficulties to capture these information and the mitigated results. Second, the task of multi-choice question answering exhibit specific particularities of the candidates. Answers can be words, values,

---

[6]We do not have yet the results of the baseline on the test set

phrases or sentences. In the case of words or values for instance, it is hard, if not impossible to represent the answer by an efficient embedding vector because of the lack of information conveyed by the candidates. Typically, our approach will always fail when answers are very short or contain only values. The third point that should be mentioned here is that MappSent didn't use any external data. This is of course an important drawback. The training data doesn't contain all the documents that might provide answers to the test questions. This is one of the clues that we let for future work. Another specificity of the multi-choice question is the fourth answer which can be of the form: "All of these", "all of the above" or "None of the above", etc. Lets see the following example:

- In the process of cell division, the parent cell divides to form the:

    1. Continuation cells
    2. Next generation cells
    3. Daughter cells
    4. None of the above

We do not take into account this particular case in which the fourth answer: "none of the above", should be addressed in a special way. This is also a drawback that we need to deal with to improve our models.

6   Conclusion

In this paper, we have presented MappSent a novel and simple approach for textual similarity and proposed two adaptations for the task of multi-choice question answering. Our approaches allow to map sentences in a joint more representative sub-space. The experimental results have shown interesting results and lend support the idea that a mapping matrix is an appropriate method for textual representation and a promising approach for multi-choice question answering task. Furthermore, no attention has been given to external data and to the particularities of the multi-choice question answering data, drawbacks that we let for future work.

References

Sanjeev Arora, Liang Yingyu, and Ma Tengyu. 2017. A simple but tough to beat baseline for sentence embeddings. In *Proceedings of the 17th International Conference on Learning Representations (ICLR'17)*, pages 1–11.

Mikel Artetxe, Gorka Labaka, and Eneko Agirre. 2016. Learning principled bilingual mappings of word embeddings while preserving monolingual invariance. In *Proceedings of the 2016 Conference on Empirical Methods in Natural Language Processing (EMNLP'16)*, pages 2289–2294, Austin, TX, USA.

Yoshua Bengio, Rjean Ducharme, Pascal Vincent, and Christian Jauvin. 2003. A neural probabilistic language model. *JOURNAL OF MACHINE LEARNING RESEARCH*, 3:1137–1155.

R. Collobert and J. Weston. 2008. A unified architecture for natural language processing: Deep neural networks with multitask learning. In *International Conference on Machine Learning, ICML*.

Amir Hazem, Basma el amel Boussaha, and Nicolas Hernandez. 2017. Mappsent: a textual mapping approach for question-toquestion similarity. Recent Advances in Natural Language Processing, RANLP 2017, 2-8 September, 2017, Varna, Bulgaria.

Nal Kalchbrenner, Edward Grefenstette, and Phil Blunsom. 2014. A convolutional neural network for modelling sentences. *CoRR*, abs/1404.2188.

Ryan Kiros, Yukun Zhu, Ruslan R Salakhutdinov, Richard Zemel, Raquel Urtasun, Antonio Torralba, and Sanja Fidler. 2015. Skip-thought vectors. In C. Cortes, N. D. Lawrence, D. D. Lee, M. Sugiyama, and R. Garnett, editors, *Advances in Neural Information Processing Systems 28*, pages 3294–3302. Curran Associates, Inc.

Quoc V. Le and Tomas Mikolov. 2014. Distributed representations of sentences and documents. *CoRR*, abs/1405.4053.

Tomas Mikolov, Ilya Sutskever, Kai Chen, Greg S Corrado, and Jeff Dean. 2013. Distributed representations of words and phrases and their compositionality. In C. J. C. Burges, L. Bottou, M. Welling, Z. Ghahramani, and K. Q. Weinberger, editors, *Advances in Neural Information Processing Systems 26*, pages 3111–3119. Curran Associates, Inc.

Jeffrey Pennington, Richard Socher, and Christopher D Manning. 2014. Glove: Global vectors for word representation. In *Empirical Methods in Natural Language Processing (EMNLP)*, pages 1532–1543.

Radim Řehůřek and Petr Sojka. 2010. Software Framework for Topic Modelling with Large Corpora. In *Proceedings of the LREC 2010 Workshop on New Challenges for NLP Frameworks*, pages 45–50, Valletta, Malta. ELRA. http://is.muni.cz/publication/884893/en.

Richard Socher, Eric H. Huang, Jeffrey Pennington, Andrew Y. Ng, and Christopher D. Manning. 2011. Dynamic Pooling and Unfolding Recursive Autoencoders for Paraphrase Detection. In *Advances in Neural Information Processing Systems 24*.

Richard Socher, Andrej Karpathy, Quoc V. Le, Christopher D. Manning, and Andrew Y. Ng. 2014. Grounded compositional semantics for finding and describing images with sentences. *TACL*, 2:207–218.

Kai Sheng Tai, Richard Socher, and Christopher D. Manning. 2015. Improved semantic representations from tree-structured long short-term memory networks. *CoRR*, abs/1503.00075.

John Wieting, Mohit Bansal, Kevin Gimpel, and Karen Livescu. 2016. Towards universal paraphrastic sentence embeddings. *Internationa Conference on Learning Representations, CoRR*, abs/1511.08198.

YNU-HPCC at IJCNLP-2017 Task 5: Multi-choice Question Answering in Exams Using an Attention-based LSTM Model

Hang Yuan, You Zhang, Jin Wang and **Xuejie Zhang**
School of Information Science and Engineering
Yunnan University
Kunming, P.R. China
Contact:xjzhang@ynu.edu.cn

Abstract

A shared task is a typical question answering task that aims to test how accurately the participants can answer the questions in exams. Typically, for each question, there are four candidate answers, and only one of the answers is correct. The existing methods for such a task usually implement a recurrent neural network (RNN) or long short-term memory (LSTM). However, both RNN and LSTM are biased models in which the words in the tail of a sentence are more dominant than the words in the header. In this paper, we propose the use of an attention-based LSTM (AT-LSTM) model for these tasks. By adding an attention mechanism to the standard L-STM, this model can more easily capture long contextual information. Our submission ranked first among 35 teams in terms of the accuracy at the IJCNLP-2017 multi-choice question answering in Exams for all datasets.

1 Introduction

Designing an intelligent question answering system that can answer general scientific questions has always been an important research direction in natural language processing. In this field, various scholars have made very important contributions before, for example, IBM insuranceQA and The Allen AI Science Challenge on the Kaggle (Schoenick et al., 2017). Multi-choice question answering in exams is a typical natural language processing task. For this task, it is required to design a question and answer system that can solve the examination of a general subject, such as biology and chemistry. The task can be considered as a binary classification that requires a system for determining whether the answer of the candidate is correct or not.

In the recent research field of question answering, various methods have proved to be highly useful. The difference between the existing methods is mainly reflected in the access to the knowledge and reasoning framework. Clark et al. (2013) proposed a method based on text statistical rules. Clark (2015) described how to obtain more information from the background knowledge base, i.e., they introduced the use of background knowledge to build the best scene. Sachan et al. (2016) presented a unified max-margin framework that learns to detect the hidden structures that explain the correctness of an answer when provided with the question and instructional materials. A system that extracts information from the corpus for automatic generation of test questions was designed by Khot et al. (2015), whereas a structured inference system based on integer linear programming was proposed by Khashabi et al. (2016). A more complex method is presented in (Clark et al., 2016). This model operates at three levels of representation and reasoning: information retrieval, corpus statistics, and simple inference over a semi-automatically constructed knowledge base.

In this paper, we mainly focus on an attention-based long short-term memory (AT-LSTM) model. Two different word embeddings are used to learn the word vectors in both the Chinese and English corpora. Subsequently, the word vectors are fed into the long short-term memory (LSTM) layer, and the attention mechanism is combined. The prediction results are output via softmax activation. There are two probabilities for each candidate: positive probability (probability of a correct answer) and negative probability (probability of a wrong answer). The sum of the positive and negative probabilities is one. The candidate answer with the highest probability of positive probabili-

Proceedings of the 8th International Joint Conference on Natural Language Processing, Shared Tasks, pages 208–212,
Taipei, Taiwan, November 27 – December 1, 2017. ©2017 AFNLP

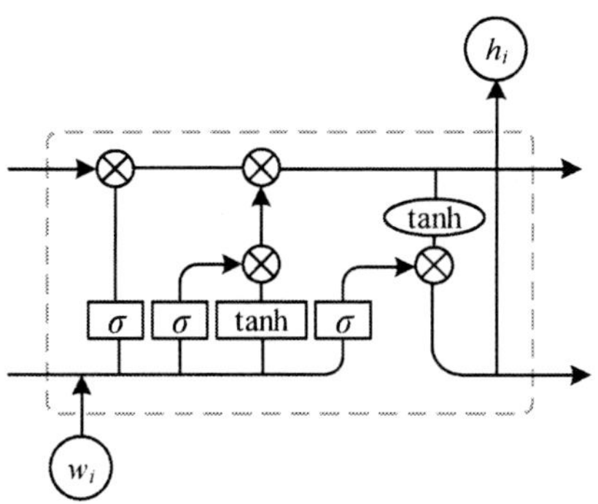

Figure 1: Architecture of a standard LSTM cell.

ty will be considered as our predictive answer. To obtain better experimental results, several models such as convolution neural network (CNN), LST-M, and AT-LSTM are employed for comparison. We also attempt to use different types of word embedding in the process. The experimental results show that the AT-LSTM model yields the best results when using GoogleNews for word embedding. The results of this model are presented in this paper.

The rest of our paper is structured as follows: Section 2 introduces the LSTM and AT-LSTM models. Section 3 provides a detailed description of our experiments and evaluation. The conclusions are drawn in Section 4.

2 Model

Three models are implemented in this competition for comparison: CNN, LSTM, and AT-LSTM models. For the two different subsets of English and Chinese, two different word embeddings are used to process the input data. The experimental results also reflect the theoretical analysis, and the AT-LSTM model achieves better results. Compared with a standard LSTM model, this model adds an attention mechanism after the LSTM layer. The input questions and answers are converted into word vectors after the embedding layer. The function of the LSTM layer is to train the input word vectors into hidden vectors. The key to this model is that the attention mechanism generates a weight for each hidden vector. The hidden vectors and attention weights are combined and passed to the following layer for calculation.

LSTM. Recurrent neural networks (RNNs) are associated with the gradient vanishing or exploding problems. To overcome these possible problems, the LSTM method was developed and it exhibited a better performance. The most significant difference between LSTM and RNN is that the former combined a processor to determine whether the information is useful or not (Sainath et al., 2015). Such processor is a memory cell. Each cell has three gates to control the transmission of information. They are called the input gate, forget gate, and output gate.

After the input data is fed into an LSTM system, the system will determine the usefulness of the information according to established rules. Only the information that is identified as useful will be retained, and the rest will be abandoned. Figure 1 illustrates the architecture of a standard LSTM cell. In the figure, w_i and h_i represent the cell unit input and hidden layer vector, respectively, and σ denotes a sigmoid function. The output of the hidden layer can be considered as the representation of a sentence. The hidden vectors will eventually be passed to the softmax layer for the classification prediction. For each candidate answer, the predicted result will consist of two parts: probability of a correct answer and probability of a wrong answer. The sum of these two probabilities is one. The answer with the highest correct probability among the four answers will be accepted.

AT-LSTM. Although LSTM addresses the problem of gradient vanishing and explosion, it is not very suitable for solving QA problems because there are very long distances involved in the QA context (Wang et al., 2016). One of the solutions is to add a mechanism of attention.

The original questions and answers are converted into vector representations by the embedding layer, and these word vectors are fed into the L-STM layer. Subsequently, the word vectors are expressed as hidden vectors. Then, the attention mechanism assigns a weight to each hidden vector. The attention mechanism produces attention weight vector α and weighted hidden representation r. Both the attention weight vector and hidden vectors are fed into the softmax layer. Figure 2 illustrates the architecture of the proposed AT-LSTM.

The attention mechanism allows the model to retain some important hidden information when the sentences are quite long. In our task, the questions and answers are relatively long sentences. The use of a standard LSTM will result in the loss

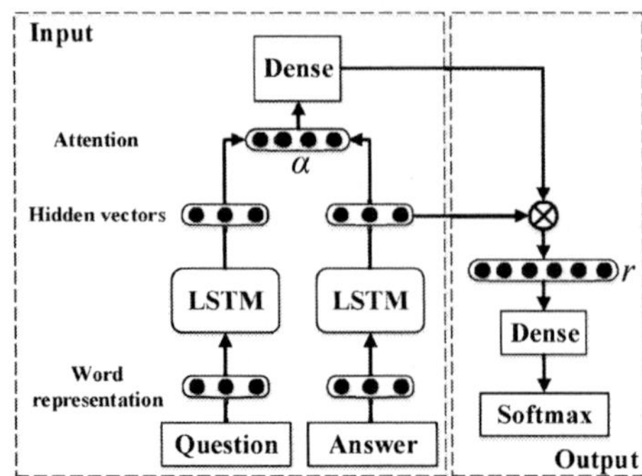

Figure 2: Architecture of the proposed AT-LSTM.

English Subset	Acc
CNN (GoogleNews)	0.275
LSTM (GoogleNews)	0.289
AT-LSTM (GoogleNews)	0.353
CNN (GloVe)	0.261
LSTM (GloVe)	0.271
AT-LSTM (GloVe)	0.307
Chinese Subset	**Acc**
CNN (character vector)	0.297
LSTM (character vector)	0.313
AT-LSTM (character vector)	0.332
CNN (word vector)	0.308
LSTM (word vector)	0.347
AT-LSTM (word vector)	0.465

Table 1: Comparative experiment results

of hidden information. To solve this possible problem, AT-LSTM is used to design the question and answer system.

3 Experiments and Evaluation

Data pre-processing. The competition is divided into two contests: English subset and Chinese subset. Our team participates in both the contests. The datasets of the organizer include training datasets, validation datasets, and test datasets. The English training data mainly contains five subject corpora: biology, chemistry, earth-science, life-science, and physical-science. The Chinese training data mainly contains biology and history. All these corpora contain the question ID, question content, four candidate answers, and correct answers. The validation data is used to initially assess the quality of the trained model and assist in the selection of the model parameters. As with the test data, the validation data is not provided the correct answer. For the English subset, we used a tokenizer to process the questions and answers into an array of tokens. The English word embedding is GoogleNews. Here, all the punctuations are ignored and all non-English letters are treated as unknown words. In the word vectors, unknown word vectors are randomly generated from a uniform distribution $U(-0.25, 0.25)$. For the Chinese subset, first, we use the Jieba toolkit to implement word segmentation on the original corpus. Then the sentences are changed into the word vectors through our own training word embedding. To obtain better training results, we increase the training data. We crwaled numerous junior high school and high school corresponding subject examination questions from the Internet. These are processed into the original training data format to train the model (Yi et al., 2015).

In this experiment, for the English subset, the original corpus is transformed into a word vector by two different word embeddings: GoogleNews and GloVe (Pennington et al., 2014). The results show that GoogleNews can be used to obtain better results. It is used to initialize the weight of the embedding layer in build 300-dimension word vectors for all the questions and answers. For the Chinese subset, we also use a character vector and word vector with two different word embeddings. The character word embedding is trained from the Chinese version of Wikipedia, whereas the word vector embedding is trained from the news (12G), Baidu Encyclopedia (20G), and a novel (90G). The dimensions of the character vector and word vector are 200 and 64, respectively. In the experiment, we notice that after the Jieba toolkit word segmentation, the accuracy of the Chinese subset is significantly improved. We combine the best results of English subsets and Chinese subsets to form our final submissions.

Implementation. The source code for this experiment is written in Python, and the main framework of the program is Keras. The backend used in this experiment is TensorFlow. We use the same AT-LSTM to obtain the results for both the English and Chinese corpora. Both results outperform the baseline. We first use the CNN model to implement this system, but the result is not good. The reason is that some texts are extremely long, whereas a few are extremely short, making the CNN model inefficient. Next, we use the LSTM model to complete this task. The results of the LSTM model are better than the CNN model, but are still unable to reach the base-line. To better solve the problem of the longer distance dependent relationship, we added an attention mechanis-

Parameters	English	Chinese
Filter number	64	64
Filter length	3	3
Dropout rate	0.3	0.1
Epoch	20	20
Batch size	32	64
Word embedding dim	300	64
Score	0.353	0.465

Table 2: Optimal parameters

Corpura	English	Chinese	All
Our score	0.353	0.465	0.423
Rank 1 team	0.456	0.581	0.423
Baseline score	0.2945	0.4463	0.39
Our rank	4	2	1

Table 3: Final testing results and ranking

m to the LSTM model. The results show that, under the same experimental equipment conditions, the AT-LSTM model can yield better results. Table 1 presents the results of a comparative experiment for an English Subset and a Chinese Subset.

The Sklearn grid search function (Liu et al., 2015) is used to determine the best combination of the parameters. Although the same model is used for both the datasets, as the two datasets in the Chinese and English pretreatment are not the same, the parameters that achieve the best results may be different. Table 2 lists the parameters of the model when the best results are obtained.

For the English subset, the best-tuned parameters are as follows: number of the filters in CNN is 64, length of a filter is 3, dropout rate is 0.3, dimensionality of the hidden layer in AT-LSTM and LSTM is 300, batch size is 32, and number of epochs is 20. Simultaneously, the optimizer is Adam, loss function is the categorical cross-entropy, and activation function is softmax.

For the Chinese subset, the best-tuned parameters are as follows: The number of filters in CNN is 64, length of the filter is 3, dropout rate is 0.1, dimensionality of the hidden layer in AT-LSTM and LSTM is 64, batch size is 64, and number of epochs is 20. The rest of the model parameters are the same as for the English Subset.

Evaluation Metrics. For this experiment, the goal is to choose the correct answer from the four candidate answers. The results of the experiment are only the two categories of right and wrong. The baseline score of the organizer is also evaluated by the accuracy. Therefore, the system is evaluated by calculating the accuracy.

Results. According to the results provided by the organizers, a total of 35 teams enrolled in the competition. As can be seen from the comparison experiment in Table 2, the accuracy of using the AT-LSTM model is the highest for both the Chinese and English subsets. The difference between the length of the input sentence varies significantly; therefore, the AT-LSTM model is used to complete the task. Furthermore, the use of GoogleNews embedding for the English subset is better than the GloVe embedding. The main difference between the two embeddings is in the training sets. The training sets of GoogleNews are practically from the news, while the training sets of GloVe are from Twitter. Obviously, the GoogleNews data source is closer to this task. For the Chinese data sets, the use of word vectors is significantly better than character vector. The meaning of Chinese words is not equivalent to the combination of the meaning of single characters. Compared with the character vector, the word vector can more accurately represent the original input information. Therefore, the results of the AT-LSTM model with Google-News embedding is chosen as the final uploaded English subset result. The Chinese subset selects the result of the AT-LSTM with our own training embedding as the final submission. Table 3 shows our final scores and ranking.

4 Conclusion

In this paper, we introduce the task of multi-choice question answering in exams. The AT-LSTM model is used to solve this problem. This model allows the extraction of the long distance dependencies. For more complex scientific questions, this model is proven to be superior to the standard LSTM. In our experiments also, the model exhibits a good performance (better than the standard CNN and standard LSTM models). In the future, we will attempt to improve the model or increase the knowledge of other corpus to enhance the accuracy of the system. Better preprocessing and more detailed word embedding are also helpful for improving the results.

Acknowledgments

This work was supported by the National Natural Science Foundation of China (NSFC) under Grants No.61702443 and No.61762091, and in part by Educational Commission of Yunnan Province of China under Grant No.2017ZZX030.

The authors would like to thank the anonymous reviewers and the area chairs for their constructive comments.

References

Peter Clark. 2015. Elementary school science and math tests as a driver for ai: Take the aristo challenge! In *Proceedings of the TwentyNinth AAAI Conference on Artificial Intelligence (AAAI-15)*, pages 4019–4021.

Peter Clark, Oren Etzioni, Tushar Khot, Ashish Sabharwal, Oyvind Tafjord, Peter Turney, and Daniel Khashabi. 2016. Combining retrieval, statistics, and inference to answer elementary science questions. In *Proceedings of Thirtieth AAAI Conference on Artificial Intelligence*, pages 2580–2586.

Peter Clark, Philip Harrison, and Niranjan Balasubramanian. 2013. A study of the knowledge base requirements for passing an elementary science test. In *Proceedings of the 2013 Workshop on Automated Knowledge Base Construction.(AKBC-13)*, pages 37–42.

Daniel Khashabi, Tushar Khot, Ashish Sabharwal, Peter Clark, Oren Etzioni, and Dan Roth. 2016. Question answering via integer programming over semistructured knowledge. In *Proceedings of the 25th International Joint Conference on Artificial Intelligence (IJCAI-16)*, pages 1145–1152.

Tushar Khot, Niranjan Balasubramanian, Eric Gribkoff, Ashish Sabharwal, Peter Clark, and Oren Etzioni. 2015. Exploring markov logic networks for question answering. In *Proceedings of Conference on Empirical Methods in Natural Language Processing*, pages 685–694.

Pengfei Liu, Shafiq Joty, and Helen Meng. 2015. Fine-grained opinion mining with recurrent neural networks and word embeddings. In *Proceedings of Conference on Empirical Methods in Natural Language Processing*, pages 1433–1443.

Jeffrey Pennington, Richard Socher, and Christopher Manning. 2014. Glove: Global vectors for word representation. In *Proceedings of Conference on Empirical Methods in Natural Language Processing*, pages 1532–1543.

Mrinmaya Sachan, Avinava Dubey, and Eric P. Xing. 2016. Science question answering using instructional materials. *CoRR abs/1602.04375*.

T. N Sainath, O Vinyals, A Senior, and H Sak. 2015. Convolutional, long short-term memory, fully connected deep neural networks. In *Proceedings of IEEE International Conference on Acoustics, Speech and Signal Processing*, pages 4580–4584.

Carissa Schoenick, Peter Clark, Oyvind Tafjord, Peter Turney, and Oren Etzioni. 2017. Moving beyond the turing test with the allen ai science challenge. *arXiv preprint arXiv:1604.04315*.

Jin Wang, Liang Chih Yu, K. Robert Lai, and Xuejie Zhang. 2016. Dimensional sentiment analysis using a regional cnn-lstm model. In *Proceedings of the Association for Computational Linguistics*, pages 225–230.

Yang Yi, Wen Tau Yih, and Christopher Meek. 2015. Wikiqa: A challenge dataset for open-domain question answering. In *Proceedings of Conference on Empirical Methods in Natural Language Processing*, pages 2013–2018.

JU_NITM at IJCNLP-2017 Task 5: A Classification Approach for Answer Selection in Multi-choice Question Answering System

Sandip Sarkar
Computer Science and Application
Hijli College, Kharagpur
sandipsarkar.ju@gmail.com

Dipankar Das
Computer Science and Engineering
Jadavpur University, Kolkata
dipankar.dipnil2005@gmail.com

Partha Pakray
Computer Science and Engineering
NIT Mizoram, Mizoram
parthapakray@gmail.com

Abstract

The present task describes the participation of the JU_NITM team in IJCNLP-2017 Shared Task 5: "Multi-choice Question Answering in Examinations". One of the main aims of this shared task is to choose the correct option for each of the multi-choice questions. We represent each of the questions and its corresponding answer in vector space and find the cosine similarity between two vectors. Our proposed model also includes supervised classification techniques to find the correct answer. Our system was only developed for the English language, and it also obtains an accuracy of 40.07% for the test dataset and 40.06% for validation dataset, respectively.

1 Introduction

In the era of computer and internet, we are getting any information at our fingertips. Besides, Natural Language Processing (NLP) is used to improve computer intelligence and to understand the natural languages given by us. If we consider information retrieval, semantic level of matching also holds a major role to retrieve similar documents (Onal et al., 2016). Question Answering (QA) as a sub field of Natural Language Processing (NLP) and Information Retrieval (IR) aims to give answer of a given question in natural language. In the present task, we proposed a method to choose correct answer in multi-choice question answering domain. First, we find the relation between the question and answers in the same vector space using cosine similarity. After that, we used a supervised classification approach to predict the correct answer from multiple options that are considered as our classes.

The rest of the paper is organized as follows. Section 2 describes the detail information of this shared whereas related work is discussed in Section 3. Similarly, Section 4 describes our proposed model in detail. Dataset information of this shared task is given in Section 5. We present results of our system in Section 6. Finally, Section 7 presents the conclusions and future work.

2 Task Overview

IJCNLP-2017 Task 5: "Multi-choice Question Answering in Examinations" challenged the participants to automatically predict the correct answer in multi choice Question Answering in exams. This shared task contains complex questions like in real exam. All questions are from the elementary and middle school level. Each question contains four possible answers. Questions are collected from different domains like biology, physics, chemistry etc. The format of the dataset is given in Table 1. In Table 1 in Correct answer column 0,1,2,3, denote answer A, answer B, answer C, answer D respectively.

3 Related Work

In recent time community question answering (cQA) plays an important role to find desired information. Many researchers proposed different type of approaches to deal with community question answering. To solve this problem most of the researcher used traditional information retrieval system.

Besides the use of neural network in information retrieval is gradually increasing because of their advantages. In the same time, distributed semantic model plays an important role to find the similarity between two sentences or documents (Sarkar et al., 2016a). Neural language model for learning distributed vector representations of

Proceedings of the 8th International Joint Conference on Natural Language Processing, Shared Tasks, pages 213–216,
Taipei, Taiwan, November 27 – December 1, 2017. ©2017 AFNLP

Quesion	Answer A	Answer B	Answer C	Answer D	Correct answer
What component of blood carries oxygen?	red blood cells	white blood cells	plasma	platelets	0
The primary component of steel is _____.	copper	iron	cobalt	nickel	3
The deepest canyon in the ocean floor.	Hellenic Trench	Philippine Trench	Marianas Trench	Japan Trench	2
Which are examples of altricial birds?	the domestic chicken	ducks	the magapodes	the Great Frigatebird	3
The nucleus contains	protons	neutrons	electrons	two of the above	3

Table 1: Multiple Choice Question With Correct Answer

words is known as word embedding. The name of those methods are the continuous bag-of-words model and the skip-gram model. These methods capture higher order relationships between words and sentences. SemEval- 2015 Task 3 on Answer Selection in cQA is similar type of shared task (Agirre et al., 2015). The main aim of SemEval-2015 Task 3 shared task was to develop a system that automatically detects the most relevant answers from the irrelevant ones.

4   System Framework

To deal with this shared task we use word embeddings to find the relation between questions and answer options. Word embeddings is well known approach for semantic textual similarity, question answering and information retrieval system(Řehůřek and Sojka, 2010; Elman, 1990). For classification, we used Matlab toolkit. [1] classification module have been used with respect to each of the corresponding runs submitted by our team to the shared task.

In this shared task, we build a complex decision tree classifier using word2vec [2] feature to predict the correct answer. Figure 1 describes our system architecture.

4.1   Distributed Semantic Similarity

Distributional semantic is very useful to capture the textual similarity between sentences. The model is mainly based on one hypothesis that the meaning of a word depends on the surrounding words. (Pennington et al., 2014) The underlying

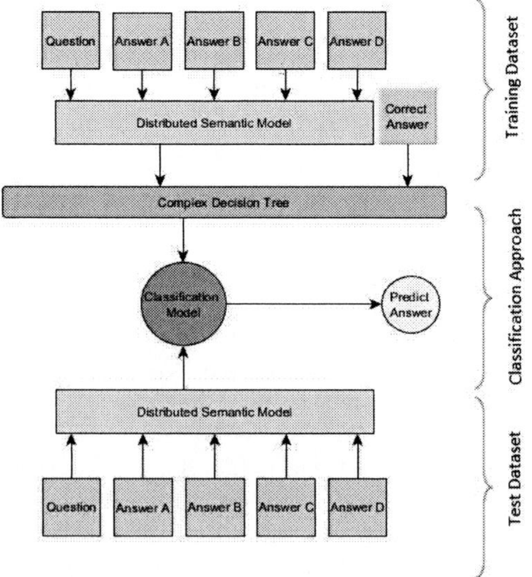

Figure 1: System Framework

---

[1]http://in.mathworks.com/help/stats/classification-trees-and-regression-trees.html

[2]https://radimrehurek.com/gensim/models/word2vec.html

idea of this concept is that "a word is characterized by the company it keeps". (Firth, 1957) Researchers are trying to improve this model that can be achieved from integrating distributional vectors semantics which is also known as word embeddings. Two such methods are the continuous bag-of-words model and the skip-gram model. These methods have been shown to produce embeddings that capture higher order relationships between words that are highly effective in natural language processing tasks involving the use of word similarity and word analogy. (Zuccon et al., 2015)

To find the relation between question and options we used the GoogleNews vectors dataset which is available on Google word2vec website.[3] The vocabulary size of this trained model is 3,000,000 word and the size of word vector is 300-dimensional. The model is trained on 100 billion words.

4.2 Classification Approach

Classification technique is used in different scientific fields to build a classification models from features of input data set. Different types of classification approach have been proposed like probabilistic neural network, rule based classifier, decision tree classifier, support vector machine to solve different types of problem (Sarkar et al., 2016b). In decision tree classification approach a series of question are asked and each time an answer is given to make a decision. Finally, we derived a conclusion of the problem. The series of question and answer are organized in the form of hierarchical structure.

For our experiment, we used complex decision tree approach to predict the correct answer. The training dataset set is used to build a classification model, which is used to predict the class labels of test dataset. The accuracy of a classification model is calculated using the count of correct and incorrect prediction by the model. .

5   Dataset

The 2017 IJCNLP Task 5 shared task collect questions from different subjects i.e. biology, chemistry, physics, earth science and life science. The variety of the questions is very challenging for the participants. The questions are given in two languages English and Chinese. We are participating only English dataset. The statistics of IJC-

[3]https://code.google.com/archive/p/word2vec/

NLP English dataset is described in the Table 2. In this shared task questions are provided in csv file where each row defines each question.

English Subset				
	Train	**Valid**	**Test**	**Total**
Biology	281	70	210	561
Chemistry	775	193	581	1549
Physics	299	74	224	597
Earth Science	830	207	622	1659
Life Science	501	125	375	1001
English Total	2686	669	2012	5367

Table 2: Statistics of IJCNLP Dataset

6   Results

In this section, we discuss about our experiment results on valid and test dataset. In the same time, we also shown the comparison between winner score and our system score on those datasets. Table 3 shows that our model gives better result with compare to winner score. Our model is not based on traditional information retrieval system. Besides our model is simple and easily implemented on different types of dataset. However, our system face problem to capture the semantic meaning of chemical equations as well as integer values.

The accuracy is calculated using the following equation

$$Accuracy = \frac{number of correct questions}{total number of questions} \quad (1)$$

Organizer implemented simple retrieval based method as a baseline, and they used Apache Lucene which is a well-known software for information retrieval. For baseline system organizer, concatenate question with option and generate the query. Next use this query to find the relevant documents. In equation 2 the query and document are denoted by q and d respectively similarity between query and document is calculated using $Sim(q,d)$. Finally, they are taking top three similarity to calculate the score using following equation

$$Score(q, a) = \frac{1}{n} \sum_{1}^{n} Sim(q, d) \quad (2)$$

7   Conclusion and Future Work

In this paper we present distributed semantic model on IJCNLP-2017 Task 5 dataset in "Multi-choice Question Answering in Exams" shared

	Dataset	
	Valid	**Test**
Winner Score	0.487	0.456
JU_NITM Score	0.407	0.406

Table 3: Comparison between Winner Score and Our System Score

task. Our proposed method achieved good result compare with winner score. The advantage of distributed semantic model is that this model is simple and robust. This model not only find exact terms from the questions and answers from resources but also find semantic information from resources. Dealing with IJCNLP dataset we observe that our proposed method can be easily implemented into complex applied systems. In the same time, we face some problem to deal with chemistry dataset because our model does not represent the chemical equations in vector space.

Our future aim is to overcome from this problem. We are trying to improve our dataset from which we build our distributed semantic model so that we can represent chemical equation in vector space. In the same this we are also trying to implement doc2vec model to deal with complex system.

Acknowledgments

This work presented here is under the Research Project Grant No. YSS/2015/000988 and supported is by the Department of Science & Technology (DST) and Science and Engineering Research Board (SERB), Govt. of India. Authors are also acknowledges the Department of Computer Science & Engineering of National Institute of Technology Mizoram, India for providing infrastructural facilities and support.

References

Eneko Agirre, Carmen Banea, Claire Cardie, Daniel Cer, Mona Diab, Aitor Gonzalez-Agirre, Weiwei Guo, Inigo Lopez-Gazpio, Montse Maritxalar, Rada Mihalcea, German Rigau, Larraitz Uria, and Janyce Wiebe. 2015. SemEval-2015 Task 2: Semantic Textual Similarity, English, Spanish and Pilot on Interpretability. In *Proceedings of the 9th International Workshop on Semantic Evaluation (SemEval 2015)*, pages 252–263, Denver, Colorado. Association for Computational Linguistics.

Jeffrey L. Elman. 1990. Finding Structure in Time. *Cognitive Science*, 14(2):179–211.

J. R. Firth. 1957. A synopsis of linguistic theory 1930-55. 1952-59:1–32.

Kezban Dilek Onal, Ismail Sengor Altingovde, Pinar Karagoz, and Maarten de Rijke. 2016. Getting Started with Neural Models for Semantic Matching in Web Search. *CoRR*, abs/1611.03305.

Jeffrey Pennington, Richard Socher, and Christopher D. Manning. 2014. Glove: Global vectors for word representation. In *In EMNLP*.

Radim Řehůřek and Petr Sojka. 2010. Software Framework for Topic Modelling with Large Corpora. In *Proceedings of the LREC 2010 Workshop on New Challenges for NLP Frameworks*, pages 45–50, Valletta, Malta. ELRA.

Sandip Sarkar, Partha Pakray, Dipankar Das, and Alexander Gelbukh. 2016a. Regression Based Approaches for Detecting and Measuring Textual Similarity. In *Mining Intelligence and Knowledge Exploration: 4th International Conference, MIKE 2016*, pages pp. 144–152, Mexico City. Springer International Publishing.

Sandip Sarkar, Saurav Saha, Jereemi Bentham, Partha Pakray, Dipankar Das, and Alexander Gelbukh. 2016b. NLP-NITMZ@DPIL-FIRE2016: Language Independent Paraphrases Detection. In *Shared task on detecting paraphrases in Indian languages (DPIL), Forum for Information Retrieval Evaluation (FIRE)*, pages pp. 256–259, Kolkata, India.

Guido Zuccon, Bevan Koopman, Peter Bruza, and Leif Azzopardi. 2015. Integrating and Evaluating Neural Word Embeddings in Information Retrieval. In *Proceedings of the 20th Australasian Document Computing Symposium*, ADCS '15, pages 12:1–12:8, New York, NY, USA. ACM.

Author Index